Conceiving Cultures

⌘

Conceiving Cultures

REPRODUCING PEOPLE & PLACES

on *Nuakata, Papua New Guinea*

SHELLEY MALLETT

THE UNIVERSITY OF MICHIGAN PRESS
Ann Arbor

Copyright © by the University of Michigan 2003
All rights reserved
Published in the United States of America by
The University of Michigan Press
Manufactured in the United States of America
♾ Printed on acid-free paper

2006   2005   2004   2003   4   3   2   1

No part of this publication may be reproduced, stored
in a retrieval system, or transmitted in any form
or by any means, electronic, mechanical, or otherwise,
without the written permission of the publisher.

A CIP catalog record for this book is available from the British Library.

Library of Congress Cataloging-in-Publication Data

Mallett, Shelley, 1960–
Conceiving cultures : reproducing people and places on Nuakata,
Papua New Guinea / Shelley Mallett.
p.   cm.
Includes bibliographical references and index.
ISBN 0-472-09828-4 (cloth : alk. paper) — ISBN 0-472-06828-8
(pbk. : alk. paper)
1. Massim (Papua New Guinea people)—Social life and customs.
2. Birth customs—Papua New Guinea—Nuakata Island.   3. Philosophy,
Massim—Papua New Guinea—Nuakata Island.   4. Nuakata Island
(Papua New Guinea)—Social life and customs.   I. Title.

DU740.42 .M353   2003
306'.089'992—dc21   2002013305

This book is dedicated to
Wycliffe (Guli) Siyae na Nuakata tomowa maudoidi

and in memory of
Antiya Meyau

Contents

Acknowledgments ix

Introduction:
Imagining the Field
1

CHAPTER 1
Tracing Nuakata
39

CHAPTER 2
Colonial Impregnations
65

CHAPTER 3
Bearing the Inconceivable
103

CHAPTER 4
Belongings
141

CHAPTER 5
Planting the Past, Tending the Future
177

CHAPTER 6
Living Death
211

Conclusion:
Remembering Nuakata
259

Notes 275
Glossary 293
References 301
Index 323

Acknowledgments

Many people have labored with me to produce this book. Without their work some of the stories and experiences of people living on Nuakata could not now be heard by those who live far beyond Nuakata's shores. First and foremost I thank the people of Nuakata for their act of grace in allowing my partner, Roger Averill, and me to live and research among them in 1993. We felt truly humbled by the hospitality and support shown to us during our stay. People's friendship and unfailing humor enriched us, making this the most wonderful and memorable year in our lives to date. We long to return.

I particularly thank Wycliffe Siyae to whom this work is dedicated. It is he who taught me about ethnography. My failings in this regard, are, however, entirely my own responsibility. Wycliffe not only worked with me on my research, he also lived with us for much of our time on Nuakata. His family offered us a place to stay, and the people of Yalasi and Bolime generously built us a house, which over time became our home. Moses Diawasi, the community health worker, generously shared his time and expertise with me. His advice was sound and welcome. For all their kindnesses and assistance with the research I especially thank Eunice Tau'owa, Malida Tau'owa, Noah Siyae, Hosea Tau'owa, Yamesi, Roger, and Sinetana, the Siyae children, Geteli, Jane, Washington (Dracula), Douglisi, Roger, Noweli, Misake, Eba, and their spouses (Justin, John, and Penina) and children. I also thank Carpenter, Malida, I'unia, Davidi, Mona, George, Sara, Emma, Getuludi, Mari, Susan, Rosemari, Thomas, Eric, Mesila, and the people of Hapela'awa'awa hamlet, including Jennifer Henry and Anne who were so helpful and hospitable when we first arrived on Nuakata. Yagu velau alimiyai. Finally I must make special mention of two other people from Nuakata. Antiya Meyau (d. 1995) shared his experiences, knowledge, and beliefs thoughtfully and generously. His life is an inspiration to me. Eba Siyae, Wycliffe's youngest sister, remains our link to Nuakata. For her friendship, love, and the memorable times together in Australia we are forever grateful.

When we stayed in Alotau on the mainland, Ken and Lisa Shultz, together with their sons, provided us with a home away from home.

Their friendship and care, together with the practical support offered by the Summer Institute of Linguistics staff, particularly Daphne Lithgow, were much appreciated. I am forever grateful to Brian and Lorraine Raisson who appeared as if from nowhere at a time of great need and delivered us safely back to Alotau. Elva and Ray Averill also provided practical and emotional support during our time on Nuakata and beyond. I thank them for the food parcels, letters, for typing my field notes, and much much more.

This ethnography neither began nor ended on Nuakata. Martha Macintyre's stories of her experiences on Tubetube first captured my imagination. Her unique ways of thinking provided inspiration, and her personal and intellectual support made the fieldwork and later the writing seem possible. For all this and her ongoing friendship, I thank her. Other people too have provided both intellectual and personal inspiration, none more than Werner and Mary Pelz. It has truly been a privilege to know them both, and it is a great sadness to me that Mary died before I completed this work. My life has been diminished by her death. The intellectual passions of Chris Eipper and Lorraine Mortimer have excited my imagination throughout my ten-year ethnographic journey. As Chris Eipper challenged me to think about anthropology's projects, Lorraine Mortimer challenged me to reflect on feminism and epistemology. They did this in the context of long-standing friendships that have provided both wonderful conversations and ongoing support. Two friends, Ann Jeffries and Di Lancashire, provided me with the intellectual support and confi-dence to embark on fieldwork. When I returned to Australia they shared my struggle to write the ethnography in a style that some may label experimental. It is true to say that without their friendship I could not have finished this book. Once completed, Margaret Jolly provided incisive comment and criticisms of the text. So too did Klaus Neumann and Henrietta Moore. Where possible I have tried to accommodate their suggested revisions.

The Sociology and Anthropology Department at La Trobe University provided a fertile and supportive intellectual environment while I was researching and writing this book. They provided some fieldwork funding. An Australian Postgraduate Award Research Award also provided funding. The manuscript was completed while I was working in the Gender Relations Project in the Research School of Pacific and Asian Studies at the Australian National University. I would particularly like to thank Margaret Jolly for her personal and intellectual support, Andrea Whittaker for her computer advice and emotional support, and Annegret Schemberg for her editing prowess and work on the text. Ria van der Zandt of the Anthropology Department in the Research School of Pacific and Asian Studies at ANU provided wonderful conversations and practical support during the six-month period that my computer crashed on a daily basis. Her efforts went beyond the call of duty.

During the researching and writing of this ethnography I have also appreciated the love and care of both family and friends. From a very young age my parents, Frank and Hazel Mallett, taught me the importance of education and the value of ideas. More than this they taught me that people and relationships are more important than anything else. I thank them for all this and their ongoing love and support. While writing chapter 6, "Living Death," my beloved aunt, Norma Mcdonald, died of a brain tumor. I dedicate that chapter to her.

Peter and Clare Averill provided all the computing equipment, advice, and backup support necessary for me to write this ethnography. I could not have written it without this help. I am also grateful to Leanne Averill-Hutton and Stephen Hutton, Ian and Linda Mallett, and Jon and Karen Mallett for their support, especially while we were living on Nuakata. For their encouragement and forbearance I thank Maria Trombin and Soraiya Christensen, Owen Wood and Cate Wotley, Beverley Van Praagh and Colin Knight, Graham Perry, Yvonne Kelly, and Peter Gaskell. I am forever grateful to Andrea Whittaker and Bruce Missingham for their friendship during some particularly stressful times. Thanks also to Doreen Rosenthal for her support.

Finally, I owe my deepest thanks to Roger Averill for daring to take risks with me and for his unfailing love and support. Not only did Roger enthusiastically embrace my suggestion to go to Nuakata, but he has also listened to, read, and edited every line I have written since. For all this, and his love and care for our daughters, Grace and Lily, I love him.

Introduction: Imagining the Field

Melbourne, November 1992—A Daydream

I am sitting in a small, open boat, perhaps a speedboat or motorized canoe. A blue calm surrounds me—blue sky and sea, made brilliant by a bright sun. Even so, I feel nervous and excited as I look out across the ocean, anxiously scanning the horizon for a glimpse of land, "the field," Nuakata—my named, but as yet unseen, destination. Fortunately I am not alone on the boat. Roger, my husband, is with me, together with two Papua New Guinean men who steer the small craft and nurture its tiny outboard motor. They are not my only sources of comfort and security. Propped against a large metal trunk, I take consolation from the knowledge that it contains my research proposal, books, and last-minute instructions on how to prepare genealogies.

The scene dissolves. A white sand beach appears. Standing on the shoreline, I extend my hand in all directions to the people who have gathered there to meet us. Moving to greet them I desperately try to radiate warmth, respect, and interest, willing people to like me. Rummaging in my bags and pockets I pull out the gifts Roger and I have brought. I am anxious, hoping the gifts are appropriate, wondering if we have brought enough. Looking around I realize that there are no women on the beach. Where are they? Why don't they come? What if they won't speak to me?

Nuakata, April 1993—A Lived Experience

Night has fallen. The Coleman lamp is lit, and our house is filled with laughter. We are gathered around a large metal trunk, playing cards.

Heavy with books, paper, and tapes, the trunk is almost impossible to lift. Even so, it makes a perfect card table for five or six players. On this particular night we are playing Oh Hell—Wycliffe, Washington, Waligeha, Roger, and myself. Wycliffe is winning, declaring himself the Oh Hell champion. The rest of us protest, promising his success will be short-lived. Later, as I place five cups of coffee on the trunk, it occurs to me that coffee and card evenings were not a feature of my prefield daydreams about doing ethnography on Nuakata!

In these reflections—one a memory of something experienced, the other a memory of something experienced only as a dream—the trunk represents a link between my imaginary field and my lived experience of Nuakata. Laden with make-believe books and preparatory notes, the fictional trunk provided a point of reference and stability for my imaginary journey to the field. Purchased at Alotau on mainland Papua New Guinea, the real trunk was initially the focus of considerable local attention partly because of its size and weight and the problems this caused in transferring it between boat, shore, and house. The trunk also attracted attention because it was locked and known to be expensive. Later, people were intrigued by its contents, for it concealed a largely inaccessible world of books—mainly novels and anthropological texts. It was home to my fieldwork equipment: a camera, tape recorder, pens and paper; the trunk also held my research plan, which detailed how I intended to relate with local people! In this sense, the trunk and its contents were objects entangled in webs of significance, solid representations of the differences—real and imagined—between Roger and me and the people of Nuakata.

However, as time passed and our relationships strengthened, interest in the trunk and its contents waned. Eventually it became a mere prop around and upon which some of the mundane but nonetheless important and ritualized aspects of our daily life unfolded. Though the trunk became a functional object, incidental to our relationships and daily living on Nuakata, my memory of the ideas raised by the books inside it continued to influence the questions I posed to people, my response to their replies, and the self-conscious reflections on Nuakatan lived experience rendered into field notes.

Placed alongside one another, these written snapshot memories of the dream and reality of my experience on Nuakata beg the question, In what ways did the field of my imagination influence the field I participated in, observed, and now represent? More generally, what constitutes fieldwork? Where and when does it begin and end? Is it gendered like the field, as some insist?[1] Indeed, what is the ethnographic field? Is it a permanent, bounded place, real and independent of the fieldworker's preconceptions? Or is it space circumscribed by the ethnographer's imagination and beliefs? Should it be thought of as a place or places? Or is it a multidimensional field of interaction and power between people, places, times, and things, squeezed into texts?[2] Could it exist on "two fronts: as a field of knowledge (as a 'discipline') and a field of action, a force field, or a site of struggle," as Scheper-Hughes (1992, 25; 1995, 419–20) suggests? Perhaps most important, how are these questions relevant to both the real and the written lives of people living and dying on Nuakata?

Questions such as these—along with the more fundamental one, Why do ethnographic fieldwork?—invite reflection on the significance of autobiography in fieldwork and writing ethnography.[3] More broadly, they invite critical reflection on the process, politics, and ethics of anthropological knowledge creation and expression in ethnographic texts. From a prior position of distance and/or inexperience, the fieldworker imagines or anticipates her invisible field of investigation, its intellectual terrain and its boundaries. She also imagines her future location, identity, and relationships in the field. These preconceptions and their associated anxieties are inevitably confronted in the field, often with far-reaching consequences for the research. Yet, this confrontation between the preconceived field and the lived experience of the field is invariably siphoned off from, or neatly partitioned in, ethnographic texts. It is rendered peripheral, if not irrelevant, to ethnographic method and anthropological knowledge creation (cf. Rosaldo 1980). Not only can these textual elisions give the false impression that the fieldworker arrives in the field bearing minimal baggage—intellectual or otherwise—but, perhaps more insidiously, they imply that whatever she brings and however she bears it, it is of little or no consequence to the participant observation and writing that ensues. In other words, the ethnographer forgets or chooses to ignore the epistemological significance of means to ends, gestation to birth, producers, and the processes of production[4] to finished products—written texts. This reinforces the related but dubious notion that fieldwork begins and ends with the arrival in and departure from a field, a specific peopled place. It is yet another means of denying the subjective and temporal dimension to ethnography. Moreover, it reinforces the view that the ethnographer alone orchestrates and performs fieldwork and fieldwork relations. In contrast, I argue that the ethnographic field, fieldwork, and anthropological knowledge encompass all these interactive spaces.

By privileging these concerns with anthropological praxis and poiesis I introduce them as themes integral to my written stories of the people and places of Nuakata, and the fieldwork upon which these stories are based. The text, the fieldwork, and these integral themes are *positioned* by and attempt to *reposition* contemporary feminist, postcolonial, if not postmodern intellectual debates. Within the disciplines of anthropology and its would-be superego, cultural studies, this postmodern intellectual climate has been inflected in vigorous critique of seamless notions of culture, society, and person. Renewed attacks on positivism, proclamations of a "crisis of representation," and an associated preoccupation with ethnography as texts and ethnographers as authors have also surfaced.[5] It is a climate "where positioning has become crucial to everyday intellectual practice" (Pile and Thrift 1995, 16).[6] As a consequence, questions about who speaks for whom in ethnographic texts with what intent and authority[7] can no longer simply be ignored—even by those who consider these textual preoccupations to be expressions of "epistemological hypochondria" (Geertz 1988, 71, 97), "falsely radical" (Bourdieu and Wacquant 1992, 72) or potentially damning authorial lapses into solipsism and narcissism (Probyn 1993; Roth 1989).

By way of response to these issues of epistemology, praxis, and politics I take the last question first, Why do ethnographic fieldwork at a moment when the ethnographic project is called into question? To answer this I return to my earliest conceptions of the field[8] and thereby trace a personal journey that began with a foray into feminist philosophy, moved into anthropological theory, then finally arrived at an imagined Nuakata. By mapping this journey here in the introduction I explore theoretical terrain that, for the most part, remains concealed in the ethnography that follows.

Surveying the Boundaries:
A Foray into Feminist Philosophy

In Search of the Gendered Subject

Pacing the long corridors of the Department of Sociology and Anthropology at La Trobe University, Melbourne, desperate for news of my research visa, I had ample time (twelve months in all) to reflect on my decision to do fieldwork. Born of disenchantment, it was nurtured by a distilled memory of fascination.

For several years prior to making this decision I was engaged in research on a critical, feminist analysis of the gendered subject. I questioned existing ways of thinking (of and about) the subject, agency, and, more broadly, the relationship between sex, gender, and the subject. I brought some basic, perhaps unsustainable, assumptions to my initial research—including a continuing belief and hope in the idea of humankind, "a unity in diversity, a pattern of variations" (Eipper 1990, 60). This belief is central to the "imaginary in anthropology" (1990, 61) and underpins much social scientific research, including feminist research.

Mine was a vague, universal notion of humankind; one in search of ways to *accommodate* differences and find a basis allowing us to respond to one another as more alike than different, more related than unrelated. Although not evident, my research was inspired by the perennial ethical question, How can people justly live with one another? I assumed that answers to this fundamental question lay in our ways of understanding persons or subjects, and from this, their needs, rights, and responsibilities.[9]

Following Mauss's (1985) seminal essay on the person and the innumerable anthropological testimonies reinforcing his basic claim,[10] I believed that notions of the person and self, and the relationship between the person and self, were socially, culturally, and historically specific. Rather naively, I also considered the term *person* to be a universally significant social category denoting the individual and material human being. The work of Kovel and Benjamin had influenced my thinking to that point (Mallett 1995).[11] Combined, their theories had offered me a reconstructed humanist vision of the gendered subject, one that straddled essentialist/nonessentialist, transcultural/cultural, and transhistorical/historical divides. Founded on the view that all human infants are predisposed to helplessness, dependence, and sociability, this subject/self is relational. It is a self or I who is not preexistent, but emerges in relation to and separation from—in recognition of and reflection by—significant caregivers in the first instance. Equally significant, it is a relational self who is conceived and develops within specific sociocultural and historical contexts. In this sense it is a dynamic rather than static, substantive self, a self in process.

In the absence of some other term to speak of individual human beings, I had seized on the universal social category of the *person* as if it were a life raft. This was a pragmatic decision that I knew to be unsustainable. I clung to this rather hollow vestige of humanism even while persuaded by the claims of Mauss (1985),[12] Lukes (1985), and others that the category itself and the "categorical identification between persons and human beings" may not necessarily exist in, or be relevant to, all societies (Moore 1994c, 32).[13] I was persuaded too by the related argument that the terms *person, subject,* and *self* are irrevocably contaminated by the Western epistemologies that reified them, if not gave them life.[14] But I suspected that in abandoning all humanist categories and constructs, I risked succumbing to a theoretical and political relativism that was ultimately nihilistic. I would come to value and promote difference rather than the creative accommodation of differences.[15]

In pursuing answers to my research questions I was forced to confront these issues. For as much as, if not more than, anything else, my questions about gendered subjects sought alternative, sustainable ways of knowing about the person, the self/I. They assumed the symbiotic relationship between the self/I and the ways the self/I is thought, spoken, and embodied. In so doing, they rode on a tidal wave of Western feminist and postmodernist criticism directed at, yet implicitly indebted to, Enlightenment and, more particularly, Cartesian epistemology.[16]

Much of this criticism focuses on the Enlightenment metanarratives (Reason, Knowledge, Truth, the Subject, the Author), their unitary, universalist assumptions, their certainties and their histories.[17] Manifestations of Enlightenment Reason—"man," belief in objectivity, binary oppositions, the privileging of vision and consciousness as a means of knowing[18]—are also exposed in these discussions, their influence in Western texts debated. By way of response to these criticisms, some postmodernist writers attempt to counter Reason's sway in Western knowing by recovering the body, the invisible, the nonrational, the "third term," "Woman," *différance* and multiple subjectivities in their theorizing (Foucault 1978, 51, 97; Derrida 1982, 21–22, 25–26; Flax 1990b, 212). Some attempt to translate these tentative and politically strategic ways of knowing into self-consciously experimental texts (e.g., Bataille, Trinh Minh Ha). In so doing they aim to subvert authorial power and epistemological authority by, among other ways, representing multiple voices in their texts, elaborating the poetics of experience, juxtaposing text with subtext(s) on the page, and writing uncertainties. Others, in turn, suggest that these theoretical/textual gestures merely represent rejuvenated forms of epistemological mastery—mastery of a kind where uncertainty is posited as the only valid alternative to certain knowledge and universal truth. For example, Heller (1990) argues that although these postmodernist theorists resist the temptation to postulate philosophical or scientific theories of the whole, or of absolute truth, they continue to assert themselves as the definitive enunciator of that which cannot be known— of the fragments and truths. Moreover, by rendering people (bodies, women, men, selves) as surfaces upon which multiple and, at times, contradictory discourses are inscribed, some postmodernist theory loses sight of—worse still, abrogates political responsibility for—the everyday experiences, the real life struggles, the defeats and victories, of living, dying people. Such experiences are lost, not between the lines or on the margin of the texts, but through the very body of these works—works that seem more concerned with the form than the content of the stories they tell. Accordingly, their refusal to speak for others also effectively becomes a refusal to speak on behalf of those whose story would otherwise not be heard.[19]

Plunging myself headlong into this sea of feminist literature, I soon found myself flailing. My progress was impeded by a lack of agreement in and across feminist and contemporary philosophical texts as to "to what" exactly the terms *subject* and *gender* refer. For example, as Heller notes, in the "contemporary French and German debates, the term subject has assumed the following meanings: point of view; individual; the 'subject' of biography; the hermeneutical subject; . . . the subject of knowledge; . . . the political subject; . . . man" (1990, 22). Some conflate subject, self, and I (as I do), variously referring to "it," either intentionally or unintentionally, as a material entity/essence or identifiable position(s) from which the person acts, speaks. Some conflate subject with subjectivity, rendering it akin to opinion, attitude, or feeling. Others reduce subject to identity, emphasizing the plural and potentially contradictory "I" constructed in and by multiple discourses (Foucault 1978).

Cartesian Methods: A Lesson in Denial

While confusion abounds as to what the term *subject/self* represents, a tacit consensus seems to exist in much of the feminist/philosophical literature about what the subject is not. The rational, universal, implicitly masculine, autonomous Cartesian "I" is emblematic of this negative vision. This rational, thinking "I" stands as a loosely defined Other or (implicit) object to many, though by no means all, of the feminist incarnations of the gendered subject that have emerged over the past two decades. For this reason I initially turned to Descartes's *Meditations,* hoping to further understand the other progenitor of these feminist accounts. Descartes's theory of knowledge, subject, and method remained as background—sometimes distant, sometimes proximal—to my subsequent prefield, field, and postfield reflections on these matters.

Fueled by Reason and fortified by the Cogito, Descartes embarked on an introspective journey in search of some irrefutable "knowledge of truth" and certainty.[20] In making this meditative journey and arriving at a new scientific method and theory of knowledge and the subject, he discarded his own confused lived experience and discounted his "age" and "maturity"—factors that, he declared at the outset, made the journey possible. By dispelling his own doubt and uncertainty, de-emphasizing the epistemological significance of his embodied existence—all that he learned from and through his imaginary, his senses and emotions—and by dismissing as irrelevant his interdependence on others, Descartes was able to conclude that the internalized God-given capacity to think is pivotal to the existence of the "I." He therefore denied that from the moment of birth the other's existence is simply there (Pelz 1992), that our earliest experiences of self and of knowing necessarily arise in relation to and with other selves.[21]

Stunted in form, but not in influence, the Cartesian subject's existence and capacity to know relied upon the subject's use of the rational scientific method. Unlike his philosophical forebears, most notably Socrates and Plato, Descartes conceived method less as "a path to be followed rationally" and more as an internalized, static "way of reasoning: a precisely ordered mode of abstract thinking" (Lloyd 1984; 1991, 168). Accordingly, neither the subject matter nor the purpose of inquiry determines the correct "order of thought." Rather, it is the "natural operations" of a unitary mind subjected to "introspection" and guided by reason that underpin this new method (1991, 168). Heidegger notes that "we first arrive at science as research when and only when truth has been transformed into the certainty of representation"—an idea initially encountered in the "metaphysics of Descartes" (1977, 127). Accordingly, "knowing establishes itself as a procedure," a set of laws that binds itself to "a projected plan of nature" or an already circumscribed field of investigation (1977, 118). It is through the projected plan and a rigorous procedure that the world of objects is represented and explained. "Explanation is always twofold. It accounts for an unknown by means of a known and at the same time it verifies that known by means of that unknown" (Lloyd 1991, 121; see also Taylor 1989, 148–58).

In reading the *Meditations* it was not Descartes's theory of the subject or "new knowledge" that made most impact on my thinking and imagining about alternative gendered subjects, but the dissonance between his theory and the evident gestatory process that brought it into being. For, unlike many philosophical treatises, the confusing bodily context, conquistadorial motivations, and mental labor integral to its development are neither concealed nor disguised in his text. As Bordo notes, the "dizzying vacillations, the constant requestioning of the self, the determination, if only temporary, to stay within confusion and contradiction . . . reveals a dark underside" to his "bold rationalist vision" (1986, 440). It is an underside rendered all the more powerful and intriguing by Descartes's efforts in the later meditations (four, five, six, and the synopsis) to deny and repress its significance to the end point of the process—a theory combining knowledge, subject, and method that disallows lived, sensory experience as a basis for knowing truth, self, and world. In other words, Descartes represents his context and process for coming to know the subject/I before declaring these experiences and processes irrelevant to the existence of the "I." Ultimately, then, in what can now be read and experienced as a postmodern twist, the form of his text belies the content of its conclusions. On the one hand, Descartes can be accused of denying the "dark underside" to his thinking and theorizing on rationality. On the other hand, it might be argued that he reveals not only the perilous doubt but also the denial of lived, sensory experience and interdependence on other people, which underpins his "bold rationalist vision."

Following my reading of the *Meditations* and related secondary texts, I returned to the feminist literature on the gendered subject, convinced, like Descartes, that ideas about the subject are inseparable from those about knowing and method. Unlike him, though, I was also sure that ideas about subject and method are contingent upon both the known and unknown motivations and experiences of us who attempt to represent the "I." As with the "self/I" these motivations and experiences arise out of, and often in response to, specific contexts and significant interpersonal relations. I was reminded too that research questions themselves, and not just the thoughts and conclusions they elicit, are historically contingent. The questions asked anticipate and constrain the answers elicited. Accordingly, when I returned to the feminist literature, I asked not just how, but why, and on whose behalf, these gendered subjects are conceived and expressed. Who or what is denied or overlooked in the process? Moreover, I sought a self/I and a means of knowing the self/I that takes account of embodied processes, praxis, and interpersonal relations.

The Sex/Gender Distinction: A Feminist Stumbling Block

It soon became clear that feminist debate on the subject, and the female subject in particular, had polarized and in some instances stalled around a cluster of interrelated issues: essentialism, female difference, the sex/gender distinction, the body, and the politics of voice (who speaks, and for whom). Of these, the essentialist debate seemed the most encompassing and divisive, for it highlighted and reinforced important political and epistemological differences between feminist theorists. Moreover, it constituted a feminist inflection of the long-standing nature/nurture, individual/society debates that continue between and within the social and biological sciences.[22]

Engaged in the fight to extend male rights and privileges to women, many early second-wave Anglo-American feminist theories of the gendered self (including feminist anthropological ones) rejected essentialist notions of sexual difference based on reproductive biology, genetics, or morphology. They claimed that by defining women in rigid, immutable terms such theories undermined their attempts to redefine "woman" as man's equal—a potentially self-constituting, androgynous agent. For this reason, they formulated diverse social constructionist theories to explain the means of "production and organization of female difference" (Fuss 1989, 2).[23]

The concept of gender and the sex/gender distinction, conceived in Western epistemology and integrally located in an "individualist problematic" (Haraway 1991, 132), proved pivotal to these strategic feminist analyses of the subject and ideologically based equality and inequality. Sex was understood as an intrinsic biological aspect of the individual person, whereas gender was considered an external sociocultural imposition; somehow internalized as an operational "state" of mind (see Gatens 1983). Like the nature/culture, body/mind, and (more distantly) individual/society, binary oppositions on which it was founded, the sex/gender distinction was sustained by the (social) construction metaphor. It is a metaphor that encodes culturally specific spatial, temporal, and ontological ideas. It suggests that things, structures, ideas, discourses, and gender are elaborated upon passive, preexisting forms, be it the body or the so-called natural world. These ontological states existed prior to and independent of their elaborations. Accordingly, the sexed body is conceived as the material foundation upon which gender identity is constructed or inscribed upon the body over time.

Since the mid- to late 1980s many feminist theorists have challenged the sex/gender distinction and the social constructionist metaphor upon which it is founded. This challenge represented part of a wider critique of the universal, "masterful" subject and the egalitarian politics that sustained him/her.[24] Committed to a politics of difference, feminist theorists resisted the efforts of (some of) their feminist sisters to construct women in the universal man's image. Indeed, they resisted feminist attempts to construct women in (white, Western, bourgeois liberal, heterosexual) Woman's image.[25] Not only did they emphasize the fundamental differences between men and women, but between women themselves—differences of class, ethnicity, age, and so forth. Much of the impetus for the initial political and theoretical challenge to the universal Woman and the (white) gendered subject came from those originally positioned on the margins of feminist debate—third world feminists, women of color, lesbian feminists, feminist anthropologists, and cultural theorists who have attempted to speak of, for, or alongside them.[26]

While aware of this work and its potential power to subvert Western, Cartesian ways of knowing, it did not initially capture my attention. Rather, I was drawn to the work of writers such as Butler, Irigaray, Cixous, de Lauretis, I. Young, Braidotti, and Flax.[27] Although theoretically diverse, these theorists are united by their efforts to restore female or, more broadly, sexually different bodies to their understanding of the subject/subjectivities and knowing. The body they attempt to recover is not ensnared by hierarchical dualisms and the constructionist metaphor that maintains them, but rather, as Grosz notes, it is the body as it is "interwoven with and constitutive of systems of meaning, signification and representation" (1994, 18). It is the sexually differentiated, or in Braidotti's case, the ontologically sexed body as it lived, enacted, and experienced. While critical of Merleau-Ponty's (1962) failure to adequately theorize sexual difference in his account of subjectivity—for using a male model of sexual experiences for representing sexuality—theorists such as Irigaray (1985a, 1985b), Butler (1990), and I. Young (1990) are variously indebted to his phenomenological theory of lived experience and embodied subjectivity (see Grosz 1989, 1994).

Despite her criticism of Merleau-Ponty's failure to differentiate between men and women's embodiment, Butler (1990) affirms his understanding of sexuality as an integral facet of people's existence, informing their experience of self and world. I. Young (1990) also stresses women's corporeal embodiment, particularly—but not exclusively—pregnant embodiment. In describing and detailing women's corporeal comportment, their movements and actions in space, Young reveals that women's embodied experiences differ from men's, and also from each other's. Her analysis is part of her broader project to subvert notions of the unitary self and reinforce the idea that "any individual subject is a play of differences," who, because s/he is not a unity, "cannot be present to itself, know itself" (see Benhabib 1992, 197–98; Young 1986, 11).

Irigaray (in what she describes as a tactically inspired feminist mimesis of phallogocentric discourses of the subject and epistemology) posits her own theory of the feminine and the female subject. She contends that woman and mother have been much maligned and denigrated as Man's mere (m)other—bearer for those that beget Wisdom, Knowledge, and Truth. Not content with an analysis of phallogocentrism in Western philosophy, Irigaray (Cixous, too) has attempted to posit an alternative female symbolism based upon women's bodies and the experience of the mother-daughter relationship. Her theory of difference is distinguished by her attempt to posit the bodily and symbolic/discursive roots of real, historically situated women. She describes femininity as "beyond definition" as plural, multiple, fluid, and heterogeneous. Women's psychology is analogous to their morphology and form, a multiplicity located in the body as a mystery that is always plural.

Not only is the body remetaphorized by these theorists but so too are the body's relations to mind, culture, gender, subjectivity, and other bodies. In emphasizing corporeality, however, writers such as Irigaray, Cixous, and even I. Young continue to present and perpetuate an understanding of the body and the subject as text. The metaphors used to describe the body, the subject, risk becoming conflated with the body, the subject.[28]

Talking about "the Body," "the Subject," "the Self"

Asked to present a paper at a feminist social theory seminar, I spoke of these, my initial efforts, to reflect on the body and gendered subjects. The first response was a rebuff: "What you have to say makes no sense to me. You speak from a completely Eurocentric position. This has absolutely no relevance to me as an Indian woman. These terms, these theories, do not speak to my experience." Several people in the group defended the ideas discussed. I could not. The statement had found its mark. In my pursuit of a universally relevant and applicable notion of the gendered subject, I had deliberately ignored, but not forgotten, non-Western and anthropological perspectives. I suspected that if I really considered the epistemological challenges they posed, I might ultimately be forced to abandon the ethnocentric language of person, self, subject, agency, even sex and gender. Believing the project to be altogether too difficult, I had contrived to study Western notions of the subject as if the West itself denoted a unified field and intellectual domain.

Like the Indian woman, but possibly for different reasons, I felt estranged from the so-called lived body described. By speaking and writing "the body" in abstract or quasi-universal terms—as a site or surface of inscription, a diffuse essence, ontologically sexed—bodies, including my own body, seemed once again to be circumscribed by the mind, rationality. Ironically, the tangible, living, paining bodies of actual situated women and men remain obscured. As Mortimer writes:

> The body reinserted into the picture is so often the reified body—like the corpse of a drowned stranger that has surfaced amongst a group of swimmers. Where did it come from? What are they to do with it? What is their relationship to it? (1990, 47)

Feeling like one of Mortimer's swimmers sighting a corpse, I stalled, wondering what to do next. Confronting my own ethnocentrism, I was forced to acknowledge the ethnocentrism of these feminist philosophical theories of the subject, body, sex, and gender—theories that claimed to disrupt Enlightenment phallogocentrism and universalism, yet for the most part ignored different (intellectual and non-Western) ways of knowing, writing, speaking, and enacting notions of the "I." I realized too that my theoretical forays had assumed a life of their own, cast adrift from their original purpose. Like Descartes's *Meditations,* the forms of my texts (written and spoken) belied their content.

Extending the Boundaries: Deciding to Do Fieldwork

Thinking Backward

Like Moore and de Lauretis before her, I understood difference to be experienced relationally, both between and within persons.[29] It follows, then, that research on similarities and differences between people can be usefully pursued and, if possible, represented by employing intersubjective methods. Wanting to accommodate difference in my own thinking and writing, rather than simply subsuming expressions of difference in an abstract, disengaged theory, I sought a broader (research and) life experience to confront these issues. For this reason I decided to invigorate my thinking among living people; to ground my explorations in time, place(s), and culture(s), in living lives—my own and other people's. Rather than starting with firm, if not essentialist, concepts of sex, gender, body, and the subject, I wanted to work "back towards them" (Moore 1994c, 27)—to discover rather than assume the relevance of these terms and concepts for people living in different contexts.

> If our *universal particularity* is to be significant, and if we are to achieve anything as a *collective singularity,* then we might best strive towards an understanding of embodied subjectivity which does not privilege gender and sexual difference unduly just because we are so uncertain what else it is, if anything, that we share. (1994c, 27, emphasis in original)

By making the decision to do ethnographic fieldwork I recognized that I was following on the well-worn heels of colonial ethnographers, past and present, who went to other, often distant, places to explore the knowledge and practices of other people, "other cultures," so that they might reflect upon, affirm, or subvert their own. But perhaps with the naïveté that remains a privilege[30] and problem of the uninitiated or inexperienced ethnographer, I hoped that the fieldwork experience would provide opportunities for dialogue, for mutual relationships, for discussion of ideas and beliefs. I hoped it would provide an opportunity to explore those experiences I share in common with people living in a different context, as well as those that render us unique, distinct from one another. I imagined that through participant observation in the daily activities of these people both the opportunities and capacity for empathetic, experiential knowledge and genuine dialogue would emerge.

Possibilities for Mutual Understanding

The hope for, indeed belief in, dialogue and mutual understanding between researcher and informants has long been held by proponents of a dialogical or dialectical anthropology, who draw on phenomenological and hermeneutic philosophical traditions.[31] Researchers persuaded by the power and efficacy of this methodology follow Gadamer's suggestion that when speakers are open to one another, do not talk past or across one another, and allow themselves to follow rather than direct the conversation, a shared world is created between participants (1975, 330–35). In this shared communicative world the authority and control of the inquiring and interpreting ethnographer are challenged, even ruptured (see Clifford 1988, 43; Dwyer 1979). This point is underlined by Fine, who urges researchers to examine "relations between" our informants and ourselves. This will "get us better data, limit what we feel free to say, expand our minds and constrict our mouths, engage us in intimacy and seduce us into complicity, make us quick to interpret and hesitant to write" (1994, 72).

Although I believed in the possibility of dialogues such as these and thought it vital to strive for this form of mutual understanding in the field, I—like Crapanzano (1992)—considered this a romantic ideal that is rarely, if ever, realized during fieldwork, let alone in ethnographic texts. For dialogues of this kind to occur, the speakers must, apart from any other consideration, be fluent in a common language. Where the ethnographer must learn a language, long experience in the field is required—a luxury afforded very few ethnographers, past and present. Moreover, I agreed with Crapanzano that dialogue "not only reveals but often enough conceals the power relations and the desires that lie behind the spoken word, and, in other contexts, the recorded and distributed word" (1992, 189).

My hope for negotiated conversations, even dialogue, in the field was underpinned by my growing awareness of the relevance of the participant observation methodology for my own research. In proposing to use participant observation and experience as a means to understanding in the field, I was influenced by my select reading of the work of Bourdieu, the "anthropologists of experience" (especially James, Turner, Rosaldo, and Jackson)[32] and their phenomenological, existential and hermeneutic philosophical forebears (Dewey, James, Dilthey, Merleau-Ponty, Heidegger, Rorty).[33] Broadly speaking, these anthropologists and their forebears contend that Western philosophy and the scientific empiricism it spawned privilege vision as a metaphor for knowledge and understanding.[34] Accordingly, the speculative scientist/philosopher observer sees, extracts, or reveals otherwise concealed facts and timeless truths. Distance and distinction are created between an active spectator and a passive recipient of the spectator's gaze. In attempting to recuperate touch, sound, smell, taste, kinesthesis, embodiment, and temporality in our ways of knowing, anthropologists who are aligned with phenomenological and existential Western philosophical traditions argue for the exploration of lived experience that

> overflows the boundaries of any one concept, any one person, or any one society. As such, it brings us to a dialectical view of life which emphasizes the interplay rather than the identity of things, which denies any sure steading to thought by placing it always within the precarious and destabilizing fields of history, biography, and time.... It remains sceptical of all efforts to reduce the diversity of experience to timeless categories and determinate theorems, to force life to be at the disposal of ideas. (Jackson 1989, 2)

Mindful that this concept of experience may be nebulous, speaking for no-body and no-thing in particular, anthropologists of experience attempt to ground their approach "in the actual events, objects, and interpersonal relationships that make up the quotidian world" (Jackson 1989, 2; see also Abrahams 1985, 48–49). In doing this they move away from the "authoritative rhetoric" and ideas of, for example, "custom, tradition, institution" (Abrahams 1985, 46), symbol, identity, even culture.[35] And they forgo the intellectual comfort that comes from stable definitions, concepts, and ideas—ideas founded on a belief in clearly bounded relationships between subject and object/other, observer and observed, fact and fiction. Instead, exponents focus upon both the substantive and the dynamic performative aspects of both everyday and occasional, extraordinary experience. The interaction between observer and observed; the tension between stasis and flux, identity and intersubjectivity; the continuity and discontinuity between disparate people's lived experience all capture their attention and imagination.

Central to this approach is the contention that ideas, concepts, or so-called facts do not and cannot "transcend this life-world" (Jackson 1989, 1). They neither mirror immutable essences nor represent foundational laws of nature or being (Rorty 1979), rather they provide a way of indirectly representing and creating meaningful connections between experiences. Experience, then, is not thought of as a neutral domain that is beyond question. While recognizing the inability of language to encapsulate experience, this method relies upon "apposite metaphors, particular ground rules, and discursive techniques," particularly narrative (Jackson 1989, 2). Metaphor, allegory, and narrative are all claimed as a means for understanding, thinking, knowing, and acting. They are not, however, posited as ends in themselves (1989, 152).

Given their interest in the relationship of body, sense, emotion, and praxis to understanding and intersubjective knowing, it is quite remarkable that these experiential and dialogic anthropologists largely overlook the ways their own sexed or gendered experience and that of their participant informants contribute to their knowing. In the texts of Merleau-Ponty, Heidegger, Dilthey, and Dewey, on whom they draw, this elision can be understood as both cause and effect of the unchallenged phallogocentrism that pervaded Western philosophical thought (see Hodge 1988; Jaggar 1983). However, it is astounding that such elisions can occur in anthropological texts written during and after the onset of the second wave of feminist theory. These anthropologists perpetuate the view that sexual difference and gender belong to women. Consideration of the relationship between sexual difference, gender, and lived experience is left to feminist anthropologists whose ideas and preoccupations have long been marginalized from the masculine mainstream of the discipline.[36]

Why Melanesia? Why Milne Bay?

Having decided to do fieldwork, the question remained, Where would I go? Several factors influenced my decision to work in Melanesia and, more specifically, Milne Bay Province—among them my awareness of the area gained from doing undergraduate anthropology courses with Martha Macintyre. As a result, some of the ethnographic writings of Macintyre, M. Young, Battaglia, Munn, Thune, A. Weiner, Chowning, Lepowsky, and their anthropological forebears Malinowski, Roheim, and Fortune were both familiar and fascinating to me. Even so, it was not until I went to and returned from Nuakata that my reading of, and between the lines of, these and other Massim ethnographies became animated.

Milne Bay was vaguely familiar to me prior to my undergraduate study. During World War II my father served in the Australian Navy and spent much of his active service at Giligili army base in Milne Bay. When I was a child he spoke little about his wartime experience. Milne Bay was only known to me through the occasional anecdotes he reluctantly volunteered—anecdotes that included memorable refrains about the jungle, pythons, and friendly, helpful fuzzy-wuzzy people.[37] Therefore, although seeming remote, even wild, Milne Bay was never completely exotic to me as a child. It was always already a colonized realm, a realm existing on the frontiers of my familial experience, my familial imaginary; a place and time that belonged, like my father's faded wartime snapshots, to World War II.

In deciding to do fieldwork in Milne Bay there was a sense, then, in which I was retracing my father's footsteps and, more significant, Martha's and the small stream of ethnographers who had gone before me to some of the many islands that make up the province. I was following and extending this ethnographic lineage. In my imagination I was journeying to a culturally distinctive place and people with elaborate mortuary ceremonies, complex forms of (Kula) gift exchange, matrilineal kinship, an ongoing practice of sorcery and witchcraft, and a history of Wesleyan Methodist Christian missionizing spanning a century.[38] But I also thought of it as a region with a violent past—a place bloodied by World War II and, before that, with a regional history of cannibalism and interisland warfare. Above all, though, I thought of it as a place or region where the similarities between the local people and myself would outweigh the differences and where, as these multiple others had testified, the possibilities for friendship and mutual understanding were real. The "field" I imagined was therefore shaped and defined in significant ways by the disciplinary field of Melanesianist anthropology and the historical experience of other people.

The Partible Person

While these factors were the most significant influences in my decision to do fieldwork on an island in Milne Bay, it was my reading of the work of Marilyn Strathern—particularly *The Gender of the Gift*—that challenged me to pursue questions about gender, person, and knowing in a specific Melanesian place, and a clearly defined time. Elaborating on themes present in her earlier work, Strathern, in *The Gender of the Gift*, explores the epistemological conundrums created by anthropology's use of Western analytical constructs to theorize Melanesian epistemology of the self, gender, agency, and gendered exchange (1988, 7). As Biersack cogently summarizes, it is Strathern's broad aim "to use 'the analytical categories in the symbolic systems of those studied' (1988, 133) to develop an 'endogenous' analysis of the status of women in Melanesia and the character of Melanesian sociality" (1991, 147). Simply put, Strathern aims to "understand Melanesians in their own terms" (Biersack 1991, 152).

In attempting this task, she acknowledges her inability to "extract" herself from the specific Western cultural way of knowing and explaining that underpins much anthropological writing on Melanesia. Wanting to sustain an ongoing argument with these Western ideas and metaphysical assumptions, she attempts to make their "workings visible," to "exploit their reflexive potential" in her own narrative. To this end she employs three analytical axes—we/they (Western/Melanesian), gift/commodity, and feminism/anthropology—to reveal the particular features and characteristics of Melanesian sociality. These binary axes are posited as textually strategic fictions, specifically elaborated in her "plot" that seeks to reveal "the contextualised nature of indigenous constructs by exposing the contextualised nature of analytical ones" (M. Strathern 1988, 8). Not only does Strathern locate these analytical constructs in the social and cultural contexts in which they were produced, but she also attempts to demonstrate their specific purpose or intent.

In strategically employing this us/them divide, Strathern does not mean to imply that Melanesian societies are "timeless" or "monolithic." Nor does she consider them static objects of knowledge. Rather, she aims to scrutinize and expose the descriptive and exegetical practices of anthropology; to highlight the reality that "our thoughts come already formed, we think through images," metaphors, and analogies derived from our own social origins. She contends that anthropological exegesis—including her own analysis—*decodes* the way people represent themselves by explicating the values, expectations, and significance that they attribute to events and artifacts. Through the writing process a "parallel world to the perceived world" is created. It is a parallel, textual world with its own demands and "conditions of intelligibility" (1988, 16–17).

In setting down the "conditions of intelligibility" for her own text, Strathern insists that the world of Melanesian persons, people, and collectivities (groups) cannot be understood through the Western distinction between the individual and society and the related subject/object, nature/culture, domination/dominated, cause/effect antinomies. Indeed, she comments that

> there is no indigenous supposition of a [static, bounded] society that lies over or above or is inclusive of individual acts and unique events.

> There is no [hierarchical] domain that represents a condensation of social forces controlling elements inferior or in resistance to it. (1988, 102)

Moreover, the Western notion of the autonomous individual person who exists "in a permanently subjective state"—the independent agent, author, or cause of his/her own actions—does not apply to Melanesian persons (1988, 338). As such, gender, values, ideas, and conventions are not imposed or constructed on Melanesian persons by an autonomous, independent society or culture. Unlike Western individuals, Melanesian persons do not conceive of themselves as "proprietors" who own or are owned by culture or society. Indeed, they do not own personal characteristics such as gender. In short, the "commodity logic" integral to Enlightenment and post-Enlightenment Western thought does not pervade Melanesian notions of personhood (1988, 322). Rather, according to Strathern,

> Melanesian persons are as dividually as they are individually conceived. They contain a generalised sociality within. . . . Indeed, persons are frequently constructed as the plural and composite site of the [consanguineal and affinal, male and female] relationships that produced them. (1988, 13)

In using the notion of sociality, understood as "the creating and maintaining of relationships" (1988, 13), Strathern provides a "mirror image" of the Western notion of society. Similarly, the "composite [Melanesian] person" is intended to critically reflect the Western individual. She argues that "creating a kind of mirror-imagery gives form to our thought about the differences" between ideas derived from distinct social origins (1988, 17). Given her sensitivity to the distinct social origins of ideas, it is somewhat ironic that the term she uses to describe the distinct form of Melanesian personhood, *dividual,* is derived from Marriot's reflections on South Asian theories of the person. Marriot states that

> persons are generally thought by South Asians to be "dividual" or divisible. To exist, dividual persons absorb heterogeneous material influences. They must give out from themselves particles of their own coded substances—essences, residues, or other active influences—that may then reproduce in others something of the nature of the persons in

whom they have originated. (Marriot, cited in M. Strathern 1988, 348 n. 7)

Following Marriot, Strathern's characterization of the Melanesian person also includes an understanding of the Melanesian notion of the body as partible, relational. It is an understanding that is underpinned by Gregory's (1982) theoretical discussion of the distinction between gifts and commodities. Strathern asserts that through social relations and material exchanges, Melanesian "persons appropriate, absorb and consume nothing other than 'things'—parts of persons/relations in attachable and detachable form" (1988, 191–224, 225–67; 1993, 90). The valued and transacted things of which Strathern speaks are not Western commodities—inanimate objects alienated from their producer and exchanged between independent individuals. Rather, they are inalienable gifts that "circulate as parts of persons" (1988, 178), thereby establishing relationships with other persons or subjects. The relationship, rather than the thing itself, is the subject of the exchange (1988, 19).

Strathern's understanding of the Melanesian notion of the person as a "social microcosm" (1988, 13, 131) both necessitates and is inseparable from her identification of a distinctive form of Melanesian agency and social action. Accordingly, the person, as a register or site of dynamic social relations, is a living expression of, and gives living expression to, those relations (1988, 131). In other words, the person's actions and interactions are not only contingent upon the actions of multiple others, past and present, but his/her actions "externalise the parts or relations of which they are . . . composed" (Mosko 1992, 702). Action is not understood as the self-determined, independent expression of a person's free will. Instead, a person's actions in any given context are evoked, generated, or caused by the particular relations that constitute him/her. In differentiating between agent and person, Strathern writes:

> The person is construed from the vantage point of the relations that constitute him or her; she or he objectifies and is thus revealed in those relations. The agent is construed as the one who acts because of those relationships and is revealed in his or her actions. If a person is an agent seen from the point of view of her or his relations with others, the agent is the person who has taken action with those relations in view. In this the agent constitutes a "self." . . . The separation between agent and the person who is the cause of his or her acts is systemic, and governs

the Melanesian perception of action. To act as one's own cause becomes an innovation on this convention. (1988, 273)

In refining her understanding of social action and Melanesian sociality, Strathern states that two forms of plurality—"the composite and the dual"—underpin social relations between single persons or collectivities (groups) in Melanesia. People move from one form of sociality to another, "from a unity (manifested collectively or singly) to that unity split or paired with respect to another" (1988, 14). Strathern insists that one of the main ways that this shift between dual and composite plurality—or between identity and difference—is conceptualized is through gender.

> Single, composite persons do not reproduce. . . . It is dyadically conceived relationships that are the source and outcome of action. The products of relations—including the persons they create—inevitably have dual origins and are thus internally differentiated. This internal, dualistic differentiation must in turn be eliminated to produce the unitary individual. (1988, 14)

Gender and gender difference are relational, according to Strathern's formulation of Melanesian personhood. Because Melanesian persons are constituted dualistically, because they are understood to comprise male and female parts/relations, it is only in specific relational contexts, or indeed through specific material exchanges, that "being 'male' or being 'female' emerges as a 'holistic unitary state'" (1988, 14). Accordingly, same-sex relations generate different "productive outcomes" than cross-sex relations (1988, 324). As persons are imagined in dualistic forms—male and female, same sex and cross-sex—a person can also be understood as embodying "one of a pair of interrelated forms" (1988, 338).

Although introduced as textual fictions—analytical axes, rather than strict binary pairs—Strathern's oppositions arguably function as suspect facts. If this is not true for the author and those who have appropriated her strategic representation of Melanesian personhood (see Battaglia 1990; Foster 1995), then it is certainly true for readers, like myself, who remain suspicious of ahistorical and unitary conceptions of culture and the person.[39] Macintyre writes:

That M. Strathern acknowledges the artifice [of "Western" versus "Melanesian"] which entails the convergence of the social, the economic and the cultural in terms of a geographically defined entity . . . does not remove the problems of empiricism—those very problems that she sets her argument against. . . . This dichotomy brings with it the complications of essentialisation and Occidentalism (Carrier 1992), and the representation of culture as ahistorical and hypostatic. It is as if the intrusion of Europeans into Melanesia, and the changes they wrought, can only be understood as epiphenomenal. (1995, 29)

Critical of anthropology's pursuit of the exotic (Keesing and Jolly 1992), and of the organicist discourses of alterity that sustain these endeavors, proponents of what Foster (1995) terms the New Melanesian History encourage (Melanesianist) anthropologists to write of the complex relations between us and them, the West and Melanesia.[40] Like Macintyre, they claim that the Western/Melanesian dichotomy essentializes epistemological, cultural, or personal differences, thereby de-emphasizing the "similarities between Melanesian and Western social realities, similarities generated out of shared histories of colonialism and commerce" (Foster 1995, 2–3; see Thomas 1991, 52–59). Arguably then, us/them dichotomies not only suppress details of the multiple intersections between Western and Melanesian peoples, they also conceal the diverse effects of these relations. As Clifford notes, those who employ us/them dichotomies present cultures "as organically unified or traditionally continuous" rather than "negotiated" and "contested" present processes (1988, 273).

It is precisely this aspect of Strathern's work that most troubles Macintyre. She claims that Strathern's presentation of the Melanesians as unified, wholesome, and devoid of conflict denies past and present (pre-/colonial and postcolonial) forms of conflict and malevolent relations in these diverse communities (1995, 33). Not only does it romanticize Melanesian sociality but it also represents an "ahistorical," if not "utopian," "reification" of Melanesian ideas of personhood and relations between persons and things (1995, 34). Although Macintyre suggests that Strathern's representation of Melanesian notions of embodiment is limited, if not inadequate, she agrees that "the construction of the person as a social being . . . is metaphorised through the human body" (1995, 32). However, she cannot accept Strathern's contention that

Melanesian representations do not objectify persons or create and perpetuate subject/object, animate/inanimate antinomies. Drawing on her fieldwork experience on Tubetube, Macintyre argues that claims to the effect that "Melanesians do not use organicist concepts as metaphors or analogies, nor make distinctions between abstract notions of 'what bodies do or symbolise' and bodies as substantial entities" are unsustainable (1995, 33). As with the related idea that Melanesians understand the physical person/body to be literally created through the incorporation of gift relations expressed through the exchange of things with others, Strathern's presentation of Melanesian ways of knowing and understanding represents "too neat an inversion of Western ideas" (1995, 33). Her claims not only imply that Melanesians think in concrete rather than abstract terms, but they also deny the influence of Western (Cartesian) ways of knowing and understanding.

Jolly (1992b) also challenges Strathern's characterization of Melanesian personhood by questioning the status of the oppositions of Western individual and Melanesian composite person. Reflecting on the significance of the notion of the individual in Western contexts, she states:

> If we look not just at liberal philosophies of the individual, and the normative structures of American psychology but at the ethnography of our daily practice as persons in relation to each other, the individual seems more permeable and partible. Do we never see persons as composites of relations? Do we not recognise agency elicited by others rather than always as the action of a motivated individual? (1992b, 146)

Contemplating doing fieldwork, I accepted many of the criticisms made of Strathern's work and remained suspicious of her reliance on the seemingly postmodern,[41] Western metaphors of partibility, multiplicity, and decomposition to represent Melanesian sociality and personhood (see Josephides 1991). Despite these reservations, I continued to be challenged and inspired by her efforts to subject "Western conceptual systems to deconstructive scrutiny" (Keesing and Jolly 1992, 241). While not persuaded by her strategic use of us/them dichotomies, I nonetheless recognized her analysis as a highly original and incisive attempt to conceive and describe Melanesian sociality. Like Foster (1995, 3–5), I saw the value of combining critical reflection on the (literary) form, structure, and terms of anthropological analysis, with an acceptance that the actions of Melanesians arise out of distinct "historical and cultural origins."

Foster argues for the development of a "New Melanesian Anthropology" that combines New Melanesian History with the Western/Melanesian distinction expounded by Strathern.

> [It] must begin with the recognition that Melanesians understand themselves and act in terms—sometimes oppositional, sometimes syncretic—conditioned by the continuing encounter between agencies of (post) colonial states, capitalism, and Christianity, on one side, and highly localised practices for making meaning, on the other. (1995, 5)

Convinced of the need for ethnographic descriptions to acknowledge colonialism's history in Melanesia, he nevertheless cautions against privileging this history in all ethnographies. To do so risks promoting the ethnocentric "presupposition that Melanesian history and culture must be construed in relation to agents and agencies *originating elsewhere*" (1995, 13, emphasis in original). As Foster (following Sahlins 1993) suggests, it risks equating "colonial history with the history of the colonisers" (1995, 14). Equally pertinent, it also implies that the history of the colonizers, both within and outside of the colonies, remained independent and unaffected by the acts, precepts, and knowledge of the colonized (see Stoler 1991). Therefore, in attempting to understand and write these histories, Melanesian ethnographers and historians alike must remain mindful that the radical oppositions between them and us are fictions. They must also remain mindful of cultural difference. Clearly then, the New Melanesian Anthropology that Foster champions poses both an ethnographic and a methodological "challenge" (1995, 16).

Like Foster, I was convinced of the need for Melanesian anthropology to make its assumptions explicit, including "what it takes to be Melanesian assumptions" (Foster 1995, 18). However, I did not believe that ethnography was best served by the self-conscious and strategic use of us/them dichotomies. Such artifice accords clarity of a type, but it is a type that, as Strathern herself acknowledges, de-emphasizes the potentially fluid boundaries between them and us. It also obfuscates the temporal, processual, and relational dimensions of ethnographic understanding.

Why Research Sickness and Health?

In defining and refining my research field, I sought a focus for reflection on local notions of the gendered self/person and the ways of knowing and acting that inform these ideas. Given my interest in the ways people conceive the relations between body, mind, and spirit, these research interests seemed best accommodated through a potentially practical study of sickness and health. By focusing on health and sickness—particularly women's experience of pregnancy, childbirth, and breast-feeding—I hoped to learn of, and subsequently represent, the lived experience of some Milne Bay women, without ignoring the related lived experience of men. By retaining a focus on men, and the relations between men and women associated with sickness, health, birth, and death, I hoped to avoid some of the problems arising from women-centered studies in feminist anthropology. Foremost among them is the conflation of women with gender and gendered subjectivity (see Eisenstein 1984; Moore 1988). Also, given my interest in Strathern's notion of partibility, I could hardly neglect men in my research.

To further my research on women's lived experience of sickness and health, I intended to study the impact of Western-style primary health care on local knowledge and practices relating to the gendered person/self. In so doing, I aimed to consider some of the factors influencing the utilization of island and mainland health services. My research agenda was thus compatible with the critical interpretive approaches to medical anthropology.

While not without their own limitations, critical medical anthropologists subject the terms, parameters, and social/political outcomes of "conventional" medical anthropological research to much-needed deconstructive scrutiny (Good 1994; Hahn 1995; Lock and Scheper-Hughes 1990; Morsy 1990; Singer 1989).[42] Exponents of this approach propose alternative research strategies and directions for the anthropology of sickness and health. These include recognition of the interconnection between microlevel and macrolevel social relations and processes, recognition of the transformative power of global capitalism, an understanding of disease as a social and biological product, recognition of Western biomedicine's attempts to dominate and replace other medical systems at all levels of health care in diverse contexts, and recognition and representation of the social-relational dimensions of people's experience of suffering (Singer 1990, 182–85).[43]

Rather than projects focused on the beliefs and practices of "alternative medical systems," critical interpretive medical anthropology concentrates on the cultural construction of all knowledge pertaining to sickness, health, and the sentient human body. Accordingly, cultural knowledge and practices are recognized as "dynamic processes" that are continually negotiated. While eschewing extreme forms of cultural relativism, it avoids the importation of Western medical concepts into the analysis of the dialogue between anthropologist and informant. Embedded in the critical interpretive anthropological tradition (see Keesing 1987), the critical medical anthropology expounded by Lock and Scheper-Hughes (1990) focuses on the relation between what they call the three bodies: the individual body, the social body, and the body politic. They suggest that critical medical anthropology must first "describe the variety of [conscious and unconscious] metaphorical conceptions about the body and associated narratives" before then showing the "social, political and individual uses to which these conceptions are applied in practice" (1990, 49–50). This approach to the study of sickness and health grew out of a critical engagement with phenomenological and hermeneutic knowledge and practices. Consistent with a Melanesian anthropology that is not wedded to the strategic use of us/them dichotomies, it came closest to my intended method of research.

Writing Ethnography

As Clifford rightly states, "ethnography is, from beginning to end, enmeshed in writing" (1988, 25). But people, places, and things are not (or not literally) texts, however integrally related they may be in both their imagined or actual manifestations. It is a point that bears reiterating at a time when discussion of ethnography has been subsumed by critical literary debate about texts and issues of authority and authorship.[44]

Two seminal works—Clifford's (1988) essay "On Ethnographic Authority" and Geertz's *Works and Lives: The Anthropologist as Author*—have arguably perpetuated the conflation of field with text, and fieldwork with writing. Using ethnographic authority as an analytic prism, Clifford explores how the ethnographer's messy research experiences become authoritative cultural interpretations. In detailing some of the theoretical shortcomings and advantages of experiential, interpretive, dialogical, or polyphonic paradigms for "embodying authority" in ethnographic texts, he reminds us that we should not mistake textual representations for the fieldwork experience. For example, he is clear that the dialogues reproduced in the text are the ethnographer's representation of dialogue and, as such, do not render the texts dialogical. But by the same token neither should we treat the issue of authority in the text as the key epistemological/methodological problem faced by ethnographers. What is or can be done in the field should not be conflated with what is or can be done in the text. The various dilemmas posed by participant observation fieldwork and the speculation and imagining that precedes it are never merely textual issues.

At one point Geertz quite explicitly states that anthropologists "have been willed, not as so often thought, a research method, 'Participant Observation' (that turns out to be a wish, not a method) but a literary dilemma, 'Participant Description'" (1988, 33). In Geertz's hands, epistemological dilemmas—associated with intersubjective knowing, the identity of the ethnographer, the ability of the ethnographer to understand the experiences of others, if not the ethnographic project itself—become textual issues of authorship, "writerly" identity, narrative, and discourse construction. Critical, even dismissive, of the self-reflexive "I-witness" experimental ethnographies reservedly embraced by Clifford (1988, 1989), Geertz argues that ethnographers deceive themselves if they believe that authorial confessions of ethnocentrism and subjectivity, and the use of transcribed fieldwork conversations, render their texts more transparent and authentic. In short, they fool themselves if they believe that "to be a convincing 'I-witness'" they must first "become a convincing 'I'" (Eipper 1996, 20; Geertz 1988, 78–79). Geertz claims that these texts risk becoming "author saturated" explorations of the self by the "detour of the other."

Geertz's criticisms are persuasive, indeed necessary, particularly if a primary aim of these texts is dispersal of authorship and authority. For, as both Geertz and Clifford recognize, ethnography remains the "virtuoso orchestration by a single author of all the discourses in his or her text" (Clifford 1988, 50). Indeed, Moore argues that even multiple and collaboratively authored texts are "far from radical," for they do "not in fact revise the standard anthropological notion of authorship, of what it is to author something, they . . . simply make it plural" (1994c, 117). Moreover, whatever the number of authors, *if* the writer(s) of reflexive ethnography believe that the "I" of the text is the same as the "I" that writes the text, then they mistake fiction for fact.

If authors of reflexive texts believe that reflection on their self/selves in the text represents a radical, postmodernist deconstruction of subject/selves, then they are deceived (see Bourdieu and Wacquant 1992; Moore 1994c, 127–28). They confuse experience with representation of that experience, but, more importantly, they fail to appreciate that the reflexive turn to oneself is born of romanticism and modernism—the modernist ideals of self-examination, and self-mastery in particular (see Taylor 1989, 176).

By framing his critique in terms of authorship and authority, Geertz, like Clifford, effectively recasts the ethnographer as author, rather than participant observer. In addition, methodological dilemmas associated with participant observation are recast as textual issues about the way experience is authorized. Although incisive, this critique of the authorization of experience obfuscates as much as it clarifies. By emphasizing the writing process, Geertz and Clifford, in their different ways, deflect attention from the integral methodological relationship between participant observation and writing (Eipper 1996; Jackson 1989, 156–87). The multifaceted nature and purpose of ethnographic witnessing are overlooked (Eipper 1996), as is its significance for anthropological knowledge creation. For ethnography "is a revelatory mode of knowledge; it results from a doubling of testimony: the ethnographer folds one kind of witnessing into another" (1996, 16). There is the witnessing that occurs in the field and the witnessing to that witnessing that occurs in the text.

> As a species of reportage ethnographic writing is *nothing* if not testimonial—this is its rationale and its virtue. . . . [I]ts epistemological status rests upon the experiential warrant which is its *raison d'être*. We trust it because it seeks to represent, if not reality (whatever that is) then the *actual*—the world as the ethnographer *engaged* with it. . . . We are writers almost by default; it is our witnessing which defines us. (Eipper 1996, 24–25, emphasis in original)

Therefore, it is not only in the text that the ethnographer must confront what it means to be a faithful "I-witness," s/he must also confront this in the field, and in later conversations and oral re-presentations of the lived field. After all, anthropology is not only a written, but also a visual and verbal tradition. These forms of witnessing rely on mutual respect and trust between informants, ethnographer, and audience. The ethnographer must then gain the respect and trust of readers, viewers, and listeners when she witnesses to her own and others' witnessing, testifies to her own and others' testimonies. While

> this may entail establishing (in certain respects almost inevitably) our authority with them, the process is not reducible to that. Equally

important in the field (if not on the page) will be our character and conduct—not to mention the enduring ether of socio-historical circumstance which informs and misinforms ethnographer and ethnographee alike. (1996, 23)

Eipper suggests that trust, unlike authority, cannot be "controlled" or "established as a textual strategy." It must be volunteered. Little is guaranteed when the ethnographer attempts to render herself a convincing "I-witness" by becoming a convincing "I." How, then, should the ethnographer bear witness in the text? How should she witness to her own and others' witnessing? What, if anything, can she do to establish her testifying, textual self as trustworthy? In contemplating this prior to fieldwork, to me the conclusion to Clifford's essay hinted at a way forward.

Experiential, interpretive, dialogical and polyphonic processes are at work, discordantly, in any ethnography, but coherent presentation presupposes a controlling mode of authority. . . . [T]his imposition of coherence on an unruly textual process is now inescapably a matter of strategic choice. (Clifford 1988, 54)

Given this, and since "naive claims to the authority of experience" (1988, 54) have been convincingly challenged, the contemporary ethnographer must first consider why she has chosen a particular way to bear witness in the text. Such a decision is necessarily contingent upon whom, what, and how she witnessed in the field and for/to whom the text is witnessing. The testifying self she textually presents is not only contingent upon personal and ethical factors, but on the context in which she writes. In choosing how she bears witness she must also consider the specific object and intended social and political outcome of the research. In so doing, she will confront, either directly or indirectly, knowingly or unknowingly, the questions, What can be known? How can it be known? Who knows? For whom is it known? If Bourdieu's pragmatic notion of methodological pluralism is extended to the ethnographic text, then the various representations of selves, of authority in the text, can be understood both as ends to strategic fieldwork means and as strategic means to epistemological, political, and social ends—be they personal, communal, or disciplinary.[45]

In wanting to tell the stories of people's experience of sickness, health, and knowing—stories that would otherwise only be heard by people's neighbors and kin—I recognized that I was committing myself to a "limited, fallible and ill-informed mode of knowledge making," one that "eschews all pretensions to absolutism and omniscience" (Eipper 1996, 22). The ethnography would not constitute certain definitive knowledge, but, rather, it would present and re-present uncertain feelings and knowing. My imagined readers, the people who would witness my witnessing, were a heterogeneous group. They included the people with whom I would research, my husband, anthropologists, feminist and cultural theorists, Papua New Guinea health administrators, friends, and family! In contemplating how to accommodate these diverse readers and readings, I was guided by several principles. I wanted all the readers to recognize and identify, at least in part, with the lives and living dilemmas of the people represented in the text, including my own personal dilemmas as ethnographer.

Clear that the ethnography would be my testimony to my own and others' testimonies, I nevertheless wished to faithfully represent what they said or did, when, where, and with whom. While I did not believe it possible to represent people as they would represent themselves, I believed it important to try to keep faith with what they said or did with me in the field (see Neumann 1992, 118–24). Following Fabian, I hoped to represent myself in the (spatiotemporal) world occupied by the people with whom I lived. Fabian argues that by rendering the other as temporally and spatially distinct from the subject, anthropology has been complicit in the Western colonial appropriations of the spaces and times of its others (1983, 143–44). He argues for the restoration of intersubjective time and communication as a form of praxis. Upon my return from Nuakata, I was so intrigued by the intersubjective process of coming to know in the field that I decided I had to attempt to represent this process in any text I produced.

Ethnographic Feminism, Feminist Ethnography, or a Feminist's Ethnography?

What happens when [a] . . . woman who experiences in her body and mind and imagination does social theory, studying human beings in society who also experience in their body and mind and imagination? Social theory, I would suggest, still tends to function as an exercise in disenchantment. Analytic mastery is the name of the game, with notions of understanding and control still closely linked. There is a kind of fear associated with admitting that we are ourselves and are, in our analysis, dealing with passionate, embodied people, prone to romanticism and capable of volatility. A kind of laundering occurs which shrinks the object under investigation. (Mortimer 1990, 45)

When Mortimer asks, What if I talked like a woman right here in public? she dares social theorists, male and female alike, to render the experience of passionate embodied humanity present in their theory.[46] Dissatisfied with social scientific approaches that objectify, partition, and launder out the emotional, romantic connections between people (particularly between mother and child), Mortimer entreats theorists to take both their own and others' lived experiences of sensual, fleshy "interactive human beings" seriously. Eschewing objectified notions of the body, mind, and imagination, she challenges us to speak of relationships—our tangible connection with one another—rather than merely chronicling the objective conditions in which these relations arise (1990, 46). Like the anthropologists of experience, it is meaning she seeks. Not the meaning that is distilled in eternal realms, providing a template for existence, but the meaning born of tangible, fleshy, finite relationships. To this end, she urges us to forsake the comforts, the certain trajectory, of traditional empirical paths and clearly bounded, objective fields of investigation—the modernist route leading to certain Certainty, Truth, Knowledge, and Freedom. In making our escape we are not compelled to retrace our steps, noting the ones we avoided on the original journey—we are spared the indifferent nihilist stomp backward over old ground. Instead we are encouraged to move along tentatively, speaking our "hopes and values," yet without sure knowledge of our destination. In committing ourselves to this path we must have the courage to challenge and replace the signposts (the language, the semantic fields) for those that follow. They, too, must do the same.

[A]s we know, the destabilisation of language may pave the way for loosening up our categories, freeing ourselves from reified thinking and closure. And this is not just a fugitive freedom. If we recognise there is no linguistic safety zone or prison house, we might put aside the fear of naming that characterises much present social theoretical discourse. (Mortimer 1990, 64)

Among many other things, the work that follows represents a response to Mortimer's dare. It is my stuttering attempt to talk as a woman, as a feminist and an anthropologist, but, above all, as someone who conceives herself as interdependent upon negotiated relationships with people, men and women, young and old alike. Certainly it is a work written by a self-identified feminist—someone who remains committed to identifying and alleviating women's oppression and empowering those who are disempowered—but is it (a) feminist ethnography? The answer to this question depends on how one defines feminist anthropology and ethnography.

Feminist anthropology is typically considered a politically motivated and informed mode of interpretation and critique of gender relations, if not women's lives in diverse cultural contexts (Behar 1995; Behar and Gordon 1995; Cole and Phillips 1995; di Leonardo 1991; Moore 1988). It is neither a unitary field nor an uncontested one. Since its emergence in the late 1970s, the political aims and theoretical foci of feminist anthropology have changed as they have influenced and been influenced by feminist, anthropological, postmodern, and postcolonial debates. Despite the differing theoretical positions and political objectives of feminist anthropologists, feminist anthropology remains broadly committed to exposing and resisting the domination of women by men. Arising out of the "anthropology of women," which sought to redress male bias in the discipline—particularly, biased ethnographic representations of women—feminist anthropology quickly developed a critique of the universal category "woman" and related claims about the universal subordination of women. Keen to avoid (further) marginalization within the discipline of social anthropology, feminist anthropology shifted its focus from women and "women studying women" to gender and gender relations. It thereby sought to engender anthropological knowledge and focus critical attention on notions of difference, a preoccupation that continues today. Contemporary feminist anthropology is concerned not just with gender differences but more specifically with the intersection between gender, race, class, sexuality, and age differences. It is interested in the way these differences are produced, and their effects, both within and between women, and between men and women. Concerned with the production of these differences within anthropological and feminist discourses, it challenges the commonly held assumption within anthropological discourse that these differences are somehow secondary to the master trope of cultural difference.

The publication of *Writing Culture* in 1986 renewed many feminist anthropologists' interest in and commitment to textual innovation. Feminist anthropologists were incensed by Clifford's (1986, 20–21) claim that they had been excluded from the book because their textual innovations were neither particularly feminist nor novel. By way of response, some pointed to the long history of innovative, experimental women's writing within the discipline and noted that even recent feminist reclamations of this work had been overlooked or marginalized. In making this critique they questioned the constitution of the anthropological canon.[47] While some examined the gendered power relations that perpetuate the "erasure of contemporary women's writing in sociocultural anthropology" (Lutz 1990), others drew attention to pathbreaking feminist anthropological contributions to theoretical debates about knowledge and representation.[48] Others, who concurred with Clifford's observations, began to explore the possibilities for and define the parameters of feminist ethnography, distinct from, yet clearly related to, feminist anthropology. Where feminist anthropology sought to understand and critique women's oppression by men, feminist ethnography was primarily concerned with the development of innovative, if not experimental, feminist ethnographic texts.[49] Several articles, one by Stacey (1988), two by Abu-Lughod (1990, 1991), and another by Visweswaran (1988), have proved pivotal to the emergence of this diverse and contested field.

Stacey (1988) argues that a truly feminist ethnography is an impossible ideal, because the feminist political imperative to promote collaborative, respectful, and reciprocal research relations and methods is at odds with the exploitation inherent to ethnographic research. Placed and placing herself in a position of power in the field, the ethnographer must constantly negotiate her potentially conflicting roles as confidant, friend/fictive kin, and researcher. These ethical dilemmas are compounded in the text that, however collaborative, ultimately and inevitably remains the product of the researcher. In both articulating and producing her own partially feminist ethnography,[50] Stacey draws on postmodernist and experimental ethnographic forms that recognize the partial nature of ethnographic truth. She argues for ethnographies that are accessible, self-critical, and mindful of the theoretical and narrative strategies they employ.

Similarly, Abu-Lughod (1990) advocates for accessible feminist ethnographies that balance literary and popularist styles, while maintaining their focus on the particulars of individual women's lives. More optimistic than Stacey about the possibilities of and for feminist ethnography, she argues for texts that are attuned to issues of race, ethnicity, class, and power relations between the ethnographer and those with whom she researches. She urges feminist anthropologists to experiment with the form of their ethnographies, while remaining sensitive to the political implications of the metaphors, the textual choices, and the narrative strategies they employ.

In considering the possibilities for and limitations of feminist ethnography, Abu-Lughod—and, to a much lesser extent, Stacey—emphasizes the ethical, political, and epistemological issues associated with writing feminist ethnography. Many other feminist ethnographers also focus on ethnographic texts, variously reflecting on the relationship between ethnography and autobiography,[51] issues of style and genre,[52] the purposes and projects of feminist ethnography,[53] modes of reflexivity, the status and political implications of ethnographic knowledge,[54] and feminist diversity.[55] Other feminist ethnographers, however, are highly critical of the apparent conflation of feminist ethnography with texts, arguing that equal attention should be given to the research process and the methods employed in the field. As such, they claim that the feminist researcher must remain aware of how she affects the research process and its outcomes. She should, they insist, be sensitive to the power relations between herself and those with whom she researches and, being concerned with and challenged by the priorities and experience of the people researched, remain open to changing her research agenda (e.g., Gordon 1993; Scheper-Hughes 1992).

Elizabeth Enslin's (1994) critique takes this approach one step further. Like many others, she claims that political issues of social inequality and injustice have become institutionalized as merely textual dilemmas in much feminist and postmodern anthropology. In this way, they have become disconnected from the practical needs and lived realities of those researched. Conceived as political interventions, these radical textual strategies are ineffective, ultimately serving little more than careerist ends.[56] Accordingly, feminist ethnography risks betraying the very people it seeks to represent and empower (Visweswaran 1994). Enslin argues for a feminist praxis that privileges practices other than writing. These, whether advocacy, mediation, translation, or other forms of practical assistance, should, she claims, benefit the community studied.

In contemplating fieldwork I positioned myself in the "awkward" (M. Strathern 1987a) yet fertile conjunction between feminism and anthropology (Caplan 1988b). Like Strathern (1987a, 1989b), I recognized that the subject matter, methods, and political aims of some feminist anthropological projects are at odds with an ethnographic agenda to identify, if not promote, difference between self and other, researcher and researched. Clearly, these potentially contradictory approaches create political, ethical, and epistemological dilemmas for the feminist anthropologist/ethnographer. However, unlike Strathern (1987a), and to some degree Stacey (1988), I believed it worthwhile to embrace the problematic and messy entanglements between feminist and anthropological knowledges and practices as way of allowing each to critique the other (Kirby 1989).[57] In short, I aimed to "engender anthropology with a feminist imagination" (Wheatley 1994). Believing myself engaged in a feminist ethnographic project, I, like Visweswaran, was mindful of the need to continually scrutinize and de-essentialize the terms and boundaries of feminist ethnography; to continually "rewrite the terms of 'home' and 'world' through a regenerated feminist praxis" (Visweswaran 1988, 112).

This work then is an attempt to foreground the relational embodied experiences of Nuakatan men and women—particularly women's experience of pregnancy, birth, breast-feeding, menstruation, and death—as a way of reflecting on my own and other people's ways of knowing and understanding notions of the self and person. But even more than this, it is an attempt to explore the often forgotten fact, reality, or truth— unpopular words in the postmodern, postcolonial milieu—that in spite of our differences we are all of women born, dependent, and in need of care. And, despite unresolvable questions about our mortality, we all face a certain death.

༛

Nuakata, October 1993—A Conversation

Shelley: We need to begin packing, if we're leaving the day after tomorrow.

Roger: We have to decide what we're leaving behind.

Shelley: And whom we will give things to. We need to make a list so that we don't forget anyone. [*Pause*] What about the Coleman lamp? Who shall we give that to? Everyone will want it.

Roger: Taubada Antiya. He'll use it himself, but he will also take it along to community meetings and church celebrations. What about the trunk?

Shelley: I don't know. Who would want it? What would they do with it anyway? What would they store in it? No one has any books except their Bible and hymnbook and what else would they put in it. No one has enough things to fill it. I think we should take it back to Alotau and give it to Ken and Lisa and the boys. They can store equipment or toys or books in it.

Roger: Wycliffe and Washington and the others could keep using it as a card table.

Shelley: They won't use it as a card table. They'll just sit and play cards on their sleeping mats. They just did that for us, because they know *dimdims* [white people] have trouble sitting on the ground for a long time!

Roger: Don't you think we should leave it here? It's really solid and indestructible. I am sure someone would want it.

Shelley: I don't know. I am just not sure that it belongs here.

Roger: What do you mean?

Shelley: I don't know. We can leave everything else behind, but somehow leaving the trunk seems all wrong. It seems out of place.

Roger: I don't understand. [*Pause*] Do you want to take it back to Australia?

Shelley: What would we do with it? No, it doesn't belong there either.

My metaphorical trunk unpacked, the baggage I carried is now revealed; what follows is a testimony of experiences shared, of my witness to Nuakatan people's witnessing.

Chapter One

≫≪

Tracing Nuakata

Arriving

As the plane began its descent toward Gurney airstrip on the outskirts of Alotau, I pressed my face to the glass straining to catch a glimpse of the view. The Owen Stanley Ranges stretched out to the west, while directly below us, at their foothills, oil palm plantations gave the landscape a strange uniformity, broken only by small village settlements and the eddies of dust churned by cars rocketing along unmade roads. To the east, coconut palms bordered Milne Bay, visible only as a sliver bathed in afternoon sun. After a year of frustration waiting for the research visa it was difficult to believe that we were finally arriving in Milne Bay Province. And difficult, too, to match my porthole impressions with those given to me by my father. Some fifty years earlier, in the dead of a stormy night, he had looked out from the airforce plane to see darkness punctuated by a row of lights. Believing it was the Gurney airstrip, the pilot descended, only to discover that the lights were hurricane lamps shining from within American army tents. The plane crash-landed at the end of the row. Remarkably, no lives were lost. A young and nervous conscript, this was the inauspicious beginning to my father's nine months' stay in Milne Bay, remembered mainly for rain, mud, malaria, and "friendly natives." How strange it was to find myself retracing his footsteps and in circumstances so utterly removed from his own. Given the circumstances of my arrival, how would I remember Milne Bay and some of its people?

Waiting for us at the airport was Linda, a missionary based at Diwala, the Summer Institute of Linguistics (Wycliffe Bible Translators) compound on the outskirts of Alotau. As for many anthropologists, the relationships between ourselves and some local missionaries proved crucial to the fieldwork. In our case, their practical and emotional support was invaluable and gratefully received. With these people we subsequently exchanged experiences and some shared understanding of daily life in remote and unfamiliar rural/island communities, negotiating the lack of familiar food and resources, the trials of language learning, sickness, and homesickness. But these were also disturbing and confronting alliances. While friendly and respectful, these relationships were haunted by a largely unspoken sense of mutual suspicion—a suspicion between anthropologists and missionaries with long-standing historical antecedents and well-rehearsed themes. Offspring of colonialism, each has cast the other as the errant sibling. Accordingly, each of the eight or so missionaries with whom we had significant contact articulated variations of the following refrain:

> Anthropologists often have a remarkable understanding of the culture of the people with whom they work. This is astounding, given their relatively short periods of time in the field compared with missionaries, their inadequate knowledge of the language, and their lack of substantial or ongoing practical and material commitment to the people with whom they work. Anthropologists use their research to further their careers, often showing little concern for the consequences of their research in the places where they do fieldwork. They sometimes attempt to revive extant cultural knowledge and practices of, for example, witchcraft and sorcery, thereby legitimating the (demonic and) potentially deadly practices which missionaries and government service providers have worked long and hard to eradicate.[1] This is indicative of a moral relativism which is reinforced by romanticized views of local people and their cultural practices. They perceive change and development as necessarily negative. Finally, many anthropologists have betrayed the friendships and support they have received from missionaries, by criticizing their work in their texts.

Recognizing these comments as truisms that preclude subtle debate, it was only through subsequent conversations and experience with local people that we realized that our own refrain on Melanesian missionaries was also simplistic:[2]

> There is much to be admired about the long-standing commitment of missionaries to the people with whom they work, including their

knowledge of the local language, and their efforts to provide practical assistance to the communities with which they work. However, they continue to enliven prejudicial and disempowering colonial relationships by foisting their evangelical agendas on people. Often patronizing, if not at times racist, they show only selective interest in, and respect for, local cultural knowledge and practice.

Not only did we harbor ahistorical and deterministic ideas about the colonizing role of contemporary foreign missionaries, but we also had not been willing to believe that the Milne Bay churches have "in many ways . . . ceased to be an alien presence" (Thune 1990, 104).[3]

Several days after our arrival in Alotau, the capital of Milne Bay Province, we met with the provincial secretary to seek approval to conduct fieldwork on one of three previously nominated islands. He was a genial man who made us feel immediately welcome. A public servant and political appointee of the national government, he was suspended three weeks later in the wake of political conflict between the provincial and national governments. Anxious, expecting to be told where I was permitted to conduct research, we were somewhat surprised by the conversation that unfolded: "So, where do you want to go?"

"If possible, we would like to go to Nuakata."

"Nuakata?—Nuakata?" He reached for a map. Like most local people we had met in Alotau, the Provincial Secretary had not even heard of Nuakata. As he placed the map on the coffee table between us, I pointed to a small speck at latitude 10°17′S and longitude 151°01′E, and repeated a well-practiced line: "It is a small island that lies in the Goschen Strait of the Solomon Sea, between East Cape [the southeastern tip of Papua New Guinea] and Normanby Island. It is roughly thirty miles from Alotau and fifteen kilometers east of East Cape."

"So why do you want to go to Nuakata in particular?"

"I would like to study health, particularly women's health in relation to pregnancy and birth. Because Nuakata is relatively close to Alotau, it is ideal for researching the relationship between mainland, Western-style medical services and traditional medicine. Anthropologists who have worked in this region say that little is known about the island. Given Nuakata's location, it has a surprisingly marginal status in the Province."

The conversation continued for a while, before the secretary extended his best wishes for the research, directed us to meet with a senior administrator in the health department, and bid us farewell. Final provincial approval had been granted, and we were free to travel to Nuakata and seek permission from the local community.

Our conversation with the health department administrator assumed a different tenor. Present with us in the tiny office were two senior health department officials, summoned to attend the meeting. Sandwiched between them, all of us facing the administrator, I could hear myself and then Roger speaking as if to persuade and convince. The administrator assumed control, plying me with questions about my research intentions. To my surprise, he revealed that he had lived on Nuakata when he was a child. He had not been back since that time; indeed, he had not been back to his mother's village on a nearby island for over twenty-five years. He told us that his education had taken him far afield to universities in places beyond Papua New Guinea. It had given him many things, both material and intellectual. Although irrevocably changed by the paths he had taken, his longing for the people and places of his childhood had never been extinguished. But the changes in him, his material and intellectual wants and needs, had become immovable obstacles blocking his return to the village. His was a homeless longing. Could we understand this? Could we write of this dilemma?

Returning to my proposed research he voiced his deep suspicion of anthropologists: "Many do not use their research findings to help the people they have lived with and many never return to the places once they have left." As evidence of this, he spoke of Malinowski and several unnamed German anthropologists who had worked on the Trobriand Islands. I was stuck for words. An inexperienced, though not uninformed or disempowered ethnographer, I was made to contemplate and bear the practical and discursive "sins" of my mostly nameless anthropological forebears. They resounded in my mind like a list of prior convictions read before a court: accessory-after-the-fact to Western colonialism through the production of orientalist, essentialist, and primitivist texts (Carrier 1992; Young 1992, 195); failure to inform participants of the purpose and outcome of study; failure to observe a duty of care for the living dilemmas faced by informants.

Although aware of my potentially compromised and compromising endeavor, I remained convinced of the need to tell the story of the encounter between small-scale, materially impoverished societies and those powerful societies conventionally, but problematically, termed the West (Gewertz and Errington 1991a, 3; Scheper-Hughes 1992; Taussig 1993). It was my intention to research and write on Nuakata and its people in a way that might value and promote their attempts to maintain autonomy in the midst of economic globalization (Gewertz and Errington 1991a). But faced with the administrator's accusations, my well-meaning (and what I later recognized as misplaced) intentions seemed like a lame offering. At the same time I wondered about the administrator's suspicion of anthropologists. Was his inability to return to his village relevant? Had his education and life-style removed him from his past, his kin, his people? Did we share different, yet related, struggles to make our work and research helpful to local people? Perhaps we were both engaged in compromising endeavors?

Searching for an adequate response, I agreed that some ethnographers had failed the people with whom they researched and voiced my hope that I would be different. At this point the administrator invited the senior health department officials to speak. Both bore obvious ill-feeling, greeting my proposed research with a disinterest that bordered on cynicism, even contempt. Staring at me, pausing as if for effect, one finally asked, "I know what we'll get out of it, but what will *you* get out of it?" "A Ph.D.," was my faltering reply. When I tentatively suggested a meeting with them to discuss regional health matters both agreed, but claimed they were too busy to make immediate plans. Faced with this perceived hostility I did not pursue further contact with them.

The tension was relieved by the arrival of Jennifer Henry, the health extension officer for Alotau District, including Nuakata. Jennifer was directed to assist us with our preparations to go to Nuakata. Having agreed to meet with the administrator before we returned to Australia, we departed with Jennifer, who talked with us for an hour or so—just long enough for the tension associated with the previous meeting to ebb away. My memory of that exchange proved harder to dispel. It remained indelibly etched into my mind—as a caution, a dare that challenges me anew as I write. Ironically, when the time came for us to leave Papua New Guinea, the administrator had been replaced by someone who showed only polite interest in my research.

During our conversation Jennifer told us that her mother came from Nuakata. Wanting to see her and needing to settle a long-running land dispute at the Nuakata aid post, she offered to accompany us to the island, so that I could seek permission to do the fieldwork. We could travel there on her brothers' *subu*—two canoes covered and joined by a flat wooden shelf and powered by a small outboard motor. We leaped at the offer. Two weeks later, in the midafternoon of 23 January 1993, we set out for Nuakata together with Jennifer and her infant daughter, her cousin-sister Anne, and fifteen or so Nuakatan women and children, who had been in Alotau selling garden produce at the market. Among them only Anne and Jennifer seemed to speak English. Together with their baggage, all the women and children squeezed under a tentlike canopy erected toward the bow of the boat. Keen to catch the view, we perched ourselves near the stern on top of several bags of betel nut. As the *subu* pulled away from the dock Roger and I felt a surge of nervous excitement. The waiting and anticipating was nearly over. Nuakata was before us, some eight or nine hours away.

Leaving Alotau behind we began our slow journey out along the bay. Ahead of us on the water was a small motorized workboat, one of many that regularly ply the waters between the mainland and the eighty-three or so islands that constitute what anthropologists term the Massim area of Milne Bay Province. I use the term *boat* reluctantly, for this vessel, like so many we had seen at Alotau's Sanderson Bay wharf, was a miserable imitation of a small seagoing craft. Fashioned with seaworthy intent, its flaking paint, rotting timbers, and exhausted diesel engine had long defeated this promise. Later when we traveled on similar vessels—overloaded with cargoes of people and goods—we discovered that life jackets, flares, life rafts, and buoys were nonexistent. Island people face considerable risks when they undertake these boat journeys to visit relatives living on the mainland, seek hospital care, and buy and sell goods in Alotau's market, supermarkets, and hardware stores. These risks were underlined for us when, several months later, during a violent cyclonic storm two boats sank. Many passengers drowned; others were taken by sharks.

Traveling close to the bay's western shoreline, we could see many small villages nestled in among the green, all set against the lush and imposing backdrop of the Owen Stanley Ranges. As night descended our attention returned to the boat. We marveled at the captain's knowledge of the sea. Steering without compass, chart, or light he guided the *subu* onward, his task eventually made easier by the rising moon and a vast canopy of stars. Casting my eyes skyward, smelling the sea, listening to the waves wash against the bow, I felt a sense of disbelief. Could this moment be mine? Could Roger and I really be living this enchanting journey?

Several hours later, Nuakata came into view as a shadow on the horizon. Its central volcanic mountain, Tanalabwa, rising 309 meters above sea level, formed a gray outline against the night sky. Its western and eastern slopes were visible as tracings that gently ambled down to the sea. In the foreground and to the west of Nuakata were three small islands: Pahilele, Iabama, and to the southwest Hana Kuba Kuba. Later we learned that Iabama and Pahilele belong to East Cape, and the fifteen people living on Pahilele speak Tewala, the East Cape language. Hana Kuba Kuba belongs to Nuakata but, like Iabama, it is uninhabited. Around midnight we approached the northwestern side of Nuakata, entering the still waters of Halewa Una bay. Unable to see the shore in the dark, the captain steered the boat toward a distant fire burning on the beach—a beacon, anticipating our arrival. As the boat approached the shore we could see several people waiting in the shadows. Once ashore Roger and I were directed to sleep in a disused trade store in Jennifer's mother's hamlet, Hapela'awa'awa.

We woke early the next morning to discover our sense of enchantment had dissipated. A feeling of apprehension had taken its place. Would we be fed? Where should we wash? How should I seek permission to do the research? With these anxieties, I tentatively stepped out into the day. To my surprise the hamlet was completely deserted save for pigs, roosters, and dogs. Not knowing what to do, I set out in search of a creek to wash. There I found Jennifer washing clothes. Neither of us said much. For my part I felt quite disoriented. Was it culturally sensitive to wash in front of her? Why was she not talking? Had I done something wrong? Sensing my uncertainty Jennifer instructed me to wash. Embarrassed, childlike in my hesitancy, I obliged, but my unease remained.

Upon returning to the hamlet I retreated inside the trade store to find Roger fully dressed and waiting. His foray outside had yielded results similar to mine. Finding the captain of the *subu* sitting smoking with a group of young men, down by the shore, he had sat down with them. They had continued to talk and laugh among themselves, largely ignoring his efforts to communicate. Finally, feeling totally out of place, he had drifted back to the hamlet. With this news I suddenly burst out crying. It all seemed too difficult. Why were these people so unfriendly? How could we live with them for a year?

Our second day on Nuakata was as exhilarating as the first was distressing. Beginning at Hapela'awa'awa and heading west we walked around the entire island, visiting most hamlets before concluding our circumnavigation at the aid post. Moses, the community health worker, accompanied us on our journey, which culminated in a community meeting at the aid post later in the afternoon. Fluent in English, Moses acted as our guide and adviser. We had been directed to choose a place to live, in the event that the community allowed us to stay. As we walked from hamlet to hamlet people received us warmly, inviting us to rest, while offering us green coconuts, watermelon, mango, or pineapple to eat. We welcomed these friendly gestures—grateful for their hospitality and refreshment on such a hot and humid day.

In making this trek we followed a well-defined path that, for the most part, traced the shoreline of the island—a round-trip of roughly fourteen kilometers that took six hours by foot.[4] We left this path at points, weaving our way along short trails that led to inland hamlets, each providing a home to no more than ten to fifteen people. These hamlets comprised two or three bush material houses, built on stumps one to two meters above the ground. Most hamlets were located less than 500 meters from the shore. As we walked from place to place we were not only struck by the changing land- and seascapes but also by each hamlet's distinctive outlook and appearance. Many were tucked away in lush bush surrounds. Some backed onto mosquito-infested mangrove swamps. Others, located fifty meters or so from narrow shorelines, had unimpeded views of the sea and neighboring islands. People clearly brought their own distinctive ways and material means to these living spaces. Some hamlets had beautiful gardens, others large houses, while others still had more modest dwellings that stood alone amid large cleared spaces.

As we moved along the main path encircling Nuakata, Moses stopped at various places to point out particular rocks or trees that functioned as boundary markers for four identified sides of the island—Bwauli, Bomatu, Bolime, and Yalasi—named after the four prevailing winds that blow across its shores. The division of the island into sides occurred in 1984 when the island's sports association decided to institute a round-robin soccer, netball, and volleyball competition. The community decided on these geographical divisions as a basis for team membership. Over the ensuing years these geographical divisions have assumed wider social significance, providing an organizational basis for communal work, local markets, and church activities.

Hapela'awa'awa, the hamlet where we began our journey, was on the northwestern side known as Bwauli, where the aid post, the main United Church at Alogau, and one of the island's three freshwater streams were located. Its bay, Halewa Una, was also the main point of arrival and departure for visiting boats. As we passed from Bwauli to Bomatu, the northwest side of Nuakata, the towering mountains of south Normanby

Island were clearly visible in the distance. Moses told us that on fine days people could sail between Nuakata and Normanby Island on their *sailau,* or sailing canoes, a journey taking three to four hours with good wind.

Leaving Bomatu behind us we moved on to Bolime, the southeastern side of the island. We had not walked far before coming across the Community Primary School, which comprised two fibro-cement and several bush material classrooms. At the rear of the classrooms was a freshwater stream, which provided a constant source of water for the schoolchildren and the three teaching staff and their families who lived on site. Near the stream was a path that scaled Mount Tanalabwa and connected the Bolime and Bwauli sides of the island. In front of the classrooms was a large grassy field used for playing soccer and volleyball. The grass was periodically slashed by older children and adults alike, equipped with their long bush knives known as 'elepa. There was also a clay netball court full of potholes and covered with pebbles and small rocks. Down by the shore and stretching out over the shallows were two sea toilets used by the children attending the school.

Two small islands, Daiwali and Boirama, located between one and two kilometers from Nuakata, are clearly visible from all points along the Bolime shoreline. Moses indicated that although they "belonged to Nuakata," only one family was living on Daiwali at that time, and no one lived on Boirama, as it had no freshwater supply. Later we learned that Australian army troops had been stationed on Daiwali during World War II—abandoned equipment testament to their stay.

The saddle of a small hill marks the boundary between Bolime and the southwest side of the island, Yalasi. There we came upon the island's second and only other United Church, located at a place named Asa'ailo. Unlike the church at Alogau, which was little more than a concrete shell, the church building at Asa'ailo, complete with painted altar rail, pulpit, and lectern, was largely built from bush materials. A concrete monument set in a garden of straggly flowers recorded the gift of this land to the church by local landowners. The church was built in 1991 by people from the Yalasi and Bolime sides of the island as part of the centenary celebrations marking the establishment of the first Methodist mission in Milne Bay Province. Until then the people of Yalasi and Bolime worshipped together with people from Bwauli and Bomatu at Alogau.

At the rear of Asa'ailo is another freshwater stream, which services many hamlets on the Yalasi side. From various points on the Yalasi side it is possible to see East Cape and the islands of Bwasilaki and Sideia. But like the view of Normanby Island from Bwauli and Bomatu, we later discovered that these isles—which act as a visible reminder of the world beyond Nuakata's shores—are often rendered invisible and unreachable by fierce storms, clouds, or haze.

Much of our conversation on the journey around the island focused on where we might live. Wanting to gain some insight into people's use of the aid post located on the Bwauli side, I felt it was important to live some distance away from it, preferably on a different side of the island. Believing it was far too presumptuous to nominate where we would live, we appealed to Moses for advice, indicating that wherever we lived I would need someone, preferably a woman, to help us learn the language and assist with the research.

Moses strongly recommended that we live with a family on the Yalasi side, explaining that "they are good people, well educated" and the oldest son, Wycliffe, would be a suitable language teacher. When we met Wycliffe at the Asa'ailo church, it was clear that Moses had already spoken with him about these two related possibilities. Quietly spoken and reserved, Wycliffe offered us a place to stay on his family's land. He assumed that "like other white people" we would want to live at a secluded site. After much discussion we convinced him that we wanted to live with local people. Finally it was decided that we could stay in his mother's hamlet, Gohiya, some 500 meters from the Asa'ailo church.

As we continued our journey, weaving our way back toward Bwauli and the aid post, we noticed the small ribbed carcasses of abandoned diesel engine boats—three in all, scattered along the Yalasi shoreline. Apparently the owners had "eaten their money," channeling their profits into food and things rather than boat maintenance. Eventually, unable to afford the necessary repairs to their wooden craft, they had sold their engines and abandoned their hulls, leaving Nuakata without a small motorized boat, a two-way radio, or practical means of transport and communication with the mainland in the event of an emergency. Nuakata was not only without a workboat but—with the exception of three individually owned large sailing canoes, able to carry up to five passengers—most canoes on the island could support only one or two people. Local people were forced to depend upon boats owned and operated by people from East Cape and Normanby Island to service their more major transport needs. When we had lived on Nuakata for some time, it became clear that, although the island lies in the well-traveled waters between Normanby and East Cape, workboats generally bypass it en route to other destinations. Workboats traveling from Alotau to Normanby, Fergusson, or Goodenough Island often break their journey at East Cape before heading north along the west coast, or east to the southern coast, of Normanby Island. Nuakata represents a significant detour, one avoided by captains unless guaranteed enough paying passengers and cargo to warrant the trip. For Roger and me at least, these rotting boats dotted along the shoreline were like monuments to the island's more affluent and independent recent past.

When we arrived at the aid post in the midafternoon, a large crowd had already gathered for the community meeting, convened to discuss the land dispute at the aid post and my request to stay and research on Nuakata. When the time came to discuss the latter, Jennifer, Anne, and later Moses spoke on our behalf, translating and explaining my intention to research women's health. As with the subsequent discussion of the aid post business, a decision was reached by consensus, with people (male and female, young and old) rising to question or make an uninterrupted comment on the matter at hand.

Discussion of our request was punctuated by laughter. As little of this was translated, we watched it all with bemused smiles. At one point Wycliffe's father looked to Roger and commented in the local language, "We know what *she* will do, but what will *he* be doing?" When the chorus of laughter subsided, Roger explained through Jennifer that he hoped to write a book. What people understood of our intentions was impossible to tell. Nonetheless they allowed us to stay and insisted they would build a house for us free of charge. We were instructed to return to Nuakata in two weeks with our possessions. Humbled, grateful, I was once again moved to tears.

When the meeting was over, Roger and I returned to Hapela'awa'awa for a swim. As I lay floating, face down in the warm water, I felt a sense of equilibrium return to my body, my thinking. For the first time I was able to reflect on the emotional roller coaster of the last three days—the ride from enchantment to disenchantment to reenchantment. How quickly the sense of wonder and promise felt on the journey was swamped by our anxiety and acute sensitivity to the differences between us and local people. And how quickly these feelings had eased when the community agreed to accommodate us in spite of, and quite possibly because of, these differences. Amid these floating thoughts Pratt's (1986) reflections on arrival tropes in travel writing and ethnographies came to mind. Prior to our journey to Nuakata I was determined not to include an arrival story in the vaguely imagined ethnography. As Pratt observes, ethnographers have long used personal arrival narratives as "emblematic self-portraits," voyages of self-discovery "to position the reader for" and lend authenticity to the quasi-scientific, "objectified description" that follows. I had accepted her challenge "to liberate oneself from them, not by doing away with tropes (which is not possible) but by appropriating and inventing new ones (which is)" (1986, 50). But having "arrived" on Nuakata—having glimpsed what I imagined some immigrants feel in their journeys to new lands—my intention seemed like a potentially disingenuous gesture to nonconformism, a denial of the ethnographic process, the ethnographer's spatial and relational journey to self-understanding and, more important, understanding and accommodation of the similarities to and differences from the people with whom she lives and works. Once again, the imagined field, the imagined text, was overturned by lived experience on Nuakata.

Language

When we arrived back in Alotau we returned to Diwala. Among those who had arrived there in our absence was Daphne Lithgow. Together with her husband David she had been working in Milne Bay as a missionary-linguist for over thirty years. Daphne Lithgow informed us that the language of Nuakata, Alina Nu'ata, is a dialect of Auhelawa, spoken by approximately 1,000 people from the Kurada and Bwasiyaiyai regions of southeast Normanby Island. Using local translators to assist her, she was developing an Auhelawa dictionary and several anthologies of local stories. These texts were intended for use in national government–sponsored preschools, operative throughout the region, including Nuakata. The programs aim to facilitate children's literacy in their local language. At that time, David Lithgow, together with local translators, was also translating the Bible into Auhelawa.

Wycliffe and his father, Noah, both of whom were engaged in Bible translation work, later articulated a contrary understanding of Alina Nu'ata as similar to, but different from, Auhelawa. They did not consider it a subordinated form or "dialect" of Auhelawa, just as they did not believe Nuakata to be a dependent branch or offshoot of the Kurada or Bwasiyaiyai communities on south Normanby Island. It was their hope that SIL (Summer Institute of Linguistics) would produce storybooks for children written in Alina Nu'ata, so that the linguistic differences and shades of meaning unique to their language could be preserved. Although involved with the Bible translation, they, like most local people I subsequently spoke with, considered it unnecessary to translate the New Testament into Auhelawa. As church services and regional church meetings (*kwato*) are conducted in Dobu, the long-established lingua franca in the region, people on Nuakata are keen to maintain fluency and literacy in this language.[5]

In addition to Dobu, many people from Nuakata speak three or four regional languages, commonly the languages of East Cape, Bunama, Duau, Ware, and Tubetube. As English is the language of instruction in community schools throughout Papua New Guinea, younger generations on Nuakata also speak English with varying degrees of fluency. David Lithgow indicated that few people within the Milne Bay region, outside of Bwasiyaiyai, Kurada, and Nuakata, are familiar with either Auhelawa or Alina Nuʻata. By way of explanation he stated, "native speakers are few and not particularly influential in the region, and certain aspects of the language are considered difficult to learn." He added that the low regional profile of these places and languages could be related to the minimal involvement of their peoples in the regional Kula trade (see Macintyre 1983). When I later questioned older Nuakatan men, they indicated that for the past seventy to eighty years Nuakata had not played a significant role in the Kula. Only two or three men had ever been involved, and the sole surviving Nuakatan participant withdrew from these exchanges over twenty years ago due to his age and transport difficulties. His children have expressed no interest in continuing his long-standing trading relationships.

From a linguist's perspective, the Auhelawa language belongs to the Papuan Tip cluster of the Oceanic group of Austronesian languages (Lithgow 1976; Ross 1988). Among the characteristic features of this cluster are subject-object-verb clauses and locative postpositions that indicate the direction and location of a subject's actions. One of the most distinctive aspects of these languages is their relatively complex possessive pronominal system that enables the expression of finely differentiated relationships between people and between people and things. Unlike English, which has only one simple form of possessive pronoun, these languages have three. The pronominal system differentiates possessive relationships according to the varying degrees of relatedness to the subject. For example, the closest, most fundamental relationships, those that are considered constitutive and integral to the subject, are indicated with a possessive pronominal suffix on the noun. These relationships include family members, both maternal and affinal, body parts, and some thoughts and feelings—what Young (1983) terms inalienable aspects of the person; for example, *tamagu* (my father), *mehena* (his or her eyes). A second class, or group of things, such as food or animals that can be consumed and transformed by the person or body, is indicated by a specific possessive pronoun positioned prior to the noun; for example, *'agu maheya* (my pig), *'adi niu* (their coconut). These pronouns may also be used in connection to a person's garden or objects of status and wealth such as armbands—indeed, any substance, object, or thing that is considered in some ways constitutive of the person. For people, objects, or animals regarded as detachable from the person, a third, standard form of personal pronoun is used; for example, *yagu 'elepa* (my bush knife). Food or animals that are intended as gifts, and therefore will not be consumed by their owner or kin, are classified with these standard pronouns.

A unique and significant feature of Auhelawa and Alina Nu'ata is its use of suffixes on nouns and adjectives, as well as verbs (Petaliyaki and Lithgow n.d.). These suffixes function as time markers, providing the listener with specific contextual information about the temporal status of the person, object, action, or state being discussed. When an action, thing, person, or state occurred and whether or not it was completed in that time is emphasized. In Auhelawa and Alina Nu'ata there are three forms of the conjunction "and" that are also selectively used to indicate whether the conjoined ideas, events, or actions occurred in the past, present, or future.

Another noted feature of Papuan Tip languages, including Auhelawa and Alina Nu'ata, is the large variety of verbs to express location or the position of people and bodies in space. In accounting for this phenomenon Lithgow, following Cappell, describes them as "event dominated" languages (1976, 162). However, when I became more familiar with Alina Nu'ata, this description seemed inadequate, for it glosses over the emphasis given to the spatial, temporal, and substantive relations between subject and object, speaker and listener. These characteristic features of Auhelawa and Alina Nu'ata seemed particularly pertinent to my consideration of notions of the person on Nuakata.

Practicing Method

On our return to Nuakata at the beginning of February we discovered that work on our house had not begun. During the next five weeks, while it was being built, we stayed at the Asa'ailo church. At night we slept in one room of the junior missionary's two-room house. We began daily language sessions with Wycliffe, which continued for several months. Needing broader assistance with the research, I asked Wycliffe if he would also be prepared to help me with translations of tapes, discuss customary knowledge and practices, and facilitate interviews with relevant local people.

Both of us were hesitant at first to make this commitment. Wycliffe later revealed that he was initially unsure of Roger and me. Accustomed to reserved and deferential relationships with *dimdim* (white people), he was highly ambivalent about having sustained contact with them. Like many people on Nuakata, he was publicly polite and respectful with *dimdim*, but privately amused by and critical of our ways of relating to people. For my part, in asking Wycliffe to be my research assistant, I was faced with a dilemma. While convinced that a female research assistant would facilitate my research with local women, allaying any embarrassment, I had the strong impression that translating and mediating *dimdim*'s agendas was considered Wycliffe's talent and lot in the community. In asking someone else to be my research assistant I risked causing widespread offense.

Experience proved these initial impressions correct. Wycliffe's knowledge of the community and long-standing interest in local knowledge and practices continually astounded me. Indeed, his knowledge and interest in "customary" matters was considered exceptional in his generation. Ethnographically inclined, Wycliffe explained local knowledge and practices carefully, methodically. He often seemed to anticipate the direction of my research, preempting my assumptions. He was also aware of my shortcomings as an ethnographer, successfully subverting my efforts to orchestrate premature discussions of local knowledge and practices. Curious about everything, I was like a precocious child who demands to know without due respect for the necessary time, place, and experiential/relational context for knowing. As I became more accustomed to the rhythms of daily living on Nuakata I tempered my research enthusiasms, becoming less directive and more content to wait for understanding to unfold. Although Wycliffe collaborated with the research and was keen for me to understand local knowledge and practices, it was clear to him that the research agenda was mine, my story of Nuakata largely shaped by my own questions and concerns, which he dutifully translated, discussed, and challenged (see Carrier 1992, 18–19).

Despite Wycliffe's qualities as a teacher and translator, the decision not to have a female assistant certainly had repercussions for the research—repercussions that Wycliffe himself anticipated. All my taped conversations and interviews with women, even in the early days when my language skills were very limited, were conducted without his direct assistance. My questions to women about their experience and understanding of pregnancy and birth, among other issues, were therefore restricted in scope. Most women with whom I spoke refused to allow me to tape our conversations. Some discussed personal issues with me in confidence, stressing that they did not wish Wycliffe to listen to, or assist me with, the translation of their taped conversations. Some women would not speak to me at all, fearing that, through Wycliffe and me, their opinion and experience might become public knowledge. Many deferred to older women's expertise in matters of contraception, pregnancy, and birth, claiming that they might not know the "proper" answer. On issues not specifically related to women, most women deferred to men.

Our decision to live among Wycliffe's family in his parents' hamlet, Gohiya, also had a significant impact on the research. Wycliffe was the eldest of nine children—six males and three females, offspring of his mother, Eunice, and father, Noah. During our time on Nuakata Wycliffe and his brothers and sisters had one living maternal uncle, Hosea; a maternal aunt or "big mother," Malida; and her husband, Antiya. Antiya was a highly respected elder in the church and the wider community. Unable to have children themselves, he and Malida had adopted a son, Roger (who was then married with one living child), and two of Wycliffe's siblings. Of Wycliffe's siblings, three were already married (Geteli, Jane, Douglisi) with nine children among them. One subsequently married during our time on Nuakata. With the exception of two of his three sisters, Jane and Eba, all of his siblings lived on Nuakata. Jane was attending Bible College on Normanby Island with her husband, John; and Eba—the youngest child in his family—was attending secondary school at Alotau.

This brief sketch of Wycliffe's family may seem peripheral to the research methods—the means of "going after" or "proceeding" to know—I employed on Nuakata. However, as I will demonstrate throughout this book, the understanding gained through participant observation and reflection is contingent. The dynamic relationships between myself and specific local people constitute a vital context for my understanding of Nuakatan knowledges and practices (see Lutz 1988). Our day-to-day life revolved around the people living at Gohiya and our near neighbors. We also had regular encounters with most people living on the Yalasi side. We had less frequent and intense contact with other sections of the island's population. More than anyone else's, then, it is Wycliffe's matrilineal and affinal families' knowledge of Nuakatan practices that I now bear witness to in the text.

Mapping Nuakata, Past and Present

Along with language learning, much of our time during our early weeks on Nuakata was spent trying to ascribe order to the unfamiliar land and seascapes of the island and its surrounds. Like our colonizing forebears, we found both purpose and solace in these seemingly quintessential anthropological tasks—preparing a census, detailing place names on a map, and eliciting information about Nuakata's territorial boundaries. Wycliffe and a band of curious male onlookers humored our initial efforts to circumscribe and know their land, patiently supplying placenames on request. Most had seen maps of the world and Papua New Guinea during their primary education. But the enlarged map of Nuakata and surrounding isles was treated like a curio—a fascinating yet poor substitute for experiential knowledge of regional weather patterns and local terrain. The map did not locate good soil for gardens, suitable trees or vines for making canoes and houses, or waters where fish are plentiful. Nor did it reveal who owned land on Nuakata, or who was entitled to occupy and work on given plots of land with impunity. People's low opinion of the map was only confirmed when they discovered several errors. The names of the islands Daiwali and Boirama were reversed, some of the contours of the Nuakata shoreline were compromised, and the position of its outlying reefs was slightly incorrect. Although marked, three small uninhabited islands belonging to Nuakata—Pali, Panamoimoi, and Awane, lying in the waters southeast of Boirama—were also unnamed and incorrectly located.

This emphasis on lived and living knowledge of the land and sea is hardly surprising in a subsistence-based community. People on Nuakata rely on their garden produce, fishing, and chicken and pig rearing for all basic food requirements, occasionally supplementing their diet with rice, sugar, tea, and tinned meat. Due to the island's soil quality, Nuakatans, unlike their northern and mainland neighbors, have been unable to generate cash income from the sale of *dimdim*-style cash crops (carrots, English potatoes, and onions). All families on the island produced and sold local cash crops (copra, smoked fish, sea slugs, woven bags and mats, betel nut, pineapples, watermelons, mangoes, scones, etc.) at the markets in Alotau, East Cape, and, more recently, Nuakata itself. However, they did so on such a small scale that the income generated by these enterprises was minimal.

Despite their perceived irrelevance to local people, I persisted with these diverse mapping ventures for some weeks, reluctant to abandon these pseudoscientific forms of knowing. Together with his father, Noah; maternal uncle, Hosea; and mother's sister's husband, Antiya, Wycliffe continued to provide assistance. These men revealed that Nuakata's regional waters encircle the island and its major reefs, stretching to the perimeter of the islands of Pahilele and Iabama to the southwest, up beyond Diligaoli and Fallows Reef to the north, around to the outer reaches of Gallows Reef in the east and just past its three small islands in the southeast.

At my request Wycliffe located and named the island's occupied hamlets on a hand-drawn map. Of the fifty-nine identified hamlets, seventeen were located on the Bwauli (northwest) side, nine on the Bomatu (northeast), fifteen on the Bolime (southeast), and eighteen on the Yalasi (southwest) sides of the island. Wycliffe explained—and I paraphrase here—that each hamlet comprises members of a given *huhu* (mother's family) and, where relevant, their spouses. Family members who are connected to one another through a shared mother and grandmother constitute a *huhu*. While the Alina Nu'ata term for mother's family is *huhu*, people on Nuakata generally use the term *susu*, which is used by many other people in Milne Bay.

Able to remember hamlet names at will, Wycliffe could also recall the names and approximate ages of all the people occupying these hamlets. Indeed, he could name the family members, for at least three generations, of every *susu* on the island. For the most part I relied on his comprehensive knowledge of the genealogies of people living and staying on Nuakata to prepare an island census. At the time of the census 385 people—180 females and 205 males—were living there.[6] Of the four sides, Bwauli had the highest population with 130 people, followed by Yalasi with 89, Bolime with 86, and Bomatu/Daiwali combined with 80 people.

As Wycliffe and I worked together preparing genograms he commented, "People and land not only belong to a given *susu* but they also belong to one of five *bwasumo* (birds)"—what I translate here, following convention, as (matri)clans. Five clans are represented on Nuakata: Lili'o

(Parrot), Bo'e (Black Crane), Ao'ao (Crow), Elolo,[7] and Manihubu (Eagle). At that time nearly half of the population on the island belonged to the Elolo clan. I subsequently discovered that the shared maternal ancestry between *susu* belonging to the same clan was generally assumed, rather than known or remembered. In fact, these were often pragmatic alliances rather than certain, substantive matrilineal allegiances. Nonetheless, clan affiliations were considered vital on Nuakata, for people from the same clan have reciprocal obligations to one another, which are realized during celebrations and mourning (as detailed in chap. 6).

Like the term *susu*, the use of birds to denote clans on Nuakata exemplifies a practice that, by both local and related ethnographic accounts, is common throughout the Massim region. In a region both linked and separated by sea, where people have a long-standing history of trade, intermarriage, and warfare (Fortune [1932] 1989; Macintyre 1983; Munn 1986), it is perhaps not surprising that birds became the totemic emblems of the various matriclans. For—like the people they represent—birds are migratory, traveling between land and sea, crossing boundaries as they seek sustenance and kin. These clan affiliations ensure that wherever people travel in the region they will be received as kin among those who share the same or linked totem. Therefore, matriclans and their totemic emblems have provided, and continue to provide, a means of defining similarity and difference between people in the region who might otherwise have no other apparent connection to one another. As on Tubetube, "today there is no intrinsic cultural significance in totems; they function as metonyms for groups or individuals and are used like names" (Macintyre 1983, 28).

Current knowledge and practices associated with these bird totems on Nuakata is seemingly a pale reflection of the totemic system that existed in the region in the past. While I have implied that birds "represent" or act as a metaphor for people's shared ancestral past, Fortune suggests that for the Dobuans of the late 1920s this shared ancestry, this "common ancestress," was quite literally "a bird," and "not a human being" ([1932] 1989, 31). As Seligman and Field observe for Tubetube (in Macintyre 1983, 26–28), so Fortune notes for Dobu: each bird had an associated fish, snake, and plant totem ([1932] 1989, 36). While free to do as they wished with their own totems, they were not allowed to eat their spouse's or father's totemic bird, fish, or snake, or use the associated plant for firewood (36). Such acts were not only considered disrespectful, but they were also seen as explicitly aggressive—an incitement to fight (Macintyre

1983). Only remnants of these beliefs and practices exist on Nuakata. People vaguely recalled that fish and animal totems were linked to bird totems, although no one with whom I spoke could remember them.

Early Settlers

Discussions with Wycliffe about the people and places of Nuakata led to conversations with his family about past settlement of the island. They told us that Nuakata was settled at Gaimanugini hamlet in Gudi bay, on the Yalasi side, during the latter half of the nineteenth century—possibly during the 1860s or 1870s. Men from the Kurada region of Normanby Island came in their canoes to fish on the reefs surrounding Nuakata. Finding a plentiful supply of fish on the reefs, fertile soil and a good water supply on the island, they decided to settle there with their families. The first settlers belonged to the Lili'o clan. According to Wycliffe's mother, people belonging to her clan, the Bo'e clan from the Siga Siga region of Duau on Normanby Island, were next to arrive. But Eunice's claim was contested by other people who commented that representatives of Ao'ao and then Manehubu followed Lili'o clanspeople.

Whatever the order of arrival, all agree that the people staying at Gaimanugini were soon joined on the island by people from Duau, Bwasiyaiyai, Bunama, and other regions of Normanby Island. Soon after the various clans arrived, everyone gathered together for a feast. Following the feast they walked together around the island, settling upon the boundaries for their respective clan lands. Each clan tells its own story of land settlement on Nuakata. These clan stories, rather than the more disconnected history of Nuakatan settlement, hold precedence in people's memory of the past. Other stories about the early settlers survive only as fragmentary narratives—snapshots of a past that seemingly holds little interest for the current generations. We were told that many of the elders who knew stories about these early settlers had recently died, taking with them their knowledge and memories of that past.

While many people claimed to have no knowledge of their early forebears, others (generally men in their fifties and sixties) stated with confidence that the early settlers were strong people—fierce warriors who instilled fear into all who visited their shores. Because their strength and warfaring prowess was renowned in the region, few people from distant places dared to engage them in warfare. Some people insist that although they were formidable warriors, their ancestors did not initiate warfare in the region. Another surviving narrative about the early settlers relates to cannibalism. According to Yamesi (the father of Wycliffe's brother-in-law), sometime during the 1880s Nuakata suffered a severe famine, which led to the emergence of cannibalism on the island. People ate their young children first. Later they went to war with neighboring places, killing and eating their victims.

Local stories certainly assume a long past history of habitation—a history that predates remembered ancestors. One such story refers to the island of Koyagaugau (or Dawson Island), which lies in the waters to the east of Nuakata. Antiya told us that Koyagaugau belongs to Nuakata because an underground, undersea pathway links the two islands. This pathway was primarily used by wild pigs during the time of the early settlers; however, prior to this, it was also used by people from both places. Antiya almost single-handedly eradicated all the wild pigs from the island twenty or so years ago. Since that time the pathway has closed.

Along with accounts of land division, warfare, and cannibalism, people readily remembered stories of Christianity and the early Milne Bay Wesleyan Methodist Church. Celebrations on Nuakata, in October 1991, to mark the one-hundred-year involvement of the Milne Bay United (formerly Wesleyan Methodist) Church in the region have ensured that these stories remain fresh in the thoughts of both young and old alike. The celebrations on Nuakata were preceded by regional centenary celebrations, which reached their climax on Dobu Island on 19 and 20 June 1991. On this occasion people from all over the region, together with former missionaries and church representatives from England and Australia, gathered to celebrate the role of the church and the work of its early colonial missionaries in particular.[8] Attention was focused on the pioneering work of its first, most visible European representative, Reverend Bromilow. Under the auspices of the London Missionary Society, Reverend Bromilow, who had arrived "together with his wife and daughter, four other Australian missionaries and 22 teachers and their wives from Fiji, Tonga and Samoa," established the first Milne Bay mission on Dobu in 1891 (Bromilow 1929; M. Young 1989b, 110).[9] Polynesian missionaries subsequently moved throughout the Massim, staking out and claiming religious territories with words and churches. By mission, anthropological, and historical accounts these colonial representatives were powerful influences for change in the region (Macintyre 1983, 280–89; 1989b, 1990; M. Young 1977, 1989b, 1990, 1996).[10] Each year, as part of the annual commemorative service on Nuakata, to mark Reverend Bromilow's work, one of the church elders speaks to the children about the missionary's heroic achievements. Emphasis is given to his role in eradicating cannibalism and instituting the current moral order.[11] We later attended one such service, where Reverend Bromilow was depicted as a savior who rescued people from savagery and depravity.[12]

Nuakata United Church

Several church elders told me that the Methodist Church first settled at Nuakata on the Bomatu side in 1892. An altar was built, and open air church services were held. The first church building was constructed in the late 1960s at Alogau hamlet on the Bwauli side. It remains today as a solid, concrete vestige of a colonial past still present.

While other organizations existed on Nuakata (e.g., the sports and youth associations, the ward authority), the United Church was, during our time there, the most visible influence on communal life. Even activities existing outside the church were brought into its temporal and spatial realms of influence when their details were announced in the notices given at the conclusion of church services. With the possible exception of the primary school, the church grounds were the only true communal spaces on the island, hosting a variety of communal activities, including feasts, working bees, the two island preschools, and meetings of nonchurch organizations. More than any other organization or activity, the church and its calendar effectively demarcated time on Nuakata into days, weeks, months, and years, rendering Sunday a non-work day distinct from other days, Wednesday Women's Fellowship day, and Saturday a time of preparation for the rest day to follow. During our time on Nuakata the church acquired a clock, so that the starting and finishing times of church services and meetings could be minuted in the records. Easter, Christmas Day, Bromilow and Harvest Day, and *mulolo* (gift-giving) were celebrated communal events in the church calendar. No other activities on the island, even mortuary ceremonies, soccer, and netball grand finals, attracted such widespread communal participation and support. Unlike these other events (with the exception of school terms), people were compelled to celebrate these ecclesiastical occasions on specifically designated days and dates.

Clearly established organizational hierarchies existed within the United Church on Nuakata. The main church, located on the Bwauli side of the island, was staffed by a full-time, fully qualified (six-year trained) national pastor. In contrast, the Yalasi church was staffed by a half-time pastor/missionary (*misinali*)—a nineteen-year-old man who had completed half (three years) of his training and was accountable to the senior pastor. Following usual United Church practice in the region, the pastor and junior pastor did not come from Nuakata, but were assigned there for three-year terms. Coming as outsiders to the community, with tenuous local clan allegiances and often no knowledge of the local language, these pastors remained marginal to the day-to-day life and work of the community (Thune 1990). Despite this, they wielded considerable power and influence in the community. As they had limited clan responsibilities and obligations, they did not participate in customary exchange activities. Their gardens and church or house grounds were initially established by local men and regularly tended by local women. They were not obliged to assist in preparation for communal feasts; however, they always presided at the main table, were given the best food to eat, and returned to their houses laden with gifts. These men, particularly the qualified pastor, assumed and were assigned "big man" (*taubada mwala'ina*) status in the community; however, they did not have the obligation of wealth redistribution that a "big man" incurs. With an annual income of roughly 600 Australian dollars, they were wealthy by normal village standards.

When asked about their primary responsibilities, both junior and senior pastor alike commented that it was their role to attend meetings and report to the regional church about the activities of the church on Nuakata. They regarded themselves as religious and moral custodians and administrators. Interestingly, the pastors did not consider preaching to be only their responsibility. In theory, at least, this role was open to male and female, young and old alike, but in practice women rarely preached, instead doing much of the invisible work for the church: preparing flowers, making gardens, cleaning the church and its grounds. Their energies were focused on the Women's Fellowship meetings that took place every Wednesday for Bible study and church fund-raising activities.[13]

Church laity are divided into nonmembers and members (*ekelesiya*), who meet at the conclusion of each weekly service. Members are privy to knowledge and decision-making power in relation to church activities. As with preaching, both men and women are entitled to hold office-bearing positions in the church, however, in practice this, too, is a male domain. There are two levels of membership. The higher level entitles the person to preach regularly, but lower level members are accorded seniority and status within the church.

The hierarchical organization of the local church merely reflects established hierarchies in the regional and national church—a level of organization that is not dissimilar to its now defunct Australian antecedent, the Methodist Church. The Nuakata United Churches constitute one section of the Bunama circuit—a circuit that encompasses Bunama, Bwasiyaiyai, and Kurada on the southern coast, and Sewa Bay on the southwest coast of Normanby Island. All the pastors working in this circuit—all men, to my knowledge—are Papua New Guinean nationals from Milne Bay Province. One qualified minister, also a Papua New Guinean national based at Bunama, administers the circuit. He alone is authorized to marry, christen or baptize, and administer the sacraments to people. A full circuit meeting, known as *kwato,* is held every three months, during which time participants from the youth groups, Women's Fellowships, Sunday schools, sporting associations, and *ekelesiya* of all member churches meet to discuss regional church activities and community. Matters of policy in relation to common or shared events in the church calendar are decided at these meetings.

The United Church, therefore, not only provided a focus for community life on Nuakata, it also provided an important context for wider regional contact. Throughout the year the various groups within the circuit gather in varying locations for specific projects or events. In 1993 there were six young people from Nuakata attending the Bwaluwada Bible College (representing one-third of the class) and two others attending an independent Bible college (Tewala Bible College) in Alotau. Some will become pastors within the circuit. As there is no scope for paid employment on Nuakata apart from cash cropping, and employment prospects on the mainland are severely limited, a career as a pastor in the United Church is a good option for some. People are given the prospect of paid, high-status employment in various locations at the end of their studies. The five Bible college students with whom I spoke indicated that apart from issues of faith, these factors influenced their decision to enroll. Several people commented that they welcome the challenge of further study—a challenge denied to them by the national education system, which sees only a very small percentage of sixth-grade students pass exams enabling them to continue their education at secondary schools on the mainland.

My initial efforts to chart Nuakata's land, sea, and familial boundaries prompted general discussion with Wycliffe, Antiya, and Noah about Nuakata's place—its social and political status within the region. These men, together with the island's elected ward councillor, indicated that Nuakata is a member of the Maramatana local council, which is responsible for administration of funds to local communities within its constituency. This local council represents people from Nuakata and the northern, or Rabaraba, side of the mainland coast, from the tip of East Cape to Yawoda. Like all the elected representatives to the council, these men were baffled by Nuakata's inclusion in the Maramatana constituency. With social, familial, linguistic, and geographical links to East Cape and Normanby Island, Nuakata could be more appropriately included in either the southeastern mainland coast (from Alotau to East Cape) or the southern Normanby Island councils. This was further highlighted by the inclusion of Nuakata in the Alotau district health department division—representing the communities along the southeastern coast between Alotau and East Cape. Although marginalized in this council, the ward councillor, together with the group of senior men that constituted Nuakata's ward authority, decided that it was still in Nuakata's best interests to remain in this constituency.

While familial allegiances across the island and region appeared strong, Nuakata's alliances with state, local council, and church organizations were seemingly disparate and arguably tenuous. Organized sporting events (e.g., round-robin netball, soccer, and volleyball carnivals) or church gatherings, which might otherwise occur with some frequency and regularity, were invariably canceled, postponed, or restricted by transport difficulties. It seemed that without a reliable, independent form of transport Nuakata was destined to be trapped in the shadows of its larger neighbors, East Cape and Normanby Island.

Fig. 1. Duwadawali Bay, Nuakata

Fig. 2. Roger, Wycliffe, and Shelley at Gohiya

Chapter Two

≥ҫ

Colonial Impregnations

Meeting Moses came as an enormous relief. It was our first day on Nuakata, when everything around us seemed strange. Until Moses arrived at Hapela'awa'awa, the hamlet where we had slept our first night, we were given a polite yet wide berth by the people around us. Clearly bemused by our presence, they were struggling to understand why we had come to Nuakata. Why Nuakata in particular? As I was feeling alien, dislocated, it was perhaps not surprising that the constellation of questions—on gender, person, women's health—that brought me to Nuakata seemed misplaced. Removed from the safety of the text (i.e., the formal research proposal) and thrust into the everyday flux of hamlet life, my questions and the anonymous medicoscientific and ethnographic facts that inspired them seemed irrelevant, foreign, contrived.[1] Most preposterous of all, however, was the assumption that my research might "assist" the people of Nuakata. No longer imaginary figures, these living people, variously perplexed, amused by, or indifferent to my research intentions, caused me to reflect again on my imposition. To this end, a dimly recalled comment by Fabian proved salutary:

> We will always be liable to be seen (correctly) as old colonizers in a new guise as long as we understand critical, emancipatory anthropology as doing *our critique* to help *them*—be they the Third World, the working classes, the disinherited, women. . . . Who are we to "help" them? We need critique (exposure of imperialist lies, of the working of capitalism, of the misguided ideas of scientism, and all the rest) to *help ourselves*. The catch is, of course, that "ourselves" ought to be them as well as us. (1991, 264, emphasis in original)

Fluent in English and able to understand Alina Nu'ata, Moses negotiated my unease with the polite self-assurance of a diplomat, fostering conversation that restored a sense of equilibrium. Twenty-two years old, and formerly from the islands of Gawa and Kiriwina to the north, he had nearly three years of experience behind him as the sole community health worker (CHW) on the island. Anthropologists were not an unknown species to him, for he had vague childhood memories of Nancy Munn's time on Gawa—memories reinforced by stories told about her by his kin.[2] As I attempted to explain my proposed research, my interest in women's health, Moses became increasingly animated, even excited. Trained for two years in Western medical practices and clearly convinced of their worth, he was critical of local customs surrounding sickness and health. Community resistance to his involvement during pregnancy and childbirth frustrated him. He nominated maternal health as one of the most important health issues on Nuakata, along with malaria and diarrheal diseases.

Oblivious to it at the time, we later realized that Moses' role with us on that day reflected his place in the community as a highly respected outsider, a Papuan familiar with the ways of *dimdim*. Regarded, in part, *dova dimdim* (like a white person), because of his education and knowledge of *dimdim* medicine, Moses was considered the obvious person on Nuakata to discern and interpret our concerns. He, in turn, subsequently perceived and represented me to the community as an ally in his struggle to improve the health of women on the island.

Talking with me several weeks later, Moses insisted that as a woman and a *dimdim* I was better placed than he, a young, single Papuan male, to acquire the respect and confidence of Nuakatan women. Perhaps I could persuade local women of the superiority of Western medical practices in relation to pregnancy and birth. However, in positioning me this way Moses evoked my ambivalent faith in Western medicine. In resisting the certainty of his convictions, I was alerted to my nostalgic hankering to uncover and (dare I say) preserve traditional Nuakatan knowledge and practices relating to pregnancy and birth—practices surviving from an idealized, and to that degree fictive, precolonial past.

Nostalgia of this kind not only assumes the existence of an imagined past, it also pretends that preservation of "culture" is possible and, more to the point, unequivocally desirable—surely nonsense on both counts. As Rosaldo explains, "mourning the passing of traditional society" and the "salvage ethnography" it has inspired have a long genealogy in anthropology (1989, 81). Spawned by the recognition of "the destructive intrusions of imperialism and its colonial regimes" in non-Western, non-industrialized societies, such a salvage ethnography is also intended as an implicit critique of "modern [and postmodern] industrial society" (1989, 82). It was from this ideological wellspring that my own nostalgia flowed. And it was a hybrid feminist inflection of this anthropological tradition that was present in my initial approach to fieldwork.[3]

At one level I wanted to believe that Melanesian childbirth practices were more authentic and wholesome experiences for Nuakatan mothers than those of their Western counterparts. I was not a pioneer in this pursuit. As Dureau (1993) observes, writers such as Mead (1949) and A. Weiner (1976) have attempted to retrieve and represent a romanticized vision of Melanesian motherhood in implicit contradistinction to the inauthentic and defiled vision of Western maternity (see also Ginsburg and Rapp 1991; Jolly 1998b; Ram 1998).

As heir to second-wave feminist critiques of Western medicine's increasing appropriation and colonization of pregnancy and birth, I was familiar with the vast literature attesting its progressive attempts to objectify and assume control over women's bodies.[4] A burgeoning literature detailing the negative impact of new reproductive technologies (NRT) on women's experience of pregnancy and birth is also emerging.[5] Accordingly, I feared the consequences of Western biomedicine's continued infiltration of Nuakatan sociality. I feared Nuakatan women would be displaced from their central role in maternity, their knowledge and expertise would be devalued and lost, and they would come to imagine pregnancy and birth as a physical event, rather than a multifaceted phenomenal experience that expresses historical relationships between people. An awareness of diverse historical precedents in Pacific and, more specifically, Massim contexts reinforced these fears (Denoon 1989a, 1989b; Jolly 1991, 1992a; Young 1989b).

During the late nineteenth and twentieth centuries, British concerns about depopulation and infant mortality surfaced in its colonies among colonial administrators and missionaries.[6] As a result Pacific mothers and mothering practices were subject to increased surveillance and modification by missionaries and colonial government personnel.[7] Environmental issues (sanitation, housing, water quality) were identified as significant factors precipitating decreases in local populations. However, explanations that focused on indigenous mothering practices—specifically, the ignorance, licentiousness, or insouciance of native mothers—received more sustained attention and responses from administrators and missionaries across the Pacific.

British colonial responses to depopulation were by no means uniform across the region (see Jolly 1998a, 1998b).[8] In Papua New Guinea colonial medical administrators were initially preoccupied with the health of expatriates and the indigenous male labor force and only turned their attention to indigenous women's maternal health in the 1930s (Denoon 1989a, 1989b). However, during the late nineteenth and early twentieth centuries Anglican and Methodist missionaries, like the Bromilows in the Massim, actively sought to transform indigenous women's maternal practices. Reed (1998, 68–69) suggests that the depopulation debates further legitimated their efforts to discourage sexual promiscuity and "raise" or "lift" the way of life of Papuan women and, through them, the village communities to which they belonged (see Bromilow 1929). Massim missionaries believed that by channeling what they considered the promiscuous sexual energies of Massim girls and women into mothercraft, domestic hygiene, alternative gardening, and health-care practices, they might arrest depopulation and win native bodies and souls for Christ (Eves 1996a; Macintyre 1989a; Reed 1998; Young 1989b).

But my nostalgic hankerings to recover Nuakatan maternity practices cannot be fully explained by my ambivalent response to Western medicine's appropriation of the maternal body. For this nostalgia was coupled with an unashamed and defiant romanticism—a romanticism that critically valorized women's experiences of maternity (Dinnerstein 1977; Rich 1976) without deeming them constitutive of the category "woman," or a defining point of "the feminine." Long fascinated by the miracle, the mystery, the sheer wonder of birth, I was drawn to the feminist literature of the 1980s that suggests that women's diverse experiences of maternity and motherhood enact and evoke distinct ways of thinking and understanding (Mortimer 1990; Ruddick 1980, 1989; Wilshire 1989)—ways that counter the dominance of reason in the Western world. Phenomenological renderings of pregnancy and birth in Western contexts challenge the notion of the autonomous subject founded on unsustainable oppositional relationships such as mind/body, inner/outer, subject/object, individual/society, nature/culture (Kristeva 1980, 1986; I. M. Young 1990). Accordingly, "pregnancy challenges the integration of my body experience by rendering fluid the boundary between what is within, myself, and what is outside, separate. I experience my insides as the space of another, yet my own body" (I. M. Young 1990, 161–63). Encouraged by Young's work, I sought to elicit Nuakatan women's embodied experiences of pregnancy and birth as a means of reflecting on local notions of the self and person. I was also drawn to, touched by, yet unable to embrace, the writings of the French theorists (Cixous 1981a, 1981b; see also Grosz 1989, 119–26; Irigaray 1985a, 1985b) and the coterie of Anglo-American theorists that joined their celebration of the poetics of the female body through "writing the body" (*l'écriture féminine*) (Mallett 1995). Wary of the mystical, essentialist proclivities implicit within their work, and the ethnocentric vision of the female bodies this has promoted, I was nevertheless inspired by their poetic reclamation of the maternal body from the clutches of phallocentrism.[9]

My romanticism was tempered by other ideas and voices. A disquieting suspicion lurked in my thoughts that my fear (of Western medical intrusions) as much as my romanticization (of the potential meanings and significance) of Nuakatan women's experience of maternity reflected a form of contemporary white female maternalism—a maternalistic (neo)colonialism.[10] It was the form of colonialism appealed to and valorized by Moses when he suggested that, as a woman and a *dimdim*, I might be able to convince local women to adopt Western medical practices. This suspicion was fueled by two sources: my reading of the writings of women of color (see hooks 1982, 1984, 1991; Moraga and Anzaldua 1983; Stack 1974) and the ethnographic writings of several anthropologists, Dureau (1993) and Scheper-Hughes (1985) in particular.

Countering romantic visions of non-Western maternity, Dureau asserts that women living in the western Solomon island of Simbo consider motherhood and maternity a "profoundly ambivalent state and relationship" (1993). Some Simbo women complain of the work load, the physical demands young babies place upon them, their diminished capacity to fully participate in community events. Others speak of fatigue and ill-health associated with pregnancy and birth. In so doing, some among them idealize Western maternity. Following Moore (1988), Dureau questions any "globalizing tendency" present in understandings of maternity, strongly suggesting "that the particular cultural evaluations, experiences and significance of maternity must be established for each ethnographic case" (1993, 31; 1998). Dureau's thoughts are supported by Merrett-Balkos (1998) who reveals that for Anganen women in the Southern Highlands of Papua New Guinea birth is not an experience that is easily romanticized, for it is potentially fraught with spiritual danger. Similarly in rural Bangladesh birth and birthing women are considered potentially polluting and therefore dangerous. Accordingly, Rozario (1998) cautions against romanticized accounts of traditional childbirth, rightly pointing out that they often overlook the difficult contexts surrounding births and the life-threatening dangers posed to mothers and their children. These themes are further elaborated by Scheper-Hughes (1985; 1992, 340–445).

Through her writing on the experience of mother love and infant death for women living in a northeast Brazilian shantytown, Scheper-Hughes challenges poetic theories of motherhood. She claims that poetic theories "do violence to the different experiences and sensibilities of poor and Third World women whose moral visions may not conform to the feminist paradigm" (1992, 341). The poetic theories to which she refers are those "proposing essential, or universal, womanly scripts" (1992, 341), in particular "Sara Ruddick's (1989) 'maternal thinking,' Nancy Chodorow's (1978) 'feminine personality,' and Carol Gilligan's (1982) 'womanly ethos'" (Scheper-Hughes 1992, 401). She argues that these and other theories of "maternal sentiment" are a by-product of a particular sociohistorical, economic, and political context. As such, they represent "an ideological, symbolic representation grounded in the basic material conditions that define women's reproductive lives" (1992, 401). For these writers, empathy, intuition, and even pacifism are celebrated as inevitable, even natural consequences of maternity—assumptions and values about maternal nature that Scheper-Hughes asserts derive from the modern Western, bourgeois family. Challenging this, she contends that the experience of maternity and motherhood may "just as 'naturally' reproduce maternal sentiments of distance and estrangement as of attachment and empathy" (1992, 403).

Scheper-Hughes posits a pragmatics rather than a poetics of motherhood (1992, 341–402)—one that attempts to understand the complex factors that constitute women's diverse experiences of maternity and motherhood, even when these understandings pose a fundamental challenge to the (feminist) anthropologist's belief about what is normal, ethical, and, I might add, desirable, even universal.

Although critical of Western medical knowledge and intervention in relation to pregnancy and birth, I—like Moses—was fearful of its absence in remote and isolated communities like Nuakata and worried by the consequences of diminished choices—itself a notion based on a culturally conceived expectation about the fundamental rights of the autonomous individual (Ginsburg and Rapp 1991, 314–15; Gordon 1976, 314–15; M. Strathern 1992). While mindful that infant and maternal mortality rates have long been used in many contexts to justify radical and often dubious transformations of maternal behavior (see Kaufert and O'Neil 1993, 537; Oakley 1980, 128; 1984, 129), I could not ignore the basic fact that many more mothers and infants die as a result of preventable medical conditions arising during childbirth in Papua New Guinea than in so-called developed countries (Gordon 1990). My concerns about the absence of Western-style maternal health care were only intensified by my knowledge of the ever-diminishing national Papua New Guinea health budget (Mola 1991, 275; Thomason and Newbrander 1991, 629) and the gap between the theoretical goals and practical realizations of maternal and child health care in rural Papua New Guinea (Edwards 1992, 1994).

Feeling a great sense of indebtedness to Moses for all his efforts on our behalf and grateful too that he understood something of my research, I did little in those early days and weeks to dissuade him from his view of my role. After all, who would not wish to be an ally in the struggle to improve people's health and well-being? While mindful that an alliance, or even a perceived alliance, with Moses might influence the course of my research, I remained confident that I could overcome any misperceptions that might arise. Like Moses, but possibly for different reasons, I assumed that because I am a woman, opportunities would soon arise with women to explain my broader interests in their customary knowledges and practices. In those early days and weeks I gave little thought and no credence to the adage that actions speak louder than words, that my actions rather than my faltering words might be construed in ways I had not anticipated.

Because I Am a Woman

But what did I mean by "because I am a woman"? How did I intend to act because I am a woman? How did I imagine people, men and women, would respond to me? What impact, if any, would my being a woman have on my research?

At one level, both in spite of and because of my theoretical ideas about these matters, I—like Moses—assumed that the partially visible form of my sexed body (e.g., breasts, body shape) together with the other implied yet invisible sexed parts and their secretions would represent and constitute me as (a) woman, and not (a) man, to the women of Nuakata. Women's early responses to me—inviting me rather than Roger to attend the Women's Fellowship meeting, urging me to bathe in their presence—encouraged this assumption. I imagined that, despite potentially different cultural discourses and practices associated with or elaborated within, upon, or by sexed bodies, I would share fundamental experiences and knowledge in common with the women of Nuakata associated with our shared bodily form and praxis—among them, knowledge of our potential to bear children. In this sense, the specters of maternity and heterosexuality infused my notion of woman (Butler 1990, 1993; Wittig 1981). Further, I assumed that these shared forms and potentialities would provide us with a basis to speak and build relationships with one another, which in turn would facilitate my research. To this end I would do as Nuakatan women do: tend gardens, prepare meals, wash clothes, attend Women's Fellowship meetings, and so on. Overlooked, however, was the reality that as both researcher and outsider I would do much that local women do not do and vice versa, and that this, too, would be interpreted by local people.

While I believed that my sexed body would constitute and position me as similar to the women of Nuakata, paradoxically I hoped that this difference would not significantly impact on my research with men. With men I wished to be positioned as an androgynous subject, with women I wished to be positioned as a female subject. In same-sex relations I wanted sexual difference to count, to render us similar; in cross-sex relationships I did not. In short, I wanted things both ways. Perhaps more accurately, I wanted my relationships with people to go all my own way, even if those ways were patently contradictory! In what might be described as magical thinking, I assumed that my relationships with men could somehow transcend sex and gender, except in specific situations where I did not wish this to occur. With women I hoped that the form of my body would count more than my actions, while with men I hoped the reverse would be true. Although I cringe at the thought, these latter working assumptions partly reflect the idea that sex/gender belongs to woman/women. Sex/gender is pivotal to women's subjectivity. It is largely irrelevant to the subjectivity of men, or relevant only as an insignificant absence or elision. I therefore vacillated between an understanding of "I"—of subject/self—as substantive, gendered, and an understanding of "I" as insubstantive, processual, and enacting. However, in living/enacting these vacillating positions, I demonstrated a consistent embodied understanding/expression of "I" as contingent, multiple. As such I demonstrated that the speaking/acting context influenced *both* how I spoke/thought about *concepts* of the gendered self/"I" and how I *enacted* self/"I."

The most obvious difficulty associated with my ideas was that they anticipated what was yet to be investigated—namely, gender, gendered identity, the gendered person/self, gender relations, sexual difference (see Moore 1994c). In casting myself as sexed, I unwittingly sought to cast Nuakatan women in my own image and form, believing that whatever the differences between us, in sharing same-sexed bodies we were more similar than different. Not only did this thinking assume the primacy of the visible form of the body to both the gendered self and gendered identity, it also posited sexual difference as a universally significant distinction, reducible to mutually exclusive binary categories (male and female) that ground all other identities and selves (see Moore 1994c). I acted and proposed to act as if the sexed body precedes and grounds subsequent lived experience, which is itself informed by sociocultural and historical discourses. As such, the body is ontologically sexed, but this does not constitute some form of prescriptive essence. Rather, it provides someone's context, position, or particular vantage point—which, by definition, is also a constraint or limitation—with/in the world. The form of the body informs without strictly causing one to act. Accordingly, sex and gender (female/woman, male/man) converge and conflate around the form of the body and diverge where and when this form is elaborated and "woman" becomes a partially stable, universal category founded on the female form/substance of her embodiment.

Having lived without scrutiny or reflection while on Nuakata, my fieldwork assumptions recall Braidotti's theoretical elaboration of Rich's (1976) notion of feminine corpor(e)ality, mixed with a dash of Foucault's (1978) discourses about sex and a sprinkle of feminist standpoint theory (Harding 1987a, 1987b; Harstock 1987). Before going to the field, I had been attracted to Braidotti's (1991) vision of embodied subjectivity—founded on the idea that the (sexed) form of the body (in)forms experience—however, I remained only partially persuaded by her broader argument. Most appealing to me was her notion of the body, cogently summarized by Moore as "an interface, a threshold between the material and the symbolic" (1994c, 18). Braidotti's "body" is neither a prescriptive essence that determines an essential subjectivity nor a blank slate upon which sex/gender is inscribed; rather, the body—in its very specificity and materiality—locates and embodies subjectivity/subjectivities (Braidotti 1989, 101). Thought of as a threshold, the body both locates and is located by its sociohistorical contexts, transforming as it is transformed by them.

But my greatest difficulty with Braidotti's argument stemmed from the very aspect of her theory that I found attractive, namely, the ascription of primary ontological status to binary (either/or, male/female) sexual difference, and specifically, the argument that the (either/or) sexed form of the body informs all other forms of difference; that form, rather than some other phenomenon, say action or relations, constitutes the most significant similarity or difference between people. That the sexed form of the body is somehow temporally prior to and therefore more significant in locational terms than other embodied forms of difference (e.g., ethnicity, disability, class) is open to dispute on a number of levels. For example, following Foucault (1978), a string of feminist authors, including Butler (1990), Haraway (1991), and Yanagisako and Collier (1987), have noted that sex is a discursive phenomenon. It is constructed in and by discourse. Accordingly, sex does not exist independently of these discourses, and without such discourses bodies cannot be sexed. It also follows that across the world multiple discourses on sex (may) exist. As anthropological and other studies testify, both the categories of sex and the features which constitute them differ from discourse to discourse, culture to culture (see, for example, Herdt 1994; Jackson 1997; Morris 1994). As Moore (1994c, 20) observes, only in theory is it possible to distinguish and prioritize discourses on sex and their effect on, in, and through bodies from those of class, ethnicity, sexuality, cosmology, and so on.

Despite these prefield criticisms of the notion of the ontologically sexed subject, this idea provided me with both a reassuring and a strategic premise for establishing relationships between myself and Nuakatan women. At the same time I also subscribed, at least in theory, to the contradictory view espoused by M. Strathern that "it remains a matter of ethnographic identification whether or not 'being a man' or 'being a woman' occupies an organizing—representational, systematizing—place in the classification of behavior" (1988, 61). Indeed, it remains a matter of ethnographic identification who and what the terms *man, woman,* and *I* designate, and whether or not they are considered static categories (nouns), fluid processes and relations (verbs), or some combination of the two.

I, Woman

My contradictory assumptions were soon challenged, and in ways that were relevant to my consideration of how gender, person, and agency were expressed and/or understood on Nuakata. After living on Nuakata for several weeks I learned that the causal statement "because I am a woman" cannot be spoken, as there is no abstract verb "to be" in Alina Nu'ata. Although the locative verb *miya,* meaning "to sit, stay, remain, dwell," passes for the English verb "to be," in certain contexts it is not applicable to the translation of the statement "because I am a woman." In both English and German, the verb "to be" formerly meant "to dwell," however this definition has arguably fallen silent in these languages (see Heidegger 1975). In contemporary usage the English verb "to be" often implies a fixed independent state (of mind, personhood) or form of existence. Accordingly, "being" is objectified as a state of the subject (e.g., I am a woman; I am happy; I am hungry); a state that can be defined and known; a state separable from the contexts integral to "its" enactment. In contrast, staying or dwelling in Alina Nu'ata is conceived as an active pastime. Place and bounded spaces are integral to staying or dwelling (see chap. 4). Unlike the English verb "to be," which functions to extract and abstract existence from the conditions that characterize it, in Alina Nu'ata the verb "to stay" assumes, rather than denotes, existence. For example, in conversation on Nuakata, the verb "to stay, to dwell" (*miya*) is often used in contradistinction to the verb "to go, to do" (*lau*). People conventionally mark their departures from one another by detailing what each of them will be doing and in what context, when they leave each other. Typically, someone may say *yamiyamiya na 'owa 'ulau* (I staying and you, you go) or *'umiymiya na yau, mata yalau yagu dalava* (you staying and I will go to my hamlet). Whether one stays, goes, or does something else does not call into question or negate one's existence. But where, when, and with whom one acts transforms the speaking/acting "I." As such, existence is inextricable from the activities, relations, and spaces that define it. This is further reinforced by the way the language is written: personal pronouns and the verbs that follow them are written as one word rather than (as in English) two words—for example, *yavahili* (I read), and not *ya vahili.*

The closest possible expression for "because I am a woman" in Alina Nu'ata is *wuwuna waihiu, yau* (because woman, I), or *wuwuna yau waihiu* (because I woman), however I never once heard this expression used.

In conversation, it was rare for the category "woman" or "man" to be explicitly invoked as a cause of behavior, even though women's and men's work and other habitual activities on Nuakata often differed. An analysis of the terms provides some insight into this. *Yau* is an absolute pronoun, meaning I, me, and mine. It is one of the three pronominal forms in Alina Nuʻata, *ya, yau, yabom*,[11] which denote the English "I." Often used alone or in expressions incorporating the personal pronoun *ya* (I)—which can only be used in conjunction with a verb, e.g., *yalau* (I go)—the absolute pronoun *yau* (I) denotes and is used in conversation to draw attention to the unified, singular and particular "I." It is the "I" that by its specific staying, actions, belongings (to people, things, places) is particularized or unified; for example, *yau, Melbin ʻainaena* (I, from/of Melbourne), *yau, yapaihowa* (I, I work). Similarly the plural absolute pronouns denote singular collectives (groups)—collectives that are unified and particularized by specific act(s), places, relations, or feature(s) shared; for example, *ʻaiwaiwaihiu Nuakataena* (we women from Nuakata).[12] As with the plural absolute pronouns that denote groups collectively constituted as one, the singular absolute pronoun *yau* may be thought of as a coalescence of activities and/or relations, unitarily embodied. This embodiment is necessarily spatial; it is located. As such, this discursive "I" (or "we") is contingent, dependent. The "I" is identified as a unity (based on, for example, sex/gender, age, place, family relationship, clan, activity, etc.) according to the speaking/acting context.[13] It is discursively constituted in relation to "you." *Yau, waihiu beibi yaʻavalai* (I, woman baby I carry it), or *waihiu, yau beibi yaʻavalai* (woman, I baby I carry it), then, is not spoken or thought as a particular ontological state of "being." "Woman" (*waihiu*) and "I" (*yau*) together here suggest or imply a unitary position or embodied context for speaking and acting in relation to specific others. This does not negate other possible unitary speaking/acting positions or dimensions of "I."

Several related points emerge from this discussion. The absolute pronoun *yau* for "I" and the contingent "I," referred to earlier when I reflected on my own enactment of "I," have much in common. In both examples the speaking/acting context is assumed to influence, if not determine, the unifying characteristic(s) of the "I" (woman, from a particular place, etc.). Multiple, alternative ways of characterizing/enacting this "I" are eclipsed in these contexts. It cannot be assumed, however, that this unitary, contingent "I" invoked in speech (i.e., the pronominal "I") and other forms of action is, or is thought to be, a manifestation of an underlying constant and coherent entity or state of being known as "self/person." The relevance, meaning and/or expression of such concepts on Nuakata remains to be established or refuted. The unitary "I," referred to here, provides the context for, and affects social action, agency, without necessarily causing a given action.

This analysis of the contingent "I" resonates with Rumsey's persuasive discussion in "Agency, Personhood and the 'I' of Discourse in the Pacific and Beyond" (2000). By referring to regional and cross-regional examples of ("direct indexical" and "anaphoric") pronominal usage, Rumsey challenges the view espoused by M. Strathern (1988), Sahlins (1981, 1985), and Mosko (1992) that there are distinctive regional modes of social action or agency. Sahlins argues that chiefly action in Polynesia is premised on a notion of "encompassment." Accordingly, chiefs use the singular personal pronoun "I" to encompass the actions of many people as their own, "summing up in their own person the lives of many" (Rumsey 2000, 102). In contrast, M. Strathern (1988) posits a uniquely Melanesian form of social action, premised on the notion of the partible person. As such, persons are understood as a composite of multiple relationships, of male and female parts that are both the "source and outcome of action" (1988, 14). While the person is composite, that person's acts are singular. It is only under the condition of unity that these "acts appear as a composite of social relations. Unity in turn hinges on agency: the agent reveals the unity for . . . it is acts which unify" (1988, 275). Thus for someone to act he or she must eclipse without denying the composite parts of him- or herself. The same is true for collective action. For example, a group of women who work collectively to raise funds for the United Church must appear to act as "one woman." While fund-raising, their cross-sex kinship ties to multiple others beyond the collectivity are necessarily eclipsed.

Rumsey argues, contrary to Mosko (1992), that these seemingly distinct forms of Melanesian and Polynesian agency are potentially compatible and allow for "moments of both encompassment and partibility" (Rumsey 2000, 101). Moreover, he claims that moments of encompassment and partibility are both "inherent in the nature of language" and the nature of agency in general, most obviously discursive agency (111). It is the latter, universalist aspect of his argument that is most relevant to this discussion of both my own and Nuakatan experience of discursive forms of social agency. Drawing on his own earlier work (Merlan and Rumsey 1991; Rumsey 1989) and linguists Benveniste's (1966 (1956), 1971) and

Urban's (1989) discussions of the meaning and use of personal pronouns, Rumsey asserts that we cannot assume that "each situated use of the personal pronoun 'I' 'indexes' or invokes a constant self." Rather, following Benveniste's dialogic and relational view of personhood, he claims that the use of "I" in discourse constitutes the speaker as a transcendent, if not "expansive," *encompassing,* subject in relation to "you." While this human subject is not *essentially* transcendent, unitary, or centered, there is a "momentary effect"—which is an inherent feature of language—whereby the act of speaking establishes the *"current* center in relation to which the values of all the other deictic terms ('here,' 'there,' 'this,' 'that') are fixed ... and in relation to which 'subjectivity' and performativity" are possible (Rumsey 2000, 110–11). By invoking the "I" in discourse, people, whatever their cultural context or language, posit themselves as unitary agents—unitary agents of speaking. This is true even when in any given speech they move between an encompassing or composite understanding of the "I"; that is, between multiple discursive positions ("projected selves" or identities). As Rumsey suggests, the transcendent, discursive "I" provides a powerful model for the construction of unitary action or social agency in general. It allows us to consider specific manifestations of encompassment and/or partibility and how they "interact with each other" in the "ongoing construction of social identity and agency" in any given sociopolitical and historical context. Most important of all in the context of this discussion of Nuakatan personhood and agency, it "enables us to consider 'encompassment', 'partibility' and 'personhood' as aspects of ongoing social interaction" rather than abstract cultural and/or metaphysical categories unique to Melanesia or Polynesia (Rumsey 2000, 113).

But this discussion of the discursive "I" and the Nuakatan *yau* tells us little about the relationship between *yau* and *waihiu* on Nuakata. It does not address what it means to speak as a woman on Nuakata. For this we need to know what the category *waihiu* denotes and how it is used. In Alina Nu'ata the noun *waihiu,* or its plural equivalent *waiwaihiu,* was used to refer to an individual (woman) or group of people (women) aged roughly between twenty and forty-five. On Nuakata this corresponds to the period of (a woman's) life when she may marry and actively bear, feed, and care for children and/or older kin. In practice, then, married, pregnant, widowed, and divorced women less than approximately forty-five years old were addressed as *waihiu.* Someone who was in this age group and whose bodily form suggested a capacity to bear children and garden produce, yet was unable to do so due to circumstances of ill health, inadvertent sterility, witchcraft, and so on, was still considered a woman—albeit a lonely woman for whom we should feel sorrow, a woman diminished by circumstance. In this sense, potential rather than actual bearing capacity was a crucial, implicit dimension of the category "woman." However, it was not its only distinguishing feature, nor was it necessarily the aspect most often appealed to when identifying or referring to someone by this term. This was contingent on the speaker and speaking context.

Used as an adjective *waihiuna* means literally "its womanliness." The adjective *waihiuna* is also placed after some common nouns (typically animals) to designate what I might term female/sex, suggesting that in Alina Nuʻata, womanliness and female are conflated. In this sense, perhaps, women's bodies are understood on Nuakata as contexts rather than essences. What women can and cannot do is contingent. To be named a woman is to be recognized as a female within a loosely defined age span or period of life, distinct from a prepubescent female child (*gamahine*), a young, unmarried female (*vahala*), an older respected woman/female (*ʻaihale*), and a very old woman/female (*ʻaiʻaihale*). To be named a woman is also to be recognized as distinct from a man—*loheya* and *loheyana* (its manliness, male), *gama* (a prepubescent male child), *hevali* (a young male), *taubada* (an older, respected man/male), and *tautaubada* (a very old man/male).

This bald description says nothing of the way these terms were used in conversation. And they cannot be understood except in conversation and the associated activities to which conversations refer, for they are relational terms. For example, the "gendered" terms used to designate older people, be they man or woman, were used as direct, respectful terms of address. However, in practice, people often respectfully addressed older, familiar others without employing these formal terms. They observed respect without giving it a gender. People rarely drew attention to the sex/gender of children, particularly young, small children, be they related to the speaker or not. And certainly I observed little or no apparent difference in the expectations of, or responses to, young children, boys or girls. They, like older, bigger children, were generally spoken of or addressed as *hedaheda* (children), *heda* (child), *natugu* (my child), or by name. It was their status as children rather than their sex/gender that was most significant to adult speakers.

While I could perceive no apparent differences in the activities younger, smaller children engaged in—typically, they trailed behind or were carried by their older siblings, played with flotsam and jetsam in the sand, ran about their hamlets or through the encroaching bush, splashed around in shallow water with other children, and so on—the same was not quite true for older, bigger children (i.e., from approximately age seven to puberty). As with the younger children, there did not seem to be significant differences in the nature of their play. Boys and girls alike played with one another in the water; created things in the sand; made grass darts, pandanus windmills, and boats; paddled their canoes around the various small bays around Nuakata; climbed coconut palms; attended to their smaller siblings; searched for seasonal food like mangoes, shellfish, prawns, and nuts; and drifted between hamlets throughout the course of any given day. What differences there were in the play of older boys and girls seemed idiosyncratic rather than gender/sex-related. Girls and boys alike were encouraged to attend preschool and primary school. If they had the ability, they were also actively encouraged and, where possible, supported to pursue secondary and postsecondary education. However, when it came to work it was clear that the adult expectations of girl children were different from those of boys. For example, I both observed and was told that from the age of seven or eight girls begin to garden with their mothers, establishing and tending their own plots with their mothers' assistance and supervision. They begin to carry increasingly weighty *boha* (bags) on or suspended from their heads. They are also expected to help their mothers scrub pots, sweep hamlets, and wash clothes and dishes. Occasionally boys volunteered or were asked to do these activities, but they were clearly not expected to perform them routinely. Daily expectations of boys were few. Their fathers or maternal uncles often enlisted them to fetch things (including firewood), climb palm trees, or fish with them; however, girls also performed these tasks.

When asked, adults invoked sex/gender as the reason for their differing expectations of older children's and teenagers' behavior. When it came to gardening and carrying garden produce, mothers explained the need to teach their daughters to do as they do. Young girls accepted that they needed to develop strength if they were to carry heavy loads on their head and neck like their mothers. The activities of teenagers were more consistently and markedly differentiated along gender lines than those of younger boys and girls. Most young people left school upon completion of their primary education, when they were thirteen or fourteen years old. While both teenage boys and girls participated in sporting and church youth group activities, girls routinely assisted their mothers with garden work, food preparation, and other domestic activities. In contrast, teenage boys spent much of their time wandering around the island with their friends; playing games; looking for betel nut, flying fox, or shellfish; fishing; and so forth. While sex/gender was invoked as the reason for differing expectations of boys and girls, boys were not considered constitutionally incapable of doing work expected of girls, or vice versa. Nor were they considered silly or inferior if they engaged in these activities. Tending and weeding gardens, cooking and food preparation, were considered optional activities for boys and men, but necessary ones for women. Of course, why this gendered division of labor existed on Nuakata remains to be explained (see chaps. 3 and 5).

In language, then, if not wider practice, sex and gender are neither distinct nor static categories on Nuakata. Multiple features or dimensions, including age, period of life, status within the community, position within a given generation, and—to a degree—someone's bodily form and condition (growing, not growing, sick, capable of bearing children, etc.) coalesced in the terms *waihiu* (woman) and, equally, *towaho* (man) and other sex/gender categories. Just as the categories themselves become meaningful in relation to one another, so, too, the embodiment of these categories is relational. The relational, conversational context determined which aspect of these terms was emphasized—which embodied dimensions were made explicit and which remained implicit (see Devereaux 1986, 69). When someone is identified as a man or woman, it seems that the respective changing bodily form is assumed to inform, without determining, his or her embodied acts. Accordingly, bodies are implicitly understood on Nuakata as enacting forms rather than static entities. They are enacting forms that enact and inform as they are enacted and informed by their historical, cultural, and relational contexts. Butler's reflections on embodiment and performance resonate with these ideas.

> One is not simply a body, but in some very key sense, one does one's body. . . . It is, however, clearly unfortunate grammar to claim that there is a "we" or an "I" that does its body, as if a disembodied agency preceded and directed an embodied exterior. . . . The "I" that is its body is, of necessity, a mode of embodying, and the what it embodies is possibilities. . . . [T]he possibilities that are embodied are not funda-

mentally exterior or antecedent to the process of embodying itself. . . . As an intentionally organized materiality, the body is always an embodying of possibilities conditioned and circumscribed by historical convention. (1988, 521)

My contact with people during those early weeks on Nuakata posed an immediate and, at times, indecipherable challenge to my assumptions about the impact of my sex/gender on my research. Nuakatan women neither used the expression "because I am a woman" nor spontaneously invoked the category "woman" or "man" as a cause of behavior. Moreover, I was never simply recognized as a woman on Nuakata, not by women, not by men, and certainly not by children. Much to my chagrin, adults of all ages initially addressed me as *sinebada*. Used during colonial times as a subservient way of addressing *dimdim* women (Macintyre 1993, 52), older, respected women were occasionally addressed this way during our time on Nuakata. Its continued use in relation to *dimdim* attested to the reality that "colonial times"—colonial relationships— have not yet passed for adult generations on Nuakata (or, at the very least, Roger and I enlivened their memory).[14] Older children simply called us *dimdim*, suggesting that skin color rather than sex/gender or any other feature rendered us different from themselves. Infants and very small children initially addressed both Roger and me with recoiling bodies and screams. Much to their parents' embarrassment and extreme discomfort, we embodied their nameless and unnameable fear and terror.

Going on a Health Patrol

Several weeks after we arrived on Nuakata Moses invited me to accompany him on his monthly health patrol of the island. I jumped at the opportunity to observe his work and so begin my exploration of the relationship between Western and local medical knowledge and practices. On this journey we met with two pregnant women in different hamlets, one pregnant with her fifth child, the other pregnant with her eighth. Speaking in halting English, Moses asked them both, "Are you feeling well? Have you been taking your chloroquine [malaria prophylaxis]? Have you been eating vegetables, protein—fish, shellfish? Have you talked with your husband about where you will have the baby? Why didn't you attend the last maternal and child health clinic?"

Shy, embarrassed, and reticent in our presence, they looked down as they mumbled their "yes" replies to these questions, one indicating that she had been too sick to attend the prenatal clinic, the other reporting that she had no one to care for her small children on the clinic day. Moses replied with an unnerving silence, commenting to me as we walked to the next hamlet that the women do not come to the aid post for the clinics, or to give birth, because their husbands will not let them. He added that, like the health patrols, the maternal and child health clinics were held on a monthly basis on Nuakata. On these occasions clinic sisters trained in maternal and child health come from the mainland to immunize children under five. They also conduct physical examinations of pregnant women (measuring fundal height, listening for fetal heartbeat, determining position of the fetus in utero), identifying those at risk of birth complications. Pregnant women at risk are advised to deliver at Alotau Hospital on the mainland.

The questions posed to these women, indeed even the order and manner in which they were spoken, expressed Moses' understanding at that time of the primary issues associated with pregnancy on Nuakata. He viewed pregnancy and childbirth as health issues. Believing himself responsible for the health needs of the community, he indicated that it was his role, first, to prevent "illness" and, second, to treat illnesses as they arose. According to Moses, illness is caused by physical factors alone. This personal view of his role and its primacy extended to pregnancy and birth. His understanding of maternity, birth, and breast-feeding and his role with pregnant women was filtered through his community health worker training[15] and the clear expectations of his employer, the Alotau district division of the Milne Bay Health Department. Reduction of maternal and child mortality, malnutrition, malaria, and diarrheal diseases had been identified as a priority for all preventive and curative health strategies locally implemented by community health workers throughout Milne Bay Province.

Aware that local women lose their acquired immunity to malaria during pregnancy, thereby placing them at risk of anemia, postpartum hemorrhage, inadvertent miscarriage, and stillbirth (Edwards 1987; Gillett 1990; Mola and Aitken 1984; Taufa 1978), Moses routinely supplied them with prophylactic doses of chloroquine. According to Moses, some women, particularly young educated women, have been persuaded by his preventive health talks and have followed his advice to take prophylactic doses of chloroquine. Some simply forget or refuse to take the tablets, complaining of their bitter taste. Moses experienced this refusal as "resistance" and recalcitrance, attributing it to women's lack of education and inadequate understanding of their bodies and the way the fetus develops in utero.[16]

Apart from malaria he stated that "the major health problems with pregnant and breast-feeding women is [poor] diet," compounded by a heavy and unequal work load compared to men.

> When [ladies] are preparing meals they give the best to the man and they have what is left. That is why their health is not really good. . . . I think on this island ladies do most of the work. [For example:] Men only clear the garden; . . . ladies dig it, plant it, weed it, and when the time comes for harvesting, they do that too. Only those responsible men help their wives in the garden, others are very slack and lazy. They expect the ladies to do the work.

Moses indicated that, unlike his advice about malaria, both his dietary recommendations and his provision of weekly "blood [iron] tablets to increase the blood system" have been generally well received by pregnant women. Critical of men's lack of understanding of the health issues associated with pregnancy and birth, Moses stated that he had attempted, with minimal success, to involve men in preventive education sessions about maternal health, nutrition, and family planning held at the aid post.

Later that day we came to Emma's hamlet. At Emma's invitation we clambered inside her house where she and her week-old baby daughter Reni were ensconced by a fire. First, Moses made his inquiries: Had her bleeding stopped? Yes. Was she having difficulty with breast-feeding? No. Was she eating vegetables? Yes. How was the baby's umbilicus? With this, Emma fiddled with Reni's clothing revealing a completely healed navel. Moses simply nodded, issued her with a child vaccination book, and told her to come to the maternal and child health clinic the following week.

Then it was my turn. Taking my notebook out and pausing for her replies, I asked, "Where did you give birth to Reni? Who was present at the time? Why are you staying inside the house? What food are you eating? What did you do with the placenta?" Although slightly embarrassed and amused by this barrage of questions, Emma answered my inquiries patiently and in turn, as might a teacher, one moment speaking from her own experience, the next offering brief explanations of custom. As she spoke she scanned Moses' face carefully, monitoring his responses. Watching her watching him, I made a mental note of her caution, suspecting she was reluctant to speak openly about customary practices in his presence.

She had given birth in her hamlet while being watched over and cared for by her mother and several other maternal relatives. Following the birth she and the baby were washed in warm water before settling down by a fire prepared inside the house. She stated, "After birth, it is our custom for mother with her baby to stay by the fire inside the house for twenty days." During this time "their mothers will care for them both." In the days that followed Reni's birth she repeatedly warmed her hands by the fire, then placed them on the tied umbilical cord. This dried it out, so that within four days it had fallen off. Emma's kin buried it in her garden to ensure that Reni "may grow to be a good gardener." For the first five or six days after Reni's birth, Emma had eaten only the boiled young leaves of pumpkins. In accordance with custom, neither she nor those caring for her had eaten fish while she was still bleeding. She commented that the smell alone could make her sick, causing her bleeding to continue. Reni's placenta was placed in a bag and hung from a tree, so that she might grow to be active and a good climber.

Before we left, Moses reiterated his instructions to her to attend the forthcoming maternal and child health clinic to immunize Reni, adding, "It is your responsibility to breast-feed when your baby needs it. Don't wait." Emma smiled. Later Moses repeated the same questions and instructions almost word for word to Emma's sister, Roda, who had given birth to a daughter one month earlier. One week later both women arrived at the aid post, as directed, for the maternal and child health clinic, apparently unperturbed by Moses' assertive, instructive style.

In his conversations with Emma and Roda, Moses' silences, as much as his questions, were revealing, reflecting strong disapproval of their decision to deliver in the village and his broader frustration about his limited obstetric role on Nuakata. With the exception of emergencies, he was only invited to visit mothers and their new babies a day or so after the birth. Moses knew from his training that the risk of death through bleeding diminished for women whose deliveries were supervised by trained health workers, and those who died of infection following birth had received much less prenatal care than other mothers (Edwards 1992; Mola and Aitken 1984).

During a wide-ranging discussion several weeks after the patrol,

Moses revealed that he had been deeply disturbed by the first village births he attended on the island.

> The first two mothers that I attended, I found out that they delivered on the bare ground like dogs, and that really shocked me. One mother had a retained placenta. . . . I managed to deliver the whole thing out, except a membrane got stuck. I was going to do a manual removal, but I am not allowed to because I did not have proper, sterile things with me. If I was only at the aid post I would do something to remove it out. . . . At another birth . . . the baby's cord wasn't tied properly . . . and it was bleeding. As soon as I got there I [tied] the cord and the bleeding stopped. [Equally disturbing was the discovery that although] the mothers of women [in labor] are present during birth, they do not help. They do not help! They just stand there or sit [some distance] away . . . and wait to receive the newborn baby. I haven't asked them why it is relating to their customs.

These experiences confirmed some of Moses' worst fears about the health risks posed to mother and child during village births, reinforcing his conviction that women should deliver at the aid post. Consistent with national findings, Moses nominated puerperal sepsis, postpartum hemorrhage, and obstructed birth as the most significant risks to women giving birth on Nuakata—risks that he claimed could be averted by allowing him to supervise and assist deliveries in the cleaner, more sterile environment of the aid post (Gillett 1990; Health 1991, 242). Although totally convinced that women should deliver at the aid post, he understood their reluctance to give birth there. He commented, "One reason is that they feel shy to come because I am a male single worker. They are shy because of the sexes, I mean making themselves public to me. If I was married it would be slightly different." Moses was acutely aware that, as in other places across Papua New Guinea, it was considered improper for local postpubescent girls/women to display the lower half of their bodies (below the navel and above the knee) to men with whom they have no sexual relationship and especially young single males such as himself. Public displays of this kind would be considered sexually provocative and a source of malicious gossip. If such views were not originally instituted by the early Christian missionaries in the Massim, then it was certainly reinforced by their efforts to discipline local women's bodies (see

Eves 1996b; Reed 1998). While respecting this custom, Moses contended that health matters, particularly maternal health matters, provided sufficient cause and the necessary context for such customs to be flouted and overturned. Committed to his work, he felt great frustration that on Nuakata, like most other rural places in Papua New Guinea, women remain reluctant to utilize maternal health services at aid posts staffed only by male health workers.[17] He knew that the husbands of pregnant and birthing women often discouraged, or even prevented, their wives from receiving maternal health care from him.

Moses' attempts to persuade women to deliver at the aid post reflected his strongly held belief that both the place of birth and the expertise of the birth attendants may influence the outcome of birth. The significance of place to the process of birth, the newborn, and its bearer was conceived by Moses in very specific ways—ways that did not accord with understandings of the integral relationship between birthplace and identity reported by anthropologists in many places across the Massim and Papua New Guinea (see, for example, Merrett-Balkos 1998; A. Weiner 1976). In his view it was not essential to literally establish continuity between the place of one's birth and the place where one grows, lives, dies—the place where one's ancestors may also have been born, lived, and died. Rather, for Moses, place of birth—in this instance, the aid post—was considered significant only as it potentially facilitated the health of the woman and child during and immediately after labor. Moses described the aid post as cleaner and more sterile than the village or village houses. He regarded cleanliness as essential to the health of the laboring woman and her unborn child; it was associated with Western-style buildings. Women could deliver inside on mats on the concrete floor, rather than outside on the ground or in their houses. In Moses' view, dogs and pigs give birth outside on the bare ground; women should not. Therefore, not only did he suggest that the aid post was a cleaner place for birth, but he also implied that it was a more dignified, if not more civilized, place. During birth, this place, rather than the village, was believed to render the pregnant woman and her unborn or newborn child more fully human.

But for Moses, birthplace issues were secondary to those about birth attendants. Who assisted the laboring woman and her child and by what means was considered most significant. Certain that Western-style medical practices and practitioners offered childbearing women and their infants the greatest chance of survival, Moses was convinced that alternative practices and practitioners exposed mother and baby to avoidable health risks. He discounted their knowledge of birth, derived from their experience as mothers and midwives, as inadequate, if not dangerous. For Moses the presence or absence of onlooking kin was believed to be irrelevant to the process of labor and birth and the health of the laboring woman and child. Only people trained in Western-style medical practices were considered appropriate birth attendants, for they could actively support and assist, rather than passively observe, the laboring woman during birth.

Moses also implied that trained birth attendants required proper equipment to adequately assist the laboring woman. "If necessary I've got proper equipment that I can use, like clean things to use—like gauze, cord, clamps. It's a bit sterile." Accordingly, proper ways of giving birth were facilitated by appropriate equipment, by the proper person in the proper place. Without these proper people, places, and things to assist childbearing women, labor presented a significant health risk to Nuakatan mothers and infants. At the same time, he ruefully noted that if difficulties were encountered during or after labor, there was only a limited array of Western medicine available at the aid post. Unlike a few community health workers working in other provinces, he had no drugs to treat postpartum hemorrhage (Edwards 1992, 79). Committed to national and regional preventive health plans and policies that emphasized the need to train local women as village birth attendants (1992), Moses remained pessimistic about the implementation of such policies on Nuakata.[18] His previous efforts to attract local volunteers to provide basic health care for people living on parts of the island distant from the aid post had met with no response. Moreover, the Milne Bay Provincial Health Department had no available funds to develop a provincewide village birth attendants training program.[19]

One Week Later: A Maternal and Child Health Clinic

A week after the health patrol the maternal and child health clinic was conducted at the aid post. Fifteen women attended, carrying their young children. Made of fibro cement on a concrete slab, the aid post was one of three Western-style buildings on the island. Small and poorly ventilated, the aid post comprised four barely furnished rooms—a consulting room with a single bench for patients and a desk and stool cobbled together from scrap wood for Moses, a completely empty room where people could stay for inpatient care, another room with a wooden slat bed, and a storeroom where basic medical supplies and equipment were kept. It had neither lighting nor functioning kerosene burners to sterilize what few medical instruments (two pairs of tweezers, a pair of scissors, and clamps) Moses possessed.

At one point in its history the aid post had a two-way radio powered by a solar panel. Several years ago the radio broke and was taken to Alotau for repairs. It was never returned. Since then the community has been without the ability to communicate directly with the mainland. With the radio gone, the solar panel was later stolen by a local youth who used it to power his cassette recorder. Despite persistent community efforts to secure its return, it too remained lost to the aid post.

Although a day had been set aside for the clinic, it did not begin until midafternoon, when all the women known to be coming had arrived. Until then Moses remained outside, close to his house, variously talking with me and relaxing with some of his friends. Withdrawing to the aid post, he systematically worked through an alphabetical list of names, seeing each woman together with her child(ren) in turn. As on the patrol, he spoke with people in English, relying at times upon several women, Emma among them, to act as interpreters. Waiting together outside the aid post for their names to be called, those assembled talked and laughed with one another. Yet much to my dismay, on the occasions when I ventured outside to sit among them, their eyes fell to ground and the talking dwindled away. Conversation inside the aid post between Moses and each of the women was similarly sparse, even strained. Women who outside had been confident, animated, became deferential and embarrassed as Moses fired yes/no questions at them to determine why they had come. At Moses' request they pointed to the problem, sometimes naming it in Alina Nu'ata—for example, cough or hot body—then waited for his response. Most striking in these exchanges were the things left unsaid, the things unable to be said.

Most who attended the clinic that day sought treatment for their children—be it immunizations or treatment for illnesses such as malaria, scabies, diarrhea, coughs, and failure to thrive. As Moses had anticipated, the two pregnant women we had seen on patrol did not arrive. Nor did the East Cape nurses. Their attendance was totally dependent upon the availability of local boats and suitable weather conditions. Aid post records reveal that during 1992 the nurses attended six times; however, during the nine months Roger and I spent on Nuakata in 1993 they did not attend once.

Moses distributed medicine and advice in more or less equal quantities. Antibiotics for infections, camaquine to treat young children with malaria, dressings and antiseptic for infected sores. But the dominant refrain repeated to each of these women, particularly the breast-feeding mothers, related to diet and nutrition. "When you follow custom children start losing weight. They will not feel well or grow. I want to see change next month."

In discussions with pregnant and breast-feeding women, Moses spoke of food as something that sustains the pregnant woman while also feeding the developing fetus/baby. Specifically, food was described and represented as a source of nutrition. The power of a particular food type (yams, fish, green vegetables) to sustain people was said to derive from its unique constellation of invisible yet loosely quantifiable constituent parts (vitamins, minerals, protein, carbohydrates, and sugars) known to disseminate throughout the body in the blood. These vital nutritional components were also said to pass between mother and child through breast-milk. Breast-milk was therefore significant as a necessary source of nutrition. Moses repeatedly urged women, irrespective of their physical or social circumstances, to eat a variety of foods—fish for protein, vegetables for vitamins and minerals, and so on—to satisfy their nutritional needs.

Confined to nutrition, Moses' advice about food took little account of the social relations associated with growing, preparing, providing, and distributing food. He contended that if uncontaminated by germs or bacteria, the various food types give rise to predictable physiological effects in healthy bodies. Food's capacity to support, strengthen, and grow healthy, living bodies was described as integral to the food itself. Accordingly, who labors how to produce food, with what intent, is deemed irrelevant to the health of the consumer. So, too, is the context in which the food is consumed. In other words, food is represented as an object detachable from its production and its producer.

Reconceiving Pregnancy and Birth on Nuakata

Climbing the hill between Yalasi and Bwauli on my way back from the aid post that day, I was preoccupied by a number of thoughts and questions. Uppermost among them were, Why were the women still so shy and reserved in my presence? Was I equally shy, or reluctant to foist myself upon them? Would this ever change? If so, when? How? Pushing these thoughts aside, I reflected on the day's activities and the health patrol a week earlier. First I was struck by the high attendance at the clinic, given the long and strenuous journey with small children that some of the women had to make.[20] Moses' conscientious attitude to the work and his provision of health care was clearly respected by the women. Even so, no pregnant women attended the clinic and, with the exception of one breast-feeding woman, no women sought medical treatment or advice for themselves. Moses indicated that some pregnant women attend for prenatal care when the female nurses from East Cape were in attendance. This attendance pattern reflects a broader national trend, particularly in rural areas. Across the country, mothers attend maternal and child health clinics primarily for curative care for their children (Health 1991, 222–23).

I was struck too by the ritualized form of the clinic, the distinctive and familiar performances of its participants, of Western medical knowledge and expertise enacted. In crossing the threshold into the aid post, Moses' casual demeanor changed. Once inside and at work, he became serious, efficient, organized. Time, which until then had stretched on seamlessly, was suddenly demarcated by everyone's knowledge of an alphabetical list of successive appointments squeezed into diminishing daylight hours.[21] Moses presided over the space and its occupants with authority, directing women where to sit with their children while he moved about the rooms freely, writing brief notes at his desk, collecting supplies from the storeroom, confidently examining, weighing, or treating children in spite of their protests. Whereas outside his conversations had meandered across many territories with no clear destination, inside they were brief, concise, and directed to a clear end point—diagnosis of illness based on a clear description of physical symptoms. Discussion was strictly confined to matters of health, precluding any sense of familiarity between the women and Moses. Women's opinion and experience was not solicited. They in turn did not question his explanations or advice, but meekly deferred to his expertise. In this intimate and confined space, both the conversational style and physical examinations themselves maximized the distance and distinction between patient and health worker. Moses' medical expertise, authority, and power seemed to converge within the aid post, where it was fully dramatized amid his equipment and supplies.[22]

For a moment my thoughts drifted back to the mainland, where a month earlier I had attended a prenatal clinic at Alotau Hospital. It, too, began in the midafternoon after a sizable crowd of pregnant women had amassed on the wooden benches outside in the waiting area. As each woman's name was called, each was directed to follow the waiting nurse. Trailing behind her, she was ushered into a curtained cubicle, told to lie down on a bed before being externally examined by nurses and nursing students, female and male. No attempt was made to engage the woman in general conversation. In this confined space the nurses maintained an efficient, almost officious, economy of words and actions. With stethoscope, medical notes, and prenatal booklet at the ready, they hovered over the named but effectively anonymous pregnant woman, silently scanning her exposed pregnant body and scrutinizing her eyes for visible signs of anemia. Fundal height measurements were taken to assess fetal growth, development, and gestation, and her swollen stomach was gently prodded and poked to determine the fetal position in utero. Many of these rituals were performed without explanation, their purpose and intent only revealed through the authoritative pronouncements that followed: "The baby is growing; you are not eating enough vegetables; you have three months before you will give birth; the baby is in the wrong position; you must give birth in the hospital;" and so on.

As the women came from varying language groups, the nurses spoke to them in a staccato English. What sense the pregnant women made of the procedures, the questions, or their parting instructions is difficult to tell, but easy to speculate upon. Without exception they did not talk except to make barely audible responses to direct questions. They simply lay there, passive, blushing, their gaze averted. Their feeling of overwhelming embarrassment was obvious for all to see. And then when final directives were issued they clambered off the bed; their slow, deliberate movements belying both their evident relief that the examination was complete and their sure wish to be gone.

Most striking about these recollections was the sense that, although distinctive, Moses' enactment or orchestration of the maternal and child health clinic on Nuakata was, in many ways, mimetic. The Nuakatan maternal and child health clinic was not unlike the Alotau clinic, which in form, organization, relational tone, even medical procedure and setting, was not unlike general outpatient hospital clinics I had attended in Melbourne. There were obvious ways in which these clinics differed, not the least being disparities in the number and training of medical personnel, clinic facilities, and the array of medicines and medical equipment.

But arguably it was the remote setting and staffing by a single male community health worker that constituted the most significant difference between the Nuakata clinic and the Alotau and Melbourne ones.

However, there were obvious structural ways in which the Nuakata and Alotau clinics were alike—the organization of time, the alphabetical listing of appointments, the arrangement of furniture, equipment, and medicines within the clinic, the constraints on movement of patients within the clinical space. But most striking of all were the similar, if not habituated, ways in which the Alotau nurses and Moses occupied and moved within their respective clinical environments. Eye contact was avoided with the person examined, except when advice was given or specific information solicited. Moses and the nurses stood over supine patients, probing, surveying, inspecting the surface of their still bodies as one might inspect and assume authority and control of an inert, dysfunctional object. When patients were present the health workers kept their bodies erect, their eyes focused, and their movements definite, efficient, contained. Their faces remained impassive, their speech uniformly modulated in pitch and tone. Their field of interest seemed bounded by the maternal body surfaces under their gaze. When pregnant women were absent from the consulting room they were uniformly referred to as "villagers" or "village women." In the same breath their lack of understanding or Western education was noted. To the observer these postures created a sense of difference and distance between health worker and patient. While the health workers enacted knowledge of the body, the pregnant women became passive recipients of this reified surface view. By the health workers' hands, through their clinical handling and comments, these women were rendered as passive, maternal bodies at risk. In categorizing them as "uneducated villagers" in need of medical care and advice, there was a sense in which the health workers infantilized these women, construed them as underdeveloped, if not slightly primitive.

In noting these similarities I do not imply that Moses, or the Alotau nurses, either unconsciously or intentionally conformed to a set of conventional ideas or protocols detailing the embodiment of Western medical knowledge and practice in these clinical spaces. Taken to their extreme, the former suggests a structuralist vision of social action that allows little or no room for personal agency and innovative social change, while the latter assumes an individual subject-agent who acts by consciously discerning and initiating behavior that may or may not be appropriate to the social setting. Both views are potentially at odds with my earlier discussion of (discursive) subjectivity agency, gender, and embodiment, to which I shall return shortly. Rather, following Bourdieu (1977, 1990a, 1990b) in particular, but also Merleau-Ponty (1962), Heidegger (1977), Mauss (1973), and Dewey (1958), and those such as Jackson (1989)[23] who have applied their work, I suggest that the mimetic actions of Moses during the clinic can be better understood as habitual practices invoked—as they themselves had been—by the setting (buildings, furnishings, equipment), the patients, and Western medical knowledge. In other words, Moses' bodily actions or dispositions within the aid post were informed by habits instilled within clinical environments. Such habitual forms of body use are necessarily relational or interactional. They arise in shared spaces or environments of people, objects, places, knowledges—what Bourdieu terms the habitus.

Bourdieu defines habitus as the "durable and transposable systems of schemata of perception, appreciation and action" arising from "the institution [or embodiment] of the social in the body" (Bourdieu and Wacquant 1992, 127; see also Bourdieu 1977, 72, 214). Through his notion of habitus he articulates a theory of practice intended to escape "both the objectivism of action understood as a mechanical reaction 'without an agent' and the subjectivism which portrays action as the deliberate pursuit of a conscious [rational] intention. . . . [It is an attempt to] escape from the philosophy of the subject without doing away with the agent" (Bourdieu and Wacquant 1992, 121). Accordingly, "to speak of habitus is to assert that the individual, and even the personal, the subjective, is social, collective. Habitus is a socialized subjectivity" (1992, 126). Bourdieu's subject and/or agent cannot be meaningfully understood as separate or distinct from the material conditions, the socially and symbolically structured spaces integral to its existence (Moore 1994c, 80). Cultural meanings and values "inform" the organization of any socially structured space, but "they are not inherent in the organization of that space" (76). It is the behavior of social actors within that environment that elicits these meanings and values. By their actions, these actors necessarily interpret and/or reinterpret the cultural meanings that inform the given space. Human action is therefore understood as historical, temporal. "It is not an instantaneous reaction to immediate stimuli . . . [for] the slightest 'reaction' of an individual to another, is pregnant with the whole history of these persons . . . , their relationship" and the historical structuring of relationships within these shared social spaces (Bourdieu and Wacquant 1992, 124).

While Bourdieu claims that the habitus predisposes or inclines the actor to habituated patterns of body use, he indicates that actors can potentially subvert these patterns by engaging in alternative activities/interpretations within that shared environment. Through their bodily praxis, people are both "informed by and give form to a habitus" (Jackson 1989, 136). Or as Dreyfus and Rabinow cogently state, "our socially inculcated dispositions to act make the world solicit action, and our actions are a response to this solicitation" (1993, 38). But this is not to suggest that these actions are intentional, formulated, and able to be articulated. For Bourdieu's theory of praxis is also a materialist theory of knowledge that owes much to Marx and Wittengenstein, but also Merleau-Ponty and Heidegger. It situates understanding in practices (Taylor 1993, 50).

> Following the program suggested by Marx in the *Theses on Feuerbach*, it aims at making possible a materialist theory of knowledge, that does not abandon to idealism the notion that all knowledge, be it mundane or scholarly, presupposes a work of construction. But it emphasizes that this work has nothing in common with intellectual work, that it consists of an activity of practical construction, even of practical reflection, that ordinary notions of thought, consciousness, knowledge prevent us from adequately thinking. (Bourdieu and Wacquant 1992, 121)

It is a materialist theory of knowledge that is perhaps more clearly articulated by Jackson, who, when commenting on the body practices associated with Kuranko initiation, notes that

> what is done with the body is the ground of what is thought and said. From an existential point of view we could say that the bodily practices mediate a personal realization of social values, an immediate grasp of general precepts as sensible truths. (1989, 131–32)

Absent from the foregoing discussion is consideration of how actors' social positions/locations influence their practices and their practical understanding. Crucial to Bourdieu's theory of praxis, this is also relevant to my reflection on Moses' clinical practices and my broader exploration of gendered subjectivity/personhood on Nuakata and beyond. Bourdieu insists that actors' practices are necessarily influenced, if not determined, by their social position in relation to pivotal cultural discourses and social relations, notably discourses of class and gender (see Moore 1994c, 77). Actors are located by and locate sociocultural distinctions and structural inequalities through their embodied practices.

By his highly focused and restrained actions within the clinic space—be it at the aid post or during health consultations in the village—Moses attempted to convince local people, male and female alike, that in his social role/position as a health worker attending to pregnant women and those giving birth, his sex/gender, sexuality, and sexual desire were nullified or rendered irrelevant. Similarly, he attempted to convey to women that as a health worker he considered their bodies, particularly their genitalia, as divisible or partible from themselves, their sex/gender, sexuality, sexual desire. Within the clinic space Moses treated maternal or diseased women's bodies as androgynous and partible—as bodies distinct from selves/persons, distinct from other bodies. While he always behaved respectfully to people outside the clinic space, he did not deliberately position himself as an androgynous subject or agent in these contexts. Ironically, then, when performing his work as a health worker, the presence of female patients caused him to act (pragmatically) *as if* sex/gender and sexuality were irrelevant to either his own actions and/or subject positions or the women in his care. Arguably this only heightened everyone's awareness that both his and their actions and/or subject positions were informed by sex/gender and sexuality in these spaces. It is a point reinforced by pregnant/birthing women's rejection of Moses' medical care. They demonstrated that where cross-sex relations occur between known adults in intimate spaces, the sex/gender and sexuality of those involved necessarily inform their actions and/or subject positions. Although they may have worried over their own health and the health of the unborn or birthing child, they were more concerned to enact proper, respectful, if not ethical, relations between Moses and themselves.

Moses' practices within the clinic space can be interpreted as strategic. By actively discouraging familiarity, especially sexual familiarity between himself and his women patients, he demonstrated a practically and theoretically informed understanding of respectful ethical relations between Western-style medical health practitioners and their patients. Typically, familiarity, especially sexual familiarity between health practitioner and patient, is actively discouraged. It is an ethical stance, which is more difficult to maintain in rural and isolated settings, where the practitioner necessarily encounters people outside the clinical setting and must relate to them in other ways.

Moses not only treated maternal bodies as androgynous, he also considered and treated them as bodies at risk. Along with the East Cape nurses, he assumed responsibility to define, assess, predict, monitor, and, where possible, prevent and manage these potential physical risks. Local customary practices were treated and construed as pernicious, static conventions that should be replaced by the "proper" and ever-developing knowledge, practices, sites, and implements of Western medicine.

By making pregnant/breast-feeding women and their infants the target of preventive health strategies, Moses, as a Western medical representative of the provincial and national health authorities, constituted these women as a unified group—a group of women who, because of pregnancy, were at risk of illness and death. This simplistic conflation of physical/biological risk with pregnancy, arguably perpetuated by the collation of narrowly focused maternal mortality statistics, has reinforced the strategic development of equally narrow medical responses focused on the individual pregnant woman. Accordingly, maternal and child health clinics on Nuakata are conducted in the belief that the most effective and efficient way of averting illness and avoidable deaths during pregnancy and childbirth was to examine pregnant women alone and target educational talks to them as a group. While men were not excluded from these clinics, in practice it was rare for them to attend with or without their pregnant wives, small child(ren), or one of their female kin. Notice of forthcoming clinics was always directed at women, suggesting that individual women were held primarily responsible for their own health—imagined as a physical/biological condition—and that of their small children, particularly while they were pregnant or breast-feeding. Moses indicated that it was the husbands' role to assist their wives, and, where possible, relieve and share their wives' burden of care. This familial hierarchy of responsibility for maternal and child health seemed based on the contemporary Western nuclear family. It took little or no account of the responsibility for care and nurture shared by the wider paternal, and especially maternal, family or *susu* on Nuakata.

Although borne by Moses and made his own, this struggle to overturn customary practices and impose Western medical ideas and practices was by no means unique to him or Nuakata. Provincial preventive health policies and strategies, developed in conformity with the National Health

Plans, which were in turn influenced by primary health-care (PHC) policies generated and instituted by international health agencies (WHO and UNICEF) whose personnel were persuaded by current Western medical knowledge and practice in relation to pregnancy and birth, informed much of his thinking and practice. Established as the paradigm of choice at the combined WHO and UNICEF conference in 1978 at Alma Ata in the then Soviet Union, the PHC policy for the developing world encouraged the provision of preventive, curative, and rehabilitative care at the local village level.[24] The PHC policy discouraged the provision of costly, and therefore unsustainable, technologically sophisticated Western medicine. Instead it sought participation of local people in the planning, implementation, and use of basic Western-style health services. Crucial to the implementation of this paradigm were community health workers, who would receive shorter and less detailed medical training than Western-style medical practitioners and nursing staff. Maternal and child health care was one of eight basic health initiatives promoted by the PHC initiative.

Once again, Bourdieu's work provides some insight here, in particular his notion of field and the relationship between field and habitus. Although it teeters toward structuralism, Bourdieu's concept of field offers a way of understanding Moses' embodiment of the field of Western medical knowledge and practice and the subfield of basic primary health care (BPHC) that neither denies his agency nor precludes a systematic (rather than systemic) understanding of his actions and the knowledge they express. When Bourdieu speaks of "fields" (Bourdieu and Wacquant 1992), discussion focuses on relations and processes rather than things and states. According to Bourdieu, a field is

> a network, or a configuration, of objective relations between positions. These positions are objectively defined, in their existence and in the determinations they impose upon their occupants, agents or institutions, by their present and potential situation . . . in the structure of the distribution of species of power (or capital). . . . As a space of potential and active forces, the field is also a field of struggles aimed at preserving or transforming the configuration of these forces. (Bourdieu and Wacquant 1992, 97–101)

While a field may be understood as "a set of historical relations between positions anchored in certain forms of power" or capital, habitus comprises "a set of historical relations 'deposited' within individual bodies in the form of mental and corporeal schemata of perception, appreciation and action" (Bourdieu and Wacquant 1992, 16). In other words, the field—in this instance basic primary health care as it relates to maternal health—conditions or "structures" the habitus. The habitus inflects the field, rendering it meaningful, as it is embodied by people who are themselves positioned in and by the field.

Each field, be it the artistic field or the field of Western medicine and its subfield of BPHC within developing countries, "prescribes its particular values and possesses its own regulative principles. These principles delimit a socially structured space" (Bourdieu and Wacquant 1992, 17). According to the position agents occupy in this space, they will work to either maintain, modify, or transform the field's existing boundaries or form.

As delegate for the field of preventive Western medicine, Moses sought to eliminate both the threat and reality of maternal and child mortality on Nuakata. In so doing he not only challenged local beliefs and practices about the place and conditions of birth but also how women should deliver, who should be present, who should orchestrate the delivery, who should provide care in what forms immediately following the delivery. His advice was not simply confined to birth but extended to pregnancy, breast-feeding, and care of the infant.

As many have observed and detailed in other social and historical contexts, Western medical knowledges and practices in general, and those associated with maternity in particular, constitute neither an ahistorical nor a disinterested epistemology/praxis. In prescribing "the way to be born," the "to be born" is also prescribed, as is the bearer. In prescribing the place of birth, the particular significance of place to birth is detailed. In declaring who should orchestrate birth, birth orchestrations are further defined. And by nominating who knows about birth, what is, can be, and should be known is specified.

During these initial efforts to explore Moses' praxis with pregnant and breast-feeding women, I gave little concerted thought to how my own actions were experienced and interpreted by local people. I gave only selective credence to the adage that actions speak louder than (faltering) words. Focused on Moses' praxis, I could barely reflect on my own. Thinking about it recently I realized that my actions and discussions during those first weeks on Nuakata must surely have reinforced the view that I was aligned with Moses' health project. For example, during this time I was confronted with people's untreated weeping sores and cuts, and malarial fevers and headaches. Wanting to respond to their need, I assumed provision of basic medical care for the Yalasi and Bolime sides of the island. I placed my faith in the medicine I knew. In addition, my trips to Bwauli to see Moses, to participate in the health patrol and attend the maternal and child health clinic, constituted my only highly visible diversion from our language learning sessions with Wycliffe. With Moses I shared an apparent ease of conversation that, except for two other people who spoke English with me, I had with no other local person at the time.

Still holding to the belief that the sexed form of my body would count for more with local women than any other dimension of my embodiment or praxis, I was reluctant to acknowledge the significance of my white skin and my comparatively big body. There was a sense in which my whiteness and my size were invisible, neutral (Frankenberg 1993, 191–243). And so when women averted their gaze from me, blushed, or gave inaudible responses to my questions, I interpreted this as shyness, in much the same way as Moses had defined their reluctance to attend his clinic or use his medicines as resistance or recalcitrance. My interpretation focused on when the shyness would end rather than its causes. Aware, at one level, that local women's shy, embarrassed demeanor embodied the deferential stance of the colonized, I was nevertheless reluctant to acknowledge that my body, my skin color evoked a history of colonial relations between white and Milne Bay women.

> Whiteness changes over time and space and is in no way a transhistorical essence. Rather, . . . it is a complexly constructed product of local, regional, national, and global relations, past and present. Thus the range of possible ways of living whiteness, for an individual white woman in a particular time and place, is delimited by the relations of racism at that moment and in that place. And if whiteness varies spatially and temporally, it is also a relational category, one that is constructed with a range of other racial and cultural categories, with class and with gender. This construction is, however, fundamentally asymmetrical, for the term "whiteness" signals the production and reproduction of dominance rather than subordination, normativity rather than marginality, and privilege rather than disadvantage. (Frankenberg 1993, 236–37)

I understood, and yet was reluctant to acknowledge, that being a woman was not enough to render me the same as the women on Nuakata. In their eyes, initially at least, I appeared as White, Other, and powerful—more different than the same. So focused was I on reinforcing the similarities between us that I was unwilling to fully admit the differences, the socially, historically, and politically important differences that exist between a white woman from Australia and the women living on Nuakata.

Fig. 3. Moses Diawasi, community health worker

Fig. 4. Mari with her baby daughter

Chapter Three

Bearing the Inconceivable

Shelley: So, how do you believe, what do you believe makes the baby? How is the baby made?
Mona: How is the baby made?
Shelley: Hmm. How does it come into the mother's stomach?
Mona: That we don't know. Our Father only knows. Our Father is to make the baby. We just our blood with that. You already know, uh? That's our difference—like this we are ladies and this ladies' children and this our children—our blood is coming . . . [unintelligible on the tape]
Shelley: So, in the past did people believe that the man and the woman made the baby or just the woman?
Mona: No, mainly the man and the woman. So was doing this, not ourselves [not just women], it formed. If we are staying ourselves we can't have a baby. Woman with a man, they will have a baby. Like this if we're single, like a young girl, that one nothing.

Not more than three weeks after Roger and I arrived on Nuakata, Mona and I found ourselves sitting together in the Asa'ailo church grounds waiting for other women to join us for a Women's Fellowship meeting. As designated leader for that day's events, she was first to arrive. For my part, the church grounds were our temporary home, a liminal place and time, where we stayed until our house was completed.[1] Mona, a woman in her mid-thirties and mother of two sons in their late teens, had taken me under her wing during two prior weekly gatherings.[2] Able to speak English, she acted as translator and teacher on these occasions, urging me to learn and use the local language. Where other women were shy and reticent in my presence, she was confident and supportive. I was enormously grateful for her efforts, as I felt quite overwhelmed and exhausted by my failing efforts to understand general conversation, especially the jokes at my expense. Effectively mute at this stage, it was she who gave me a voice, albeit a whisper, and the ability to "hear" these women whose language I could not discern.[3] She gave me some hope that eventually these other women would become less timid and embarrassed in my presence. Much later I learned she was from East Cape. Before moving to Nuakata nine years earlier, she had worked for a time as a nurse on the mainland. Although she understood Alina Nu'ata she rarely spoke it, preferring to use her own language—Tewala. Sitting, waiting with Mona, practicing words, naming things around us like a child might with a parent, I asked her to do an interview with me about childbirth, pregnancy, and conception. The preceding transcript is an excerpt from that interview, my first interview on Nuakata and one of only a handful conducted in English. Barely able to speak Alina Nu'ata, let alone think or imagine in it, I resorted to my own. While I knew this endeavor was premature, I was anxious to begin my research, to justify my presence, to vindicate people's act of grace in allowing us to stay. Although committed to a way of understanding that emphasizes lived experience and participant observation, rather than contrived expositions of local belief, I had grown impatient. Wondering how I would ever witness or participate in the activities of birth, let alone conception, I opted for a known path—a formal interview. How ironic that my quest for Nuakatan gendered identity began with a woman from another place—a woman with some experience and training in Western medical thought and practice! Whose ways of knowing about whom, or what, did I elicit?

~

Talking with Mona, the tape recorder running, I was suddenly confronted with my inability to pose a question that might reveal her way of understanding conception rather than my own.[4] Even this dilemma reflected an assumption of difference in our beliefs, a we/they, Western/Melanesian opposition, that I not only rejected but also wished to subvert. By asking, How is the baby made? I introduced a construction metaphor that was momentarily confusing, if not nonsensical, to her.[5] In Alina Nu'ata there are several commonly used words for make: *'abi* (to build), *'abilau* (to start or begin to make), *'abimamole* (create), and *paihowa* (work, make, or do). Apart from these, many verbs include the idea of making in their semantic field. All are derived from the two verbal prefixes *'abi* (to touch, by hand) and *'abiye* (to cause an act by your actions; to cause to become by your actions); for example, *'abiyemodi'ini* (to make or cause to become angry). *Paihowa* is used as a more general term (a performance or action metaphor) to denote working, doing, or enacting of any kind, and as such can imply making in its meaning. However, *'abi*, used alone or as a verbal prefix, specifically refers to making or building with the hands. It is akin to the word *manufacture* in English, which is derived from the Latin *manus* (hand) and *facere* (to make). While this direct link between making and the hands may now be only implicit in English, it remains explicit in Alina Nu'ata. Building/making is literally a tangible activity that a person or people "do" by hand. Something is made by the hand of somebody from some thing or things. A visible change in activity or state of something/somebody is caused by the tangible actions of some thing(s) or somebody. Mona was clearly perplexed by my use of the metaphor "to make," for I could have been literally asking, "By whose hands is the baby made?" or less specifically, By what means or activity is the baby done, made, created? Struggling, and without understanding the basis of her apparent confusion, I tried again, this time inadvertently introducing the idea that an already formed baby is somehow ontologically external to the mother. It comes into the mother's stomach from another place.

Clearer about my intent or meaning, Mona adapted or expressed her answer in the terms implied by both the word *paihowa* in Alina Nu'ata and my original use of the metaphor "to make." In her subsequent responses to questions she used "making" and "doing" interchangeably to convey enacting. She stated that she does not know how the baby is made, how it comes to be inside the mother's stomach. Not only does she not know but it is not something that can be known, or perhaps not something that she even cares to know. Only God the Father knows. Only God "makes" babies. By our menstrual blood we—Mona and I, and all "ladies"—are the same. But our common menstrual blood also renders us different from those without it—presumably men, children, and girls who have not yet menstruated. This blood goes toward the child. As such, our common menstrual blood truly renders women the same when its purpose is enacted or realized within us. But at that point, she looked at me quizzically, "You already know, uh, [the purpose of menstrual blood, about conception]?" In other words (i.e., the unspoken words of gesture, facial expression, laughter, tone), Why ask these questions when you already know the answers? For what reason or purpose do you want to know? If you already know these things, what do you hope to find by asking me? Are you tricking me, embarrassing me, trying to confirm that we are the same, different? What motivates your inquiry?

Deeming Mona's question a distraction, I ignored it, only to be confronted by it time and again as I talked with women about conception. Embarrassed, they looked away from me, saying *bada 'uhanapui* (already you know). What I did not understand at that time was that the verb *hanapui* (to know) refers to certain, unequivocal, authoritative knowing/knowledge. *Hanapui* is both a stative and an active verb, a state of knowing and the act of knowing. Daphne Lithgow indicates that it may also be a noun, but in my experience this form was used infrequently in conversation. *Hanapui* is knowing with certainty that an event has transpired, a boat arrived, a story remembered correctly, and so on. It is knowledge of something complete or completed. It is not opinion, understanding, or belief. People may know without understanding or understand without knowing.[6] *Hanapui* can also refer to knowing/knowledge that may be inherited or offered as a gift; knowing/knowledge selectively and discriminately passed down familial generations to specific family members. Knowledge of this kind, which may include such things as magic, stories, or customary practices, is, in other words, an alienable possession, owned but able to be imparted to selected persons if the knower so chooses. For example, one young woman said that her knowledge of love magic came from her maternal uncle, who had given it to her because she had shown great kindness to him over a number of years. *Hanapui* is also the type and way of knowing that *dimdim* are believed to possess or enact (i.e., knowledge, experiential or inherited, of how things are made or work, knowledge gained from books, be it the Bible, school books, the newspaper). An older man, who spoke with me at length about magic, commented to me one day: "You *dimdim*, your knowledge are in books, but ours are given to us by our ancestors. Some of us know them, some of us do not." However—and this is most relevant to my interview with Mona—someone does not generally insult others by soliciting knowing/knowledge of this kind when he or she already knows the information or ideas. When one does this, one is said to be *politiki* (politicking)—seeking knowledge to increase one's power, wealth, or advantage in a given situation or circumstance. Ignored at the time, Mona's question, You already know, uh?—implicitly, So, why do you ask?—now challenges me from a distance, inviting a response. What did I already know about conception?

Shelley: What part of the baby comes from the woman and what part of the baby comes from the man?
Mona: Because this blood is working toward it, we will stop our blood flowing.
Shelley: Menstruating. Yes, but some people in Papua New Guinea say that the mother's body contributes the blood of the baby and from the father's body contributes the bones. Do you think that here?
Mona: No, that one we can't give our—what?—bones to them one nothing. Only God knows what he's doing, the baby. We can't do any baby, nothing. We just our blood only working, men's blood and our blood its working. Its new blood already with the eggs, the eggs [tape becomes unintelligible] . . . Our Father only making our—what?—person, who makes me. That one makes egg, neck, our shoulders, our arms, make our stomach. Everything he make until nine months he already finish our body. That comes, we give birth. No one in our stomach, we never do anything. Only God makes us.

Dissatisfied with Mona's explanation of how the baby comes into the mother's stomach, I then focused my questions on the contribution of men and women to conception. By querying whether men and women contribute different parts to the developing fetus I signaled my interest in gender difference and identity, inviting Mona to reveal local beliefs about the essential, substantive differences between men and women. My questions to Mona shifted between "how," "what," and "from whom," between the process and the substance or constituent parts of conception. They inadvertently invited a materialist understanding of conception, conflating "the conceived" with "the individual person," and, in so doing, suggested that he or she is, quite literally, a confluence of substances or substantive forces (e.g., eggs, sperm, spirit, God). Substance, so imagined, comprises immutable and essential matter—matter fundamental to human existence, natural matter that underpins culture. Knauft writes:

Our own individualism and personal atomism are so ingrained that the independence of the single body as a biological entity goes without saying; the conceptual isolation of the body and its identity with an individualistic self seem as natural to us as they do foreign in other cultures. Consider, in contrast, societies in which the body is at heart socially and collectively constituted. Its physical make-up, including its gender, is not deep-sealed at the moment of conception, but arises sequentially depending on the actions and thoughts of relatives, spirits and the person him or herself. (1989, 201)

At the most basic level these questions assumed that the people of Nuakata think about conception—that ideas about conception matter in everyday life. Not only did the questions posed imply what mattered (i.e., the confluence of substances), but, more to the point, they implied how it mattered. They were founded on the assumption that, when dissected and analyzed, conception beliefs would reveal aspects of the constitutive, gendered ingredients, be they literal or symbolic, of Nuakatan personal identity and, more broadly, Nuakatan sociality. Therefore, not only did I anticipate the content and form of these beliefs, I also anticipated their purpose and/or significance.

With the benefit of hindsight—born of distance and time—it is perhaps too easy to criticize the loaded nature of these questions. However, I believe it is important to examine my underlying assumptions, for not only do they show that Mona's answers were constrained by the questions posed but they also reveal aspects of what I already "knew," without listening, about Nuakatan conception beliefs. My assumptions, both conscious and unconscious, were not without precedent or their own convoluted past. It is a past that includes Western definitions of conception, my prefield reading of Massim ethnographies, and broader anthropological debate of conception beliefs. As conception is increasingly understood in scientific terms in the West, new dilemmas arise for anthropologists exploring conception across varying cultural contexts. In speaking about the "concepts, the words, and the methods that the 'profession' [of sociology or equally anthropology] employs to speak about, and to think the social world," Bourdieu indicates that "language poses a particularly dramatic problem for the sociologist: it is in effect an immense repository of naturalized preconstructions, and thus of preconstructions that are ignored as such and which can function as unconscious instruments of construction" (Bourdieu and Wacquant 1992, 241).

In English, conception is understood as both the act of conceiving an entity or thought, as well as the entity or thought itself.[7] It is both a state of being and the state of coming into being, a noun incorporating its verb, a state and a state of action. Conception carries with it notions of joining together and taking in—a taking into the womb, or a taking into the mind. But the meaning of conception in Western thought has not remained static over the centuries. Use of this term across a variety of texts dating from the fourteenth through seventeenth centuries (detailed in the *Oxford English Dictionary*) reveals an understanding of conception as simply a beginning, or the womb's reception and embrace of the seed. In contrast, contemporary English definitions reflect an understanding dominated by a medicoscientific metaphor that details the constituent substances (the ovum and sperm) and the end point of the process (the fertilized egg) from which the physical (sexed) individual is formed.[8] Hence, at one level, we (in the metaphorical West) have come to attribute our individual existence to the coalescence of biological substance—a coalescence arising and completed during a single act of sexual intercourse. Our essential biological identity, conceived as the very ground of our being, is founded on the unique conjunction of both maternal and paternal substance—sexed substances that are different. Moreover, as feminist writers such as Martin (1987, 1991) and Haraway (1990, 1991) argue, the metaphors employed by Western biomedical discourses to describe these sexed substances and the processes by which they unite are founded on culturally specific and phallocentric definitions of male and female.

This emphasis on substance has recently been made even more explicit by the proliferation of new reproductive technologies that disconnect the substance of conception from its usual process, bypassing sexual intercourse as the means by which ovum and sperm unite and subsequently divide. As Western medical science moves from a macroscopic to a microscopic vision of human life, especially human procreation, it takes its fetish for dissection of lifeless or fragmentary, disconnected bodies to ever new depths.[9] This quest to categorize and map the invisible substrata fundamental to human conception, collected and isolated in a petri dish, is underpinned by the broader scientific premise that in reducing matter (including human matter) to its smallest component parts we may better understand and control it. However, by focusing on substance, the context and process of human conception is both deemed and rendered less significant to human identity and sociality. Scientific explanations of conception have reduced it to a potentially discernible moment—distilled time—distinct from the gestation process that ensues. Imagined as somehow separate from conception, gestation is rendered a time of development—a time bounded or completed by birth, itself a distinct event. Exploration and understanding of conception within Western medical science is therefore occurring in ever-contracting visual, temporal, and spatial fields, with inevitable consequences for our understanding of both conception and human life. For example, in discussing the implications of the new reproductive technologies for kinship in contemporary Euro-American society, M. Strathern comments that

> however one looks at it procreation can now be *thought about* as subject to personal preference and choice in a way that has never before been conceivable. The child is literally . . . the embodiment of the act of choice. . . . [S]o also those not born by them, and . . . those not born at all. (1992, 34, emphasis in original)

In the West, knowledge of our substantive constitution, our actual maternal and paternal inheritance, is generally considered important, if not pivotal, to individual identity. Among other ways, we give expression to this belief when we look for resemblances between ourselves and our parents; when the adopted child searches for its "natural," "biological" parents; or when the older child or adolescent declares to a stepparent that they have diminished parenting rights because they are not a "real" parent.[10] Current research in human genetics is advancing this belief through its efforts to list, categorize, and map the human genetic template upon which individual variations, representing a confluence of maternal and paternal genetic characteristics, are inscribed. There is a sense in which knowledge or awareness of our substantive maternal and paternal inheritance is considered the foundation, the substrate upon which our identity or multiple identities are elaborated and thought (Rapp 1995; M. Strathern 1992).

Perhaps this belief in the relationship between knowing our substantive inheritance and formulating our identity should come as no surprise given that an analogical link between conception as thought and conception as the biological creation of the child/person is present in the English definition itself. Is it stretching this point too far to argue, then, that in the post-Enlightenment West Descartes's *cogito ergo sum* (I think therefore I am), formulated in response to a journey through and beyond existential doubt and uncertainty, has a contemporary elaboration, namely, "I think and know the substantive facts of my conception, therefore I am truly conceived"?

Intrigued, if not seduced, by Descartes's legacy, anthropologists have long sought to understand and categorize knowledge and cultural practices. Such a project has been part of a broader, often implicit, agenda to define what is human—to define the person and/or dismantle the concept of the subject. In Melanesian anthropology many of these issues came into focus through the debates surrounding the (anthropological) doctrine of the Virgin Birth, perhaps more accurately termed the doctrine of insubstantial paternity. This doctrine first emerged around the beginning of this century when anthropologists documented beliefs that detailed the "possibility of conception taking place without insemination" (Leach 1967, 39).

Noted by Roth[11] in the Australian aboriginal context, and later seized upon and elaborated by Hartland and Frazer, this doctrine, by equating scientific knowledge with civilization, asserted that ignorance of the so-called facts of physiological paternity necessarily signified primitivism. Championed by early anthropological cultural evolutionists eager to trace a developmental continuum between the civilized and native/savages, defective scientific knowledge of paternity was presumed to be a feature of matrilineal societies, regarded at the time as the earliest, most natural, and therefore most primitive form of kinship organization (Jorgenson 1983a, 2). At the other end of the evolutionary scale, civilized cultures were defined by patrilineal kinship in which a scientific knowledge of paternity was seen as central. Malinowski's (1932, 1948) dogmatic assertion that the matrilineal Trobriand islanders believe there was no biological connection between father and child further substantiated these ideas. He wrote that "without doubt or reserve . . . the child is of the same substance as its mother, [whereas] . . . between the father and the child there is no bond of physical union" (1932, 3).[12] Preoccupied with the sociological significance and meaning of indigenous knowledge and beliefs, Malinowski later actively dissociated himself from these ideas:

> In future we should have neither affirmation nor denials, in an empty wholesale verbal fashion, of native "ignorance" or "knowledge," but instead, full concrete descriptions of what they know, how they interpret it, and how it is all connected with their conduct and their institutions. (1932, xxviii)

Leach (1967) reignited this debate in the 1960s with the publication of his celebrated article "Virgin Birth." At stake in the furore that subsequently erupted were epistemological issues central to the anthropological project. Earlier opposition to the doctrine of the Virgin Birth focused on the accuracy of the supportive empirical accounts (Leach 1967, 46 n. 1; *History of Anthropology Newsletter* 1996, 3–11).[13] Leach, while sharing this skepticism about the empirical claims (1967, 41), focused instead on the ideological significance of conception beliefs, both for the anthropologists and the societies they studied. In repudiating evolutionist arguments, he directed his invective at Spiro and "all the neo-Tylorians who think like him" (1967, 40). According to Spiro, native accounts of procreation that do not accord with the scientific facts of life should be accepted as empirical evidence of native ignorance of paternity, rather than, as Leach suggested, "formulations of structural relationships" (Spiro 1966, in Jorgenson 1983a, 2–3). Spiro (1968) believed science to be the arbiter of truth and by implication a higher form of knowledge. He used it as a yardstick by which all cultural ideas (which he believed were founded on empirical knowledge) could be compared. For his part, Leach, not unlike the mature Malinowski (1932), claimed that, as ideologies or social dogmas, conception beliefs pertain to a structured cultural whole.[14] They are internally motivated cultural facts that fit together; they reveal social relationships. For this reason, their meaning and internal connections must be understood in their own cultural context, and not in relation to an externally imposed scientific schema that postulates "causes and ultimate origins for the facts under observation" (Leach 1967, 39). To do otherwise is to impose ethnocentric explanations from the outside, bolstering the identity of the anthropologist and the society to which she belongs by representing native knowledge and, by implication, native people as something less, as defective or simple.

Where Spiro believed science to be the liberator of the inviolable, universal facts of nature, the discoverer and custodian of truth, Leach reified the internal structural coherence of culture, of cultural facts. Facts themselves were not at issue between Leach and Spiro, the principal protagonists in this far-reaching debate. Rather, it was the nature, interpretation, and status of facts that proved contentious.[15] Leach suggested that what was "really at issue is the technique of anthropological comparison which depends in turn upon the kind of 'meaning' which we are prepared to attribute to ethnographical evidence" (1967, 40). Believing in the possibility that anthropologists can understand another culture from within, he implored anthropologists to "remain skeptical and positivist," to resist the temptation to "inject magical causal explanations from outside" (1967, 46). For Leach it was imperative to understand the cultural context for beliefs as much as the beliefs themselves. In this sense, he, like Malinowski before him, sought to explore both the similarities and the differences between people's lived experiences. Accordingly, he argued, all beliefs, including those of the anthropologist, should be subjected to scrutiny and understood in terms of their social meaning and significance. Among other things, Leach concluded from this debate that "anthropological theories often tell us more about the anthropologist than about their subject matter" (1967, 46).

Leach's claim that it is possible for the ethnographer to understand another culture from within has been rendered highly contentious and problematic by postmodernist and postcolonial debates within and beyond anthropology.[16] However, his exhortation to ethnographers to scrutinize their own assumptions surely remains salutary advice for the discipline.[17] It remains especially pertinent to contemporary analyses of conception beliefs, for it seems that—with the exception of writers such as Wagner (1983, 75)—basic assumptions about conception and the way conception beliefs are collected and analyzed (who asks what, when, where, and with what interpretative purpose in mind) remain underexplored in ethnographic texts.

For example, the link between the confluence of substances and identity or, more specifically, between knowledge of substantive constitution and identity has been a recurring theme in contemporary discussions about conception within Melanesian anthropology (Jorgenson 1983a; Knauft 1989, 204–11; M. Strathern 1988). Ethnographers, including myself, have often blithely assumed that the substance(s) of indigenous conception beliefs are significant primarily because they reveal the foundations of identity, whether that identity be biological, spiritual, or based on gender or kinship. Not only is knowledge of conception beliefs assumed to be constitutive of identity and difference, but ethnographic accounts have frequently implied that this knowledge is widely and uniformly held throughout the community studied. As Knauft (1989) observes, if we combine Jorgenson's (1983b) discussion of the differing views of conception offered by Telefol men and women, with Wagner's (1972, 1981, 1983) claim that beliefs do not remain uniform or static, but are always changing as they are used, we can quite reasonably assume that multiple conception beliefs may exist within a given community.

It seems, then, that if we are to challenge our most basic assumptions about conception, a number of questions must be leveled at our analyses. Do the detailed expositions of the meaning and significance of the substance(s) integral to conception beliefs reflect local or Western assumptions about the relationship between sexed substances and identity? Do our analyses privilege substance because the meaning of conception in Western cultures is pervaded by an increasingly detailed medicoscientific metaphor (i.e., the formation of a viable zygote by the fertilization of the ovum by the sperm)? Does the form our analyses take (i.e., dissection of the component parts of conception beliefs) reflect the increasingly specific content of contemporary English definitions of conception? By dissecting these beliefs in and beyond the field and making them the object of intense scrutiny, are we enhancing or depleting their local meaning and significance? Finally, could analyses that focus on the place or the process integral to conception, or the context in which conception beliefs are culturally elaborated, be equally pertinent to a shared understanding of the local meanings of conception beliefs?

While these assumptions, implicit to my own culture, no doubt affected the questions I posed to Mona, they did not directly influence the content and composition of my inquiries. My prefield reading of Massim ethnographies not only influenced my choice of questions, but it also led me to anticipate the form and content of Mona's responses. For example, Battaglia writes that the people of Sabarl believe that "human beings are conceived when 'white blood' (father's blood) co-mingles with 'red blood' (mother's blood) in the heat of sexual intercourse" (1990, 38). Eventually these bloods descend into the womb, where they separate into white and red, masculine and feminine body parts. The skeleton is formed first, thereby acting as a "support for the red flesh and organs." Later, grease or fat is added, and this is said to "thicken the watery, fishlike infant blood," strengthening the bones and generating heat. It is said by some people that this grease is derived from "subsequent acts of intercourse, supplementing or completing the fetal body." Battaglia (1990, 50) argues that Sabarl conception and gestation beliefs "reiterate" M. Strathern's contention that, for Melanesian gift-based societies, "relations between opposites produce an object (such as a child) which in being neither of them is also their relationship objectified and thus both of them. The product appears as an addition to their identity" (M. Strathern 1987b). Battaglia adds that "the child in this model is only half of the 'relationship objectified'. The other half is the *self sufficient* [and, for the duration of pregnancy, 'androgynous'] mother" (1990, 50). Throughout gestation a mother is "both parents," substituting natural substances for semen, rendering them masculine and "therefore compatible with the masculine components" of the fetal body: "She is Creator . . . the agent of her own and her child's creation" (1990, 50).

Alternatively, Macintyre writes of Tubetube that "until recently, conception was equated with quickening and was deemed to be the soul or life-force entering a congealed but unformed accumulation of maternal secretions in a woman's womb" (1988, 51). It is unclear from Macintyre's account what precipitates the movement of the soul or life force into the womb. She notes that the relationship between mother and child is pivotal on Tubetube, for it is the maternal body that was believed to provide

> the essential substances for the formation of bones and flesh, thereby forming an inalienable relationship based on shared substance. . . . The mother/child relationship created an essential identity which, in a literal sense, was perceived to inhere in the individual's bones from the time they were formed *in utero*. (51)

As with the documented beliefs held on Sabarl and Vanatinai (Lepowsky 1993, 84–87), on Tubetube it is repeated acts of sexual intercourse that ensure the growth of the fetus into a fat and healthy baby at birth. Thus, intercourse between a man and a pregnant woman was considered the active force or relationship creating fetal growth. Despite the reported importance of such a relationship in this matrilineal community, a father's relationship to his child was considered "tenuous" and contingent upon the marital relationship. Both Fortune ([1932] 1989, 43–56) and Thune (1980, 81–89) emphasize the marginal status of fathers in relation to their children, attributing this in part to their questioned paternity. Thune (1980) posits maternal blood as the primary source of *susu* identity on Duau.

> Blood is inherited from one's mother at conception, being identical to her blood and hence necessarily identical to that of any of her *susu* mates . . . [Blood] alone is acquired from another person, and in the case of a woman, it alone can be transmitted to another person. Identity of blood within the *susu* implies . . . a physiological unity. [T]he possibility of bilateral inheritance of blood [is rarely considered]. (1980, 81–89)

While these anthropologists do not necessarily ignore the process of conception, substances rather than processes act as the prism through which both the acts of conception and the relationship between conception beliefs and identity (be it gender, kin, or spiritual) are analyzed. Following their example, I pursued descriptions of substantively constituted gender identities and consciously sought to compare Nuakatan conception beliefs with those documented for these other southern Massim communities. On reflection, though, the question most needing to be asked is, What are the implications of using substance as a prism through which the process of conception is considered, rather than the inverse? More specifically, is this emphasis relevant to Nuakatan understandings and beliefs?

When asked what body parts were contributed by both man and woman to the baby, Mona responded with a seemingly oblique reference to the work of menstrual blood and women's actions to ensure this work is realized. Mona specified that a woman's blood, her period, will sense the arrival of the child and respond by moving toward it. Because menstrual blood directs its work toward the baby—this is its purpose, its reason for existence, its labor—a pregnant woman stops her blood from flowing. When menstrual blood moves upward, a woman will definitely know she has a child within her body. The concealed child's presence is therefore known by its effect on/in the mother's body. The presence of the child causes its mother's menstrual blood (and parents' co-mingled blood) to work on its behalf. But a woman does not consciously or knowingly direct her menstrual blood toward the child. In this sense the pregnant woman does not cause her own actions on behalf of the child, although she may be considered, in M. Strathern's terms, an agent. Strathern argues that in the Melanesian context "an agent is one who acts with another in mind, and that other may in fact coerce the agent into so acting" (1988, 272). "Agents do not cause their own actions; they are not the authors of their own acts. They simply do them. Agency and cause are split" (1988, 273). Strathern also differentiates between agent and person. A person is defined by the "relations that constitute him or her." In objectifying those relations he or she is revealed as a person. An agent, in contrast, "is construed as the one who acts because of those relationships and is revealed in his or her actions." Accordingly, a person is an agent when his or her relationships with others cause him or her to act. An agent is a person who acts with those relations in view. "In this, the agent constitutes a 'self'" (1988, 273).

Mona commented that only a woman, together with a man, may have or possess a baby. When a man and woman come together in sexual intercourse, God "does" a baby. Their combined blood works or labors toward the baby, making new blood, growing the egg. The egg, by Mona's account, is the starting point for the baby and made by God alone. Blood works for and grows the baby, but the baby is not a direct consequence of that co-mingling blood. Mona's discussion of blood emphasized growing the baby rather than the baby's growth. Growing does not inhere in the baby (fetus) but occurs through the combined labor of maternal and paternal, cross-sex blood. Sexual intercourse is the crucial context for and enactment of this labor. Blood, specifically menstrual blood and semen, does not provide the substantive identity nor, indeed, the form of the baby, but it does grow the child within the womb. Without stating it, Mona implied that the mother's womb provides or acts as the necessary context for this growing to occur.

Mona stated emphatically that women or men alone or together cannot "do" the baby; they cannot do anything to create the baby. They cannot bring it to pass, contribute parts to it, or complete it. Men and women cannot make something from nothing; they cannot make matter. While the child remains in the womb their actions merely anticipate—prepare the ground for—and grow the child. "Only God knows what He's doing, the baby." God forms the baby. Because He does the baby, only He knows what He is doing. He starts, makes, and completes the body, the baby; the baby is a consequence of His doing. Mona's use of the performance metaphor "doing" is instructive. Implied here is an integral, dialectical relationship between knowing and doing. Without knowledge of the "what" of doing, doing cannot occur. Inversely, without doing the "what" of knowing, knowing cannot be fully realized. Knowing is the effect of doing, as doing is the effect of knowing.[18] Perhaps it follows that because a man and woman alone or together cannot "do" the baby, they cannot know (about) conception. Mona implied that their knowledge of conception extends only to what they do to create the context for conception and growth of the baby to occur.

Shelley: God makes us. Umm . . . is that what you've always believed?
Mona: Yes.
Shelley: Always? Is that what you were told when you were a little girl? Or did your mother believe something different about how you were formed? Or did she believe what you told me?

Mona: I told you that's how the baby is started growing like that, inside our stomach. God made earth and from there he made Adam . . . [tape unintelligible]—Adam only man he will stay, woman talking with him nothing. But what he do only himself. No one to stay with him. So God made—what?—girl or woman to stay with him. He made her from one rib there, so he took from man's rib, that one he put it, so man he has eleven ribs so always girls like mens because the one part they got it and they put it two. [Laughter] So ladies they want men and men they want ladies. So everything we never made, only God made us.

Frustrated by my resistance to her answers and conscious that I was seeking some other explanation for conception, Mona, her voice bespeaking exasperation, finally gave me what she believed I wanted to hear, what she knew I knew: an account of the (second) biblical creation story. Waiting together in the church grounds for the beginning of the Women's Fellowship meeting, it was a fitting time and place to recount this story. In her telling Mona emphasized neither Adam's creation, the garden of Eden, nor woman's role as Adam's helper in the garden. Rather, she drew attention to Adam's state of aloneness. Because Adam is alone, God makes woman "to stay with him." Because woman is created from man's rib, men and women are by themselves incomplete. For this reason they want each other—indeed, need each other. Perhaps it is not surprising that in a community where loneliness and being alone is anathema, an undesirable state, Mona emphasizes both Adam's need for a woman, and woman and man's mutual need and desire for each other. This mutual need of, or interdependence between, man and woman is a recurring theme expressed throughout all aspects of Nuakatan sociality.[19]

However strategically motivated, Mona's responses to my questions about past beliefs nonetheless reflected her current beliefs.[20] In telling the biblical creation story she not only demonstrated her biblical knowledge—knowledge that is generally assumed to impress *dimdim*—but, more important, she offered an account that would bring us together, render us similar, an account we could share. Sensing my feeling of dislocation or marginality, perhaps she sought in this and other conversations around that time to highlight the similarities between us by rendering potentially strange or different beliefs and practices familiar, commonplace. While these gestures were gratefully accepted by me in other contexts, in this particular conversation they were received with great ambivalence if not obvious disappointment. Unbeknownst to her, in those tentative days early in my fieldwork, expressions of difference provided purpose, confidence. Unsure of my place in the community, my way forward as an ethnographer, expressions of difference provided activity as it begged to be documented. It relieved the waiting, made tiresome, at times, by my own impatient expectations.

While clearly motivated by contradictory political and epistemological assumptions—some conscious, others not—my appeal to Mona's inherited beliefs, to cultural difference, was in part a sincere attempt to further understand the historical context of her present beliefs and practices. It was an attempt to consider how past beliefs impinge upon present ones, and the inverse, how the present influences and interprets the past. I sought to contextualize and understand current beliefs about conception as a starting point in a process of intersubjective, dialectical knowing.

Reflecting upon the "conditions of possibility of intersubjective knowledge," Fabian contends that "somehow we must be able to share each other's past in order to be knowingly in each other's present" (1983, 92). Taken literally this statement implies several things: people's past influences their present; in order to be knowingly in each other's present, people must share aspects of their past with one another; and, perhaps most significant, intersubjective or dialectical knowledge is made possible when ethnographer and interlocutor experience a shared past and present.[21] Fabian writes:

> Time is . . . needed for the ethnographer to become part of his interlocutor's past. . . . If it is true that ethnography, in order to be productive, must be dialogical and therefore to a certain degree reciprocal, then we begin to appreciate the epistemological significance of Time. (1983, 90)

But the question still remains, What does it mean to *share* in Mona's past? In this particular conversation I assumed that to elicit her cultural inheritance was to invite her to remember it, if only in fragments, in spoken, narrative form. I overlooked the idea that this inheritance may exist only as it is enacted or performed (see Dening 1996; Turner 1986). And, at one level, I denied the possibility that our pasts may be linked through shared religious ideas and practices. Also, although sincere, my attempt to understand Mona's inherited beliefs was neither naive nor innocent, for, as earlier indicated, the "past" I attempted to solicit was already prefigured by my reading of Massim ethnographies. Thus, while Mona and I shared the present, our knowledge of each other was constrained by the intrusion of my past—a past glimpsed by her only through the questions that sought to conjure her "present" beliefs.

> The object's present is founded in the writer's past. In that sense, facticity itself, that cornerstone of scientific thought, is autobiographic. This, incidentally, is why in anthropology objectivity can never be defined in opposition to subjectivity, especially if one does not want to abandon the notion of facts. (Fabian 1983, 89)

Mona could not possibly know that, in asking those questions about conception, I was being haunted by the ghosts of an anthropological past, assailed by the phantoms of a "postcolonial" present. While eager to elicit Mona's understanding of Nuakatan conception beliefs, spoken as it were "in her own voice"—a voice that renders colonialism mute—I was unable to "hear" her responses. Listening for difference, I was deaf to the familiar. I dismissed Mona's God as a mere Western contrivance, a vestige of colonialism imposed upon core conception beliefs. In so doing, I was trying to both distance and distinguish myself from colonial enterprises, past and present, and invoke a postcolonial present purged of imperialist influence and power. Living at that time in the shadow of the church, hostage to its subsuming evangelical rhetoric, I took refuge in the subversive, if not, redemptive, idea of the traditional. While I knew this intellectual shelter to be temporary, unstable, exclusive and excluding, the prospect of comfort, albeit ephemeral, was difficult to resist. Suspending my disbelief in the unitary person, I tried to resuscitate true Nuakatan identity by appealing to a nonspecific past; an imagined "real time" in which unified beliefs existed as a cohesive force, binding a community of believers who lived in a pure, undefiled space/time. Despite my disavowal of notions of culture with a capital C (i.e., culture as a core set of overarching, "superorganic" ideas [Jackson 1989, 121], shared meanings or organizing principles [Fabian 1983; Keesing 1974, 1990]) I was seduced by their legacy. In anticipating Mona's voice, unique, pure, and strong, I inadvertently invoked an-other echo of my own (see Carrier 1992).

Keesing states that "the invention and evocation of radical alterity"—cultural difference and the exotic "radical other"—have been, and remain in veiled guises, central to the anthropological project (1990, 46). Whether proving that "cultural conceptions of personhood, of emotions, of agency, of gender, of the body are culturally constructed" (as "symbolist/interpretive modes of anthropology" attempt), or refuting the ethnocentric presumptions of Western thought (as postmodernist anthropology presumes to do), "non-logocentric alterity"—difference, in other words—is invoked (1990, 47). Keesing suggests that this dubious project is advanced by "reified" notions of culture as "a culture," "an agent," "a collectivity of people" who are in essence a unity (1990, 48). A key element of this idea of "culture" is the assumption that it exists in a distinct spatiotemporal realm—a realm diversely embodied by its participants.

This view of culture has been questioned by many Pacific historians, notably Thomas (1991, 1994), Carrier (1992), Dening (1980; 1996), and Neumann (1992). Dening, following Wagner, observes that "culture is a stranger's invention: it is the sense of wholeness and integration an outside-outsider or an inside-outsider develops" (1996, 57). Carrier is critical of anthropologists' "tendency to hypostasize the Other, to bestow upon the alien society a timeless concreteness [and to] see the societies . . . [studied] in terms of [essentialist] states of being rather than in terms of contingencies and historical processes" (1992, 13). He writes that this "tendency to essentialization can produce in anthropologists an unwillingness to focus on aspects of society that are recent innovations, under the assumption that because they have not been present for a very long period of time, they must be transient and illegitimate, inauthentic" (1992, 14). Keesing and Jolly concur with this critique, similarly urging anthropologists to

> take a more processual, dynamic view of how human populations create order and meaning, a view that focuses on internal contradictions and cleavages as well as on coherence and consensus, and on the production and reproduction of symbols, then the engagement of contemporary Melanesians with capitalism, the world system, postcolonial states, and Christianity. (1992, 227)

Aware that my interview with Mona was constrained by my inability to formulate appropriate open-ended questions, I sought Wycliffe's help to translate my questions on conception and birth into Alina Nuʻata. His response was telling. Though happy enough to assist me, he remained skeptical about the responses I would elicit. "People do not think about conception; they do not know about these things," he suggested. Without hearing or discussing Mona's words, Wycliffe echoed their sentiment; conception is not known or thought, therefore explanations or understandings of conception are rarely and/or reluctantly given. As if to confirm this disinterested knowledge, Wycliffe sought clarification of the names of some body parts from his mother, father, and big father, including the word for conception.

Despite his cautionary words I determined to substantiate the assertion that "people do not know (about) conception" by posing similar questions to other women. Searching for appropriate, neutral questions for Wycliffe to translate, I suggested: How does the baby happen? How does it come to be inside the mother's stomach? Can you tell me about how a baby is formed? Is it formed from the mother, the father, or how? Wycliffe's translations literally asked: Can to me you say how baby it starts/begins? How your understanding when child, its mother, her stomach (womb) it starts/begins? How the child it is placed inside? How your understanding this? Father from him, or maybe mother from her, or how your understanding?

Anxious to respond to several women who had offered to talk with me about childbirth, and having only two months of language learning behind me, I paid little attention to the form or meaning of Wycliffe's translations. I simply transcribed them into my notebook for easy reference. Many months later, frustrated by my inability to formulate open-ended questions (e.g., Can you tell me about . . . ?), I reexamined my original conception questions and Wycliffe's translations, looking for clues. Only then did I appreciate the subtle shifts in meaning between the two. Where I spoke of forming in the sense of shaping or fashioning, Wycliffe translated this as placing or putting inside. Also, where I used the expression "tell me about," Wycliffe translated this as "how your understanding when . . ." "To speak about, or of, something" implies a temporal and, especially, spatial distance/distinction between the speaker and the spoken, the knower and the known. When questioned, Wycliffe indicated that in Alina Nuʻata there is no equivalent form of "to talk, think, speak, know *about.*" Perhaps the closest equivalent is encapsulated in the expression *yanuwanuwatuwuine,* which may be translated as "I thinking-feeling it," or "I thinking that one/that thing." When this particular expression is used there is a sense that the subject's thinking goes toward something. However, Wycliffe did not use this expression in his translations. Instead he invited the listener to locate or contextualize her understanding in the time and place of conception. Where I sought authoritative knowledge, Wycliffe's questions sought understanding born of experience, of doing.

Wycliffe used the word *nuwamasele* to denote understanding. In other contexts *nuwamasele* can also mean something like opinion, attitude, or meaning. While Wycliffe's translation was appropriate in this context, it is important to note that the English "understanding" and the Alina Nuʻata *nuwa* are founded on different metaphors—metaphors that express semantically significant differences. Pelz states that, in English, "understanding" means to stand under or place yourself below the thing that you are trying to comprehend; in German, *verstehen* (to understand) means "to stand in the place of, put oneself in place of" (1974, 84; personal communication, 1996). Used as either a verb or noun *nuwamasele* is derived from two words: the stem *nuwa-* and *masele*, which means light, outside, to bring out into the open, visible. For example, *ʻabiyemasele*, which combines the verbal prefix *ʻabiye* with *masele*, means to explain, to make clear, to make visible, to sweep or clean around. In this context the term *masele* implies that when the "to be discerned" is brought out into the open or becomes visible, then it becomes clear, discernible. Once outside, things become visibly appreciated or understood. The stem *nuwa-*, however, proved more difficult to translate. My efforts to understand its meanings and uses sparked some lengthy conversations with Wycliffe, his birth father, Noah, and his highly respected big father, Antiya.

A man in his sixties, Antiya was locally renowned for his efforts, some twenty years earlier, in eliminating all the wild pigs on the island. His hunting exploits and subsequent dissection of the pigs gave him widely recognized knowledge of pig and—by association—human body parts. At first he, together with Wycliffe, translated *nuwa* as the heart organ. As an example, they added that just after a pig has been killed and the fat is cut away from its flesh its pumping heart (*nuwapo*) is clearly visible. The translation of *nuwa* as heart initially caused me some confusion, for people on Nuakata also use the term *ʻate* for this part of the body. Wycliffe explained that when David Lithgow began work on the translation of the Bible into Auhelawa he, together with local assistant Bible translators, decided that "heart" would be better translated as *ʻate*—as it is in the Dobuan Bible. Lithgow concluded that, like the term "heart" in the English Bible, *ʻate* denotes a center of emotions or feelings. In making this decision to replace *nuwa* with *ʻate* the translators chose to ignore the fact that *'ate* means liver in Auhelawa and Alina Nu'ata! Indeed, *'ate* denotes feelings—emotions that arise from the liver (and not the heart), embodied feelings.[22] For example, *'atemuyamuya* (liver/feelings paining) is used to mean empathy, pity, care for someone in trouble, the ability to feel and identify with another human being's pain. *Atehawawali* (liver, reddish) is used to describe rashes and skin diseases that occur when someone is fearful, and the embodied feelings of fear and/or anxiety.[23]

This translation of *'ate* as liver and embodied feelings is by no means unique to Nuakata. Macintyre notes that on Misima island *'ati/'ate* means

> emotion; compassion; the ability to imagine and thereby identify with other human beings; by association with the idea of individual response it approximates the concept "personality" in English. The word is from the Proto-Oceanic word meaning "liver" and until recently referred to that organ as well as the abstract meanings. Largely because of mission teachings that located emotional response in the heart, the majority of Misimans now think of *'ati* as meaning the heart. The same shift in meaning has occurred in Dobuan and Ware languages in the Massim region. (1990, 91)

Antiya, Noah, and Wycliffe later elaborated upon their initial translation of *nuwa*, stating that it means the place where the thinking combined with feeling arises, the place from which wanting, wishing, and longing (desire) stem. It is also a general term meaning the inside of the body. For example, *nuwatuwudawani* is a noun meaning, quite literally, the thinking-feeling/wanting hidden from family elders. It is akin to lust. The words for chest (*nuwa'epo*) and kidney (*nuwamagi*) both take *nuwa* as their stem, as do the words for thinking (*nuwatuwui*) and a multiplicity of nouns and verbs that denote feeling/living states—for example, *nuwavitai* (heavy heart), *nuwadaumwali* (calm heart), *nuwanuwapuyo* (virginity/chastity)—and characteristic personal styles or ways, such as *nuwadobi* (humble), *nuwapotapota* (stubborn).

Common to many languages throughout the Massim, the term *nuwa/nua/nuatu* has been previously discussed by several Massim ethnographers. Commenting on the meaning of *nua* on Tubetube, Macintyre notes that "the *nua* . . . [or the mind] is thought to be physically located in the body" (1987, 208), and more specifically "in the heart" (1987, 209). Elsewhere she notes that in Tubetube "heart" is *nuwapou*, literally, "thought egg." She suggests that the meaning of *nua* overlaps or correlates with like terms in other Papua New Guinea languages and cites as an example the word *noman* found in the language of the Kawelka (Hagen) people (see A. Strathern 1972, 143–44; M. Strathern 1968). *Noman,* like *nua,* means "both will and social consciousness" (M. Strathern 1987a, 208). Reflecting on the term *nuatu* which is used on Misima, Macintyre states that it means "mind; will; capacity for thought and intention" (1990, 91). She adds:

> This term now incorporates the Western concept of the "brain" and is one which has definitely altered over time. In normal everyday speech it refers only to abstract, mental processes. One elderly informant suggested to me that in former days, before Europeans taught people about brains, Misimans believed that the heart was the seat of thought. . . . I cannot confirm this. He did suggest however, that consciousness was not deemed to have anything to do with the brain/mind, but was a sensory capacity of the body, usually explained with reference to the eyes. (1990, 91)

In writing about Sabarl, Battaglia (1990) points to the distinction between *nuwa-* and *nuwo-* in the local language. *Nuwo-* means "mind/cognition," a "capacity for ordered thought." The root of *nuwotu* (thought) is "understood as an organizing experience—of 'focusing' or 'assembling' distinct perceptions and ideas and gathering them together into one homeplace." In contrast, *nuwa-* means "a capacity for feeling" (1990, 55). She suggests that "as the life of the mind invokes images of convergent thinking, divergent images predominate in the realm of 'feeling' and 'emotions' (*nuwa*)" (1990, 56).

While Wycliffe and Antiya stated that *nuwa* could denote the mind—described by me as a place where thinking occurs—they claimed that in the past, if not the present, the people of Nuakata did not associate the mind or thinking with the brain (*'uto*). Wycliffe was well aware of the *dimdim* belief that knowledge and thinking stem from the brain. He gained this awareness through his involvement in primary and, especially, secondary education as well as Bible translation work. Moreover, he readily accepted this idea as fact. But in Nuakatan thought, thinking—which is considered inseparable from feeling and emotion—is not clearly linked to a specific body part. Rather, it is, as Macintyre has recorded for Tubetube and Misima, thought to occur within the body as a whole. On the basis of these discussions and references to other Massim ethnographies, *nuwamasele* can be considered both the state and the process where concealed, inner, or undisclosed thinking-feeling is brought out into the open, made visible. Accordingly, understanding may be possessed and enacted. It passes from within the body to outside it and is directed toward or "situated in" the space of the thing or event understood. On the threshold between the inside and outside of the body, or moving between the two, understanding may be possessed as a semi-alienable or alienable form/process. It is not indissociable, and therefore it is not fundamentally constitutive of the one who possesses it.

Satisfied that I was able to express my basic conception questions in Alina Nuʻata, I was less than confident about my ability to understand people's replies. When I asked Wycliffe to assist me with some early interviews, he agreed, but his subsequent absence on these planned occasions confirmed my suspicion that this was a culturally inappropriate request. Much later he explained that men and women do not generally "speak together [of] these things," and, by implication, I should not speak (of) these things with other men. "This [is] our custom, our way." Indicating that his presence could cause embarrassment and disrespect to the women concerned, he then commented, "I already know about conception and birth. I learned about the ovum and the sperm, and the process of fertilization in science classes at secondary school." He added that if I wished to learn customary understandings of conception, gestation, and birth, I should speak with women who have been pregnant and given birth in their village, for "they understand these things." Other people—girls, childless women, men—"do not know [and therefore cannot speak of] these things, for they have not done them."

Here again the relationship between knowing and doing, and understanding and doing, was highlighted. Many other people subsequently drew this to my attention. For example, one young woman of fifteen, Roda, laughed when I asked her about conception, pregnancy, and birth. Embarrassed, she stated that she was too young to know about these things, even though she had witnessed several of her mother's pregnancies and births. Another person poured scorn on a young woman who had spoken with me about pregnancy and birth, with words to the effect, What would she know, she has only one child! And so it became clear that if I wished to elicit Nuakatan ideas about conception I needed to speak with women who had given birth many times.

Over time and through experiences such as these I came to better understand what it means to think, know, and understand on Nuakata. Only those with personal experience gain a legitimate right to speak with authority about an event, practice, or belief. Understanding arises from doing or participating. Although *nuwamasele* rather than *hanapui* best describes understanding derived from lived experience, in practice people often use either word interchangeably to refer to this form of knowing/understanding. Almost without exception, however, *hanapui* is used to refer to inherited or acquired knowledge, which is known but not necessarily understood. Most important, in the context of my research I learned that without my own personal experience of conception, gestation, and birth, I could only hope to know Nuakatan beliefs and practices without understanding them.

Some time later, still seeking an exposition of conception beliefs similar to those documented by other Massim ethnographers, I questioned Wycliffe about the meaning of the word for conception. As our conversation unfolded it emerged that the word for conception, *lagahi,* is derived from the verb *laga,* which means "to go up inland, away from the sea." This was a revelation to me. Expressed in these terms, conception refers not to substance, but rather to activity or process—doing or social action; the journey of the unnamed, undisclosed, to an inland place. It is movement of an already "assumed" (person? baby? mother? thing? spirit?) away from the exposed reaches of the sea toward the enclosed, concealed realms of the bush. For local people "inland" has many tangible associations. The inland is generally familiar, known, or possessed clan land. While by day it is a friendly, if not benevolent place, nightfall can render it hostile—a realm to be feared. Not only do ill-disposed, ancestral spirits linger in the bush at night but so do witches, who lay invisible traps for unsuspecting night wanderers. "Up inland, away from the sea" is also the place where most gardens are located on the island. And people may steal away during the day into their garden or the bush to engage in sexual intercourse (*'apali*), in secret. As in other Massim island communities of the past (Lepowsky 1993; Munn 1986), people retreated inland for safety during times of warfare, for there they were hidden from the stranger's view. Indeed, it can be dangerous for strangers to venture inland into the bush without first rendering themselves familiar to Silopan, the custodial spirit of the island's central peak, Mount Tanalabwa. Strangers can make themselves identifiable to Silopan by eating a particular leafy vegetable that grows on the island. People should show due deference to Silopan by speaking quietly when deep in the bush.

Understood thus, the inland is both a place of refuge, privacy, growth, and sustenance and also a realm where an attitude of caution and respect should prevail. The suggestion that conception is imagined, not as a confluence of substances, but rather as the movement of the "assumed" from without to within, from outside to inland, from open space to a concealed place, is reinforced by the words associated with pregnancy and birth. The verb for pregnancy, *hiuma,* means they plant in the ground. By Mona's account, menstrual blood stops flowing to signal the baby's arrival and works toward the baby to grow it within the womb. Known as *heda yana 'abaeno* (literally, child, its sleeping place) or *'abanatu* (literally, child's place), the womb is an enclosed and enveloping space, a sealed place where the child sleeps and is grown until completion. The large clamshell (*godugodu*) is used both in popular speech and also in stories and legends to denote the womb. *Godu* means "to break, snap." The word for abortion or miscarriage, *goduyoi,* uses the stem of this word, thereby likening miscarriage and abortion to the irrevocable breaking or snapping apart of the tightly sealed halves of the clamshell.

Elaborated in these terms, conception is associated with a journey inland, a journey and a place familiar to those who make daily treks inland to, among other things, tend gardens. Perhaps this journey signifies the journey of the baby inland into the womb. The suggested relationship between the beginnings of the baby and the journey to a concealed place of growth and sustenance points to the broader significance of metaphor to thinking and understanding. Considered by Jackson to be a pivotal aspect of thinking about self, person, or people, anthropomorphic metaphor is a "verbal correlate" of patterns of bodily use and social interaction within the habitus (1989, 145–49). Following Bourdieu (1977), Mauss (1973, 73), and Dewey (1929), Jackson understands habitus as patterns of body use generated and informed by both intentional and unintentional habits that are "instilled within a shared environment" of everyday practical activities (1989, 128). Interactional, these habits are linked to the immediate world of people and things. Accordingly, metaphors express the distinct habits, rhythms, structures, material features, landscape, and relationships of everyday life in the particular social and linguistic contexts from which they arise. As such, metaphors are "situated" and "socially constituted" (1989, 141). They may simultaneously express bodily, social, economic, political, gender, spatial/geographic relationships, without exhausting other possible meanings.

Jackson contends that metaphor is not a "way of saying something 'in terms of' or 'by way of' something else" (1989, 142). Not "merely a figure of speech, drawing on an analogy"—itself denoting resemblance or similarity—metaphors must, instead, be apprehended "nondualistically," not as an "arbitrary or rhetorical synthesis of two terms—subject and object . . . which can be defined more realistically apart from each other, but [as] a true interdependency, [and identity] of mind and body, Self and World," body and landscape. "Metaphor reveals unities; it is not a figurative way of denying dualities. Metaphor reveals, not the 'thisness of a that' but rather that 'this is that'" (1989, 142)—that mind is body, conception is to go up inland. "Means of saying things," metaphors are also "means of doing things"; they are instrumental—means to an end rather than ends in and of themselves.

According to Jackson, metaphor is "a part of all thought" (1989, 145). However, in everyday communication in "both literate and nonliterate societies," the real connection between what he—adopting philosophical metaphors—terms *domains of being* (e.g., the human body and the landscape, or animals and human beings) generally remains implicit (1989, 143). It is passive and quiescent rather than active and explicit. In other words, people do not draw attention to the link between the domains. Although ordinarily quiescent, mundane metaphors may be activated under certain conditions or in certain contexts—particularly in times of crisis—to effect and mediate change in people's behavior and relationships (1989, 144).

Although the literal translation of conception as *lagahi* came as a revelation to me, Wycliffe cautioned that this meaning holds little significance for local people. He commented to the effect that "people do not think the word like that, they only speak it, use it." I wondered what he meant by this statement. Was he suggesting that the people of Nuakata did not think or enact the relationship between conception and *lagahi* (going up inland)? Was he saying that there is no such relationship between conceiving and going inland? Perhaps he was suggesting that the relationship should be understood as an analogy, or figuratively? Perhaps, like Wittgenstein (1953), he was advising me to look for the use of a word rather than its meaning. Or was he simply stating that, in pragmatic terms, an understanding of this relationship is irrelevant for the purposes of communicating (about) or doing conception? While I did not solicit answers to these questions, some clues lay in the conversation that ensued.

As I recall, Wycliffe's initial statement was followed by discussion of our early language learning sessions. Laughing, he indicated that I always wanted to learn the meaning of single words, together with the rules and laws of language. My way, he suggested, was not the best way to learn or understand Alina Nu'ata. It was only by making mistakes, by listening, speaking, and doing it that I would learn it properly, that I would speak as others do. Reflecting upon his comments and upon the word for conception, which sparked this conversation, I realized that neither I nor those to whom I spoke used the word *lagahi* when speaking about how the baby begins. Indeed, people did not ordinarily speak of conception. Rather, conception was known or understood by its effect—pregnancy.

If my conversation with Mona stood out as an important moment, one in which I was confronted by my own assumptions, then these brief comments made by Wycliffe constituted another moment of equivalent and related significance, as they made me examine the value I placed on the analysis of language, specifically metaphor, as a means of cultural translation. This conversation made me scrutinize how I was interpreting life on Nuakata. Preoccupied by the task of learning to speak, I was seduced, charmed by the power of words. Perplexed, even disappointed by the absence of distinctive Nuakatan conception beliefs, I had attempted to excavate the seemingly dormant, if not fossilized, word for conception in the hope of extracting a deeper metaphorical meaning. Following in the spirit of anthropologists, such as M. Rosaldo (1980) and Lutz (1982), and cognitive linguists, Lakoff and Johnson (1980) among others, I had set out to trace the ontology of conception, to identify a central conceptual schema underlying it, by mapping the semantic fields of related metaphors. While I believed then, and continue to believe now, that this is a potentially fruitful, although not unproblematic, way of elucidating cultural meanings, Wycliffe's statement warned me against privileging the meaning of single words removed from their social, pragmatic, and linguistic contexts. Although a useful heuristic device, interpretation of this kind risks mistranslation and misreading. Words become reified as the repositories of static meaning—"instruments of reflection," a "mirror of nature" (Rorty 1979) rather than, as Malinowski suggested, "a mode of action and not an instrument of reflection" (1922, 312). Wycliffe's comments acted as a restraint to my impulse to privilege elaborations of difference and revelations of the exotic.

Of course these reflections in the field were not without precedent for me or anthropological debate. Mindful of both the potential and actuality of cultural mistranslation born of linguistic incompetence, and fueled by the quest for the exotic, Keesing (1989b) urges anthropologists to be cautious with their necessarily fragmentary and limited linguistic data or evidence. He directs his strongest cautionary refrain to fieldworkers who seek to document, understand, and interpret "cultural symbolism, cosmological systems, or cultural constructions of 'self' and 'person'" (460). At issue here is the analysis of what Lakoff and Johnson (1980) term "conventional metaphor"—metaphors that "are not creative extrapolations from literal use" but are embedded within both the semantics and the grammatical form of the language (Keesing 1985, 205–8; 1989b, 463). Lakoff and Johnson (1980) assert that conventional metaphors are systematic; they underpin our language, our speaking and our thinking. Whether employing "body parts," "spatial imagery or physical acts or states," one domain of experience (the source domain) is used to represent another (target domain), be it "temporal relationships, social relationships, [or] inner states" (1980, 463). Keesing (1985) warns that metaphors may be so deeply conventional that we need to carefully consider whether or not they are constitutive of experience or thinking. Rather than the "frozen residues of old belief" (1985, 208) they may be semantically irrelevant, effectively dead or at least unrecognizably transformed. Therefore, we need to adopt an attitude of caution or skepticism in reading cosmological or metaphysical significance into conventional metaphors. This should not, however, be interpreted as a call to abandon such projects. Keesing calls for the mapping of metaphorical schemata in non-Western languages in the way elaborated in Lakoff and Johnson (1980) and Lakoff (1989, 473).

> The metaphoric systems of particular peoples are *expressions* of their culturally constructed worlds as well as the reverse. . . . [D]ifferent metaphoric schemes in a particular language may themselves be connected in systematic ways reflective of cultural-conceptual systems that underlie them. Metaphors, that is, are constructed in terms of, as well as themselves being constitutive of, a people's view of the world. But that does not mean that we can easily infer from the metaphoric usages

the systems of cultural assumption—if any—that underlie them. Nor does it mean that all native actors necessarily share assumptions about how the world works, despite being able to use the linguistic coin of the community. (Keesing 1989b, 463, emphasis in original)

Jackson (1989) recognizes that we may misread active meaning in the merely conventional, but also says because it was once there, it can always be revitalized or enlivened. Fernandez (1989) is also less interested or persuaded by the "dead metaphor trapped in convention" idea. Responding to Keesing's words of caution, Fernandez stresses the "pragmatics of metaphor" and the need

> for an enduring anthropological interest in human playfulness and human capacity to create or enliven metaphors and to build universes on such grains of sand. . . . [T]he study of the conventional structures of dead metaphors should be enlivened by the field study of the "play of tropes." . . . [We should] complement the cognitive enterprise and its attention to those recurrent cultural moments and cultural movements in which something new and lively and colourful is created out of—to use the linguist's metaphor he evokes—the "bleached bones" of the past. (1989, 470–71)

The Conceived, Borne

One day, two months or so after our arrival on Nuakata, I summoned the courage to visit Emma in her hamlet on the Bolime side of the island. Nervous about my language skills, I put my list of questions about conception, pregnancy, and birth, my language notebook, and my tape recorder in my backpack and set off alone to talk with her. The well-defined path to Bolime passes through several hamlets before tracing its way up a short steep rise, through dense bush filled with towering rosewood trees and other splendid tropical hardwoods. At the top of this rise, which marks the border between Yalasi and Bolime, you can see in the foreground the densely forested island of Boirama and, in the distance, on the horizon, the outline of Tubetube—where Martha Macintyre did her fieldwork. Looking out to sea on this day, catching my breath, I thought first of Martha going before me to Tubetube, and then of the small stream of ethnographers that had previously journeyed to other islands in Milne Bay Province. I remembered accounts and photos of Martha's friendships on Tubetube, her fictive kin, her house and village, her boat journeys. Standing there, scanning the horizon, my memories of her Tubetube pictures and stories were enlivened just as my Nuakata friendships and stories were now unfolding, taking shape, finding words. Malinowski's words, "Imagine yourself suddenly set down surrounded by all your gear, alone on a tropical beach close to a native village" (1962, 4), came to mind. I realized, then, that a transition had occurred without me really knowing or noticing it. I was no longer imagining the field, but living it, living on Nuakata. I was no longer imagining myself as a fieldworker through the texts and testimonies of my anthropological forebears. I was doing fieldwork. Running down the slope to Emma's place, my arms and legs barely in control, my backpack straining against its harness, I felt once again what a privilege it was to stay in this place, to share this time with people. If, as anthropologists say, fieldwork is a rite of passage, then this journey to Emma's village marked a moment in my own conception as a person who does ethnography—a person privileged to hear, see, and create stories with other people.

My arrival in Emma's village was announced by barking dogs. I can barely bring myself to classify them as such, for dogs on Nuakata are miserable, mangy, dispirited creatures—mere shadows of their (comparatively) pampered Western cousins. Seated outside under her house, with her mother and several small children, Emma welcomed me warmly. In her late twenties, divorced, she had recently given birth to her fifth child, Reni, a daughter (see chap. 2). Like Mona, Emma had made discreet efforts to befriend me during Women's Fellowship meetings. She too spoke English, but used it with me sparingly, to explain unfamiliar Alina Nu'ata words.

Before long Emma, Reni, and I retreated inside the house where we talked together about a range of things, including conception, pregnancy, birth, marriage, and my own marriage ceremony. During the conversation I asked her, "How do you understand the baby starts?" Emma replied:

> A baby begins when a man and woman marry. If a man and woman go together, then a child will arrive. The woman's period will sense the baby and go up to the baby. Then the woman will know. She will feel the baby within her. Then the woman has found the baby.

Emma did not offer an explanation for the creation of the baby, stating in this and subsequent conversations that she didn't know or understand these things. However, she did speak of the "arrival" of the baby. The word she chose, *mahalava,* is used to describe a person, spirit, or thing coming to a hamlet or place from outside, or someone arriving from another island or place. *Mahalava* means to happen, to occur, to become present—although not necessarily, to materialize—in a place. At first the baby arrives without the mother's knowledge. It is for her to discover its presence (*lobai*) by its effect within her own body. Emma's use of the term *lobai,* meaning "to discover or find," is revealing, for it makes the point (reinforced by other women) that she does not cause the baby, nor make herself pregnant, but, rather, discovers its concealed presence within her.

Like Mona, Emma stated that a child "arrives" when a man and woman marry and come together in sexual intercourse. Her reference to marriage was knowing, and strategic. She wanted me to understand that, although her relationship with Reni's father could not be publicly acknowledged, this was only a temporary situation. For at that time she and Reni's father, Apolosa, were privately preparing for their noncustomary church marriage, planned to coincide with the visit of the regional United Church minister from Bunama on Normanby Island, later in the year. Unlike usual Nuakatan marriages, which occur outside and without reference to the church, Apolosa and Emma—both church members—intended to have a marriage sanctioned and officiated by the United Church. Not only would this legitimate and consolidate their status before the church, but it would also reinforce Apolosa's and, by implication, Emma's standing within the community. This and subsequent conversations about her wedding plans were only possible because I was an outsider in the community without familial or clan ties—a *dimdim* who was assumed to be associated with, and supportive of, the church and its activities.

According to Emma, then, this active coming together of man and woman creates the conditions of possibility for the baby's arrival without necessarily creating the baby. Captivated by Reni lying between us I did not think, at the time, to ask how a baby arrives/arises inside the mother, or where it comes from. Nuakatan beliefs about the cause or means of human procreation were rendered irrelevant to me by the presence of a child already conceived and born. The present, undeniable needs of the conceived—in this case a tiny, weeks-old baby girl—overshadowed speculative discussion about how she was formed. For the first time I understood a prevailing form of pragmatism, that the ever-presence of the effects of conception (babies, children, adults) rendered questions about their cause unimportant. Such pragmatism is sustained by the knowledge that the creation of babies occurs, but cannot be known. It is only when the conceived is brought into the open, made visible, borne that the constitutive conjugal relations and acts that prepared the ground for it are revealed (see M. Strathern 1988, 316–17).

Following her own account of conception, Emma asked me to explain how the baby starts. Aware that I was a married woman, thirty-three years old, and without children, she did not attempt to elicit understanding born of my lived experience of conception, gestation, and birth. Rather, she appealed to my learned knowledge *about* these issues. Reluctant to be positioned as an authority, or to reinforce the view that this knowledge should be privileged as fact or truth, I prefaced my reply with, "Some *dimdim* understand that the baby starts when . . . " While unsure whether or not this preface achieved its desired effect, I was confident that the ensuing explanation did not reinforce Emma's presumptions about the status of my *dimdim* knowledge of conception. Launching into a description of sexual intercourse, the journey of the sperm to the egg, fertilization, and implantation, in broken Alina Nu'ata, I was forced to resort to indecipherable diagrams and gestures, before we both abandoned the exercise in fits of laughter. But I was not yet off the hook. Clearly relaxed and feeling more confident in my presence, Emma carefully scanned my face as she asked, "Why do you have no children?" Still laughing, I offered an obvious, easy answer—*'ai 'auhi, ya paihowai* (I use contraception). But this did not satisfy her, for it failed to explain why I chose to study women's stories of conception, pregnancy, and birth and did not become pregnant myself. Specifically, it did not explain why I sought an understanding of these issues through others' experiences rather than my own. It also failed to acknowledge the implications of this choice for Roger and me, and our families. A lengthier conversation ensued!

Bearing the Inconceivable

As I was preparing to leave Emma's hamlet, I noticed a basket lying on a mat under the house. Like the bags used by women to carry garden produce it was woven from coconut palm leaves, but in a different style. Rectangular in shape, its weave was more pleasing to the eye. Taken by its appearance, I asked Emma what it was used for. She told me that it was a carrying basket for Reni. Her mother made it when Reni was born. Although primarily used for carrying new babies, this type of basket can also be used by women to carry yams from the garden at harvest time. She added that some, but not all women on the island, continue to use these bags for carrying babies or yams.

While interested to learn that freshly harvested yams and new babies may be carried in this style of basket, and intrigued by the possible significance of this practice, this did not occupy my thoughts on the journey home. Nor did I focus on Emma's claim that she did not know (about) conception—a claim that, as Wycliffe had anticipated, was repeated by every woman I subsequently asked about these things. Instead, my thoughts centered on the familiar and recurring image of women returning home from their gardens bearing heavy baskets of food on top of, or slung from, their heads. This image, combined with that of Emma carrying Reni in her basket, caused me to reflect on the Alina Nuʻata word ʻavala (to give birth). Used to describe a women's bearing during pregnancy, ʻavala is also used more widely to mean "carry" or "bear." While men carry things (their personal bags, bush knives, wood for canoes or houses, fish, pigs, children, and particularly older infants), they do not generally, or routinely, carry newborn babies, garden produce, or weighty bags or parcels. And, of course, they do not bear unborn babies within them. These "bearings" are carried by women alone. A woman carries the conceived baby—inside her womb. After birth women continue to carry their babies until they can stand alone, just as women continue to carry food from their gardens that nourishes and sustains their growing children. For women, then, bearing a baby is not confined to labor and giving birth, but is an ongoing activity that precedes and extends well beyond birth—and for women, too, it is bearing rather than conceiving that can be enacted and, therefore, known and understood.

But these musings still left me puzzled by Emma's use of the word *mahalava* (arrival) to describe how the baby begins. Several weeks later, Iʻunia, the adoptive mother of Emma's fourth child—a woman in her mid-forties, who came to Nuakata from Duau (on Normanby Island) in her early twenties—took me aside to tell me that many people on Nuakata do not understand conception properly. She indicated that because people on Nuakata, particularly the younger generations, are disinterested in customary knowledge, they are forgetting what people on

Duau still know to be true: "Babies' spirits are sent by the spirits of the mother's maternal ancestors." The spirit of the baby "arrives" within the woman after she and her husband have intercourse.

I'unia's comments were consistent with A. Weiner's (1976) totalizing description of conception beliefs on the Trobriand Islands. Accordingly, the spirits of maternal ancestors implant the baby's spirit within the body of its mother. Like Emma and Mona before her, I'unia also implied that sexual intercourse creates the possibility for the baby to arrive, but it does not create or cause the baby. A man and woman do not decide to "do" and therefore have a baby—(the spirit of) the baby comes to them from another source.

Her comments and my earlier musings on women's multiple and related "bearings" brought to mind the story of Bulelala, told to me by Wycliffe as an aside in an earlier conversation about women and witchcraft.

> Bulelala is a spiritual belief that all people on Nuakata believe to be true. Bulelala is a legendary flying woman, a spiritual woman. She used to carry a basket of food, which meant that it was going to be a good harvest. When Bulelala flies (at night), it is really bright across all of Nuakata. She flies two times a year—every harvest when the yams are growing and starting to mature. If she flies south, [i.e.,] north to south, it won't be a good harvest. She flies like shooting stars—but shooting stars are not bright. She flies in a long line over the top of Yalasi, Bwauli, Bomatu. She will fly and then go down for two or three seconds and stop. If you stay (and listen) for a minute you will hear her put her basket of yams on the ground. It sounds like thunder. This year she came two times, but mainly to Duau and not Nuakata. Last year when there was a drought she did not come. It's a sign, *mahuli*, of a good harvest. Her basket is as big as this house. She carries two baskets, one a bit bigger and one a bit smaller, one on her head and one on back. All the spirits of the yams, she takes them down this way. Now it doesn't happen often, but before she often used to fly.

In telling this story Wycliffe had explained that "yams are like children." Like people "yams have spirit." Yams are the "most important" food grown in the garden. Men and women together usually plant their seed yams. Later when they have grown they are generally harvested by women. They can be stored to eat or given to people. "People give their best and their first harvested yams to the church as *mulolo*—a love gift, an offering—just as Abraham offered up Isaac, his first-born son, to God." Wycliffe also added:

> The story of Bulelala is a legend, but a true legend because people believe. Those who do not believe do not hear her. Those who know the story of Bulelala to be true have heard her and seen the night sky lit up. They have seen that a good harvest has followed. Bulelala comes from Duau, where custom continues to be strong. Because most people on Duau continue to believe in her, she comes to them more often.

While told in a different context, the story of Bulelala, together with Wycliffe's accompanying explanation, resonated with and unified key aspects of the explanations of conception given by I'unia, Emma, Mona, and Wycliffe. If, as Wycliffe suggests, yams and children are understood as analogous, then the story of Bulelala arguably highlights the significance of women's bearing, carrying, and supporting roles in relation to growing yams and "en-wombed" or unborn children. Wycliffe's comments also reinforced the idea that it is men and women together who "prepare the ground," make a place, for growing yam seeds and unborn babies. Buried within the soil, the yam seed divides and multiplies when the spirit woman Bulelala arrives, carrying the spirits of the yams on her back. When she deposits her bags on the ground, the yam spirits enter the concealed seeds or growing yams, causing them to multiply, ensuring a bountiful harvest. Just as spirit is vital to the yam so it is, by I'unia's and Mona's accounts, vital to the baby concealed within the womb of its mother. The story of Bulelala also reinforces the idea that the yam/baby spirit is ontologically distinct and detachable from, if not prior to, the growing yam/baby. This view was consistent with Mona's, I'unia's, and Emma's descriptions of conception, suggesting that, like contemporary Tubetube ideas described by Macintyre (1995), Nuakatan ideas of the person express physical/metaphysical, body/spirit, mortal/immortal dualisms, consistent with Christian ideas of body and soul.

> This physical/metaphysical divide sits easily with Christian ideas of body and soul that are today spoken of in church sermons, or in any context where human mortality is an issue. Perhaps they reflect a century of missionisation and the acceptance of Christianity. . . . [T]his

dualism of body and soul, which we consider to be a hallmark of Western thought, is now claimed by Tubetube Christians as "something we always had," entirely consonant with what they think of as precolonial ideas of human mortality and the eternal existence of spirits of the dead. (1995, 41)

But the story of Bulelala also highlights an important distinction between I'unia's and Mona's understandings of conception. Mona suggested that God the Father makes the egg from which the baby is made. In so doing she revealed the influence of both Christian cosmology and Western medical teaching in her thinking on the person. I'unia, though, implied that this was not a proper customary understanding of conception. Just as the spirit woman Bulelala brings spirit to the yams, it is the maternal ancestors, and not a single paternal God, who brings spirit to the "en-wombed" baby.

I'unia clearly believed in, and sought to retain, an original, authentic, if not static and essentialist, Nuakatan understanding of conception—customary understanding that, like the story of Bulelala, stemmed from Duau. Far from obfuscating what is, can be, and has been known about conception, I'unia's essentialist thinking arguably added another perspective to the multiple, dynamic, and syncretic knowledge of conception on Nuakata.[24]

Chapter Four

✺

Belongings

Identity and difference are not so much about categorical groupings as about processes of identification and differentiation. These processes are engaged for all of us, in different ways, with the desire to belong, to be part of some community, however provisional. Belonging invokes desire, and it is in this desire that much of the passion for difference resides. . . . [T]he question of where and to what I belong involves . . . a consideration of position and location. (Moore 1994c, 2)

belong: **1.** (foll. by *to*) to be the property or possession (of). **2.** (foll. by *to*) to be a member (of a club, etc.). **3.** (foll. by *to, under, with,* etc.) to be classified (with) . . . **4.** (foll. by *to*) to be a part or adjunct (of) . . . **5.** to have a proper or usual place . . . **6.** *Informal.* to be suitable or acceptable, esp. socially . . . *belonging:* . . . secure relationship, affinity . . . *belongings:* . . . the things that a person owns or has with him[/her]; possessions; effects. (*Collins English Dictionary,* 1985)

Five weeks after our arrival on Nuakata we prepared to move from the church grounds to our newly completed house at Gohiya—Wycliffe's mother's hamlet (*dalava*).[1] Although a small journey of maybe 800 meters, it represented a significant move, but not necessarily in ways I had anticipated. In asking to be housed in a hamlet we sought a more intimate appreciation of daily life on Nuakata, particularly, but by no means exclusively, the lives of women. By making the move to Gohiya, though, we not only sought to position ourselves optimally for the research but also hoped to find a place (a home), a sense of belonging among Wycliffe's family, rather than living on the margins of the community beholden to everyone passing by the church. We yearned for intimacy with people, an intimacy that explored, tolerated, even celebrated, the distinctions between us and them, while creating a space—a time and place—for an inclusive we to emerge. A romantic, utopian hope? Yes. But our hope nonetheless.

Ethnographers have long testified to their fictive kin status in the communities in which they have worked. Such status carries a power that extends beyond the ethnographic field, to the more academic reaches of the discipline. Intentional or not, testimonies to acceptance, to belonging—genuine participation, and not just observation—in the field are used to lend authenticity and authority to ethnographers' subsequent textual representations and interpretations.

This multifaceted hope for belonging, first ignited in Melbourne when the field and its people were still mere imaginings, was fanned on Nuakata by what can best be described as a fortuitous coincidence. Wycliffe's younger brother and older maternal cousin/brother were both named Roger. They were the only people so named on the island. From our earliest days on Nuakata, my husband Roger was instructed to address these men as *'waligeha* (namesake). At first this term merely seemed quaint to us. Surely, we thought, it simply made explicit the familiar and respectful practice of naming children after familial forebears, friends, or significant people, living or dead. During the building of our house, however, when Roger's senior *'waligeha* took him under his wing, taking great pains to explain and teach him various house-building skills, we began to suspect that this relationship was significant in ways not quite so familiar. Early discussions with Wycliffe about *susu*, clans, and names reinforced these thoughts, our hopes.

Susu *Belonging*

Wycliffe revealed that namesakes generally, but not always, belonged to the same *susu* and/or clan. By way of explanation, he added that *susu* means breast and breast-milk as well as mother's family. People who belong to the same *susu* share the same mother, while those belonging to the same clan—*bwasumo* (bird)—merely share the same maternal ancestors. Therefore, Wycliffe's mother, Eunice; her brother; her sister and her sister's children; and, indeed, Wycliffe's own brothers and sisters all belonged to the same *susu,* as did his adopted brother, Nowel. (When Nowel's natal mother, a member of Wycliffe's clan, became ill following his birth, Eunice breast-fed and subsequently cared for him.) Wycliffe's mother's brother's children, however, did not belong to his *susu,* for they did not share the same mother. As such, these cousins could not claim a place on Wycliffe's mother's and maternal uncles' land. Only those who belonged to his *susu* could claim a place on *susu* land.

Paraphrased above, Wycliffe's succinct explanation of the meaning of *susu* was consistent with more detailed accounts given by some Massim ethnographers (Fortune [1932] 1989, 3–6, for Dobu; Macintyre 1983; 1988, 51–54, for Tubetube; and Thune 1980, 81, for Duau). Without directly stating it, Wycliffe implied that to share the same mother was to share common breast-milk, to be breast-fed from the same source. In both a literal and symbolic sense, breast-milk flows between mother and baby, feeding their relationship as she, too, had been fed and nurtured by her mother. The breast-feeding relationship is enacted down through and across the maternal generations, nurturing *susu* belonging and consolidating the recent ancestral past in present *susu* relations.

Accordingly, a person addresses his or her mother and mother's sisters as *hinagu* (my mother). When having to distinguish between mothers—if, for example, more than one are present at the same time—the terms *hinagu 'agu taulabalaba* (my birth mother),[2] *hinagu mwala'ina* (my big mother, i.e., mother's elder sister), or *hinagu habaluna* (my small mother, i.e., mother's younger sister) are used. However, people avoid using these more cumbersome terms in day-to-day conversation. Therefore, a mother's sister(s) would be considered mother(s) just as the children of these mothers are all considered brothers and sisters, for they have been breast-fed by the same grandmother or maternal source. For example, the same-sex siblings of one's birth mother or mother's sisters are called *tahigu* (my sister/my brother). Cross-sex siblings are addressed as *lougu* (my brother/my sister). An older sibling can address a younger sibling of different sex as *lougu tahigu*. Similarly the younger sibling can address the older sibling of the opposite sex as *lougu tuwagu*. In contrast, the (non-*susu*) children of a person's mother's brother (cross-cousins) are addressed as *nibaigu* (my cousin). The different terms for same-sex and cross-sex, younger and older siblings as opposed to the general term used for all cousins imply, without specifying, that sexual difference and age constitute significant dimensions of *susu* relations (see Munn 1986; M. Strathern 1988). It could be said, therefore, that maternal breast-milk and the breast-feeding relationship, more than blood or semen, underpin familial/*susu* belonging and relations on Nuakata. In this sense, someone's existence (especially outside the womb) is not independent from *susu* relations or *susu* belonging[3]—both are nurtured in infancy at the mother's breast.⁴ It is in the places where people stay that *susu* relationships, *susu* identity, find expression and form. This aside, my reflection on Wycliffe's explanation reifies and idealizes the literal (substantive) significance of breast-milk and breast-feeding to *susu* belonging on Nuakata, for in practice—in daily living—many exceptions to these generalizations were accommodated. For example, unlike Nowel, most adopted children were taken into their new family after they had been weaned. In those instances when a child's adoptive mother came from the same clan—but not the same *susu*—as the birth mother, the child was generally considered to be a member of both its birth mother's and adoptive mother's *susu*. While the adoptive mother had not breast-fed the child, she had, by her distant maternal link to the child's birth mother and her feeding and nurturing role, rendered the child a member of her *susu*. Although unclear, it seemed that the adopted child was also entitled to claim land belonging to either its adoptive or natal mother's *susu*. In one example of which I am aware a female adopted by a woman belonging to the same clan as, but different *susu* than, her birth mother's was only given land belonging to her birth mother's *susu* when she herself had children. By claiming her place on this land she apparently forfeited her claim to a place on her then deceased adoptive mother's land. While an important means of establishing *susu* relations, the substantive breast-feeding relationship was clearly not the only means of establishing and feeding this form of belonging to the *susu* and *susu* land.

In explaining the significance of *susu*, Wycliffe implied that, as in other Massim communities, land and *susu* belonging are crucially linked on Nuakata (Fortune [1932] 1989; Macintyre 1983; Munn 1986; Thune 1980). People are born into, nurtured, and grow up within a matrilineal social environment—a dynamic world of *susu* relations grounded and expressed in domestic landscapes and living arrangements. Accordingly, everyone possesses a living place—a preconceived relational place in his or her *susu* and a place to live on *susu* land. It is through living on, and being sustained by, this land, together with other *susu* members, that someone's *susu* relations and belonging are continually defined and redefined throughout life. Further, it is through people's relationship to the land of their maternal forebears that continuity between past and present, the living and the dead, is maintained and remembered.⁵

While all members of a given *susu* share a common identity and a place on the land, it is usually women who continuously occupy it. They are also responsible for the day-to-day tending of both family gardens and hamlet spaces. Given that women also cook the vast majority of a family's meals, wash clothes and dishes, and take primary responsibility for the care of children, it is not hard to see their relationship to the land and their role in everyday life as central, if undervalued. Women are the foundation of the matrilineage, but like many foundations their work is often unnoticed, if not invisible.

Men have a different place, position, or role in the matrilineage of their birth. Although many, like Noah, are considered controllers of *susu* land in their generation, they, together with their brothers, grow up in the full knowledge that much of their adult life will be spent living among nonkin (affines) in their wife's village. In this context they are always different, outsiders who gain respect, identity, and power among their affines through their work, namely, fishing, building houses, making copra, clearing and establishing new gardens, and caring for their families. While women also spend periods of time living with their affines, where they, too, must prove themselves through hard work, they usually spend the greater part of their domestic lives among kin on *susu* land. Where women provide stable points of reference for the matrilineage, men are more mobile, circulating and establishing themselves in other places, where they must attempt to balance affinal and matrilineal obligations to sisters and their offspring. When senior adult members of the matrilineage live in other places, day-to-day decisions that affect the *susu* and the organization of its land are made by the most senior members currently "staying" on the land. Decisions or disputes with far-reaching consequences are settled, where possible, by senior members of the *susu*, regardless of residence.

Wycliffe insisted that although people are entitled to a place on land belonging to their *susu*, they cannot simply assume a place on their birth father's land, particularly after his death. In granting permission for children to live and work on their father's *susu* land, members of his *susu* show respect for, and recognition of, the work contributed by the children's mother and maternal kin to his *susu*.[6] In other words, unlike their place in their mother's *susu*, children's place, their belonging, in their father's *susu* is contingent upon the labors of their parents—particularly their mother's and, later, their own—on behalf of their father's *susu*.

While a person's relationships to the people and places of his or her matrilineal *susu* are the ground of that person's living and staying (*miyamiya*),[7] his or her paternity and paternal kin are not irrelevant or unimportant. This point is reinforced by people's use of their father's first name as surname. Only by the efforts of a birth father (*tamagu 'agutaulabalaba;* literally, my father, the body/person that gave birth to me) to prepare the ground for his child (conception) can the child's place and belonging with(in) its mother and her *susu* arise. The continuity of a *susu* and the belonging shared by its members is contingent upon the labors of affinal kin who support but do not belong to it. Unlike the relationship with a mother, who by bearing and breast-feeding nurtures and sustains the belonging to people and place shared between herself and her child, the father's relationship is more tenuous, more contingent. As Fortune ([1932] 1989, 5–30) describes for Dobu, a man's natural, obligatory, familial responsibility lies with his sister's children rather than his own, for they belong to his *susu* (cf. Battaglia 1985).

In discussing the relationship of both mothers and fathers to their children, Wycliffe, his mother Eunice, and another woman, Malida, highlighted fathers' caring for (*'ita'avivini*) and giving (*mulolo*) to their children. For example, Wycliffe suggested that "a mother cares (*'avala*) for her child—every time she washes the child, feeds him with good food and forbids him not to do those sorts of things (that will give him or her) a headache. A good mother always looks after baby in whatever he does, so he or she will not get accident or sickness."

It is a mother's role, together with other *susu* members, to feed and sustain her children. Eunice suggested that in the past "a mother had many children, but not so many that she made herself weak and therefore unable to look after (*'avala*) them properly." In contrast, Malida emphasized that a father is "kind, generous, caring (*'ita'avivini*), tender-hearted and hard-working." According to Wycliffe, "a father freely *gives* to his children.[8] He is different to a mother. He always shows the child the things that are suitable for him/her. . . . He teaches him/her culture. He protects him/her from having sickness, makes sure that the child eats properly."

While these accounts suggest that both mothers and fathers care for their children, the selective use of terms for a mother's and father's caring was instructive. The word *'ita'avivini*—derived from *'ita* (to see) and *'avivini* (to care)—quite literally means "see and care." This word is used to denote a father's care for his children or a grandfather's care for his affinal grandchildren. It is also commonly used to describe looking after things, such as a radio or bush knife. There is both a temporal and contingent dimension to this term. It implies a response to the visible, the apparent—a temporary response. In practice, many fathers on Nuakata demonstrably cared and provided for their children on a day-to-day basis and assumed an active role in the decisions affecting their well-being. In contrast, *'avala* (to bear, carry, give birth to) is generally used to describe women's (and in some instances men's) care for members of their *susu*. Rather than being a specific response to a visible need, the carrying and bearing of a mother is foundational, continuous.

There is a certain freedom and flexibility in the father-child relationship that is absent between mother and child. Unlike the response of a mother, whose daily care and nurture for her children is assumed, obligatory, for they simultaneously sustain herself, her children, and their *susu*, a father's response to his children is contingent. A father may express this negatively as indifference and disinterest, or positively through everyday activities associated with the care and nurture of his children. His children may help him with the same sense of spontaneity and affection shown to them. An example of the nature of this relationship was illustrated by Wycliffe's naming of his canoe. Soon after our arrival on Nuakata, Wycliffe built a new sailing canoe (*sailau*). When he finished it, he called it *gwama'idou*. Translated, this expression means "boy he cries." Wycliffe explained that when a child cries for fish his or her father sees his or her hunger and responds by taking to his canoe and finding fish for the child to eat. This is the love a father gives to his child(ren). Such a relationship creates interdependence and indebtedness. A father's love, his gift to his children and their *susu*, is acknowledged during life and especially upon his death by members of his wife's *susu*. For example, his care and support of his wife and children may entitle him to land use and influence among his affinal kin. Upon his death, his children and/or his widow express appreciation for his love/gifts by the presentation of reciprocal gifts (*mulolo*)[9] to his *susu*. These gifts of yams (if available), rice, and pigs both formally and respectfully acknowledge a father's contribution to his children and affines while absolving their debt to his kin.

The differing relationships of mothers and fathers to their children are by no means unique to Nuakata. Thune (1980, 80–84) states that on northeast Duau a father's relationship with his child is described by a term that means both "voluntary or freely given love" and "to give gifts." This contrasts with the "required nurturance" provided by *susu*. Macintyre (1983, 51–53) indicates that the same distinction applies on Tubetube. Indeed, as on Nuakata, a linguistic/social distinction is made on Tubetube between a more permanent, maternal care that builds and sustains and a more temporary yet altruistic form of care in which a father seeks to protect and preserve his children as he watches over them (see also Battaglia 1985).

Naming Place, Placing Names

That people's existence—their living and staying—on Nuakata is never disentangled from *susu* and clan belonging is further reinforced and expressed by people's names and the relational terms used to address them. Wycliffe indicated that two personal names were bestowed upon a child at birth: a *susu*/clan name that could only be spoken by members of the same clan and a public name that, with some important exceptions, everyone could use.[10] Just as people's use of public and *susu*/clan names to address those belonging to their own clan named and gave voice to the vital source of belonging they shared so the silence accorded to those names by those from other clans gave silent respect to the distinctions between them.

Public names were often new or novel, taken from other sources beyond Nuakata,[11] for example, "Sydney" from Sydney Harbor bridge, or "Maino," representing the initials of five matrilineal family names. Arguably these distinctive public names anticipated individuality. Indeed, in some instances, they seemed to preempt the embodiment or practice of this individuality. For example, Wycliffe was named after the Wyclyffe Bible translators (also known as the Summer Institute of Linguistics or SIL), who have been engaged in Bible translation work across the Massim for over three decades. Wycliffe's paternal grandfather had been a local pastor, who worked throughout the Bunama circuit of the United Church on nearby Normanby Island during the time Reverend Alfred Guy worked as a missionary at the Bunama Methodist mission around the turn of the century. Wycliffe's father, Noah, was a Christian actively involved in local and regional church affairs and committed to translating Methodist hymns into Alina Nu'ata. In naming his first-born son after the Bible translators, Noah had hoped Wycliffe would grow up to become involved in Bible translation work, thereby following in both his own and his father's footsteps. Whether by coincidence or coercion, this has, in fact, eventuated.

Although not a routine occurrence, any person could have his or her public name in common with one or possibly more members of his or her *susu,* living or dead. When this did occur, as with the two Rogers in

Wycliffe's mother's family, it was understood as a gesture of affection and respect for the living person whose name and matrilineage the newborn child shared. The subsequent relationship between living namesakes was grounded by this initial gesture made by the newborn's parents. Together with the name, this affection and respect constituted a significant part of the newborn's matrilineal inheritance. Like a seed planted in soil this inheritance, if nurtured, was grown, transformed, and revealed over time by the living *'waligeha* relationship.

While people did not always have their public name in common with a *susu*/clan member, they always shared their *susu*/clan names with a matrilineal forebear either living or, more often than not, dead.[12] Hence, *susu*/clan names were not randomly inherited. Named at birth, female children inherited the names of female forebears and male children inherited the names of male forebears, suggesting that the sexed form of the body was recognized and named at birth. Each name not only carried the memory, however vague, of the more senior or deceased forebear, it also denoted the relational place that the particular forebear occupied within the *susu* of his or her birth. For example, Wycliffe is the first-born child of his mother, Eunice, who is herself the fourth- and last-born child of her generation. Eunice has a brother and sister still living. Another sister died before reaching childbearing age. Unable to become pregnant, Eunice's living sister Malida (now deceased) first adopted the senior Roger and later Eunice's third- and fifth-born children: Jane and Douglas. As first-born boys in their generation of the *susu*, senior Roger and then Wycliffe are regarded as the senior members of the *susu*. Accordingly, Wycliffe was named after his mother's brother (MMB), a man who occupied a similar position of seniority in his generation. When their mothers' and grandmothers' generation have died out, Wycliffe and senior Roger are expected to assume primary responsibility for control of the land and any disputes arising among members of the *susu* or between their and others' *susu* from the same or different clans. Known, then, but rarely spoken, these *susu*/clan names recalled and made present particular living pasts of a given *susu*. Not only did this naming practice reinforce a sense of continuity between past and present generations of a given *susu*, but, equally, it gave living expression to the realized hopes for, or past anticipations of, future generations.

Another example is instructive. Two of Wycliffe's three sisters had children. Jane, the younger of the two with children, had one child named Sydney. About nine, he was the first-born boy and second-born child of his generation. As such, he will be expected to assume some senior status among his generation of the *susu* when he becomes an adult and, more particularly, when he is among the oldest surviving generation. Geteli, the second-born child (and first-born female) of Eunice—and the older of Wycliffe's two sisters with children—had five children: four girls (Linda, Jesili, Viki, Maino) and a boy named Brian, the last-born. Brian shared his *susu* name with Wycliffe. By naming him in this way Geteli and her husband demonstrated respect for Wycliffe while also signaling Brian's potential place among his generation of the matrilineage. For example, while Geteli's first-born child (and the first-born child of her generation), Linda, aged eleven or twelve in 1993, will almost certainly have some senior status within her generation of the family, there was talk that Brian may also assume senior responsibilities, given that he was the first-born boy of the first-born woman in that generation of the *susu*. It remains for Brian to find, claim, and realize this relational place, identified and named at birth by his living matrilineal kin as his potential inheritance. He must grow and be grown into this relational place or role. Whether or not a given child assumes the relational place within his or her matrilineage foreshadowed by the *susu*/clan name bestowed upon it at birth is contingent upon many factors, including the child or adult's individual or particular qualities, where he or she lives during adult life, and who remains living in the generation (see Macintyre 1983).

For the most part, people's identification with familial land is prescribed by preexisting and predefined matrilineal kinship/clan relationships. In a very real sense this identity, at once familial and individual, social and cultural, is embodied—grounded upon the age, sex, position of a person in the nuclear and extended family (first-born, second-born, etc.), and his or her living relations. People are born into, nurtured within, and grow up amid a matrilineal social world—a dynamic world of social relations that are inscribed upon and expressed in the fluid organization of domestic landscapes and living arrangements. In such a world every person has a place—a place to live throughout his or her lifetime and a preconceived place in his or her wider maternal family or *susu/huhu*.

Given this understanding of these naming conventions, it made some sense to us that in sharing a nominal, if not a birthing and feeding, inheritance Roger—my husband—potentially belonged to his two namesakes' *susu*. It remained for him and the members of this *susu* to recognize this association. The questions that troubled Roger and me, especially early on, were, Would this potential relationship be recognized, realized? If so, how? Would this relationship be directly acknowledged when we moved to Gohiya? Where, and with whom, would this place me? Did the instructions given to us about addressing each other have any bearing on these matters?

Naming Distinction(s)

Around the time Wycliffe instructed Roger to address his namesakes as *'waligeha,* his father Noah, among other senior people, suggested that Roger and I should address each other respectfully as *mwanegu* (my spouse). Noah explained that from the moment a marriage is declared by senior members of the woman's *susu* the newlywed couple should not address each other by name, even if they had always done so in the past. Rather, they should show respect for one another and for each other's *susu* by using the relational term.

Encouraged to address each other by the relational term, it was also explained to us that married couples do not generally touch each other or express physical affection for one another in public. The taboo on touching in public applied to unmarried and married, old and young couples alike. Eager to please, trying not to offend our hosts, we conformed to these practices. While we experienced the immediate distancing effect of these conventions in our own relationship, we remained uncertain of the significance of these practices for couples on Nuakata. After some months we realized that, although no couples flouted the convention about touching in public, many (especially younger couples) did not use the relational term *mwanegu* to address one another. Most circumvented this practice by using either nicknames or no names at all. When I questioned them about this, they explained that younger people found this term awkward and old-fashioned. Having grown up and gone to school together they (like us) were reluctant to speak with each other in such formal, respectful ways. Even so, they did not use their spouse's public name, and they always employed formal, relational terms of address when speaking with members of their spouse's *susu*.[13]

Wycliffe explained that a person (male or female) addresses the women that his or her spouse calls mother (*hinagu*) as *yagulauwa*. The men that his or her spouse calls father[14] are addressed as *bwasiyagu*. A same-sex sibling of his or her spouse is called *yagu'iva,* and a cross-sex sibling is called *'agu yaiyewa*. He or she can only address those sisters-

and brothers-in-law who are not consanguineal relatives of his or her spouse's *susu* by their public names. This is permitted only when the particular in-law is not otherwise related to that person. When the spouse's sibling is still a child, the person addresses him/her as *natugu,* and he or she in turn is addressed by the child as *tamagu* (my father) or *hinagu* (my mother) until the child reaches adulthood. Women who marry into a *susu* are called *hinevela,* men are called *wohiwa.* As with the naming conventions associated with use of *susu*/clan names the use of relational terms of address with one's in-laws and spouse expresses respect for and distinctions between people belonging to a *susu*/clan other than one's own.[15] These inviolable naming conventions, (p)reserved for *susu* and affines, drew attention to the centrality of relational forms of belonging on Nuakata, reinforcing the notion that *susu* belonging is necessarily defined in contradistinction to affinal kin.[16] A *susu* can only establish its unique identity in relation to and connection with other *susu.* Without these relations a *susu* cannot actually reproduce itself. Marriage to nonkin consolidates and further defines kin relationships by making the essentially dialectical relationship between identification and differentiation, similarity and difference visible, tangible.

For this reason marriage between people of the same clan, particularly those who can trace their descent from a shared ancestor, meets with strong disapproval and a loss of respect for the couple involved. Such marriages are regarded as incestuous, for rather than strengthening and regenerating the unique identity of the *susu*/clan they diminish it, forcing it to feed upon itself. To my knowledge there was only one marriage of this nature on Nuakata at the time of our stay. The couple in question had been married for ten years or so, and this despite attempts at the time of their marriage to prevent the relationship. Wycliffe's family were related as affines to the woman in this partnership, and while they liked her husband, they expressed their diminished respect for him by calling him by his name, rather than addressing him respectfully by the various terms to denote in-law/affinal relationships.

Making Place(s), Placing Belonging

Completion of our house not only brought to a close our very public sojourn at the church but also marked the end of an intense period of labor by Yalasi and some Bolime people on our behalf. Over a five-week period women wove the coconut palm mats for the external walls (*bili-*

bili) and ceiling of the house, while men collected and erected the necessary timbers from the bush: hardwoods for the stumps (*logidi*) and floor joists (*pulipuli*), split black or betel nut palm for the floor (*heva*), and saplings secured by vines (*'uwe* or *wetuhu*) for the rafters and wall braces. During this time we accompanied men on some of their many forays inland in search of bush materials. Beginning their treks on well-established trails, they soon left the paths behind and plunged deep into the bush, confidently forging ahead until they reached an area where specific trees or vines were known to be growing. Once located, these plants were chopped down, stripped of bark, then carried back aloft on men's shoulders through the tangle of undergrowth. What was to us a dense and seemingly impenetrable thicket of green and brown was a known, habitable, and negotiable world to our guides. These men knew the land, particularly their own *susu* and clan land, as I might know the streets, shops, houses, and gardens of a familiar urban landscape. They knew the land and its names just as many knew the names and something of the genealogy that connects each person to *susu*/clan land on the island.

All this constituted strenuous work in windless and oppressive February heat. As participant observers and direct beneficiaries of this collective labor we felt overwhelmed by people's generosity. Our completed house was a silent yet powerful testimony to this communal gift of labor and time, and to the relationships forged during and by its construction. The effort to build our house was made even more significant by the knowledge that men did not generally rely on group labor to build houses. It was considered an able man's responsibility to shelter himself and, where relevant, his spouse, children, and dependent (female or infirm) members of his *susu*. A man working alone on Nuakata would therefore find, chop, and carry the necessary timbers and vines from the bush and construct the house with only limited help from female kin (his spouse or members of his own *susu*) to make the walls and roof. For this reason new houses took many months, and in some instances years, to build. When a man sought help with the building of his house from male members of his *susu*, his wife and female kin were expected to provide meals for the workers. Where help was sought from non-*susu* men, payment of meals, tobacco, and money was made. Men were also primarily responsible for building other structures on Nuakata, including yam houses, shelves or tables for feasts or parties, small shelters for people to rest in their gardens, copra smoke houses, enclosures for pigs, canoes, and so on. In the past men also built small, one-room houses for new mothers to stay for the first months of the newborn baby's life. Commenting on men's broader responsibility for building on Gawa Island to the north, Munn states that "it is essentially men who construct bounded ... protective ... spaces. ... [W]omen are those protected by these masculine acts" (1986, 34). While men build essential, temporary dwellings on *susu* land, it is through women's labors in the garden, hamlet, and giving birth that the continuous occupation of this land by members of the *susu* is ensured.

To my knowledge, only church and school buildings, including pastors' and teachers' houses, have been built on Nuakata by unrecompensed communal labor. Home to communal activities or workers, these buildings were considered the responsibility of the community, particularly those who attended church or had children at school. Because my research activities were also believed to have a communal focus and benefit, the community as a whole agreed to build our house without cost. As it turned out, the people of Yalasi, coordinated by senior men living in or closely associated with Gohiya, assumed primary responsibility for the task. In building the house a sense of community—the community of Yalasi and Bolime, if not Nuakata—was re-created and reinforced. Once completed, however, the working group dissipated and returned to activities based in or around their own familial hamlets. With them went the visible, tangible, and practical sense of community created in the building work—so, too, our initial sense of belonging on Nuakata.

Although freely given, the gift of the house was made with some expectation of reciprocity. Along with their minimal daily payment of a small ration of tobacco in recognition of their efforts, people subsequently made requests for goods, knowing that their past labors obliged us to be generous. By freely responding to our state of dependence the workers staked a legitimate claim for our future assistance.[17] Seen in this light, people's contribution to the building of the house was calculated and strategic. Indeed, some people subsequently sought to exploit their initial acts of generosity by returning to our house time and again, simply to ask for goods. Such a materialist interpretation of these events, though, belies or, at the very least, fails to capture the subtleties of the experience. Though valid, it offers a diminished explanation of the "spirit of the gift," failing to appreciate both the expectation and the intention of some of the gift-givers and recipients in anything other than logical, rational terms. For in building the house people recognized our most basic need, and by satisfying that need honored us as they honored themselves. In this particular context, free giving was not an act that disavowed recognition and acknowledgment, but rather invited potential or ongoing interdependence. It remained for us to recognize their acts, to honor and, in some small way, reciprocate them.

Like many places throughout the Massim, houses on Nuakata were rectangular in shape and built on stumps (*logidi*) a meter or so above the ground, so that air could circulate freely through them. Ours was no exception. When high enough, the area underneath houses offered animals and people alike welcome respite from the sun or rain. Where possible, their gable roofs (*nuwanuwa*) were made of sewn sago palm leaves (*'atovi*) and their walls fashioned from the split stems of sago palms. These coverings were more durable than the coconut palm alternative, which lasted for only twelve to eighteen months. However, sago palm was not plentiful on the island, and people were often forced to use woven coconut palm as a more temporary covering for the outer walls and ceilings. Forced to survive high winds, tropical rain, intense heat, white ants, and the wear and tear associated with their human inhabitants, houses had a life span of five to ten years. While people repaired their houses, these repairs merely delayed rather than prevented their inevitable decay. Because Nuakatan houses were temporary sheltering places, left to wither away and rot when their useful life was over or when one of their occupants died, it was the land itself, rather than the structures built on it, that carried and sustained the shared, ongoing history of a given *susu*. In stories of the past, legends and ancestral histories, houses were merely incidental to the places and events described. In contrast, the land and its markers (distinctive trees, rocks, rock formations, caves, etc.) provided permanent sites of remembrance for a continuous past, present, and future history of *susu*, clans, and community.

Including an enclosed veranda, local houses commonly had three rooms separated by three-quarter-height internal sago palm walls. Therefore, with three rooms and a veranda, our house was by Nuakatan standards quite spacious. Despite our protests to the contrary, several senior men insisted that, like other *dimdim*, we needed a big house to store all our things. Moreover, they told us that, unlike Papuans, *dimdim* have a great need to be alone—a need that is satisfied by retreating inside their houses. Houses on Nuakata were used as sleeping, recuperative places rather than living, staying spaces. Most had a single open entrance (*'awa*), which could be covered by a woven coconut palm screen in the event of bad weather or if the residents were away. Some had a sandbox hearth inside, which was lit when the sleepers were cold or sick. People rarely ventured into or gathered inside each other's houses. With the exception of those such as Wycliffe and his father, who worked inside on Bible and hymn translations, houses were rarely used as working places. People generally only remained within houses during the day to rest or take shelter. The area around rather than inside houses formed the living/staying space for each hamlet. As such, the external rather than the internal boundaries of Nuakatan houses provided a backdrop or context for people to sit, smoke, chew betel nut, talk, eat, rest, and muse.

As well as its distinct size and proposed use, there were other features that rendered our house slightly different from the usual Nuakatan dwellings. Where local houses had simple pole ladders (*'amwaha*, path) at their entrance (*'awa*, mouth), ours had flat wooden stairs, with a carefully fashioned balustrade, built to reassure and stabilize the passage of tentative *dimdim* feet. The stairs opened out onto a small porch especially designed to offer shelter for people awaiting permission to enter. At the entrance to the house there was a decorated half-door with an internal wooden latch, described to us as a deterrent to dogs, children, and other unwanted guests. Generally, only the small, single-room trade stores on Nuakata had wooden doors with padlocks. When we protested that "we don't need to keep the children out," others older and wiser pointed to the children's unguarded gaze—their unrestrained fascination with us and our things. While embarrassed at first by these conspicuous representations of our difference, we later conceded that all these concessions befitted our needs.

Responsibility for the design and construction of our house fell to an elderly man from a neighboring village, a boatbuilder affectionately known as Carpenter. He gained his nickname as a result of his training in carpentry during World War II. Showing us through the house the day before we took possession, Carpenter suggested that one room was for sleeping, one for storing our things, another for working. He strongly suggested that we place a curtain across the door of our bedroom and the storage area, so that all our things could remain hidden from view. While Nuakatan houses generally had concealed storage spaces within them, it was unusual for them to have whole rooms designated for this purpose. Apart from anything else, people did not generally have enough belongings to warrant this use of space, storing food, such as yams, sweet potatoes, and pumpkins, in yam houses on the edge of hamlets.

Sleeping Place(s)

As someone long used to a private, if not secluded, sleeping space the sleeping areas in Nuakatan houses were immediately noticeable to me. Like in so many so-called third world places, couples with children—be they parents and children, or grandparents and grandchildren—generally slept within a single room with few, if any, windows. These were highly restricted places. Unless otherwise granted permission by the adults sleeping in the house, no one other than *susu* members entered this space.[18] People slept on individual sleeping mats woven from pandanus by adult women and older female adolescents. Few had sheets or mosquito nets to cover them. While most adults recognized the need to protect themselves and especially their children from mosquitoes,[19] nets were generally not considered a spending priority for people's extremely limited funds.

Where possible and convenient, sexually active young men slept in bachelor houses, separate from their parents, with brothers or cousin brothers. Sexually active, unmarried young women often had their own rooms within familial houses or slept in enclosed cooking areas. More rarely they slept in otherwise vacant hamlet houses. These sleeping arrangements recognized and facilitated conventional sexual, relational practices between unmarried men and women, explained to me by young and old people alike. Their descriptions matched those of Fortune ([1932] 1989, 22) for Dobu and Munn for Gawa (1986, 35–36). Arriving under the cover of night, when the inhabitants of the hamlet had retired to sleep, a young man would quietly join his girlfriend in her room or place. He would stay with her until the early hours of the morning, stealing away before dawn when those sleeping in the hamlet stirred. There was much incentive for him to escape the hamlet undetected, because if caught by the young woman's mother or maternal kin he could be forced to compensate members of her *susu* with gifts (of yams or other highly valued food) or to marry the young woman. What was an unrestricted place for the young man by night was a highly restricted place by day. Occurring under the cover of darkness, in enclosed yet barely private rooms, the intimate relationships of the night between unmarried men and women were ostensibly invisible in the light of day. Discussed only with very close friends, these (sexual) relationships were unable to be acknowledged in any public place, day or night, without causing disrespect to the couple and their kin.[20]

Like sexually active young women, newly married or childless couples such as Roger and I generally slept in their own room or, if possible, their own house in their respective natal hamlets. The need for a place—their own couple space—in each other's natal hamlet was deemed necessary, as young couples during the early years of marriage usually alternated their residence between their respective *susu* hamlets. Only when they had several children did they settle for more protracted periods of time on (generally) the wife's *susu* land. When I asked people to elaborate on the newlyweds' need for their own room or house when staying with kin, most looked at me as if I was stupid, their expressions implying, What can you be thinking—anyone and everyone knows young couples need their own, private space!

While certainly considered "important" at the time of our stay on Nuakata, newlyweds' need for a secluded place within each other's natal hamlet was, arguably, essential in the more distant past. Asked to remember aspects of this ill-defined "past," Eunice confirmed what anthropologists have described for other parts of the Massim (Battaglia 1990, 31, 108–18; Fortune [1932] 1989, 6; Lepowsky 1993, 107–8). When staying with their in-laws, newly married young women were expected to prepare food, cook, collect firewood, sweep hamlet spaces, and provide garden produce for their senior female in-laws. Among other activities, young men were expected to prepare gardens, make houses, and provide fish. Both were expected to contribute to the gift exchanges of pigs and yams made by their affinal kin during mortuary feasts and to fully participate in other collective endeavors engaged in by their spouse's *susu*, such as making sago (*labiya*). During the first year or so of marriage the young man/woman could not eat in sight of his or her in-laws, and was not even entitled to share the food produced by them. Food had to be "stolen" or secreted away by the spouse, to be eaten in private. He or she was also not permitted inside the houses in the spouse's natal hamlet and was expected to tread carefully and cautiously on the in-laws' hamlet land.[21] In short, marriage alone did not give newlyweds a respected relationship, place, and space among their affinal kin. This could only be gained by deferring and giving respect to their senior in-laws. After a year or so of marriage senior members of a *susu* would invite their new son- or daughter-in-law to eat with them. By permitting their young in-law to openly share food with them, senior in-laws declared the newlywed worthy of a legitimate place among their *susu*—as an insider/outsider prepared to work on behalf of the *susu*, rather than a stranger, neighbor, or friend. From that moment on, the newlywed could begin to move more freely (although not without some restriction) around his or her spouse's *susu* hamlets.

Reflecting on the past relationships between newlyweds and their senior affinal kin, Eunice described them as onerous. While she acknowledged that many of these practices were continuing on Nuakata in modified ways, she implied that senior people's expectations of their junior in-laws had significantly altered over the years. A newlywed junior in-law was still expected to prove him- or herself to be hardworking and uncomplaining when staying in his or her spouse's natal hamlet, otherwise he or she would become the subject of covert (and at times overt) criticism and gossip. While a junior in-law was no longer expected to eat "stolen" food in a secluded place within an affinal hamlet during the first year or so of the marriage, he or she was generally expected to take food from the pot or communal dish after everyone else. He or she should never appear greedy. Similarly, while a junior in-law had far more freedom to move about and congregate with affinal kin within their hamlet(s), he or she was not allowed the same freedom and confidence to move about in hamlet houses as those *susu* members who belonged there. Although some of the expressions of respect had changed or been abandoned over the years, the need to maintain respect for senior affines, and indeed all senior people within the community, kin and nonkin, remained unchanged. Until new spouses had demonstrated respect for their senior in-laws by proving themselves to be hardworking and uncomplaining they occupied a marginal position, status, and praxis in their spouse's natal hamlet.[22] When, later in the year, Nowel (Eunice's adopted son) and Susan married and came to live at Gohiya for a time, they had to negotiate and establish their place on Nowel's *susu* land in the ways Eunice had earlier described.

Several weeks prior to their marriage Wycliffe told us that when his father (Noah), returned from the church meeting at Bunama (southwest Normanby Island), Susan would come to live at Gohiya in recognition of their new, wedded status. While their intended marriage was news to us, it was not a complete surprise, for I had heard rumors from several women that Susan and Nowel were lovers. Several weeks earlier I had learned that Susan was pregnant. (She had one child by a previous marriage.) Wycliffe explained that "when they learned from Nowel that Susan was pregnant, his father, mother and Nowel's birth mother had met with Susan's relatives to discuss and organize the marriage." Neither

Susan nor Nowel was present at the meeting, and it was unclear to me what, if anything, they were told about its outcome. We were instructed to remain silent about these plans. Three or four days following Wycliffe's announcement, Noah returned from Bunama; still, though, no marriage occurred. Several weeks elapsed before Wycliffe arrived at our house early one morning with the news that "maybe Susan and Nowel got married last night."[23] He explained: "Yesterday as Susan was making her way back to her hamlet after church, Geteli (his sister) captured her. Susan was made to stay at Gogobohewa (Geteli's hamlet) until Nowel was brought there to take her back to Gohiya last night when it was dark." Once at Gohiya, Susan and Nowel slept together in the vacant house.

On the first day of their marriage Susan and Nowel remained together at Gohiya playing draughts all morning. This was a strange sight. Until that day Susan and Nowel had largely avoided or ignored each other in public. So this act in and of itself drew attention to their transformed relationship. In the early afternoon Nowel went off to work in his garden and Susan worked at Gohiya, preparing food for that hamlet's residents (i.e., her new in-laws). After the food preparation was completed, she swept the hamlet, washed dishes, collected firewood, and spent some time weaving new sleeping mats for herself and Nowel. When it became time to eat, she waited until everyone had sufficient food before taking some for herself. When I spoke with her later that day she explained that the marriage had occurred "according to custom." She had been surprised when Geteli "captured her," but she had been expecting something to happen—"either Nowel would have been forced to stay at her hamlet or she his." While she and Nowel had more or less chosen each other as marriage partners, they had not chosen the timing for this event. This decision rested with senior members of their respective *susu*.

Following their marriage, Susan and Nowel remained at Gohiya for five days. During this time Susan worked tirelessly around the hamlet, while Nowel went to his garden on a daily basis. Nowel's trips to the garden represented a significant change in his daily behavior. Until his marriage, Eunice had tended his garden. He had rarely ventured there, spending much of his days with his friends, playing soccer and volleyball, fishing, talking, making copra, looking for cuscus, and generally roaming about. All this changed immediately and dramatically after his marriage; so, too, his relationships with his friends and brothers. While he continued to talk and joke with them as before, he was no longer free to wander around (*'ilowolowohi*) with them,²⁴ but rather was busy proving himself to be hardworking and responsible. No one found this dramatic change remarkable, although some young men with whom I spoke mourned the implications of his newfound marriage status for their friendship with him.

After their stay at Gohiya, Susan and Nowel moved to Susan's hamlet Pahilele, on the Bolime side of the island. They took with them a basket of yams, a stem of betel nut, and a rooster. These were gifts from Nowel's *susu* to Susan's. After these gifts were presented, a small party, arranged and attended by members of Susan's *susu*, was held for the newlywed couple. When Susan and Nowel returned to stay at Gohiya one month later, they brought with them a return gift for Nowel's *susu*, one that perfectly matched the original offering. Wycliffe stated that by matching the gifts equally the different *susu* showed respect for one another and recognized the mutually beneficial relationship created by the joining of one *susu* to another. Accordingly, for Susan's *susu*, not only did Susan and Nowel's marriage and pregnancy make it possible for Susan to reproduce a birth family of her own but, more important, it ensured the continuation of their *susu* in future generations. By making gardens, looking after children, and assisting members of Susan's *susu*, Nowel would also contribute to the care and sustenance of Susan's *susu*. For Nowel's *susu*, Nowel's labors with and for his in-laws could, if performed conscientiously, create a sense of indebtedness that his in-laws would feel compelled to recognize and redress. As Macintyre (1983) writes in connection with Tubetube, this sense of indebtedness may be counterbalanced by the bestowal of usufructuary land rights to the non-*susu* male—a gift that enhances his place among *susu* and affines alike. Susan's labors for Nowel's *susu* were also potentially significant, as they could relieve the burden of cooking, gardening, cleaning, and contributing to feasts carried by senior affines.

Talking Place(s)

Standing together with Carpenter on the veranda of our house the day before we moved, he explained that, unlike the rest of our house, it was a place for people to come and sit. Verandas were a common feature of Nuakatan houses, but generally only inclement weather rendered them communal spaces. Built for a communal purpose, it was perhaps not surprising, then, that—whatever the weather—our enclosed veranda was subsequently used as a gathering place. And, unlike many other people—particularly older men, and women of all ages—the men who worked on the house subsequently felt free to congregate there without any sense of embarrassment, presumption or trespass. Similarly, young people also felt free to congregate on the verandas in the young men's house at Gohiya, the junior pastor's cookhouse at Asaʻailo church, or indeed other "bachelor" houses located elsewhere on the island. There they talked soccer, told stories, played cards or draughts, or listened to music with friends. Married people, whatever their age, shared no such ease inside the houses of their affines or friends. Their activities and freedom to associate wherever they wished seemed constrained by marital, affinal, and *susu* responsibilities. Those houses where married or senior adults and their children slept seemed highly restricted places. Only those who slept in them had freedom to move within their confines. Others, including other *susu* members, moved within them only upon invitation.

Cooking Place(s)

Once our house was completed and just before we moved in, a small three-walled kitchen (cooking shelter) was erected beside it. Built at ground level on a bed of dirty gray sand, this shelter was, at different times, claimed as a home by several flea-infested dogs and extravagantly colored snakes. Of these, the fleas were the most successful and persistent squatters. The floor was subsequently covered by crushed coral in an effort to still the fine clouds of dirt stirred up by the slightest movement of people or animals. Although small by Nuakatan standards, our cooking shelter was by no means unusual. Many hamlets had enclosed cooking houses, several, including Carpenter's, with makeshift ovens made from concrete and/or tin drums. Cooking pots, enamel dishes, and an assortment of crockery were also stacked inside these areas on specially built shelves made from coconut palm. So, while our cooking house was not unusual, it was more common for people to cook outside on a fire lit between three stones, positioned in a sheltered area close to the house. Because the area close to the fire was often a focal point for people to come and sit, and because sparks from fires represent a threat to people's houses, women kept these areas meticulously clean, constantly clearing away food scraps and other debris. Such cleaning efforts were complemented by scavenging hamlet pigs, dogs, chickens, and, occasionally, cats.

The decision as to where to place a cooking fire was generally made by the women of the hamlet. Rolling the three stones into a triangular configuration, roughly eight inches apart, they nonchalantly rocked them to and fro until satisfied that their position would ensure optimal heat and stability for the cooking pots. When Roger and I first attempted to position stones in this way, our efforts were met with laughter and disbelief by several onlooking women. Incredulous, they were at a loss to explain why such a simple activity, so taken for granted by them, was so difficult for us. What was a fluid, seemingly unthinking activity for them was for us a measured and quite difficult task—one requiring several attempts and much discussion. When we attempted to solicit these and other women's knowledge and expertise about making good fires, they only laughed more and urged us to watch and then copy them when they did it again. Where we attempted to extract and abstract knowledge, rules, and guidelines for making good fires, they simply urged us to make one—to know by doing (see Jackson 1989, 119–55). Much the same occurred when we initially attempted to light fires, scrape coconut flesh, when I peeled and cut vegetables or supported small baskets on or from my head. Our ways—more particularly my ways, for all these activities were typically engaged in by female children and young and older women on Nuakata—lacked local women's rhythm, style, and strength. My movements embodied the differences between us—differences in doing, living, and knowing that arose in the present, but embodied a distinct past and foreshadowed distinct futures. For example, I was told that I could not carry heavy baskets on my head for I had not done this as a small girl and young adult as local women had done. Therefore, I could not hope to carry heavy baskets at my age. Basket carrying aside, I could transcend some of the differences in doing, living, and knowing between myself and other women by making fires, collecting appropriate firewood, and, eventually, by making fires as they did. My participation in activities typically associated with women on Nuakata was encumbered by my ethnographic agenda to decipher or entice people to reveal the meaning or symbolic significance of the activity we were engaged in—to separate out what is known through the body and what is understood by the mind. This even when I, like Jackson, rejected a way of thinking about symbols that

> ranks the idea over the event or object, while privileging the expert who deciphers the idea even though he or she may be quite unable to

use the object or participate in the "symbolic" event. In short, I object to the notion that one aspect of a symbol is prior to or foundational of the other. . . . In my view, utterances and body movements betoken the continuity of body-mind, and it is misleading to see the body as simply a representation of a prior idea or implicit cultural pattern. Persons actively body forth the world; their bodies are not passively shaped by or made to fit the world's purposes. As Merleau-Ponty puts it, "Consciousness is in the first place not a matter of 'I think that' but of 'I can.'" (Jackson 1989, 136)

Seeing Places

Aware that *"dimdim* like windows," Carpenter had asked us how many we wanted and where we would like them placed in the house. Mindful of the need for ventilation and, as he had discerned, wanting to look outward, to glimpse the beautiful view of ocean and trees, to observe what was going on around us, we asked for five windows. Carpenter's expression of surprise indicated that we had asked for more than even he had anticipated, more than he considered necessary or appropriate. Local houses had few windows. Conversations with Eric (the island's land mediator and a practitioner of local medicine) and Wycliffe suggested that this may be a legacy of the fragile yet lingering belief—perhaps more aptly described as a doubtful suspicion—that flying witches enter houses at night while people are sleeping, causing sickness to some or all of the inhabitants. This, I was told, was one reason why people preferred not to sleep alone. Eric and Wycliffe claimed that some people attempted to prevent these unwelcome intrusions by making protective magic to render their houses invisible to these malevolent spirits.

Wanting our house to be close to the beach, we had asked Carpenter and the other senior men to construct it about thirty meters from the water's edge and with windows facing the sea. The other four houses in Gohiya at the time were clustered together close to the undergrowth, toward the foot of a large hill. Worried our house (if positioned where we had suggested) would be buffeted by cyclonic winds and lashed by rain coming in off the sea, the senior men decided to build it midway between the shore and the other houses. In the end, none of the windows faced the sea. When high winds and sheeting rain arrived sometime in April, we quickly understood why many of our requests about window placement had been ignored. We realized too that, as people live outside and around rather than inside their houses, decisions about the number and placement of windows are not determined by the need to maximize natural light or provide the most favorable, unrestricted outlook from the house!

It was not until much later in the year, though, and in a very different context, that I began to appreciate how strange our request for a framed vision of the sea must have seemed to our hosts. Often when walking with people, resting on a ridge or saddle of a hill before making our descent, my companions invariably stood on the path, head down catching their breath, while I, more exhausted than they, would wander off to take in the view of the undergrowth below and the sea, dotted by distant islands, stretching out to the horizon. On one such occasion—a fine, sun-drenched day—Wycliffe, Roger, and I stood on the ridge overlooking the bejeweled waters of Hapelaʻawaʻawa bay, on the northwest side of the island. The trees in the foreground acted as a frame to our view of the dazzling bay. Taken by the beauty of this scene, Roger and I were surprised when our exclamations to this effect were met with indifference from Wycliffe. The conversation that followed underscored the multidimensional nature of his (in)difference.

Wycliffe explained that people on Nuakata rarely noticed or drew attention to the beauty of the scene, partly because these scenes were familiar, and therefore unnoticed, but also because the word they might use to say that something looks good (*namwanamwa*) is not equivalent to the English word *beautiful*. Rather, it means "good, right, and proper relations," something like "in harmony with." Wycliffe implied that the view from afar, the view looking down upon—indeed, the whole idea of a detached view of a beautiful vista—was not highly valued on Nuakata. This, it seemed, was not their preferred perspective. He added that people would rather be paddling on the sea, or in it, fishing, diving, or (especially the children) swimming. Only then might they feel moved to exclaim of the sea that "its appearance is good" (*ʻana ʻita namwanamwana*).

These reflections were as much a comment about a participatory relational aesthetics as they were a participatory knowledge and knowing. They brought to mind Jackson's experience with his daughter when doing fieldwork in Firawa.

> Not long after beginning fieldwork in Firawa in 1969, I, a creature of a deeply ingrained cultural habit, climbed the hill overlooking the village to *get things into perspective* by distancing myself from them. From the

hilltop, I surveyed the village, took panoramic photographs, and achieved my bird's-eye view, believing that my superior position would help me gain *insights* into the organization of the village, when, in fact, it was making me lose *touch* with it. Ten years later I was living in Firawa with my wife and daughter, Heidi. One evening Heidi and I climbed the hill above the village. No one else ever did . . . I asked Heidi what she thought of the view. "It's all right," she said, "except you can't see anyone in the village from here." And indeed there was no human movement visible; only the smoke from cooking fires. (1989, 8, emphasis in original)

Jackson notes that ten years together with long experience living with people in the village had given him a different orientation to both the village and to knowledge and knowing. In this time, and through his lived experiences with these people, he had "cease[d] to be a detached observer and become a part of Firawi" (Jackson 1989, 8). He "recognized the village as a second home," as a *"lived space"* that can be understood from within and among, rather than looking (down) upon it from above and afar (see de Certeau 1988). Following Dewey (1929), Bourdieu (1977), Fabian (1983), and Foucault (1980), among a coterie of others, he eschewed "the spectator theory of knowledge," the theory of knowledge that privileged vision as a means of knowing and controlling how and what can be known. Instead, he sought a means of understanding that relies on all five senses and arises from lived experience. He sought to reclaim an understanding of knowledge as a "mode of being-together-with" (Jackson 1989, 8), of living together with.

All this caused me to think again about windows, the way windows are used in Nuakatan houses and the way Roger and I used the windows in our house. As people rarely stayed in their houses during the day, there was little opportunity or inclination for them to look out from within on what was happening outside. Indeed, as Wycliffe's comments about the view suggested, this was clearly not their preferred perspective. But when, on the odd occasion, someone did look out from a window, his or her body would invariably be extended outside as far as possible, minimizing the distance between the self and the world outside and eliminating some of the restrictions to vision posed by the window frame. Necessary for ventilation, windows were also used to throw or pass things in and out of houses. As such, these framed spaces did not represent impermeable divisions between the inside and outside of the house. As our time on Nuakata progressed Roger and I also found ourselves using them in this way. In fact, apart from our early weeks at Gohiya, we rarely used our windows to look out at what was going on, preferring to move out of the house to look and/or participate in what was happening. Used for looking out upon the outside world, our windows positioned us inside and at a distance from the people and places beyond their frames. It seemed that our original desire for windows, reflecting an impulse to observe living places at a distance, to map rather than live in or embody the place, was receding.

Living Places

Known as *ba'uba'uyai*, the area in front of houses and adjacent to the path that circumnavigates the island was communal space where people gathered freely without inhibition or restraint. The area in front of our house and behind the other houses at Gohiya was no exception. A particularly large, sandy space, it was perfect for volleyball games, kick-to-kick soccer, or marbles. Later in the year some of the children played night chasy between the darkness and a beam of light cast onto the space by our Coleman lamp. When games of volleyball involving large numbers of young people occurred there, older men and women would posit themselves on the margins of this space, in the shade of a tree or under the young men's house at Gohiya. Seated there, talking, laughing, or making asides about the games, they invariably ground away at betel nuts using a diverse assortment of mortars and pestles, the slow, rhythmical pounding of nuts providing a counterpoint to the frenetic movement of the players.

In contrast to the *ba'uba'uyai* space in front of our house, the area behind it (close to a small creek) was not treated as a communal area. With the exception of Wycliffe's family, people only ventured there if Roger or I was present. Although perhaps more cautious and tentative in relation to our house and its immediate surrounds, people's movements in nonfamilial hamlets were marked by a similar observance of palpable yet invisible boundaries. For example, if the land between houses was a communal path, then people walking through the hamlet congregated in these areas without hesitation. However, in hamlets where this was not the case, generally only *susu*, affinal relatives, close friends, and in some cases neighbors moved freely yet respectfully in these familiar spaces. Non-kin tended to wait for an invitation, be it verbal or nonverbal, to enter enclosed or semienclosed hamlet cooking areas. This was especially true when people were eating. Neighbors or visitors hovered around on the margins or wandered off, waiting for the meal's completion before joining them.

Clearly, these boundaries between the inside and outside of the house, the front and back of the hamlet, or between houses were not static or fixed. They remained permeable to *susu,* semipermeable to affinal kin, and a discernible restraint to all the other visitors who entered a given hamlet. But they reflect even more subtle matrilineal relationship divisions and distinctions than this suggests. As already alluded to, boundaries shift according to a person's age, current relational status, and also the particular occasion or time of day or year. Only the *susu* of a given hamlet can facilitate boundary crossings for nonkin visitors. Transgression of these boundaries by adults is most often expressed by gestures of disapproval and the language of silence. Children and visiting anthropologists alike learn these boundaries through experience, over time.

Battaglia (1990, 31) claims that on Sabarl, hamlet spaces and dwellings are gendered places. For example, she states that the interior of hamlet houses is "the domain of feminine activity and influence" as is the "shady underside of the house where women gather to talk and tend their children." In contrast, the "bright, hot exterior space, and all that is public, including the shell of the house" are said to have "masculine connotations" (1990, 32). On Nuakata I found no clear evidence of a simple public/private gendered division of space. Males and females alike moved through hamlet spaces with similar constraints and freedom. Certainly gardens were women's domain, the site of their knowledge, expertise, and work. Even these, though, were not exclusively female realms. Men always assisted in garden preparation, and many married men tended their own yam, sweet potato, or tapioca gardens. Perhaps it could be argued, however, that areas within a given hamlet are gendered spaces at specific times of the day or in specific contexts. For example, women rise early, often long before men, and wash dishes left from the meal on the previous night. Clothing may be washed, fires lit, and food prepared long before others rise. In this sense it is a female time of day, oriented around the hearth, the clothesline, and the shelf where dishes are stored. Similarly, during parties in which food is prepared, women hover around the rear of the hamlet, near the kitchen or hearth while the food is cooking.

Men usually stay well clear of these areas and activities, except if they are directly involved in killing, butchering, or cooking pigs.

Walking Place(s)

Paths (*'amwaha*)[25] lead into and out of hamlets in all directions. Some connect with the main path that traces its way around the island. Others lead directly to gardens, neighbor's hamlets, or areas where people defecate and urinate. Still other paths weave their way inland, over mountain saddles to the other sides of the island. People use communal paths linking the various sides of the island, even where these paths deviate through or cross hamlet land. Tracks linking neighboring hamlets are generally used by their respective inhabitants. Although other people are free to use these paths, they usually enter non-*susu* hamlets by the most communal route. Paths to gardens are used by the owners and custodians of the land (*susu* and their immediate affinal kin). Others are not strictly forbidden to venture on them, but they would rarely have good cause to take themselves to nonkin land. People say that in the past, and to a limited extent today, many people protected their gardens and the paths leading to them with magic. Non-kin outsiders must, therefore, approach these areas with some trepidation or, at the very least, respect for they risk persistent illness if they become ensnared in this magic. Paths leading up into the bush where people defecate or urinate are used by *susu* and affinal kin. Visitors may venture inland for these purposes, but they generally use communal land or return to their own land to relieve themselves.

And so, while paths connect or join people to places and one another, they also divide the social and physical landscape, testifying to matrilineal organization and communal relationships that inscribe differences on the land. Paths are boundary markers, but they are also transitional spaces. Distinctions between the four sides of the island, kin and nonkin, friend and acquaintance, neighbor and nonneighbor, communal and familial, are not only encoded on these pathways but also reinforced by people's movement along them. Paths that by day hold little fear for the traveler may become places of fear and dread for the lone walker at night. Movement, plays of light, smell, sounds, and undergrowth spill over into these cleared spaces posing an unseen, invisible threat. In this context fear is grounded in the belief, or surviving remnants of the belief, that witches roam these paths at night, seeking out and performing bad magic upon the vulnerable walker.

Moving Place(s): Making House(s) (a) Living Space

On the actual day of our move to Gohiya we rose early and hastily packed away our sleeping gear. By the time we had finished breakfast, a small crowd of helpers had arrived—members of Wycliffe's family and their immediate neighbors. As box after box was carried out of the church house, a steady procession of our possessions trailed along the path to Gohiya. Embarrassed by this conspicuous display of material belongings, I hid inside the pastor's house, ostensibly dismantling our mosquito net. As I fiddled with the net, an earlier conversation with Wycliffe gnawed away at me. When asked about the difference between Nuakatans and *dimdim* he commented with words to the effect that

> during the 1940s a Papuan man was sentenced to death in Port Moresby. In his defence he produced two sweet potatoes: one brown, one white. Cutting them in half, showing them to the crowd, he said, "You see, both are red inside." This is what I think about *dimdim* and Papuans—they are different on the outside, but on the inside they share the same blood. Apart from this, the main difference between *dimdim* and Papuans is things. *Dimdim* have more things for themselves. We sometimes call Papuans who get and keep things for themselves *dova dimdim* [like white people].

Wycliffe had stated what Carpenter had implied in the design of our house: that the way things are possessed constitutes the most significant difference between Papuans and *dimdim*. It is not merely that *dimdim* have more things, but, more important, that they get and keep, procure and store this "more" for themselves. Thinking about his comments later that day as we unpacked the boxes of food in the storage room and positioned the trunk of books on the veranda, I realized that in many ways our belongings both constituted and constrained our sense of belonging on Nuakata. Unsure of local food supplies and believing it presumptuous to expect people to feed us, we had arrived on Nuakata with enough rice, tinned fish, coffee, and tea to sustain ourselves for eight weeks.

As it turned out, our decision was vindicated, for a drought in the previous year had delivered an extremely poor harvest. For the first three months of our stay people mainly ate tapioca, coconut, and, in the first six weeks, a small amount of seasonal fruit. Fishing was irregular during this time. While seemingly necessary, our "things" effectively rendered us independent, self-sufficient, and without genuine need of other people's support. In other words, our things assumed the place of people; they replaced or substituted for people, especially kin. Perhaps this explained why people had not yet questioned us about Australia and, more particularly, our families in Australia; why at times we felt like we were considered totally independent, autonomous people who had materialized from nowhere and no one in particular. Perhaps people believed that we treated our anonymous possessions as constitutive, inalienable, or indissociable aspects of our selves; that we possessed our things like they possess body parts, spirit, *susu*, clan, and affinal relationships. Our things, rather than the relationships that produced them, were our belongings. Relations with inanimate things rather than animate people defined and identified us; it seemed our things erased the desire, or at least need, for relationships. (Possession of this kind is not to be imagined as proprietal; see Strathern 1988, 158.) Although this was all mere speculation on my part, it served to remind me that if we were to realize our hope for a newfound sense of belonging, the way we negotiated our relationship to the things in our possession would be crucial.

Living at Gohiya at the time of our move was Wycliffe's mother, Eunice, a woman in her early fifties, birth mother of eight, adoptive mother of one, and the most senior member of the matrilineage staying in the hamlet.[26] The land at Gohiya belonged to her *susu* and, more broadly, the Bo'e or Black Crow clan—the smallest of the five clans represented on the island. Across the island there are seven hamlets currently located on Bo'e territorial land. Many years earlier Eunice's matrilineal forebears had secured the land at Gohiya by making a gift of pigs, yams, *mwali* (Kula arm shells), and *bagi* (Kula necklaces) to the original owners (see Macintyre 1983). It was unclear to me how binding this exchange would be in the future. While in the past this was a conventional means of transferring land between clans, the land mediator, Eric, informed me that arrangements such as these were now a common source of dispute and conflict between clans across Nuakata.

Eunice, her elder sister Malida, and elder brother Hosea were themselves the senior owners of significant tracts of Yalasi land. In 1991 they gave some of this land to the Yalasi church at Asa'ailo, and some had been acquired by other *susu*/clans, as Eunice's forebears had done for Gohiya. Eunice's *susu* occupied four hamlets on their land: Gogobohewa, where her brother lived; Gohiya; Hagovi 1, where Malida and her husband, Antiya, lived; and Hagovi 2. Of these, Gohiya—located in the middle and separated from the others by a ten-minute walk and several neighboring hamlets on either side—was the focal hamlet, at least during our stay on Nuakata. This, though, was not the case in past generations. Eunice indicated that Gogobohewa was the place where the family first settled on the island—the place where memories of their forebears coalesced. Some of these memories she preferred to forget. Based at Gogobohewa, her mother's generation were notorious sorcerers and witches, "humbug people" by Eunice's account. In settling at Gohiya, and not Gogobohewa, Eunice had determined to put distance between herself and the past relationships and practices of some of her forebears.

Also living at Gohiya at the time of our move was Eunice's husband, Noah, whose maternal and paternal kin came from Bunama on the south coast of Normanby Island. A church elder and former primary school teacher, he spent his days writing hymns, doing Bible translation work, attending church meetings, baby-sitting one or more of his grandchildren, and occasionally assisting his wife in one of her gardens. Although a senior member of his own matrilineage, Noah had lived at Gohiya for over thirty years. His story was by no means unusual among those men who had come to Nuakata to live when they married. Newly married couples generally move between the husband's and the wife's village for the first years of their marriage. They often stay for several months in one place, maybe longer, before shifting again. But when people such as Noah marry partners from other islands they tend to stay in each other's place for extended periods of time before moving. This pattern may continue for many years until they have many children, at which point the couples tend to establish themselves on the land of the wife's *susu*, either in an existing village or a new one.

Gohiya was then also home to three of Eunice and Noah's six sons—Washington (twenty-seven, divorced);[27] Roger (Waligeha) (twenty-four); Nowel (twenty-three)—and their grandson, Sydney, aged nine. Noah, Eunice, and Sydney slept in one house, while the three young men slept in another. Eunice and Noah's youngest child (a daughter, Eba, fifteen) was living on the mainland at Alotau, where she attended Cameron High School. Their second-born daughter Jane (twenty-eight) and her husband, John, were attending a Bible college at Bunama on Normanby Island. They returned to Gohiya during term holidays. At that time their seventh-born child—a son, Misaki (twenty-two)—was living with senior Waligeha, his wife Sinetana, and their daughter Viki (thirteen), a ten-minute walk away at Hagovi. For several weeks at a time the fifth-born child of Eunice and Noah, Douglas (twenty-five)—together with his wife, Penina, and their two small children, Bunedia (six) and Jema (two)—would come to stay. And a month or so after our move, Wycliffe returned to Gohiya to live. Eunice gardened, cooked, and washed for them all!

These fluid living arrangements were by no means uncommon on Nuakata. Apart from the daily responsibilities and obligations associated with subsistence and child care, *susu* and affinal relationships ebb and flow with the weather and the seasons. The harvest of highly valued and storable root crops, such as yams, sweet potato, taro, and pumpkin, occurs in the months between July and September/October. At this time women are often assisted in their gardens (*'oyai*) by their spouses, older children, and other *susu* men. Prior to the harvest proper, husbands and/or *susu* men may build a new yam/food house to store the crop. In the months following the harvest, from October through January, new gardens are cleared, burned, and organized in preparation for the planting of the new crop. It is primarily men's responsibility to prepare new gardens, and as this involves extremely strenuous activity, *susu* and affinal men work together to clear the land—felling and burning the trees and undergrowth. Women assist the men as they work and also provide food for all the workers. At this time of year it is work that draws families together. December, January, and February are generally very hot, still months. Women rise even earlier than usual and go alone to their gardens, returning to the village before the hottest part of the day. Afternoons are often spent sitting in the shade talking and chewing betel nut with neighbors and kin. Children play together in the water, men may dive on the reefs, and, if there is a breeze, young men go sailing in their *sailau*, or sailing canoes. Cyclonic weather patterns are a feature of the months between April and October. This is also the season for the southeast wind—a wind that sweeps across both the Yalasi and Bolime sides of the island. During this time strong winds often prevent men from fishing, thereby significantly reducing the level of protein in people's diet.

In the days and weeks immediately following the move to Gohiya a tide of depression swept over Roger and me. Having anticipated intimacy with Wycliffe's family, that we would experience a newfound sense of belonging, we were initially disappointed. For at least two or three weeks we were given a wide and respectful berth by the older generation, particularly Wycliffe's mother and big mother who did not venture near our house. Not knowing our place with Wycliffe's mother and father, we in turn remained at a distance, making only very tentative gestures toward them when they were sitting/staying close to their house at the rear of the hamlet. During this time Roger continued to be called *'waligeha* by Wycliffe's family and affines, and I became nameless to most adults, *dimdim* to the children, and on occasions *'waligeha* or *'waligeha mwanena* (namesake's wife) to Wycliffe's kin. Our place, our belonging among Wycliffe's *susu,* remained undefined and undeclared. Still holding to a rather essentialist, proprietal view of land and self, we had assumed that people's and, especially, our belonging resided in locating themselves/ourselves on the land, rather than in the living relationships between *susu* and affines forged on, in, and through the land.

No longer distracted by the house building and regular trips across to the aid post, I was also forced to confront the full irony of my situation. Doing a project primarily committed to the study of women, I found myself in a hamlet where I was one of two females! Added to this, my research assistant was a male, and I was potentially a fictive affine! Although I could see the humor of my situation, and although I knew that my plight was by no means uncommon for fieldworkers, this knowledge did not relieve my dilemma. I was uncertain what to do next. How and with whom could I do as women do on Nuakata?

For a long time after our move, Eunice's work, like the work of other women, remained more or less invisible to me. Rising around daybreak, she often greeted the day before her tardy and contrary roosters and long before others in the village. Staggering from my bed after these same perverse roosters had gathered under our house to announce a dawn already past, I would look out the window, only to catch sight of Eunice, bush knife in hand and *boha* (garden bag) on her back, setting out for one of her gardens. Behind her, washing would be done and left hanging limply on the line. The dishes from the evening meal would also be washed and stacked to dry. All this before her husband, five sons, and grandson had barely stirred. Not so in Geteli's hamlet Gogobohewa, a kilometer away. There Geteli and her husband, Justin, were woken early by the demands of a hungry breast-fed baby and four other small children. Where possible, one or occasionally both of them would steal away to their gardens around dawn, returning in the early morning before Linda, their eldest child, had left for school. When the weather was favorable, Justin often paddled his canoe out of the bay and fished while the water was still calm. Otherwise gardening was postponed to around 7:30 or 8:00 A.M., when the children had eaten and Noah, their maternal grandfather, was able to look after the baby. While I often did not see Geteli trek to one of her gardens on the steep slopes at the back of Gohiya, the lilting sound of Noah singing a lullaby over and over again to the baby told me she was there.

Given Eunice's obvious work load, I was reluctant to add to her burden by trailing along beside her as she went about her daily tasks. And opportunities were few to accompany my immediate neighbors on their regular treks to the garden. Like Eunice, they rose around dawn and set out alone for their gardens to complete their work before the rising sun brought the full heat of the day. Paths that just prior to dawn carried a traffic of single young men returning from their sexual forays in the hamlets of their girlfriends were suddenly alive with young and old women intent upon the garden work that lay ahead of them. Many hours later these same women returned, often cast in a stoop by the weight of garden produce bursting from *boha'wo,* bags strung around their shoulders and foreheads. No one rushed to relieve their burden, for it was considered theirs alone to carry. Longing to accompany them to these invisible yet seemingly bountiful places and eager to learn about this pivotal aspect of their daily work I approached Geteli, who had befriended me, and asked if I could accompany her when she went to her gardens. Geteli was bemused by my request. "Why?" she said. "Because I want to see and understand your work," I managed to reply in faltering Alina Nu'ata. Geteli exclaimed with words to the effect, "But there is nothing to see!" Laughing, she agreed to take me several days later. That day came and went without the trip eventuating. My disappointment was relieved by the knowledge that, like Eunice, Geteli's heavy work load, caring for and feeding her five children, husband, maternal uncle Hosea, and elderly adoptive father, was constant. Her days were filled with gardening, food preparation, washing dishes and clothes in the creek, breast-feeding, and tending to the sporadic needs of her other children. Undeterred, I decided to make another arrangement with her; and I also decided to ask Sineliko—a young woman who lived in a neighboring hamlet.

Chapter Five

≥⊊

Planting the Past, Tending the Future

Following Wycliffe's recounting of the Bulelala story and his comments that "yams are like children," that, like people, "they have spirit" (see chap. 3), I speculated that on Nuakata pregnancy was analogous to gardening.[1] My reading of Massim ethnographies bolstered this working hypothesis, for example, Battaglia's comments that people on Sabarl "think of their growing food, [and particularly yams] as being 'like children'" (1990, 94). As gardeners they consider themselves to be nurturing parents who will be nurtured, in turn, by their offspring or produce. Similarly, Thune (1990) writes of Loboda village, Duau, that yams are spoken of as human beings and, as such, possess spirit. In describing the sacred quality of gardens on Dobu, Fortune declares that yams are considered "humans in metamorphosis" ([1932] 1989, 95); they are "personal beings in metamorphized forms" (101). Only those possessing knowledge of garden rituals know how this transformation occurred within their own matrilineage. Each *susu* passes on to its members (male and female alike) its own strain of seed yams. When people marry they plant their own seed yams in separate gardens from those of their spouses, thereby ensuring that their seeds remain within, and may be continuously passed down, their matrilineage.

Aware of this, and because in Alina Nu'ata the word for pregnancy, *hiuma*, means "they plant in the ground or under the soil,"[2] I reasoned that an intimate knowledge of planting would beget local knowledge of pregnancy. It would provide insight into the relations between men and women, *susu* and affine, mother and child, enacted and expressed through childbirth. Most important, I hoped that gardening and birthing knowledge and practices on Nuakata would express local understanding of the gendered person/self. I needed to understand knowledge and practices associated with pregnancy, contraception, birth, *and* gardening (e.g., garden selection, preparation, weeding, harvesting), taking careful note of who plants what, how, when, and for whom. For this reason, among others, I wanted—needed—to accompany Geteli, Sineliko, and Eunice on their treks to their gardens. Although founded on insubstantial evidence, this hypothesis subsequently functioned as a concealed reference point for my parallel investigations of Nuakatan gardening, pregnancy/childbirth knowledge, and practices.

Pregnancy and Kastom

Soon after our move to Gohiya I spoke with Susan, who was then aged twenty-one, divorced, and the single mother of a son, Rex, aged three. Susan volunteered to speak with me about her experience of pregnancy and childbirth. I asked her, "Are there any things that you do, any foods that you don't eat, or any special customs that you have when you are pregnant?" Focusing on the things that she did while pregnant, she replied in Alina Nu'ata:

> When I [am] pregnant (*yahiuma*) I don't walk about too much. I walk only in the daytime and then I return to my village. I cannot walk at night in case I accidentally break a spider's web. Also, I cannot eat food that is forbidden. I cannot eat fish. If I eat it, then an accident might happen.

In this conversation Susan spoke of "doing" or "enacting" pregnancy—*yahiuma* (I pregnant). Although a common way of describing pregnancy on Nuakata (i.e., as a stative verb), women also referred to pregnancy as a state or condition that is their semialienable possession: '*agu hiuma* (my pregnancy). Like food planted, grown, and later ingested by the gardener and her kin, the active state of pregnancy transforms the woman as she, in turn, transforms it. Pregnancy was temporarily of, but not completely indissociable from, the (pregnant) woman. Susan refrained from eating fish, shellfish, and squeezed food during pregnancy, for she knew they would make herself and her unborn child sick. When asked, she could not explain these customary practices, imparted by her mother and sister during her pregnancy. Susan practiced these customs without contemplating their possible meaning or wider cultural significance. These, she said, were the only customs associated with pregnancy that she practiced.

Later in the year, however, when she had remarried, was two or three months pregnant, and was living at Gohiya, Susan also demonstrated her belief in the relationship between place and maternal health during pregnancy. Having lived at Gohiya for several weeks, she became ill. On Eunice's advice she returned to her matrilineal hamlet at Bolime. Explaining the move, Eunice told me that a pregnant woman should stay in, or return to, her natal hamlet when she feels sick. Even if the pregnant woman is not sick during pregnancy, she should return to her hamlet to give birth. Both the woman and her unborn baby will be healthier when staying in their own hamlet, with members of their *susu*. Female members of her *susu* will care for her and tend her gardens if she is too sick or too big to work. When pressed for a reason why, she simply said, '*wuwuna yadi dalava*' (because it's their hamlet). Although she did not elaborate, it seemed that not only does the unborn child already belong to its mother's *susu*, but it has a place within her womb and the *susu* hamlets where she lives, stays, and belongs. Carried by its mother, the unborn child stays where she stays, belongs where she belongs, is grown by the food grown on her land.

Seeking to understand Susan's fear of walking at night and breaking the spider's web, I asked Eunice to explain this custom. Dismissive, she described it as a belief akin to superstition. Later in the year, Mari—a woman in her mid-twenties who was then about seven months pregnant with her third child—gave the following explanation.

> If we are walking about and a spider's web gets us, then when its our time for giving birth we will not be able to give birth properly. The baby will go down and get stuck. That's why we don't go for a spin at night, because if the spider gets us it will make us bad. That belief remains with the older women, but now in this time the "light" has increased, prayer has become meaningful to each one of us and so when we go for a spin at night and the spider gets us, it will be all right when we give birth. Before, in the time of our ancestors, it was bad. At that time they forbade women, if they were pregnant, from walking around in the night. This time it's a bit all right.

By Mari's account, her ancestors thought that spiders' webs effectively, if not actually, penetrate the bodies of pregnant women, ensnaring their unborn children, thereby preventing birth. More recently, however, the power of these ideas has diminished as a result of people's belief in a Christian god. They no longer need fear the night, for they walk in the light of God's care. Because of her belief in God, then, Mari did not follow customary practices in relation to pregnancy. While she did not doubt the power of these ancestral beliefs, they were, for her, effectively obsolete. When asked if she knew and/or practiced other customs relating to pregnancy Mari told me:

> If we are pregnant we eat plenty of food. In the past some pregnant women were staying and they fasted from some foods. They said, if they are pregnant they cannot eat plenty of food, especially fish and shellfish. They won't eat fish and shellfish, in case their children develop sores. It was taboo for women to eat these foods. That was an old custom of our old mothers, in their time. At this time we can eat any kind of food. Myself, I eat all kinds of food, fish and shellfish. Sometimes if we want we eat, and sometimes if we don't want then we don't eat. If we eat and we are vomiting or we don't feel like a particular type of food then we won't eat it. If we feel like roasted food or cooked food we will eat it.

From my observations and discussions with these and other women of both Susan's and Mari's as well as Eunice's generations it seemed that observance of customary practices associated with pregnancy was a matter of personal and familial belief on Nuakata. All these women regularly attended the United Church and Women's Fellowship meetings and identified themselves as Christians. Only some considered these customary practices to be incompatible with Christian beliefs. The range of foods eaten by pregnant women was not only contingent upon their belief in the efficacy of food taboos, but also determined by personal and familial circumstances: who was willing and able to assist the pregnant woman in her garden, the seasonal availability of food, family size, and the attitude of the woman's husband and kin to her condition. Some men, for example, were very supportive, assisting their pregnant wives in the garden and fishing regularly, while others seemed indifferent.

When discussing pregnancy with these women, I, and they in turn, employed the term *kastom*. People spoke of "our *kastom*" or "our ways" to describe specific practices enacted or done within their *susu*, clan, generation, on Nuakata, across Papua or the Milne Bay region. The meaning and use of this term was unstable, differing according to the context in which it was spoken and the speaker. It was used to unite and divide or oppose. It was not a neutral term. For example, when spoken of in church or by Moses in relation to local health practices, *kastom* was often used pejoratively, denoting un-Christian or uneducated practices and values (cf. Dureau 1994, 15–18; see Keesing 1989c; Keesing and Jolly 1992)—barely civilized, traditional ways that should be discarded. In these contexts *kastom* was not thought of as practices unique to or constitutive of the contemporary Nuakatan community or culture. Rather, speakers implied that *kastom* referred to relics of a primitive—Papuan, if not national—Papua New Guinean past. By continuing to practice *kastom*, Nuakatan people and, by implication, Papuans and Papua New Guineans aligned themselves with this primitive past rather than a developed, civilized future. However, often these same speakers identified some Papua New Guinean, even Melanesian *kastom* as preferable to and distinguishable from *dimdim kastom,* most notably the *wantok* system in which people are obligated to care for family and friends. In addition, when describing feasts and mortuary ceremonies to me, people used this term to positively identify modified contemporary forms of Nuakatan mortuary practices. On these occasions *kastom* functioned as a synonym, of sorts, for an objectified culture—for collective practices that variously reinforced a sense of belonging to the people and places of Nuakata and/or Milne Bay (see Foster 1995; Keesing and Tonkinson 1982).

Teachers and, through them, children at the local primary school represented *kastom* as practices that the people of Nuakata *have*. For example, to fulfill a national education agenda, arguably conceived by postcolonial elites living and working on the mainland, the school designated each Friday as a cultural/*kastom* day. Girls dressed in grass skirts and boys wore pubic coverings made from pandanus. A part of the day was devoted to performance of local dances, songs, stories, and occasional demonstrations of "traditional" yet still commonly practiced ways of lighting fires, hunting, or fishing. Performed out of their usual context, these activities were identified and reified by teachers as *kastom*—ways that constitute unique and desirable aspects of Nuakatan culture. By performing these customary practices the schoolchildren would preserve and repossess them as a source of cultural identity and unity. While these ostensibly benign practices were designated and quarantined as cultural, other customary practices, particularly those considered harmful to people's health and nutritional status (e.g., chewing betel nut, practicing all forms of magic, using barks and plants for health purposes), were declared uninformed and therefore expendable. Adults and children alike found custom/culture days amusing, if not quaint. In my presence at least, children felt self-conscious, even embarrassed, when I saw them clothed like their forebears. Despite their reservations older people felt these events gave them the opportunity to tell and thereby pass on their stories. For this reason they continued to give this practice their tacit support.

Through the primary school cultural days and the preschool indigenous language program, culture on Nuakata was constituted as a set of benign customary practices. People were encouraged to imagine their forebears and, by implication, themselves as a collectivity with commonly held ideas and practices. Construed as extrinsic to people, as an overarching system, Nuakatan culture comprised a shared language and mainly traditional customary practices that were selectively and strategically revived and appropriated. It was worn, performed, and spoken. It was also Christian. In reinforcing, if not inventing (see Keesing 1989a; Wagner 1981), a unique Nuakatan culture, educators were effecting a broader sociopolitical agenda, one born of the colonial critiques central to the Papua New Guinean Independence (Crocombe 1994; Lindstrom and White 1994). Local people were actively encouraged to take pride in their island and those foundational stories, practices, and rituals of their forebears that were compatible with Christian beliefs. It was hoped that this pride would keep young people at home, on the island, committed to maintaining and developing their local community, rather than drifting to the mainland centers in search of illusive paid employment and an independent urban future.

In other contexts, *kastom* was not strictly construed as things to be "had," as my questions and the *kastom*/culture days at the school implied. In these instances, *kastom* was represented as dynamic practices. As with the paths forged by people that socialize or inhabit the landscape, *kastom* was spoken of as "ways" to be followed (*kastom 'umulitaedi*) or respected (*'uve'ahihiyedi*). They were respectful or "proper" ways of living and staying on Nuakata, ways that preceded those currently living and staying there. They were conventional ways or paths, enacted by those that came before and reenacted and transformed by those that follow (see Wagner 1981). Often these ways were specific to men, women, children, members of a *susu* or clan. In respecting them, people evinced sociality. *Kastom* belonged to people, but, more important, to "time(s)" embodied and inhabited by people. Like Mari, people described them as belonging to "the time of our ancestors." As these temporal embodiments passed away, so too the customary practices disappeared, unless, that is, they were reembodied, reenacted, and retemporalized by those that followed. By enacting these ways, continuity between past, present, and future generations was consolidated, if not created. While *kastom* was not spoken of as created or authored by people, these practices are selectively known and enacted by some people. These people were described as the "owners" or, perhaps more accurately, the custodians of this knowledge. Owners of this knowledge are entitled to recompense for enacting customary practices, and they alone choose who, if anyone, may be given this knowledge in subsequent generations. This knowledge is typically, but not exclusively, passed on, through what Lindstrom (1994, 74) describes as a customary apprenticeship relationship, to a worthy junior member of one's *susu* or clan. Often money, goods, and services are exchanged for knowledge. Like Wycliffe, people may be given certain *kastom* knowledge without receiving either the right or the capacity to enact or practice it.

When I asked Susan and Mari what *kastom* they had, or "did," in relation to pregnancy, I appealed to a notion of *kastom* and, by implication, culture as discrete practices constituting a corpus of collectively constituted and potentially cohesive, traditional cultural beliefs, possessed by local people. As with my efforts to understand notions of the gendered person on Nuakata, I sought to uncover, penetrate, dissect, and extract the meaning of these customary practices as one might crack a code. I construed them as functional and strategic practices, logical means serving identifiable and purposeful ends. I invested these practices with a meaning and significance that were independent of their enactment.

M. Strathern (1988) claims that assumptions of this kind are peculiarly Western, stemming from the "commodity logic" that pervades Western thought and economic practice. Accordingly, people living in the Western world imagine that there is an overarching system of relationships variously called *culture* or *society* (see also Rosaldo 1989, 32). Imagined as real, as a real source of understanding, practices, and values, this abstract system is believed to impose itself upon people; it does things to people, compelling them to think and act in certain ways.

> Western people imagine themselves as double proprietors. On the one hand they naturally own themselves, and their personal attributes,

including their gender. On the other hand, their capacity for communication with one another is based on their common ownership of a culture. But if they own culture, culture also owns them. Proprietorship thus introduces the subject-object relation, in which either may become a thing in the hands of the other. . . . [Culture] stands as a thing over and beyond them. (M. Strathern 1988, 322)

Strathern's analysis of the commodity logic implicit in Western thought, particularly evident in notions of culture, society, the subject, self, or even personality, rings true. Certainly some of my questions about *kastom* manifested this understanding. However, the idea, which is not necessarily Strathern's, that proprietal notions of society and subject are the only ways Western people understand themselves, others, and their different worlds, is problematic. It takes little or no account of people's differing circumstances and the complex and often contradictory stances they assume in their worlds. In drawing a sharp distinction between Western and Melanesian ways of knowing, between Melanesian sociality and the Western notion of society, Strathern also states that Melanesian communities lack both the language and the concept of culture or society, either their own or others. This proposition is both unsustainable and mystifying in the contemporary Nuakatan context. As illustrated above, *kastom* and the often related term *culture* have multiple meanings on Nuakata, some of which approximate a proprietal view of culture (see Foster 1995). The term *kastom* was differentially employed on Nuakata, as elsewhere in Melanesia. Sometimes it was used to differentiate between past and present, Christian and pre-Christian, Papuan and *dimdim,* ideas, values, and practices. Other times it was used as a "pan-Melanesian re-presentation of the past . . . —[an] idiom of resistance to colonial and postcolonial domination" (Dureau 1994, 15).

Believing there was more to be told about women's experience of pregnancy on Nuakata, I attempted on many occasions to question Wycliffe's sister Geteli about her five pregnancies. However, unlike discussions of other aspects of her life, she did not, and seemingly would not, elaborate on her pregnancies. My questions about pregnancy always seemed out of context, going against the tide of our conversations and our lives; she was breast-feeding her nine-month-old child at the time and had declared that he was to be her last-born child. Pregnancy was therefore the last thing she wanted to think about, and I had only an intention to become pregnant, but had no lived experience to share. In responding to my persistent inquiries, she, like so many others, deferred to older women's expertise, changed the subject, or remained silent. She repeatedly insisted that women do not speak (about) their pregnancies with one another, except to comment on their health or perhaps where they intend to birth. Should they wish to talk further, they do this with one of their female kin, particularly their mothers. Ordinarily, then, there is little cause to speak of pregnancy on Nuakata. Pregnancy is simply done, lived. It is not highlighted or reified as a discrete and distinct event in the life cycle of mother and child as my questions inferred. The child within the womb is grown until it is born. The unborn is not imagined as a developing fetus, and the process of growth is not cause for speculation, but is accepted as necessarily concealed and known only by the swollen stomach of the mother and the movements of the unborn child.

Geteli's responses to my questions about pregnancy matched my stymied attempts to go to the garden with either her or Sineliko. Frequent requests were made and countless arrangements forged. Each time, though, I found myself left behind in Gohiya. This became a standing joke between Sineliko and me. She took great delight in "tricking" me. With Geteli it was a slightly different story. Sometimes she claimed that she "forgot," or "saw me working with Wycliffe" and did not want to interrupt. Most times, however, she told me that there was nothing for me to see or do, she was only weeding. But this was clearly not the case. Her baskets were always laden with food. Amused by the image of myself as the witless anthropologist badgering Geteli to show me her gardens, I also despaired of ever going there, of ever learning more about the relationship between gardening, pregnancy, and birth.

Blocking Pregnancy

One day, six months into my fieldwork, while walking over to the school with my neighbors Malida (a woman in her early fifties) and her younger sister Rosemary (a woman in her early forties), Malida pointed out several plants known and used by women to prevent pregnancy. I was stunned. I knew women used local plants and roots for this purpose, but my efforts to discover what they were and how they were used had, until then, gone unrewarded. While some younger women, both married and unmarried, reluctantly confessed that they used plants to prevent pregnancies, my attempts to question them further met with embarrassed silences or evasive asides.

No doubt they were concerned that in revealing their contraceptive practices I and— perhaps more significantly—Wycliffe (and through him other people on the island) would become privy to their ordinarily unspoken decisions about these matters. Perhaps women's reticence to speak on these issues was also born of historical resistance to colonial and particularly Methodist missionary intervention in maternal practices, including indigenous fertility control (Ram and Jolly 1998; Reed 1998; Eves 1996a). Colonial opposition to indigenous fertility control was widespread across Melanesia. Jolly (1998b) and Dureau (1998) indicate that in Fiji, Vanuatu, and the Solomons, for example, indigenous forms of fertility control were vigorously opposed by Methodist missionaries and colonial administrators concerned with depopulation. Dureau (1998, 253) notes that in the Solomon Islands Methodist missionaries disavowed these practices, as they were "immoral, promoted promiscuity, . . . involved pagan invocations" and diminished men's marital authority. Women on Nuakata may also have assumed that my beliefs about indigenous fertility control coincided with the views espoused by my white forebears in Milne Bay and contemporary community health workers, such as Moses. At a time when overpopulation is of vital concern to the national government, indigenous fertility control has been targeted in family planning programs. Maternal and child health workers consider these practices unreliable at best; at worst they pose a serious risk to women's health.

But Malida, finding herself alone with me that day (save for her sister) and seeing the plants growing along the path we were taking together, took the opportunity to describe and explain their use. Standing with these women, plants in hand, I sensed that these explanations of *'ai'auhi* (contraception) were offered as a gift, as an expression of gratitude for things I had given to her and her family. It was an understanding implied by Rosemary when she commented that Malida's extensive knowledge of contraceptive plants is locally recognized, sought, and valued by other women. It was further reinforced by Malida herself who, when Roger and I were finally leaving the island, thanked me profusely for the *mula-mula dimdim* (Western medicine) that I had given her family. Only then did I fully appreciate that on that particular day Malida had offered me a gift in kind: a gift that acknowledged and deepened our neighborly relationship, one that, to my mind, far exceeded my own, thereby creating anew my own sense of indebtedness.

Totally unexpected, this gift was immensely satisfying. Months of frustration and impatience dissipated in a moment. I understood then that in asking younger women, not only was I asking them to reveal private decisions pertinent to them at the time but, more important, I was seeking explanations from those with limited experience. For them to discuss these issues with me was to show disrespect to their elders, such as Malida, who had greater knowledge and experience. Moreover, I realized I had sought explanations from people prematurely, before mutual trust had been established. Like knowledge of magic and other forms of medicine, knowledge of 'ai'auhi (contraception) primarily belongs to those women who have inherited it from one of their kin.

The word 'ai'auhi is a composite of the two words 'ai and 'auhi. Auhi means to block or cover by oral means. Ai, however, has several associated meanings. It may be used as a verbal prefix meaning "in the process of doing something—a state of becoming which implies transformation." Ai is also an exclusive form of the absolute or free collective pronoun meaning "us, we," as in 'ai Nua'ata 'ainaiena, tenem 'awalo (us, from Nuakata, we say that). Ai is also the verb "to eat." When it is reduplicated, 'ai'ai means eating or food. Eating or ingestion is believed to transform food into blood. Collectively, the meanings associated with the word 'ai'auhi (contraception) and, indeed, the word yaipoine (sterility) suggest that the ingestion of particular food blocks the blood, thereby inhibiting the growth essential to pregnancy. Understood in this way, contraception is not necessarily believed to prevent conception, but it does block pregnancy.

Buoyed by Malida's gesture, I was unable to recall all that she told me at the time. The next day I visited her hamlet, where, among other things, she detailed how these plants are used. Rosemary also contributed to this conversation, but often deferred to Malida's knowledge and experience. In the course of this conversation they described three forms of contraception: one a temporary contraceptive and two others that cause permanent sterility.

> The leaves of one plant known as *edewa salana* (dog's teeth) are cooked in water. When their cooking is finished we drink two cups of the "water" in the morning and two again at night. Because this plant's "power" is so strong, women will become permanently sterile (*yaipoine*) [from *poi* meaning to pluck or rip off flowers, to tear open] after drinking it. (Malida)

> Another plant with thorny leaves and flat leaves [is used as a temporary contraceptive for both men and women]. The flat leaves are female leaves and the thorny leaves are male leaves. If women drink the [soup

made from boiling the] flat leaves, then they will "find" a child. If they drink [the soup made from boiling] the thorny male leaves, then they will not "find" a child. In the same way if men drink [the soup made from] the flat leaves, then they will not "find" a child. If they drink [the soup made from] the male leaves, then they will find a child. We [make this soup by] putting either flat or thorny leaves together with a small section of the stem into a pot and cooking it with food. (Malida)

One plant called *manihubu gigini* (sea eagle, handle) grows upward like a vine and has sharp leaves which can spear us and draw blood. When the moon goes down, when it sets, then we get some betel nut and we chew it together with a small section of the root of this plant. We are chewing, we are chewing and the moon rises again until it is a full moon. We stop chewing and we eat fish. The full moon is finished and it sets and we chew again, but we fast from eating fish. Then the moon rises and we eat fish and the full moon finishes, and then we will not "find" any children. We chew that thing it runs through the blood to the womb and we cannot "find" children. If she chews and then eats fish, then the blood will go to all of the body and affect the power of the plant. (Rosemary)

Rosemary's reference to fish echoes the taboos about eating fish during pregnancy and immediately following birth, upheld by women such as Susan and Emma. In the course of our conversation, Malida explained that fish blood is thin, that it makes human blood run, causing bleeding to continue and the power of Papuan medicines to dissipate throughout the body (cf. Battaglia 1990, 79). Neither Malida nor Rosemary could explain the relationship between the ingestion of these plants and the lunar cycle. They accepted and enacted these practices without questioning them. Malida, Rosemary, Eunice, and several younger women all indicated that many women use plants to prevent pregnancy before marriage, to delay pregnancy after they have weaned a child, and/or to prevent them from having more children. While *'ai'auhi* was widely practiced by women, it seemed that they rarely discussed it openly with friends or members of their *susu*. This was especially true of young women with two or three children. Some of these women feared criticism from members of their *susu,* especially their mothers, who may have wished them to strengthen the *susu* by contributing many children. When necessary, young, single women discussed *'ai'auhi* with their sisters and friends, but like their sexual practices they attempted to conceal their use of it from family members.

Apart from these local forms of *ai'auhi*, three forms of Western-style contraception were also available from the aid post—condoms, the contraceptive pill, and Depo Provera injections. Away from the island for four months during 1993, Moses conducted no family planning health education clinics during our time on Nuakata. He did, however, offer advice to people, especially women, during consultations at the aid post. One family planning clinic was conducted by Moses at the aid post in 1992 and was attended by thirty-six women. Discussion focused on the need to reduce family sizes to ensure the sustainable health of, and sources of nutrition for, themselves and their families. Moses explained how to use the three available forms of contraception, stressing their safety and reliability in contrast to indigenous methods of fertility control. Without knowing exactly what these local forms of contraception were, he claimed that they posed health risks to women. During 1992, eight women requested contraceptive advice and assistance from Moses. Five initially chose to use condoms, one chose Depo Provera injections, and two opted for the pill. Only one married male inquired about contraception, and he asked Moses for condoms. A total of twenty-seven condoms were distributed to people in that year. Of those women who sought contraceptive advice, it seems only one woman—who was using the contraceptive pill—continued to use the contraception provided by Moses. Frustrated by poor responses to his family planning efforts, especially men's refusal to attend family planning clinics, Moses explained that men are reluctant to take responsibility for contraception, believing it to be within the woman's domain. He added that many men and women still wished to have large families, so that children and grandchildren will care for them in their old age. He also indicated that understandably women are very embarrassed to talk with him about family planning issues. Of those that do, some complain that their husbands are resistant to family planning, especially condoms.

Birthing

> So we are pregnant. When we start missing our monthly period we already know that we are starting pregnancy at one month. Then we start counting the months until nine months. Our stomachs grow big like balloons and then we know that in two or three weeks' time we'll

give birth. If we are going to hospital, then on the eighth month they'll send us there. If there are no boats, then we'll give birth in the village. At that time our husbands, brothers, or mother's brothers should, or at least they used to, build our small house. In that house they prepare our bed for giving birth. They prepare a fire so that we might sleep by it or warm ourselves. Then when we are ready, when the time comes, we'll call our mothers to come and sleep [in the hamlet] and we'll give birth. We lie down and the baby will be pushing and we will be crying and shouting because it is painful to us, until the membrane ruptures and the baby comes out. Somebody will hold the baby and the baby's cord will be cut. Then we wait for the baby's bag. The baby will be placed on its bed. The baby's bag will come out. Just like we give birth to the baby, so the baby's bag we are borning that one too. They prepare us. They clean away our blood. They change our clothes and then they take us to our sleeping place by the fire. They put us on our bed and they take our rubbish away and throw it. Sometimes they put the baby's bag inside a basket and hang it on a tree, sometimes they dig a hole [and put the bag inside it]. If we hang it on a tree, then that means that the baby, boy or girl's blood will always pump. [He or she] will always think, "I want to climb coconut tree, betel nut or mustard tree." (Excerpt from initial interview conducted in English with Mona, described in Chapter Three)

Hopeful that I might witness a hamlet birth, I asked Mari where she intended to deliver her baby. She was one of five pregnant women from the Yalasi and Bolime sides of the island and one of only three (from these sides of the island) who gave birth while we were living on Nuakata. She told me that her first child was born in her hamlet, her second in the hospital, and this child, her third, would also be born in the hospital. As with her last delivery, she and her mother would go to Alotau during her eighth month of pregnancy, where they would remain with friends or relatives. When the time came for her to deliver she would move to the hospital, where they would stay until five or so days after the baby was born. Much preparation was required to execute this plan, for, like all pregnant women delivering in the hospital, she and her mother needed to carry enough food with them for the duration of their stay in Alotau. She stated that, despite all the preparation and inconvenience, she preferred giving birth in the hospital rather than the hamlet, because

In hospital we get help. They give me medicine and injections, so that after I have given birth I won't be cold. After five or ten days I can leave the hospital and return to the village. But if I give birth in the village, I will have to stay by the fire for one month to warm up.

Mari's expressed beliefs about hospital births and her history of childbearing were by no means unusual among the young mothers with whom I spoke. Without exception these women had given birth in their matrilineal hamlets, watched over by their respective mothers, maternal uncles, husbands, and often several women with some locally recognized skill in delivering babies. Most of the younger women, though, had also given birth in the hospital. For example, Geteli had her first child in her hamlet, but because she was ill throughout her second pregnancy she delivered this child in the hospital. Her third, fourth, and fifth children were all born in her hamlet. Susan indicated that she intended to give birth to her next baby in the hospital, because she would be given assistance if difficulties arose during her delivery. Like the other women, she had neither asked about birth nor been told what to expect before giving birth to her first child, Rex. When birthing Rex on the ground outside her house, she was greatly shocked by the experience and pain of birth.

Susan, like the other women with whom I spoke, did not seriously consider giving birth at the aid post. Apart from feeling "shy" with Moses, she indicated that the hospital was better supplied with medicines, equipment, and female nursing staff to help her. The help received in the hospital was clearly welcomed by these women, even when it meant that they were forced to birth while lying on their back with their legs in stirrups. While they valued the expertise of the female nursing staff during hospital deliveries, it was the availability of *dimdim mulamula* (Western medicine) that they considered most important. Unlike at the aid post, or in their hamlets, an injection would be given immediately following the birth to stop their bleeding.[3]

Sinetana indicated that there was another important reason why young women often preferred to deliver in the hospital rather than their hamlet. When giving birth in her hamlet, a laboring woman may be assisted by one or more of her mothers. This assistant would stand or sit behind the woman and wrap her arms around the laboring woman's rib cage and sternum, pressing down on her stomach in an attempt to squeeze the baby out. The attendant often ignored the woman's contractions. An extremely painful practice, it was one that younger women sought to avoid.

Given these experiences and apprehensions, it seemed somewhat surprising that pregnant women did not always choose to deliver in the hospital. However, factors such as money to pay for boat fares to and from the mainland, accommodation on the mainland while they await the birth, sufficient quantities of available garden food to last their month-long stay, and familial circumstances, including the attitude of their husbands, impacted upon their decisions. Also, like Eunice, women thought that, where possible, the newborn should be carried and born into the land of its matrilineal forebears, its mother's and grandmother's place; the land it may claim as shared inheritance; the land that will sustain its living and staying, and where it will be buried together with these same kin when its time is over. However, children born on the mainland, or in places other than their own matrilineal land, were believed to have no lesser claim to that land than those born in matrilineal hamlets. Accordingly, who bears a child is more important than where it is birthed. And as the decisions to deliver in the hospital reveal, people believed that birth on matrilineal land did not always guarantee the health and safety of the mother and unborn child. Like Moses, women recognized that in certain circumstances hamlet births posed a risk to their safety and the safety of their unborn child.

Some women indicated that complications during a prior village delivery (long and difficult labor, retained placenta, excessive bleeding following birth, etc.) prompted them to go to hospital for their next birth. Others indicated they had been advised to deliver in the hospital by Moses or the maternal and child health nurses. All mentioned that they made this decision during their pregnancy because their blood was "small" or "thin" or simply "no good." They were "not strong." Malida commented:

> In the village there is no Papuan medicine to stop women from bleeding after birth. All they can do is make a big fire to dry their blood out and drink hot water to stop them from bleeding. They must not eat bloody food, especially fish, until their bleeding has stopped, because their blood might run. For this reason they remain in the house with no windows and only a small amount of air.

References to blood and strength were a recurring theme in all my conversations about pregnancy and birth. It was a theme made more intelligible by knowledge of the etymological associations with the word for blood in Alina Nuʻata: *ʻwapina*. The stem of this word, *ʻwahi*, also constitutes the stem of *ʻwahiala*, meaning strength, energy, vitality, and *yawahi*, meaning breath or life force. This etymological link between blood, breath, and life force expressed local understanding of the integral, indissociable relationship between these aspects of a living, staying human being. Blood, strength, and breath were thought to diminish with old age and finish at death with the cessation of embodiment. In this sense, blood and breath were understood as temporally constituted. People thought that blood was generally not static. Only in sickness was it thought to settle in a given place in the body. Accordingly, during life, blood travels along paths. Ideally these paths are straight; however, if they should deviate, become narrow or circuitous for any reason (e.g., during pregnancy and birth), then someone's energy, strength, and living will be depleted. Blood, strength, and life force may be depleted or enhanced by many means, as they are contingent upon the actions of the living person and multiple others, both the living and the dead.[4] Given this understanding of blood, it is not surprising that women show no reluctance to take the blood tablets, in contrast to the malaria prophylaxis, supplied to them by Moses during their pregnancy.

As discussed in chapter 3, blood was considered essential for the arrival and subsequent growth of the child within the womb. Without blood the "en-wombed" child cannot live. This blood, the blood that makes new life possible, that enlivens the child, and from which new blood first springs, was thought to be a combination of female menstrual blood (*ʻwaiena bwadana*) and male "semen" blood (*molo*). As the difference in names suggests, *ʻwaiena bwadana* (menstrual blood) and *ʻwahina* (blood) were not considered one and the same, although when spoken in English the same word, "blood," was used, thereby glossing over the difference. Similarly, semen and blood were not thought of as equivalent. Accordingly, when male and female "blood" come together as a result of sexual intercourse, new blood is formed, the child's blood: *ʻwahinana* (its blood), and with it growth of the child. Inalienably possessed by the unborn child, this new blood is subsequently "made" and strengthened by repeated acts of sexual intercourse and the labors of both mother and father to grow the child's blood within and later outside of the womb. Therefore, although possessed by the child, blood was, in the first instance, understood as the consequence of his or her parents' labors and, later, the labors of many other kin—male and female, *susu* and affine— on his or her behalf.

People implied that the child's growth in and outside the womb is facilitated by the efforts of birth parents and their kin to feed the child. Food is transformed in someone's stomach before passing into the blood and thereby circulating throughout the body (see Macintyre 1988, 55). While the women I asked did not discuss how food enters the placenta (*tamumu*), whether or not it is transported via the mother's blood, they did comment that food consumed by a pregnant woman enters and fills the placenta. As the use of semialienable possessive pronouns implies, both the placenta and the umbilical cord, *'ana pehipehi* (his or her umbilical cord or navel), belong to the child. For example, when talking in English, both Emma and Mona described them as the "child's bag." Mona commented that "just like the baby we borning the baby's bag too." Just as mothers carry and replenish the baby and its bag of food within the womb so, too, they continue to carry, prepare, and cook food for their child once it is beyond the womb.

Indissociable from the conditions of its making, blood, on Nuakata, can be understood as representing the life, the strength, the (fluid) unity that arises from difference shared—the difference between a childbearing woman and an adult male, the difference between menstrual blood and sperm, and the difference between *susu* and affine. As Macintyre (1988, 53) suggests for Tubetube, "blood provides the metaphor for socially created relations between people of different *susu*," and food is the means by which these relations are maintained, replenished, and transformed. Here M. Strathern's argument is also compelling in the Nuakatan context. Strathern (1988) suggests that blood is the metaphor for dyadically conceived relationships. The source and outcome of actions, these relationships produce persons who inevitably have dual origins and are thus internally differentiated. The unitary individual is produced when this internal dualistic differentiation is eliminated or, as I would suggest, overlooked. In reproducing yams and children this internal dualistic differentiation must be re-created or, perhaps, recognized. On Nuakata people also used blood as a metaphor for humanity. For example, on several occasions members of Wycliffe's *susu* commented to both Roger and I that "you [exclusive plural absolute pronoun] are whites (*'omiu dimdim*), we [exclusive pronoun] are Papuans (*'ai Papuan*), but we [inclusive plural pronoun] are one blood (*na hesi 'ita'wahina 'ehebo*)." Whereas *susu* (breast-milk) passes down through and across the generations of a given matrilineage, constituting the matrilineage and ensuring its continuity, *'wahina* (blood) passes between male and female of different matrilineages, making new life possible.

Just as pregnancy (alone) did not constitute someone as a woman/female on Nuakata so, too, the act of giving birth or bearing a child did not constitute a woman as a mother (*hina*). For example, people addressed their mother's sister as *hinagu* (my mother) even when she was unable to become pregnant or give birth, as was the case with Wycliffe's mother's sister. Where the conversational context demands, they differentiated between their mothers by adding the adjectives "big" or "little" to denote their birth mother's older or younger sister. They also addressed women of their mothers' generation within their clan as mother. While an expression existed in Alina Nuʻata for birth mother, *hinagu ʻagutaulabalaba*, and birth father, *tamagu ʻagutaulabalaba*, in practice these were rarely used. Nuakata had such a small population that awareness of any given person's birth mother was generally common knowledge, particularly among the adult members of the population. Apart from this, the distinction between birth and nonbirth mothers was afforded little attention, as both were accorded equal respect.

While rarely used as terms of address, the existence of terms to differentiate between birth and nonbirth parents indicated that the distinction had meaning and significance on Nuakata. Translated, the expression *ʻagutaulabalaba* means something like "the one who effects my birth." *Agu* is a semialienable possessive pronoun meaning "my." *Tau* is a widely used noun stem, which means both "body" and "one who . . ." (see chap. 6). While both a birth mother and father (*ʻagutaulabalaba*) were believed to effect the birth of the child, people did not speak of a birth father as literally giving birth to or bearing his child. Three verbs, *ʻavala* (to bear or to carry), *labahi* (to birth), and *labalaba*[5] (the transformative time of birthing), were used to refer to the process of giving birth, yet only *ʻavala* conveyed the pregnant woman's, or birth mother's, sense of pain, struggle, and labor associated with bearing or birthing. Only birth mothers were said to carry or bear their children in this sense.

Unlike *ʻavala*, which was used to draw attention to the woman's embodied experience of the process of birth, *labahi* and *labalaba* were used to emphasize the temporal process and time period of birth, culminating in the child becoming born (*tubui*). *Labalaba* can denote the mother's time, baby's time, or the shared time of birth. While the pregnant woman was said to enact the process of birth (*ʻilabalaba*), it was believed she did this on the child's behalf. As such, the unborn child was believed to initiate the process—it decides when to be born by its mother. In other words, as with the flow of menstrual blood to the womb, people understood a mother to labor at her unborn child's behest. Used in the context of birth, *tubui* refers exclusively to the liminal state and time of the child immediately prior to, or after, birth. Hence, whether unborn or just born, the child is considered *tubui*—imminent. Similarly someone whose death is imminent is often referred to as dead.

Unlike a birth mother, it was not said of a birth father that he enacts the process of birth (*'ilabalaba*). As stated in chapter 3, his actions to grow the child within the womb are believed to make the birth possible. In this sense he is recognized as *taulabalaba,* one who enables the child to cross the boundary from the inner, concealed, "en-wombed" world to the nurturing containment of the outside world. The actions of both birth mother and birth father to effect the child's birth were represented as semialienable possessions of the child—that is, these actions transform as they are transformed by the child, making the child's temporal embodiment possible. Their actions and/or those of their kin are believed to influence the child's decision to be born. In these contexts personal agency and/or will is contingent on the acts of others. For example, several people commented to me that some children delay their birth until all their living kin, particularly those belonging to their *susu*, have arrived in the hamlet to welcome them. During our initial interview Mona stated:

> Sometimes [a] baby likes its father. That's why if they go somewhere and the lady wants to give birth, she will walk around for a day or two days waiting for the baby to come. So then we will call the husband and say, "Come and sit near your wife and she will give birth" and then he will come and she gives birth. Sometimes like that, babies like their father. They stop us from [helping them] to come out because they like their father. Sometimes babies never think anything and we give birth.

Doing Pregnancy and Birth

Throughout June, July, and August a craze swept across Nuakata—or at least that is how I first experienced it—reminding me of the fads of my schooldays, when swap cards would suddenly and inexplicably be replaced by yoyos. Across the island, people could invariably be found sitting together, laughing and joking, with single loops of string in their hands. Adults, and to a lesser extent children, were doing the cat's cradle, or *'ai'abi,* as it was known on Nuakata. *Ai'abi* literally means building, or making in process. In their hands, between their fingers, string representations of houses, turtles, cats, drums, paddles, bananas, Tanalabwa (the mountain on Nuakata), islands, flowers, chestnuts emerged. Roger joined in on several occasions, offering the only configuration he could remember from childhood: a cup and saucer. This sent people into fits of laughter, partly because it lacked the sophistication of their own designs, partly because of Roger's performance, but also because it seemed such a strange and silly *dimdim* thing to make.

Perplexed by this fad I initially asked Wycliffe and later several older people to explain. These conversations went something like this:

Shelley: But why is everyone doing this?
Interviewee: Every year before the harvest we do this to make the yams grow.
Shelley: How does it work?
Interviewee: We don't know, we only do it. Our old people did it and we do it.
Shelley: Do you believe it's true? Do you believe it makes the yams grow?
Interviewee: I don't know, we just do it.
Shelley: Who does it?
Interviewee: Everyone can do it: women, men; some children, they do it too.

It seemed yams did not simply grow of their own accord, but were grown by imaginative, laboring hands. Just as Wycliffe and others "did" *ai'abi* without understanding how it worked, I watched people do it with a sense of perplexed fascination.

One August morning, sitting at the back of Gohiya with six or seven members of Wycliffe's *susu*, Roger and I found ourselves spectators to an uproarious "session" of *ai'abi*. People seized upon bits of string and quickly wove their designs before challenging us to guess what they had made. In the midst of this commotion Eunice motioned to me and laughingly dared me to watch her, saying *'uita 'waihiu 'ihiuma* (you watch, woman is pregnant). With this she formed an *ai'abi* sequence that began with the "pregnant woman" and then transformed before us into increasingly complex string configurations representing the woman and baby at *'waiena ehebo* (one month), *'waiena bwau* (two months), and so on, up to and including the ninth month of pregnancy. Then, with a triumphant flourish, she declared *'iavalai* (she gave birth). Releasing the configurations held by her fingers, she revealed a single, whole loop of string, stretched taut over and between her outstretched hands (see figs. 5–14).

As I watched Eunice make pregnancy and birth with her hands, as I delighted in the ever more complex "en-wombed" "baby" unfolding between her fingers and the "woman" or "mother" transformed by this process, I saw in those ephemeral loops of string a shared vision of pregnancy and birth. It was a vision that had stubbornly defied my attempts to elicit it with words and explanations that had unraveled before my best efforts to penetrate or "understand" it. It was a vision Eunice dared me to see.

Excited by this string revelation of pregnancy and birth, I dashed to our house, grabbed the camera, and ran back and made Eunice repeat each stage of the sequence so that I could capture it all on film. When it came to the final shot of "birth," I ran out of film! My efforts to encapsulate it were thwarted.

> Truth is on the margins. It is lost when it is claimed. . . . Can our discourse be likened to these string figures, a game we play with words, the thread of an argument whose connection with reality is always oblique and tenuous, which crosses to and fro, interlacing description with interpretation, instruction with entertainment, but always ambiguously placed between practical and antinomian ends? If so truth is not binding. It is in the interstices as much as it is in the structure, in fiction as much as in fact. (Jackson 1989, 187)

Happy Birthday, Dimdim!

One afternoon as I was passing Mari's hamlet on my way back to Gohiya I bumped into her on the path, cradling a new baby in her arms. I was most surprised to see her, for I knew she had gone to hospital at Alotau, but had heard no news of the birth or her return to Nuakata. Mari explained that she had only just returned to Nuakata several hours earlier, together with her new baby, a little girl. Delighted to see them both, I fussed and fawned over the baby, straining to catch a glimpse of her face half hidden in the folds of a blanket. Several minutes elapsed before, noting Mari's marked embarrassment, I toned down my response and made my good-byes. It seemed that my celebratory response to the new baby was exaggerated, foreign to her. Still feeling enthused by my dis-

Fig. 5. Eunice Tau'owa demonstrating Ai'abi (cat's cradle) beginning

Fig. 6. One month gestation

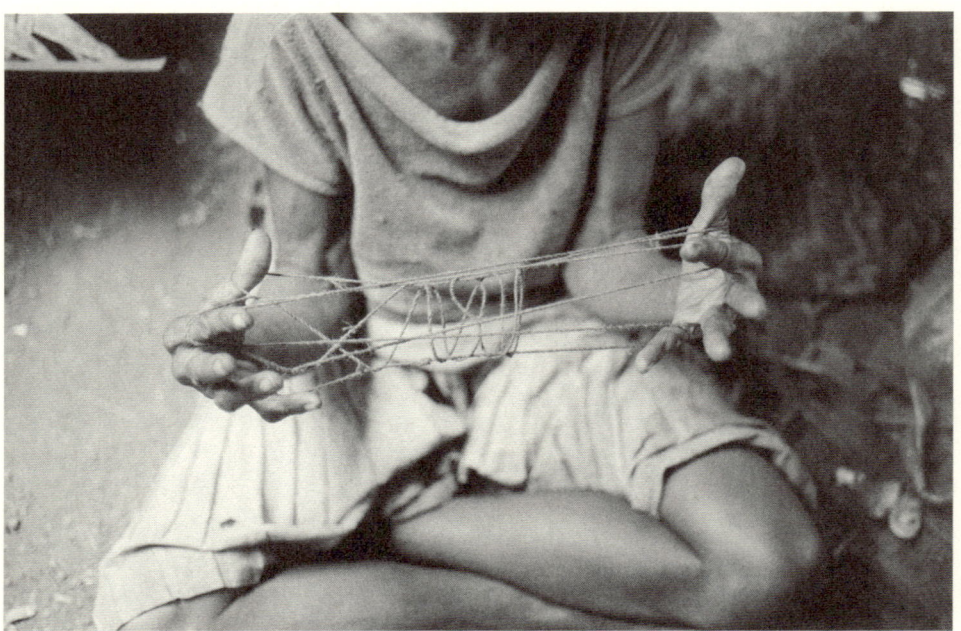

Fig. 7.   Two months gestation

Fig. 8.   Three months gestation

Fig. 9. Four months gestation

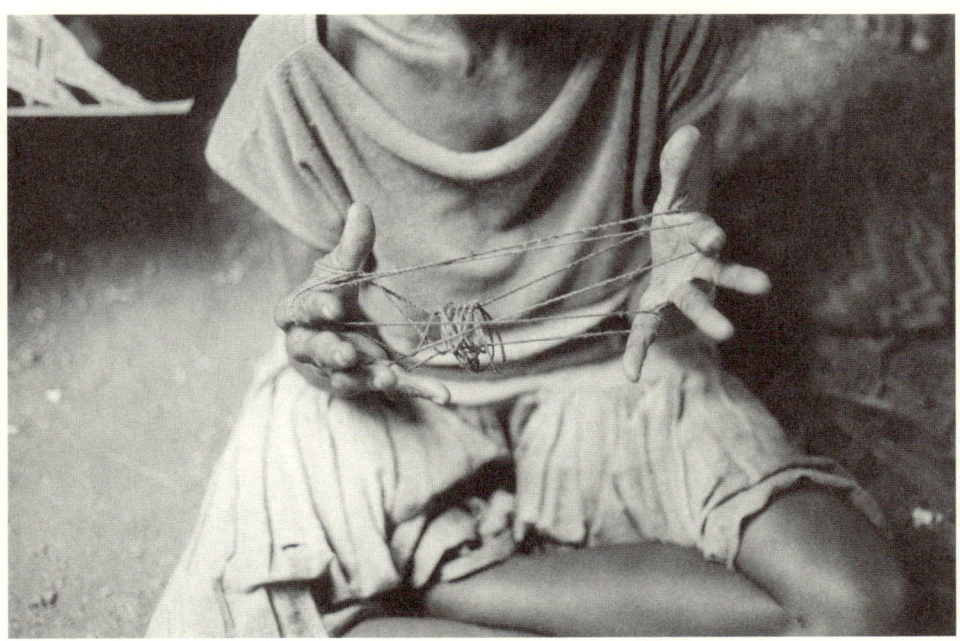

Fig. 10. Five months gestation

Fig. 11. Six months gestation

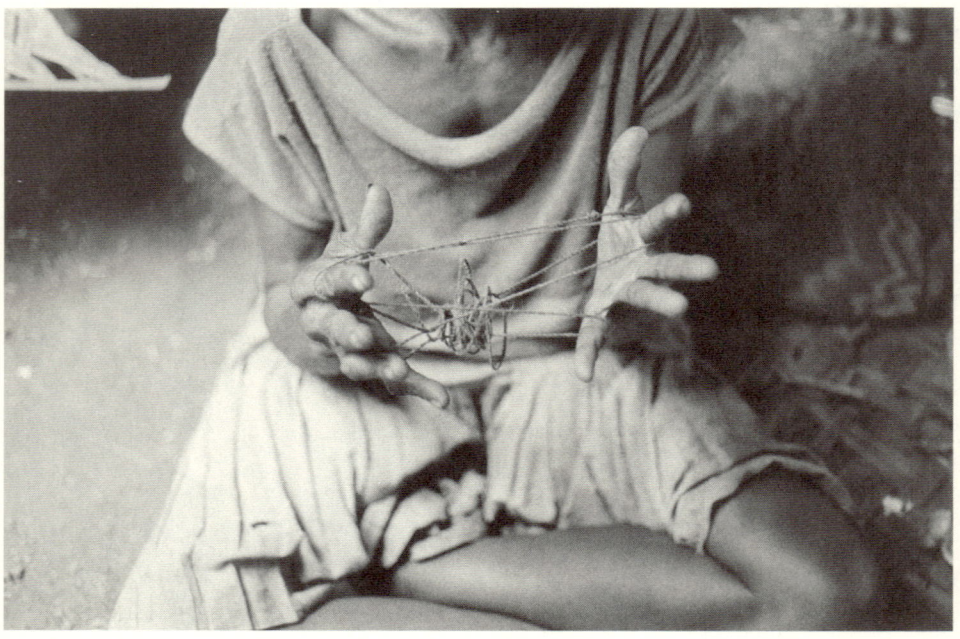

Fig. 12. Seven months gestation

Fig. 13. Eight months gestation

Fig. 14. Nine months gestation

covery, I walked back to Gohiya to tell Eunice and Geteli the news of Mari's return. While not greeting my news with total indifference, they certainly did not appear to share my sense of celebration and excitement. When asked whether they would visit Mari and the new baby, both indicated they would wait until she returned to the Women's Fellowship meetings or church. Their response was not unusual. In fact, all those with whom I subsequently spoke who were not members of Mari's *susu*, or affinally related, seemed disinclined to visit her in her hamlet. Several weeks elapsed before Mari emerged together with her new baby. During this time, the regular sight of several of Mari's female kin washing diapers in the creek reminded me that although she had delivered in the hospital she and the baby were still considered vulnerable to sickness and in need of care and protection.

When Mari did emerge to attend a Women's Fellowship meeting, the women offered her genuine yet, to my mind, muted congratulations. Like their initial responses to the news of the birth, they showed real, but seemingly restrained, interest in her newborn daughter. As with Emma and her baby Reni earlier in the year, both Mari and her baby were happily yet quietly assimilated back into the group, and from there back into the wider community of people living on Nuakata. In contrast, I had attempted and expected others to herald the birth event, to conspicuously welcome and laud the new life, to celebrate the birth of a new and unique member of the Nuakatan community. But birth does not inspire these responses on Nuakata. Birth is an occasion of great happiness for the birth parents and members of their respective *susu*, but, to my knowledge, is not celebrated by conventional rituals or gift-giving to the newborn, to the newborn's parents, or between members of its *susu* and affinal kin. Birth is cause for greatest celebration among members of the newborn's matrilineage, for the newborn's presence evokes the past (both living and dead) and invokes the future of the *susu*. Living members of the *susu* variously become mother, father, uncle, grandparent, brother or sister, and so forth in the newborn's presence.

My experience with Mari on the path, coupled with people's response to news of the birth, made me recall my earlier birthday celebrations and the ensuing discussions between Geteli, Wycliffe, and me. Learning of my birthday, Geteli had arranged a family party inside our house. Chickens were killed and cooked, vegetables, sweet potato, and tapioca prepared, and the twenty or so members of Wycliffe's family and in-laws gathered inside our house. Clearly unsure of what they should do, or what should happen on these occasions, all those present followed Geteli's muted orchestrations. After covering our table with a cloth provided by her mother, she carefully laid out all the food in an assortment of well-preserved enamel serving dishes. Each person was given a plate and fork and was instructed to wait for me to serve myself before the children and older people were served. In the crowded room conversation was constant, friendly, yet polite and subdued. Immediately following the communal meal everyone, except Geteli and several of her children, departed to do other things. Deeply touched by Geteli's act of love and friendship, designed to allay any sense of homesickness I might feel on the day, I was also embarrassed by the selective attention the birthday celebrations accorded me.

That my embarrassment was justified was later reinforced when Geteli and Wycliffe commented that until recently birthdays had not been noted, remembered, and certainly not celebrated on Nuakata. In explaining this, they stated in separate conversations that it is highly unusual to draw attention to someone by celebrating his or her living/staying when this living/staying is incomplete or unfinished. They added that people do not like to stand out from others. It is not only considered inappropriate but also dangerous to draw attention to either oneself or another in this way. Such attention distances and distinguishes someone from the rest. Wycliffe concluded, "We only do this when someone dies." On other occasions it may evoke gossip, jealousy, envy, and the illness and/or misfortune that accompanies these responses.

Wycliffe implied that (birthday) celebrations to mark someone's actual birth, the coming into life, "the life," or the time elapsed since the birth were considered premature, presumptuous, and misplaced on Nuakata. People did not speak of their own or others' "life" in such abstract, or static, categorical terms. Instead, they spoke of someone's living or staying. Nor did they speak of life beginning at birth or ending at death, or attempt to celebrate or distinguish that "life" as if it were a possession made and claimed by the living individual. Rather, they spoke of someone's living/staying, his or her ways. Attention was focused on "living" rather than "life," action rather than state, the individualizing activities of someone, rather than the individual person as such. This living/staying was considered contingent upon the actions of others, of those that made one's birth possible, that support one's growth, the affinal kin that one joins with to make new "living" possible by replenishing one's living *susu*, and, for some, the inspirational work of a Christian God. Only when someone's living was completed, or finished, could his or her "life" be encapsulated and celebrated as it was mourned by all those who expressed or enacted the loss of their particular living relationship with the deceased. In other words, "the life" was understood by diverse expressions of its loss in and by "living" people. Living, therefore, was contingent on relationships with others.

Of course there were more obvious historical reasons why birthdays were not remembered or celebrated on Nuakata. Before colonization, time was not siphoned through a calendar of progressive, numbered days, weeks, months, and years; its inflections were not charted by a clock that rhythmically and relentlessly pursued the infinitesimal moments of its passing. In Alina Nu'ata the word for time, *hauga,* is one and the same as the words for weather and lifetime. To speak of one is to invoke the others. People looked to one another and to the sky, the sea, and the earth for signs of time's presence, its past, and its future. These land-, sea-, and skyscapes enacted time's repetitions—its recursion—with infinite and spectacular variety. Seasons were known and named by the arrival of certain winds, the blossoming of plants, the presence of certain fish in the sea, the proclivity for storms, heat, or rain. The lunar cycle and the yearly arrival of the southeasterly wind further divided time. The transitions between day and night—predawn, dawn, morning, midday, early afternoon, late afternoon, dusk, evening, midnight—were determined by the varying lights cast by the sun's trajectory across the sky.

Alone or in concert, these expressions of both space and place constituted time's scapes, its familiar rhythms. While they continue to do so in the present day, time is now also measured by numbered days, months, and years, all named in English. Some people wore watches for decorative purposes, and the starting time, day, and date of church meetings was recorded in the minutes of these events. Maternal and child health clinics relied on a calendar to organize the timing of events. Birth dates were noted in the Birth Register compiled at the aid post, and parents also generally recorded the dates of their children's births. Given these changes, and given that segments of radio programs on the regional Milne Bay radio station and of the local mainland paper, the *Eastern Star,* were devoted to birthday greetings, it is not inconceivable that the time will come when people's birthdays will be widely acknowledged, if not celebrated, on Nuakata.

Confronted by a persisting notion of time, weather, lifetime, as repetitious or recursive, and with an understanding of death as the moment for collective reflection on and encapsulation of someone's life and living, I was forced to abandon the notion of life cycle as a guiding point for my research. My experience in the field confirmed what I only suspected prior to fieldwork, namely, that—as the writings of Massim anthropologists attest—death was the most significant prism for understanding one's life and living, if not the gendered person, in Massim communities. Nuakata, I had discovered, was no different in this regard.

The Garden at Last!

This realization coincided with my first trip to the garden with Geteli, which occurred toward the beginning of August. Having long exhausted my petitions to this effect, I was greatly surprised when Geteli arrived at Gohiya one day and volunteered to take me to one of her gardens on the slopes behind her hamlet, Gogobohewa. I resisted the impulse to ask, "Why? Why now?" and seized the opportunity with a sense of genuine enthusiasm and relief, mingled with a stream of silent mutterings about the virtues of patience!

The path to Geteli's garden began at the rear of Gogobohewa and passed by her husband's small tapioca plantation, before rising steeply to a small plateau, where a new yam house had been built by her brothers. Inside the yam house, pumpkins and a small collection of yams from the gardens of Eunice, her older sister Malida, and those of their daughters Jane and Geteli had been arranged in discrete piles by Malida, the most senior woman in the *susu*. These, I was told, were the first produce from the imminent harvest. In the coming weeks and months the yam house would be filled with pumpkins, sweet potatoes, and yams. Some yams would be set aside for future consumption, some for gifts to affinal kin, and others for the church. (Indeed, Wycliffe commented one day that the first yams from the harvest are given to the church in the same way that Abraham offered God his first-born son, Isaac.) When all the yams, pumpkins, and sweet potatoes were harvested, preparations for next year's gardens would begin. After Geteli had selected her garden plots (her own and one for each of her children) in consultation with her mothers and sisters, she would ask her brothers, husband, and fathers to gather at the plots on nominated days to fell trees and saplings. While they axed the trees, she and younger female members of her *susu* would slash away the undergrowth with their bush knives. Later, when the undergrowth had dried out, the plots would be burned, after which she and her husband would prepare them for planting. A month or so later all this occurred as Geteli had described, although there were many more helpers than I had anticipated. Geteli's sisters-in-law and cousins assisted her brothers, husband, and uncle with the clearing work, which was conducted in a spirit of great reverie. This work done, they all gathered at Gogobohewa to eat a meal prepared by Geteli, her mothers, and her sisters-in-law (see Fortune [1932] 1989, 105).

From the yam house, the path to Geteli's garden plunged inland through dense, entangled undergrowth. As we slashed our way forward, Geteli's backward glances in my direction alerted me to her concern about my safety. Perhaps this concern had thwarted my earlier attempts to make this journey. As we burrowed further inland Geteli confirmed what was clearly apparent by the nature of our journey. People other than kin are free to walk on this land, owned by members of her matrilineage; however, in practice this rarely occurs. Occasionally Geteli's husband or brothers trekked to these gardens, though she generally worked there alone.

Emerging from the canopy of vines and branches and the thicket of low-lying plants obscuring the path, we came to a semicleared, sun-drenched area: last year's garden, overrun by "weeds," but still dotted with pineapple plants, watermelons, sugarcane, a local leafy green vegetable, and several areca (betel nut) palms. Around the trunks of these palms were large bows made from dried strips of pandanus—a signal to would-be climbers or intruders that the palms and their produce were owned. Seemingly embarrassed by this haphazard assortment of plants and weeds, Geteli continued onward. As we passed through this area she pointed to two gardens on our left—one, her mother's, the other, her sister Jane's—neatly laid out on two adjacent slopes. Jane was living at Bunama at that time, but her mothers, Eunice and Malida, tended her gardens on her behalf. Five minutes later we reached Geteli's garden, also a picture of order. Although encircled by a tall forest of trees, the lush assortment of plants was bathed in morning sun. Like the two gardens we had seen minutes earlier, and others visible from the path encircling Nuakata, Geteli's garden was laid out in the grid pattern previously described by Macintyre for Tubetube (1983, 58–59). Larger felled trees acted as a border or boundary between the encroaching forest and the garden. The trunks of smaller felled trees divided the plot into squares measuring approximately one and a half square meters. The garden was planted with banana, tapioca, pumpkin, sweet potato, snake beans, thorny yams, seed yams, 'aibika, and peppers. There was not a weed to be seen. As with all the other gardens I had seen on Nuakata, banana palms, and tapioca were dotted around the periphery of the plot. Although some were planted toward the middle, they were planted on the edge of each square, consistent with an earlier comment made by Wycliffe that these plants "protect" the carefully staked and precious yam vines, generally positioned toward the center of the garden.

Standing, surveying the scene, noting Geteli's veiled pride in her work, I began to appreciate why this moment—this journey—had taken so long to eventuate. I saw for myself what was meant by her exclamation, "But there is nothing to see!," made in response to my first request in late February to go with her "to see her garden and understand her work." At that time her new gardens had been planted for only two or three months. From her point of view, there really was nothing for me to see in her gardens and certainly little I could do there. The effect of her labor to plant and weed the garden—and that of her husband and brothers to initially clear and prepare it for planting—was concealed within the ground, growing. Decimated and depleted by the drought of the previous year (1992), her old gardens, which continued to supply her family with food, had contained little more than tapioca. Although a staple subsistence crop, tapioca is generally regarded as inferior food to the other root crops, especially yams. Therefore, at the time of my earlier requests, there was little growing in her gardens from which she could take pride. My requests had been premature.

But Geteli's pride in her garden work was not the main issue that seized my imagination at that point. Rather, it was the thought that, from Geteli's point of view, I could only really understand her garden labor through its visible effects or outcome. Planting and gardening must be understood through harvesting and the harvested produce, just as the concealed work of pregnancy and conception could only finally be understood through its revelation: birth, the newborn. So, too, someone's life/living is finally understood in and through death. I realized, then, that in relation to gardening, pregnancy, birth, and notions of the person, Geteli and I had been approaching understanding from opposite directions. Impatient, I had sought understanding before rather than after the event. She was inviting me to look backward to understand what had gone before, while I had asked her to look forward to anticipate and imagine an abstracted, nonspecific version of what was yet to come. While skeptical of the notion of life cycle, I had nonetheless clung to some of its progressive, developmental, and categorical, epistemological assumptions.

Having stood there for several minutes, Geteli and I moved into the garden. She recovered a long metal digging rod from the bush and proceeded to demonstrate how to dig for thorny yams. Handing the rod to me, she instructed me to dig in a particular patch of soil. While I did this she inspected her pumpkin plants and yam vines, assessing whether or not it was time to harvest them. After this, she too dug for thorny yams and sweet potatoes, using her bush knife as a digging stick. As we worked she told me that had Roger and I arrived on Nuakata while gardens were being cleared, one would have been prepared and planted for us. After twenty minutes or so we had uncovered enough yams and sweet potatoes to fill two baskets. Only when she began to set aside a sizable portion of the harvest for Roger and me, and when on the return journey she selected a pumpkin for us from the yam house, did I realize that by resisting my earlier requests and taking me to the garden at that time of year Geteli had combined the showing of her garden with a giving of its produce. In doing this, she recognized and affirmed the relationship we shared. I knew, then, that it was no coincidence that she took me to this garden, her garden, rather than her children's gardens or the garden planted and tended by herself and her husband. Closer to us, the latter was located on the mountain path joining her mother's hamlet, Gohiya, to her husband's *susu* hamlet, Le'amatapouwa, on the Bwauli side of the island.

When I had repeatedly asked Geteli and Sineliko to take me to their gardens I had been hoping to learn gardening practices through seeing them. I had also been attempting to confirm the related hypotheses that an analogous relationship exists between pregnancy/birth and planting/harvesting—that knowledge of gardening would beget knowledge of birthing on Nuakata. But there, in the garden with Geteli, I began to realize that although I understood what this might mean in theory I had not known how to negotiate it in practice. If I had, I would have understood my initial presumption in asking Geteli and Sineliko to take me to their gardens, Sineliko's evasive rejection of my requests, and Geteli's deferred response. For this (actual and epistemological) journey to and from Geteli's garden demonstrated to me that, like other *susu*-owned land, gardens were considered places that supported the relational and temporal products they bear—be they children or yams.

Chapter Six

✍

Living Death

At eleven o'clock on a Friday night in April 1993 drums sounded across Nuakata informing people that someone had died.[1] A little later a messenger arrived at Gohiya with the news that a boat carrying the body of Eric's father had arrived at Tutuma, the hamlet of his widow. People were called to Tutuma for the *'waliwali*, the singing until dawn, to comfort and give company to Eric's father through the long, lonely hours of the night. Hurriedly changing their clothes, they gathered betel nut and tobacco and hunted for torches and batteries that might last the hour-long journey to the Bwauli side of the island. Roger and I had never met the deceased—a man in his early sixties—as he had passed away two weeks earlier during an extended stay with his granddaughter in Port Moresby. He was known to us only as the father of Eric—the island's land mediator and a local healer. On Nuakata he had lived in his wife's hamlet, which was some distance from Gohiya. Consequently we had barely met or said *"yauwedo"* (hello) to most of his kin. They were anonymous to us, people with whom we had no direct connection or responsibility. More than a little excited by our first opportunity to witness mortuary ceremonies and having sought and been granted approval to attend, we were anxious to join the procession of mourners. But still recovering from bouts of malaria, we decided to sleep and make the journey soon after dawn.

Wycliffe revealed that beating drums announce to the wider community that someone has died. Messengers from a paired matrilineage of the deceased take the news to people around the island and to family members living in other places. While messengers spread the news, summoning kin to mourn, women from the deceased's *susu* prepare him for burial—washing, adorning, and then dressing his body in fine clothes, before placing him on a stretcher covered by a newly woven mat. Devastated, distraught, and wounded by loss, the deceased's *susu* abandon their daily routines and gather together in the house with their loved one, crying out (*'wo'e*) to him in their grief and pain. In the midst of this desolation and turmoil, clan members from this paired matrilineage act to fill the breach, caring for their distressed relatives as they fulfill their responsibilities to prepare and bury the dead. Their actions restore some strength and wholeness to the wounded *susu* by orchestrating the burial rituals, which facilitate transformation of the deceased from a *susu* member living and staying with them on Nuakata to an ancestral spirit living and staying with clan ancestral spirits in the realm of the dead.[2]

On hearing news of the death, other people make their way to the deceased's hamlet to demonstrate sympathy for those left behind. More important, they go to mourn, to offer solace to the deceased through the long, lonely hours of the night. As night falls people congregate in the hamlet singing hymns together until dawn.[3] The deceased's spouse, together with members of his *susu*, keep vigil around the body, wailing, joking, and remonstrating with him. As dawn breaks many of the singers lapse into sleep or stumble home to rest before the burial, which usually takes place later that day or the next. In keeping with other Massim communities little, if any, nonessential work is done by others on the island at this time, for people demonstrate respect for the deceased by their quiet inactivity (see Wagner 1989, 255).

Dawn arrived, and after a hasty breakfast we set out for Tutuma on the northwest side of the island. Two-thirds of the way there, we passed through Eric's father's natal hamlet Gaimanugini, where the burial would take place later in the day. It was deserted, except for a lone woman who remained in the cemetery tending the garden around the graves. The hamlet was immaculate. The large area of ground in front of the houses was covered by freshly laid crushed coral, and the garden in the adjoining cemetery had been cleared of weeds. We walked quietly through the hamlet, only to learn much later that people show their respect for the deceased by skirting around the perimeter of his matrilineal or *susu* hamlet.

Wycliffe, his father (Noah), and big fathers (Antiya and Yamesi) stated that paths habitually taken by someone, particularly those leading in and out of his hamlet, should be avoided in the days and weeks immediately following death. His house—particularly if he was married—should be closed and abandoned to disintegrate and rot. People should approach his hamlet quietly, talking and acting with restraint. They should not climb or throw at fruit trees or coconut and betel nut palms; nor should they eat fish and shellfish. Most important, people should refrain from those activities by which the deceased is known and remembered. These expressions of respect (*bubuli*) should be observed until the burial feast is completed. Around this time fish is cooked by the paired matrilineage of the deceased's *susu,* and one member will visibly engage in the activities previously associated with the deceased. With these signs enacted, "forbidden things become unforbidden."

On Nuakata people spoke of someone's particular ways, his typical response to given situations, his relationships with people as paths (*yana'amwaha'amwaha*). These ways, these paths habitually taken or enacted, characterize someone's living as distinctive. Although possessed, someone's "paths"—unlike his body, spirit, or *susu* relationships—were not indissociable from him. Rather, like food grown for personal/family consumption, they were often spoken of as intimate, mutable, semialienable possessions, possessions that transform as they are transformed by whoever owns them, where, when, and for what purpose. Some paths were spoken of like food grown to give away—they were possessions that created and maintained connections between people (see Lithgow 1976; Young 1983, 20–26). Established and transformed by walking them, doing them, paths traced the territory of someone's living (see Young 1983, 25). The territory expressed the living as the living expressed the territory. This territory is grounded at birth in *susu* relationships, on *susu* land, and gradually extended beyond this with lived experience.[4] Paths, therefore, were the means by which someone's *living* was known and described, and upon death these paths or ways became the means by which his *life* was recalled.

From within the Western tradition it is tempting to consider paths a metaphor; namely, that someone's "ways" are like (but not equivalent to) the paths she takes in her daily travels. It is seductive to think of paths as a metaphor for an inner state or personality. But on Nuakata, people spoke of paths *as,* rather than merely *representing,* someone's ways (see chap. 3). When asked, Wycliffe stated that there is no word for personality in Alina Nu'ata. "We can only describe someone's ways in a sentence." For this reason, it would be a mistake to consider paths and personality as interchangeable terms. Indeed, it would be a mistake to forget that the term *personality* (the state of being a person) is itself a metaphor.[5]

Amwa'amwaha was founded on neither the notion of an internal personality nor the abstract category "person." Although people who have received primary school education know and can employ the term "person" when speaking in English, people rarely utter this word on Nuakata. There is no equivalent generic term in Alina Nu'ata, only a collective noun, *tomowa,* which was used in specific contexts—stories, sermons, conversations, or community meetings—to refer to either human beings in general or a mixed group of people. The same is true elsewhere in the Massim. For example, Battaglia (1990, 55) notes that on Sabarl, where there is no generic term for "the person," the word *tolomo* is used in certain contexts to denote "mankind." According to Thune (1989, 174–79), on northeast Normanby the term *tomotai* refers to human beings, dwarfs, elves, witches, and the *behai* variety of yams. Kuehling (1998, 33–36) also claims that on nearby Dobu Island, the word *tomota* is a generic gender-neutral term denoting person or human being, supernatural being and yams. Person and human being are conflated in her account.

On Nuakata, people or ancestors belonging to the same clan were generally addressed as *boda* or, in the case of ancestors, *bodaowa* (*boda–o–wa:* group of people–plural marker–completed past marker). As previously discussed (see chap. 2), particular human beings or people were referred to, described, and identified in terms of their particularities, be it their relationship to the speaker(s), their age and stage of life, sex/gender, marital status, the hamlet where they live, or their typical ways or activities. The communicative context—who was speaking to whom, when, where, and for what purpose—influenced what "particularities" were highlighted. For example, it was said of someone: *'iya loheya* (himself a young man), or *tenem vahala, 'ana'amwa'amwaha yababana* (that young woman, her ways are bad). Others were described as *tenem tauve 'ita* (that teacher), or *'iya tau modi'ini* (himself the angry one).

These latter descriptions all utilized the noun stem *tau,* which means both "body" and "one who . . ." The phrase is completed with a particular action, activity, or way of doing things (anger, humility, teaching, leading, joking, etc.) associated with (the) body or "the one who" enacts it. Accordingly, (the) body gives form to activity, embodies or bears activity,[6] and the embodiment of this activity becomes a means for describing, defining, if not identifying, someone in a given context. Bodies were also described in other ways. For example, people referred to one body as either *hi* (they) or *i* (he/she/it). In the Nuakatan counting system, twenty is *loheya ehebo,* where *loheya* denotes a young man in his twenties or early thirties. Twenty is equivalent to the sum of one man's fingers and toes. A related variation of this idea is encountered in descriptions of the number of people in a group. Take, for example, the expression "the three of you" found in English. Its equivalent, the expression *'amtautonuga,* comprises the plural form of "you" (*'am*), followed by *tau* and the number of people, whatever number that may be. It literally means "you, one who is three" or "three bodies are (as) one."⁷ In these contexts, then, (a) body is generally understood as (a) "one" that is both singular and plural; (a) unity based on the sum of its plurality; (a) collective that is also (a) unity.

The masculine inflection given to body in the counting system is by no means coincidental, as it is also embedded in the respectful term of address, *taubada,* for a senior man. The association of man with body was also expressed in the link between men and sorcery, women and witchcraft. Sorcerers were believed to act on or affect body/bodies, whereas witches were believed to act on or affect spirit. In both cases the effects were known through their embodiment in the victim or target. While it was possible for women to be sorcerers and men to be witches, this was highly unusual. But bodies, as such, were not spoken of as masculine or feminine. In conversation, the sex/gender of the body was assumed without being specified. It could only be known or inferred from the context.

Body/bodies were rarely spoken of as abstract or general categories or forms. Unlike some contemporary feminist philosophers, people on Nuakata did not refer to *"the* body" or "*a* body," because those articles do not exist in Alina Nu'ata. Body or bodies could not be distanced in this way from the people who enacted and possessed them, but were always described as inalienable possessions, whether spoken of in the plural, for example, *taudiwo* (their bodies), or in the singular, for example, *taugu* (my body). This necessarily raises the question of ownership— to whom does someone's body belong on Nuakata? The answer to this question has implications for issues of morality, agency, and subjectivity. A dead body (*taumwalowoi*), which may be referred to as such only by members of his clan, was both claimed and spoken of as owned and possessed by that *susu*/clan. While someone's living body certainly belonged to the one who speaks of it as "mine," for example, *taugu* (my body), the one who feels its pain in death as in living, it also belonged to his *susu* and clan. Although it was recognized that someone's living was made possible by the combined labors of *susu* and affine, male and female blood, affinal kin could not claim or possess someone's body as their own. Only the *susu* that bore the infant/child and/or adult could make such a claim. And they alone were entitled to bear this body to the grave.

While the abstract concept of the autonomous individual person did not exist on Nuakata, people clearly recognized and affirmed each other's embodied, enacted individuality or particularity. Singular human beings were understood to be relationally constituted, and their paths/ways, their things, their unique location or position among their *susu*, clan, affines, and the community at large particularized or individualized them. This notion of particularity or individuality was not equivalent to the Western individual or person, regarded as an autonomous agent or author of one's own actions. But people did recognize that there were some on Nuakata who acted *as if* they were autonomous. While older people accused some younger people of this behavior, it was not simply considered a generational phenomenon. Such people were identified as *dova dimdim* (like white people), because they acted selfishly,[8] on their own behalf, as if they did not belong and, therefore, have responsibilities to others. Equally, white people who acted with others in mind, as if connected and responsible to and for other people, were identified as *dova Papuan* (like Papuans). Singular human beings on Nuakata were, therefore, recognized as capable of (both causing and effecting) autonomous action that was motivated by their own wishes, wants, or desires. But this is not to suggest that an ontological basis for such action or desires was proffered by people on Nuakata. Clearly, M. Strathern's (1988) and Battaglia's (1990) contention that in Melanesia relational notions of personhood preclude the understanding of, or belief in, the unique individual cannot simply be discounted in the Nuakatan context, however it cannot be claimed with confidence.

And so, the paths taken by someone on Nuakata, his habitual ways, his relationships with people and things, constituted the territory of his individuality. In the prevailing Western intellectual culture of the "text" it may be tempting to understand someone's "ways" on Nuakata as inscribed on the landscape—an inscription that upon death is first honored, then erased by living kin. However, this metaphor, like that of personality, implies an imposition upon, rather than interpenetration between, human beings and land. It construes the land as a surface, a blank slate upon which a life is written, rather than a dynamic, inhabited place. It was this individual habitation which was forsaken when those paths could no longer be walked, enacted, or embodied. And so, the customary practice of avoiding the paths of the deceased, of closing and abandoning his house, respected the particularities of the lived life, acknowledging that the paths established and enacted in life necessarily discontinued and decayed in death.

Passing through Gaimanugini, we rounded the nearby point and met Roger's senior namesake, his wife, Sinetana, and Antiya coming from Tutuma. Singing and chanting over Eric's father's body had ceased with the dawn, and preparations were under way to transport the coffin by boat to Gaimanugini for burial. As a senior member of Eric's father's clan and a *galiyauna* responsible for the burial of the deceased, Antiya was needed at the cemetery. Although he was too old to carry and bury the dead, his fellow *galiyauna* valued his long experience and advice in these matters. Waligeha told us that he and his wife were making their way to Tutuma to assist with the cooking preparations for the burial feast. Although Waligeha, at least, was from a different clan than his father's—and therefore not strictly obliged to assist with the cooking preparations—it was clear to us that he did so out of respect for his father (Antiya), the dead man, and their clan. Standing together on the path, musing over the news, the others prepared to go. Disappointed at having missed the activities at Tutuma, we joined their solemn procession back to Gaimanugini.

Waligeha—and later Wycliffe, Antiya, and Yamesi—told us that preparations for burial occur in the cemetery adjoining the deceased's main *susu* hamlet and are overseen by several senior clan members—male or female. As owners of the deceased's body it is they who control events, deciding where "their body" will be placed, when, and by whom. At all times they tend "their" body lovingly, respectfully, for the spirit of the deceased (together with the ancestral spirits) is known to dwell in the hamlet with his living kin until *tau'ala'alahi,* the resurrection or transformation feast, which is generally held five or six days after burial. The disembodied spirit roams freely, watching over the unfolding events to ensure that his body, living, and living relationships are duly honored by *susu,* clan, and affinal kin.

By honoring the deceased's body, the embodied life already past, the clan also honors the collective body—the living *susu*/clan. In so doing they enable the living spirit of the deceased to readily join with the community of living *susu* and clan spirits at Mount Bwebweso, the realm of the dead. If people fail to properly honor the deceased they may invoke his wrath, causing his spirit to remain at Nuakata, creating havoc and mayhem. Acts of retribution by this spirit may make the living sick or even cause them to die.

The task of handling and tending a dead body is considered so important that each matrilineage appoints two *galiyauna*, senior men responsible for carrying the dead.[9] The *galiyauna*, assisted by other male clan members, also dig the grave. One of these men, the senior *galiyauna*, generally the most senior member of the paired matrilineage, carries the head and shoulders of the deceased and is known as *galiyauna mwala'ina* or big *galiyauna*. The other man, *galiyauna habuluna*, or small *galiyauna*, carries the deceased's lower body and legs. He is generally a less senior member of the paired matrilineage and, therefore, less experienced in the practices associated with burial. These are representative positions of great honor, responsibility, and risk, and for this reason the work of the *galiyauna* is watched closely and judged critically by others, especially members of the deceased's *susu*. The deceased's body—its smell, fluids, and flesh—is considered powerful and potentially dangerous. *Galiyauna* must show great respect and care to the deceased, for they are at constant risk of becoming ill themselves or making others ill. If the body is treated disrespectfully, as though dispossessed, the risk of illness to the dispossessors is magnified. This illness is spiritually mediated. Therefore *galiyauna* must protect themselves and others by observing strict food taboos (i.e., eating only roasted foods and refraining from all meat), burning leaves and plants to disguise the smell of the body, saying 'oba (magic words), and remaining distant from all others for a designated period of time after the burial.

Feeling like conspicuous intruders, we sat on the ground in the shade toward the rear of the hamlet, in the area where women were preparing food. We waited. As we waited we watched from a distance. Antiya and several other senior men from the clan were ambling around the cemetery, discussing where to dig the grave. Time dawdled by. People dallied over their preparations, working silently or speaking with one another in hushed tones. Others simply sat, their eyes drifting around the hamlet or scanning the sea for a sign of the boats. A sense of distilled inactivity prevailed. No one within earshot spoke of the death or mentioned Eric's father's name. If people spoke at all they spoke of the mundane tasks before them. In their silence I remained alert, vigilant, and tense. Having discarded my notebook and camera as a gesture of respect, I was placing considerable and undue faith in my ability to remember salient details of the events about to transpire. I told myself over and over again, reciting it like a vivisectionist's mantra, that nothing should be overlooked or considered insignificant.

Wycliffe stressed that while the presence of friends and nonclan mourners at the *'waliwali* and initial burial feast brings honor to the deceased, it is considered highly disrespectful for these people to name the dead and his passing. When declaring someone's passing, the word for death, *mwalowoi*, is used very selectively. Only the owners of the body, the *susu* and clan of the deceased—people who belong as one to another—pronounce the death of one of their kin, and they alone can utter his name. Unlike its English counterpart, *mwalowoi* does not mean a cessation of life, ceasing to be, but translates literally as "a return to before." Implied is a movement toward—or, perhaps, a return to—a prior time, place, or state. But who or what moves, to where, or when, remains implicit rather than explicit in this literal translation.

How or why naming the dead and declaring death causes offense was not explained. But, as these naming practices were consistent with the prohibition preventing use of *susu* names by non-*susu* members, it seemed likely that naming the dead, like naming the living, indicated the relationship between people. Perhaps naming the dead also highlighted the particular loss, exposing and thereby deepening the wounds felt by the remaining, living *susu*. By avoiding the name, people avoided provoking the sadness and distress this name evoked for the living *susu*. They also avoided causing offense to the deceased's spirit who, lingering in his hamlet until the burial feast is completed, may be distressed at leaving his loved ones behind. Perhaps, too, the declaration of *mwalowoi*—the return to before—can only be recognized and confirmed by the living members of the deceased's clan and *susu*.

During the mourning period and beyond, affinal kin refer to the dead by the term of address they used in life. People whose names are the same or sound similar to the recently deceased's may change their name in an effort not to offend. Others show respect for the dead and bereaved alike by referring to someone recently died as *'asiyebwa*.[10] When normally used in conversation, this word means "to be sick" or "sickness," but when used without personal or possessive pronouns it denotes, without being equivalent to, what English speakers call "the corpse." Named in these ways, someone recently dead, but not yet interred, was not simply understood as a dead body, a disembodied spirit, or even a confluence of relationships already past. Rather, as the detached term *'asiyebwa* suggests, the recently deceased was, for a time, the embodiment of sickness and depletion.[11] Wycliffe stated that at the time of burial this sickness passes into the ground, where it slowly decays. People never eat garden produce grown in or around their cemetery, for they risk illness by feasting on the flesh of their ancestors.[12] However, they will plant and harvest seed yams there, in order to replenish and multiply their seeds for future planting. And so it is understood that the flesh of *susu* and clan life permeates the soil, replenishing the ground on which living *susu* and clan stay. While the flesh decays and with it the combined labor of matrilineal and affinal kin, the bones of the deceased remain as permanent, if anonymous, testimonies to the living *susu*.

Later on, well past the time of burial and when the flesh may well have rotted away, people unrelated to the deceased say his time is over, finished, completed (*yana hauga'i'ovi*). As discussed in chapter 5, *hauga* also means weather in Alina Nu'ata. Weather and time are believed to have their seasons, their cycles, but each repetition is considered unique. Each has its consequence felt long after it has passed away. As indicated by the use of *yana*, the distant possessive pronoun, someone's time (*yana hauga*) belongs to him only in an alienable sense. Unlike body and spirit, or particular relationships with matrilineal kin, someone's time is not an integral, fundamental, or inalienable aspect of him. It is time potentially shared by or between others. Time assumes embodied forms; however, the particular, fleshy forms of these embodiments are transient, ephemeral, finite. Understood this way, time is embodied, and embodiment is temporal. In time someone is grown, nurtured, and sustained into mature embodiment, and in time his strength diminishes, dissipates, and finally ceases before his body withers away. Somebody's lived time must be completed by all those who mourn his passing. His past ways and obligations must be completed by living kin.

More than an hour passed before the boats carrying the coffin and the mourners rounded the point and moored in the waters directly out from the hamlet. Two *galiyauna* from the Ao'ao clan carefully loaded the coffin onto a dinghy, brought it ashore, and placed it under the house adjoining the cemetery. With the deceased temporarily laid to rest and watched over by female kin, the *galiyauna* joined the four or five men in the cemetery who were digging the grave. In the coffin's wake came the principal mourners: Eric's mother (the widow) and her seven adult children—five daughters and two sons. As Eric's mother stepped ashore, dressed in a black calico skirt, black T-shirt, and a black cloth covering her head and face, a wave of grief flooded the hamlet. From behind the veil anguished cries pierced the stillness, disrupted the waiting, announced the loss. Unable to stand or proceed alone, she was supported by her daughter on one arm and a female member of the Ao'ao clan on the other. Her sense of desolation and distress was palpable. With halting steps the three disconsolate women—widow, sister, and child—traced the path already taken by the *galiyauna*. Although a relatively short distance, it was an arduous crossing punctuated by mournful wailing that seemed to ebb as it flowed.

Death creates rupture among the living. Living kin, *susu* and affines alike, must cope with the loss from their lives of someone with particular "ways," but they must also adjust to the loss of someone who is a visible, tangible, and unique confluence of living social relationships. Those relationships actively created in life, between someone and his friends and affinal kin, are actively unraveled upon death. No longer able to do things together, the relationship dissipates, then finally disappears.

Wycliffe, Antiya, and Yamesi stressed that while the clan honor the dead by claiming his body and his name as their own, the widow (or widower)—as principal mourner—honors and respects the spouse by the observance of customary mourning practices and by visibly displaying grief. For a widow, in particular, the death of her husband ushers in a period of intense mourning. It is a bleak transitional time, culminating in the dissolution of the obligatory, reciprocal relations between herself (and her kin) and her husband's *susu*. Bound to stay in her husband's hamlet for the period of mourning declared by his kin, the widow dwells there on the margins, redefined to her affinal kin as "our widow" (*yamahiwape*).[13] During this time, particularly immediately following death, she does not wash herself. She "does not make herself properly." Nowadays she dresses in long dark clothing, but in the past widows wore ankle-length grass skirts, and their faces and bodies were smeared with a putrid mix of ash and coconut oil. Now, in the day(s) leading up to the burial, a widow stays with her husband's body, her desolation evident. Unclean, unkempt, unable to eat with her affines or eat produce from their gardens, she dwells among them at their behest, a living testimony to loss. Unable to return to her *susu* at this time, she belongs with neither affines nor *susu*, but remains in a liminal state, neither dead nor fully alive, a nameless outsider—a living embodiment of her husband's death, the loss experienced by his *susu*, and the imminent dissolution of his affinal relationships. With her spouse and their living relationship now lost to her, her accepted place within her husband's hamlet forgone, it is her grief alone that recalls her marital identity—an identity, a place, a confluence of reciprocal relationships that fade away with the withering of her sorrow.

Swamped by emotion from this coffin-bearing tide, by the sight of the grieving widow and children, my perspective suddenly dramatically changed. There, amid people in obvious distress and pain, my sense of anticipation and curiosity about the forthcoming events evaporated, leaving a feeling of disgust in their place. Confronted with people's real, tangible loss, their wailing and tears, their attempts to cling to the body, to summon new life from it, to forestall death—feelings and responses familiar to me—I questioned my right to be there. How had I ignored the reality that this was a time of real loss and vulnerability for the bereaved, a time culminating in the final passing from sight, touch, smell, and sound of someone unique, known, and loved? By what leap of the imagination, by what violent act of abstraction had I hoped for a death, imagining the bereaved as disembodied representatives of distinct mortuary rituals; as cultural icons rather than living, loving, fleshy human beings? In remembering this, how should I respond? How best could I respect the dead, the bereaved, the living? By my presence or my absence? On what grounds would I base this ethical decision? My own? The people of Nuakata's? Anthropology's? How should I enact and negotiate the irreconcilable tension between my participation and observation on Nuakata in this particular context? Uncertain and unable to voice my plight to those around me, I remained in the hamlet, my dilemmas unresolved.

Faced with this ethical dilemma, I reflected on the ambivalence, the agnosticism that pumps at the heart of the participant observation methodology. Participant observation is both a contradiction in terms and a contradiction in deeds. When its epistemological pretensions are taken as real possibilities, the participant observation method offers the ethnographer hope for a truly empathic understanding and knowledge of the people with whom she temporarily lives. There is the suggestion that by placing herself with, and participating in, the daily lives of people, the ethnographer may become so familiar with these lives and their living that she understands them *almost* as they understand themselves. The method as such invites the ethnographer to strategically play with the incongruities between her life in the field and the one beyond its margins—to temporarily suspend disbelief, to partition and immobilize doubt, to assume faith, in the interests of an arguably "purer, deeper, more authentic" participatory understanding. This form of participation—life, living in the field—is totally dependent upon relationships of mutual intimacy and trust (Eipper 1996; J. Weiner 1998).

But the ethnographer does not only participate. She also observes. Participation is a vantage point from which to view and speculate upon shared lives. In observing while participating the ethnographer-observer not only sees but also selectively attends to and filters what comes before her, rendering it irrelevant, salient, incidental. Through speculation she makes an object, an event, an experience of her participation (see Abrahams 1985; Jackson 1989, 51). The speculation born of participant observation is not subject to the same constraints as participation. The ethnographer may subsequently question and challenge practices and, in so doing, liberate her disbelief, mobilize her doubts, and disavow her faith. Observation of this kind necessarily compromises both participation and the understanding born of participation by consolidating imagined boundaries and reinforcing the space between observer and observed. This space is neither vacant nor neutral. Its definitions and boundaries are contested, negotiated, as often the observer is also the observed. As such, it is an intersubjective, social, and ethical space. Perceived as distance, the space bolsters difference; perceived as proximal, it solidifies similarities. If under observation's sway participation and the trust on which it is founded become mere playful performance, serving purely epistemological interests, then the ethnographer risks bad faith. Not only is she ethically compromised, but she also jeopardizes her relationships with people and the very understanding that flows from such relationships.

Floundering in this maelstrom of emotion, I looked across to Roger's senior namesake, hoping for reassurance, some indication that it was appropriate for us to stay and bear witness to this grief. But his thoughts seemed elsewhere. His face was awash with pain. Cast into the distance, his eyes *seemed* to reveal the haunting story of his own grief and loss—the sudden, inexplicable "passing" of his fourteen-year-old daughter less than a year earlier.[14] Following his gaze, I recalled my grandmother who had died soon after we left Australia. Sitting with head bowed, these griefs—Eric's father, Waligeha's daughter, my grandmother—felt as one. But a short time later, when this burst of feeling had passed, I wondered at my presumption. Then, Waligeha's grief and my own *seemed* not one but two—similar yet distinctly different—losses. Of course there were many obvious ways in which this was true, not the least being that, in contrast with Waligeha's loss, the death of my aged and infirmed grandmother was expected, anticipated, although none the less mourned. Above all I realized that Waligeha's loss must be understood in the knowledge of his absolute certainty that death was not a cessation of living but the joining of the deceased with matrilineal kin already gone before. Although I was attracted to this understanding, I did not share Waligeha's comforting certainty—the certainty of his inheritance. But this certainty did not only bring comfort, it also brought inconsolable sorrow. Sure of his daughter's place among her *susu*, in the realm of the dead, Waligeha was sure too that her place in this realm was not his. Waligeha's abiding love for his daughter—a love that enacted and substantiated his paternity in the realm of the living—was eternally thwarted by her death. In the realm of the dead his daughter had no tangible need of his care and nurture. I imagined, without knowing, that this loss must be akin to amputation. Like the phantom limb, the nurturing love remains, longing to give form and movement to its impulses.

Unlike someone's *susu* relationships and identity, which were considered continuous—an irrevocable birthright that conferred a distinct, identifiable place among the living and the dead—affinal identities, established through marriage or one's paternal inheritance, were considered ephemeral, discontinuous, insubstantial. Marriage relationships replenished living *susu*, because without in-marrying spouses a *susu* could not regenerate. Marriage relationships directly regenerated a *susu* by reproducing offspring and indirectly replenished them by the additional labor power they contributed to the husband's and wife's *susu*. However, the regenerative power of the marriage relationship was lost upon the death of one partner.

Absorbed by these griefs, it was some time before I was aware of Roger's discomfort beside me. Suffering from a malarial headache and no longer able to countenance what felt like voyeurism, he decided to discreetly slip away and return to Gohiya. Not wishing to offend or draw undue attention to ourselves, I stayed behind. Roger's passage out of the hamlet was immediately noted by people with concern and what seemed like disappointment. When I offered an explanation in English to one young man, originally from Normanby Island but at that time living in Port Moresby, he boldly dismissed my suggestion that people might resent our presence. On the contrary, he said, "They felt thankful and honored by your show of respect. Where is your camera? Why don't you take photos?" Looking around I noted that others there—kin from Moresby—had cameras and were taking photos freely. I reasoned that as kin of the deceased man their actions were permissible. Surely, though, it was inappropriate for me to behave in a similar fashion. "And why," I asked rhetorically, "should our presence bring honor to the dead man and his kin? We did not know him." Raising his eyebrows the man replied, "But you are *dimdim*." At that moment my attention was drawn back to the widow.

Assuming their place by the coffin with women from the dead man's *susu*, the widow and her daughters (also dressed in black) continued their vigil by the body. As people came to sit with them for a while, some praying, some bearing flowers, many crying over the body, the widow's wailing reached a crescendo before trailing away as the sympathizers moved on. While all this was happening Eric and his older brother, John, together with their families, positioned themselves on the shoreline, some distance away from their mother and sisters. Talking quietly among themselves, they seemed like marginal bystanders to the unfolding events. Seated close by was a senior man from the Ao'ao clan, who was instructing Anne's father (also a member of the Ao'ao clan) and—through him—Anne, a woman in her late thirties and first-born in her generation, in the customary ways to respect the dead. Around this time the two *galiyauna*, working in the cemetery under a fierce sun, took a break from their digging and returned to the area close to the house and the coffin. They took great care to avoid direct physical contact with people, particularly the mourners. As the sun rose higher in the sky and the mound of earth grew in the cemetery a stream of people trickled into the hamlet, many bearing food to contribute to the burial feast.

Wycliffe later told us that the current practice of burying the dead in horizontal graves, six feet deep (some with concrete headstones), in a cemetery on the margins of the main *susu* hamlet, was termed missionary-style burial. While he did not know when the old burial practices finished and this new form of burial began, he attributed the changes to the missionaries.[15] Yamesi together with his friend David (the brother of Antiya)—senior men in their mid- to late sixties—spoke with me several times about the old ways, the burial practices they had witnessed as boys. Yamesi said that

> in the past *galiyauna* dug the grave maybe three and a half feet deep. The *galiyauna* himself went down into the grave and then the *taumwalowoi* ("the one gone before," the deceased) was carried and placed inside the grave. From his nose down they put him down in the grave and they sat him there. The *galiyauna* stood and straightened up the dead person from his neck down, and the head [of the corpse] came up, outside the grave.

Present during one of these conversations, Wycliffe added details told to him by his grandfather:

> When they were putting the dead body vertically inside the grave, all the owners of the dead body watched and if the jaw of the dead body fell, and the head *galiyauna* did not use his own mouth [to reposition it], then he was not considered a good *galiyauna*. Also if fluid escaped from the mouth of the corpse at this time, then the *galiyauna* had to drink it.

Once the corpse was positioned correctly, then, according to Yamesi, "they closed the grave with timber and covered the body with earth, and the head [which was outside] they covered with a *'walata* [or pot]." During a later conversation Noah, in consultation with Antiya, further explained:

> The head *galiyauna* slept with his head on his right hand which rested on top of the right hand side of the *'walata*. This sleeping arrangement remained until the head rotted and popped off—maybe several weeks. The men slept in a line maybe up to twelve men, six on either side of the *'walata*, and at either end of the line there had to be an actual sorcerer. When the person with his head on the *'walata* coughed, then everyone had to turn over. When he wished to relieve himself, the next man in line would take his position until he resumed. The person who rested his head on the *'walata* listened for rumbles like thunder as the

body rotted. When they heard this, they then knew that already there were worms inside. They would build a small hut to protect themselves from rain, and when they opened the *'walata*, the worms would shoot up out of the head, hit the roof and fall on them. They did not kill them, as the worms would die naturally themselves. If the worms landed on them, it was a sign that they were doing their job well. They are said to be good *galiyauna*. During this time the *galiyauna* would observe strict food taboos. They would eat only roasted food, no protein, no coconut cream. They used different smelling trees and special magic words to hide the smell and protect them.

According to David, only the *galiyauna* would chew, smoke, and eat roasted food. Their helpers would eat porridge made out of taro. Every day they had to kill a pig for those helpers until the head came off. All of, say, Nuakata would bring food to them, not just the owners of the body. Yamesi continued:

> Once the body rotted, the person who was resting his head on the pot would take the *'walata* off, pull the skull off and take it to one big river. They would take the rotten flesh off with their mouths, not their hands. . . . They would not close the grave where the body was buried, for later they would take out the bones and use the grave again for another clan member. These bones would be buried elsewhere.

Repugnant to me, these burial practices were also repugnant, even ghoulish, to Wycliffe. It was a shared reaction matched only by Wycliffe's horrified response to the discovery that in Australia, as in other parts of the world, some people cremate the dead. While I offered a range of explanations for the practice of cremation—pragmatism (e.g., space and money), religious disavowal of burial, respect—my justifications were met with utter disbelief and disgust. Wycliffe's reaction reflected his understanding of the relationship of the dead to the living, death to life, body/bodies to spirit(s). He, like his elders, noted that in the realm of the living, people necessarily comprise both body (*tau*) and spirit (*'alu'alawa*). In this realm only people possessing exceptional powers (witches and sorcerers) can, in certain contexts, dissociate their spirits from their bodies. Upon death, however, people's spirits are no longer bounded or constrained by their bodies; their spirits remain, free to roam in the realms of the living and the dead. While people's living bodies or embodiments discontinue in death, their bones remain. For this reason, Wycliffe believed that, where possible, dead bodies should be left in *susu*/clan ground so that their flesh may decay and rot leaving the skull and bones placed in the ground. There they remain as a permanent yet, more often than not, anonymous expression of both their own living past and that of their *susu*/clan. In one sense, then, this past—now interred, but previously retained in skull caves—quite literally grounds the lives of those kin already present and those kin yet to come.

Just as my attempts to explain why people in some cultures cremate their kin did not satisfy Wycliffe so his claim that the historical practices of the *galiyauna* were simply signs of respect seemed inadequate to me. He, like his father, big father, and uncles, spoke of their sense of relief and gratitude that these onerous burial practices had ceased with the missionaries. Repulsed yet captivated by the (imaginary) image of decaying flesh held in the mouth of the *galiyauna* as he prized it away from the skull, it was some considerable time before I could shift "my gaze" peripherally to review the context for such practices. For, like my colonizing forebears—missionaries, explorers, anthropologists, and government administrators—I was intrigued, perhaps even seduced, by the specter of this historical Other, realized in these seemingly barbarous acts. I was, however, also suspicious of the subject inquirer this Other reinforced. It was this suspicion that forced me to look once more at this spoken, barely remembered, yet discontinued past.

Imagining that past, I allowed myself to contemplate if my (and, more important, Wycliffe's) response to the historical practices of the *galiyauna* had been shared by his forebears. Perhaps these acts, compellingly repulsive in and of themselves, were curious acts of devotion, expressions of care made all the more powerful and poignant by their dangerous, transgressive quality. Perhaps the actions of the *galiyauna*—positioning the jaw with their own jaw, drinking the putrescent bodily fluids, resisting the impulse to brush away showering worms engorged with the festering flesh of the deceased—were unparalleled marks of love and respect, revealing the deceased as one with the *susu* and clan. Maybe these practices revealed *galiyauna* as people, more specifically men, who literally and metaphorically embraced death and the deceased in order to facilitate its transformation from corpse to ancestral bones, embodied to disembodied spirit, and to aid the deceased's journey from Nuakata to Bwebweso. Perhaps, too, the honor and respect granted to *galiyauna* for their courage in handling the potentially dangerous corpse was enough reward for them to undertake these horrible duties.

Such an interpretation of the historical practices of the *galiyauna* is consistent with anthropological reappraisals of the transgressive nature of cannibalism and the significance of its social memory (Arens 1979; Macintyre 1995, 34–39). Seen in this light, cannibalism's greatest insult was to treat the other, the slain enemy, in a way that contemptuously gestured to the respect and care shown by *galiyauna* for a deceased body belonging to their clan. Acts of cannibalism, of appropriating and feasting on the flesh of an enemy, defiled the deceased's body and, by implication, his *susu* and clan. Unlike usual treatment of the corpse, the body of the deceased was handled and ingested as a dispossessed object or thing. In so doing, his relatedness and belonging to *susu* was desecrated, denied. Just as the acts of the *galiyauna* can be considered unparalleled expressions of respect and relatedness, so cannibalism can be thought of as an unparalleled mark of disrespect or transgression that literally disembodied, depleted, and disempowered not only the dead but also his living relations. Defiled and diminished by this act, the afflicted *susu* and clan could only restore themselves by retribution enacted in kind.

During my time on Nuakata, cannibalism, the collective memory of it, acted as a powerful and persuasive trope, one hostage to evangelical Christian rhetoric. Along with witchcraft, magic, and sorcery it was regularly cited as a forbidden, demonic practice, hostile to the Christian God and His church. Its eradication by the missionaries is celebrated as marking the community's delivery from a depraved and primitive past.

In the early afternoon, women from the Yalasi/Bolime and Bwauli/Bomatu Women's Fellowships entered the hamlet, bearing crosses, wreaths, and bouquets of flowers. Walking in two lines, headed by the United Church pastors, they approached the coffin and the mourners, singing a hymn in full voice. The pastors discreetly withdrew. Assembling around the coffin, the widow, and her daughters, the women stopped singing and paid their silent respects to Eric's father, carefully placing the flowers on his coffin and the surrounding mats. Several women prayed, then singing rose up again, this time seeming to gather and hold the widow's grief in a chorus of support, a hymn of solidarity.

Their declaration complete, the Women's Fellowship quietly retreated to an area close by, where people had been invited to sit for the church service preceding the burial. A senior male from the Ao'ao clan opened the service in prayer. The head pastor then addressed those gathered in Dobu (the church language), before the head deacon delivered a longer, impassioned speech about the glory of God. The same member of the

Ao'ao clan closed proceedings with a prayer. The service over, attention turned to the owners of the body. People watched and waited silently as the *galiyauna,* instructed by senior kin, made their preparations to move the coffin toward the grave.

Wycliffe indicated that it was usual for the deceased's body to rest on a narrow stretcher lined and covered by sago palms and mats. Following the church service, the *galiyauna* raise the stretcher to shoulder height and begin the journey to the grave. He, and later Noah and Yamesi, explained that women, together with their infants, stand on the path leading to the grave. At the appropriate time these women carry their infants underneath the stretcher as a gesture of respect to the deceased. In a taped interview conducted with Wycliffe and Noah several days after the burial, Noah stated:

> After death the spirit of the deceased, together with their ancestral spirits, gather in the hamlet of the deceased and remain there for three or four days until the feast known as *tau'ala'alahi*. These spirits are visible to small children in the night. Children wake up crying because they are frightened of them. They are not visible to bigger people.

Wycliffe added:

> At the time of a death, ancestors may want to come and take the child's spirit away with them, because they may feel that the parents of the child are not looking after the child properly. [People] believe that most of the spirits like small children. . . . By walking under the body it shows a sign of respect to it. . . . If ancestors come and get the spirit of the child we use the word *labavai*. It occurs without people seeing or knowing. It doesn't mean that the child will die, but their spirit will be affected. Maybe the ancestors will carry the spirit away and they will be patting the spirit—looking after the spirit in their hands. Physically the child will be crying all the time.

In a taped conversation with Yamesi in our house several weeks later, Yamesi suggested:

> Maybe the ancestors . . . will come because the child's parents may be smacking and scolding the children. Parents can tell that this has hap-

pened because the child won't be eating properly; its health, its look not good. And then the parents must take the child to anyone who knows the *'oba* for *labavai* and [maybe] they will call the child's spirit back or call them to leave the baby girl or boy and go back to their place, and then the child will be healthy again (*tubuiuyo*). This sickness won't happen by itself, only if parents aren't looking after the child properly.

Wycliffe, Noah, and Yamesi all implied that when taken by ancestral spirits, the newborn/infant's spirit is separated from the body. The boundary between the body and the spiritual realm is rendered permeable. Dispirited, the newborn's body becomes depleted, sick, and may even die. Young children are considered attractive to ancestral spirits, as they are playful and unspoiled by living. Wycliffe explained that, unlike most older children and adults, small children can see spiritual things—ancestors, dwarfs, and fairies—"because [they] . . . aren't mature, they can't think yet," and they cannot protect themselves. By providing good care and demonstrating respect for the deceased, the infant's kin protect her from ancestral spirits. The spirits of ancestors, witches, and other things are known to take or interfere with the spirits of older children and adults. However, such acts were not termed *labovai*. Wycliffe insisted that the term *labovai* only refers to the acts of ancestral spirits to take the infant's spirit and the "bad feeling" arising in the infant as a result of this action. *Vai* means "to take or get," and, as noted in chapter 5, the stem word *laba* means "line." It is used in the words *labalaba* and *labahi*, which denote the temporospatial process of birthing, of crossing the line between inside and outside, between the unborn and born state, between concealed spiritual realms and the visible, embodied realms of the living.

Hoisting the coffin on their shoulders, the two *galiyauna* carried it toward the grave site where Antiya and several other senior men were gathered. Women trailed behind, carrying flower arrangements and a bowl of yams. Then came the widow and her children, followed by a procession of people—kin from Port Moresby and nearby Normanby Island, and friends and kin from Nuakata. Reaching the grave, and with burial imminent, Eric's mother asked the owners of her husband's body if they would open the coffin, so that she could see him for one final time. Without lowering the coffin to the ground the two *galiyauna* prized open the lid. A hubbub developed around the widow as she stepped forward toward the coffin. As the cloth covering the deceased's face was peeled back, powder was released into the air to protect people from the smell of the body, now dead for over two weeks. Senior men burned fine smelling leaves, waving the smoke around to discourage flies. Seeing her husband for the first time after his long absence in Port Moresby, glimpsing his face withered and cast with a deathly pallor, Eric's mother let out a desperate, agonized cry. Rising to a pitch, her cry once again pierced the air, this time puncturing the seamless flow of events delivering the body to the grave. It was as if in that fleeting, shrill moment the gravity of her loss was realized, the finality of death faced. Stricken, she collapsed into awaiting arms. Following their mother, the man's daughters also stepped forward to see their father, and they, too, were overcome with grief. Bracing themselves against the force of this grief, the two *galiyauna* closed the coffin and, together with their kin, moved silently onward to the grave. As the powdered haze fell to the ground the distraught widow and her weeping daughters were assisted back under the house. Brian, the junior pastor, offered a brief prayer for the deceased man. This completed, the two *galiyauna*, advised by senior men at every turn, gingerly lowered the coffin into the hole, resting the casket on the deceased man's sleeping mat that lined the grave. New mats were produced and placed on top of the casket.

Wycliffe later explained that the deceased's body is carefully placed in the grave so that the head points in the direction of the rising sun. Like the sun, the spirit of the deceased is believed to rise beyond the grave. At the end where the head is buried a pot of roasted yams is placed on top of the grave by the members of the deceased's clan. Known as *tamahina* (literally, father, mother), or "food for a journey," this pot of yams is placed there to sustain the deceased during the journey to Bwebweso, the realm of the dead. It is considered "spiritual food." Like the deceased's body, the yams will rot away, but their spirit sustains the spirit of the deceased (cf. Fortune [1932] 1989, 181).

Reflecting on the "olden days," Wycliffe and Yamesi told me that their ancestors believed that on the journey to Bwebweso people's spirits came to a fork in the road. At that intersection two paths diverged, each with a spiritual woman guarding their entrance. On the right-hand path stood Sinelautegege, a good spiritual woman, who waited to claim people who had been good (e.g., those who have lived humbly and in harmony with others) throughout their lives. Sinelautegege washed people, making them clean, so that they may enter Bwebweso with joy. On the left-hand path stood Sinemuyamuyalele, a bad spiritual woman, who took those who have been bad (e.g., sorcerers, witches, those who have killed others) throughout their lives. Sinemuyamuyalele took them to the fire where they burn. Later, they went to the bad spiritual place, an unnamed place close to Bwebweso.

What little was known of Bwebweso at the time of my stay on Nuakata was based on the eyewitness accounts of people who were long dead, among them Yamesi's mother. In the past, those who knew the necessary magic journeyed there to visit their kin. These people described it as a "nice place," where there was "no rubbish." "There's no bad things there and the people are nice, friendly. People do not go to the toilet there; . . . there is no night, only day" (Wycliffe). Yamesi added, "At Bwebweso all the clans have a tree and if one of the leaves or branches fall off, then the people staying there say, 'Tomorrow one of our friends will join us here.'"

As people trickled back toward the hamlet I, too, withdrew from the grave. Remaining at the site were the two *galiyauna* and senior male members of the clan. Positioning myself within view of the grave, I saw them place some of the dead man's belongings in the grave. Not long after, I was tapped on the shoulder and invited to come and eat. Ushered into an enclosed veranda, my hosts then left me alone to eat. Once again I had occasion to ponder my position, my difference. Singled out as a guest of great importance, amid a gathering that included kin who had traveled from distant places at great expense, I felt acutely embarrassed at this show of respect.

Later, when I reflected on burial practices on Nuakata past and present, it seemed that just as women on Nuakata bore children/kin into the realm of the living so—through their representatives Sinelautegege and Sinemuyamuyalele—they bore the spirits of their kin into the realm of the dead. But as indicated earlier, the spirit's embodiment—and later its liberation from temporospatial, bodily constraint—was only made possible by the complementary, supportive activity of both *susu* and affinal men. *Galiyauna,* past and present, delivered the deceased's body to the grave. In the past these men subsequently removed the deceased's skull, then carried it in secret to a river or the sea, where it was washed, anointed with coconut oil, and adorned with flowers. At that point—according to Wycliffe (speaking in English)—

> [t]he two *galiyauna* would remain concealed from view until their preparations were completed. Then the sister, mother or uncle would be crying and she would go and look for them. She had to be a well-prepared woman. She had to put some things around her body (leaves, magic words) to protect her from the men's power. Because the two *galiyauna* had fasted they had different spiritual power. She would find them, and when she found them, they would all come to the village and the skull would be carried by the head *galiyauna*. When they came into the village, all the women had to leave the village. Only women who knew the magic and could protect themselves could stay. When they came, they sat on shelves made by owners [of the skull] and they chewed areca nut. Then the village elder would take the spiritual power away from the *galiyauna*.

The responsibility of the two *galiyauna* for carrying the deceased's skull did not end with the delivery of his skull to his *susu* village. One journey remained: a journey undertaken during *guyau*, the final feast of the mortuary sequence. Wycliffe translated *guyau* as gift or offering, thanksgiving for the spirits. During this feast the senior *galiyauna* carried the skull of the deceased to the sacred skull cave of his clan and placed it there with the anonymous skulls of his maternal forebears. There the skulls remained, a permanent testimony to an embodied ancestry, a reminder of lived time, long past. Through the actions of *susu* women and men, the journey taken by someone into life, then later to "the before" of death, was made possible. Although the burial and birthing practices of *susu* women and men have changed over time, women have continued to carry and give birth to children, thereby reproducing and sustaining their living *susu*, while senior men have continued to assume responsibility for carrying their clan's dead.

With the burial complete, the hole filled, attention turned back upon the principal mourners: members of the dead man's *susu*, the widow, and her children. For the first time Eric and his brother moved to sit with their mother and sisters under the house. Senior women from the Ao'ao clan placed red hibiscus in the mourners' hair and then washed their hands. This done, final preparations for the communal feast began. Women who had been busying themselves with the food laid banana palm mats on the ground in two long lines. Women sat at one mat and men at another. Tapioca, pumpkin, and sweet potato were distributed evenly along these mats. Two smaller mats with rice, a small amount of tinned fish, and a plentiful supply of tapioca and pumpkin were laid out on higher ground closer to the houses. Men from the deceased's clan sat at one, and the pastors and deacons from both the Yalasi and Bwauli churches sat at another. Grace was said and the meal began. Solemnity gave way to restrained levity.

Wycliffe explained that as a sign of respect, a sign of living diminished by loss, the principal mourners—generally the widow/widower and children of the deceased—observe food taboos until the feast known as *bilai*. The owners of the dead body cook the food for this feast. It is following burial. During this period of fasting the principal mourners are forbidden from eating highly valued foods, such as taro, yams, sago, fish, or protein of any kind. At the feast the owners of the dead body wash the hands of the widow and her children, thereby signaling to their kin that they are able to eat freely once again. In the distant past the widow observed these food taboos until the final feast of the mortuary sequence.

Immediately following the meal speeches began. After some initial words by the head pastor, the brother of Eric's father spoke, thanking people for their work and their respect. Eric then rose to his feet. Speaking tenderly of his father, he explained that he and his brother and sisters wore black on that day as a sign of respect and remembrance for a man who would do anything for them when they were children. If they wanted a coconut he would climb a coconut tree. If they wanted fish he would go fishing. "But now," he said, "we wear a red hibiscus to cancel out the black, to celebrate our father's life, to signal an end to mourning. Now we will return to our village and wash and eat. We will wear red hibiscus so we don't feel sad when we return to the village." Eric was followed by his brother John, who stated that their mother had only learned of her husband's passing when the boat arrived at Tutuma the previous evening. The family had gone to great lengths to keep the news a secret from her. When I had questioned people about this decision, everyone assured me that this was for the best. "Otherwise she would be crying and mourning and fasting for many days prior to the burial." "By this time," they said, "she will be too tired [to mourn properly]."

Wycliffe, Antiya, and Noah later confirmed what these comments implied. It is crucial that the mourners, especially the principal mourners, demonstrate or perform their grief properly during the ceremonial events associated with death and mourning. In other words, they must do and be seen to be doing things respectfully. In making this point I do not wish to infer or suggest that a distinction between real and false, inner and outer feelings exists on Nuakata, but rather to assert that mourning at once expresses the personal, familial, and communal implications and ramifications of death on the island (Abu-Lughod and Lutz 1990; Appadurai 1990).

Like all performances, mourning performances on Nuakata are validated by their audiences, their witnesses. On Nuakata, these witnesses are both visible and invisible and include the deceased, his *susu* ancestors, and living *susu*/clan. Following death, the primary task of the community of mourners is to visibly affirm what was previously assumed, namely, that someone's living, now past, previously and uniquely enlivened particular *susu*, affinal, and other communal relationships. Integral to the deceased's former life/living, these relationships or pathways are integral to the living of those who remain behind. In this way, these people are depleted or wounded by the loss. Paths linking them with the deceased are now closed. It is only by publicly recognizing the nature of these wounds that their cause is fully revealed and respected, thereby preventing further development of the wound and making possible the process of restoration of the living and the transformation of the dead. Through death and mourning the life of the deceased and his *susu* is widely acknowledged and valued. By respectfully testifying to the former relationships and ways of the deceased, his life is completed by those who mourn him. The mourners, in turn, are accorded prestige by the deceased's living *susu* and spared retribution by the spirit of the deceased and his ancestral spirits.

Finally, a woman from Gaimanugini thanked all those who had helped with the preparations for the funeral. Then Antiya rose to speak. He, too, thanked people for coming and now urged us to return to our hamlets, as the day's proceedings were over, the sun was setting, and for many the journey ahead was long. As he sat down members of the widow's *susu* stepped forward and presented members of Eric's father's *susu* from Normanby with a bale of rice and a pig for them to take back to Normanby for a feast to commemorate his life.

Wycliffe explained that unlike the prestation of love gifts (*mulolo*) buried with the deceased—generally mats freely given by members of the deceased's *susu* and people close, but often unrelated to the deceased—the gift-giving by the widow (or widower), her children, and their *susu* to the deceased's *susu* is conspicuous. Neither Wycliffe nor his father knew the name of this gift. As personal expressions of love, of deeply felt affection for the deceased, *mulolo* are given without expectation of repayment. These gifts, and the bonds they represent, may be recognized and appreciated by the place given to the giver at the ensuing mortuary feast. In contrast, the affinal prestation of pigs and yams (and/or rice) to the deceased's matrilineage is given in recognition of the deceased's prior contribution to his affinal *susu*. The broader meaning and expectation created by gift-giving remains implicit rather than explicit, for this gift occurs in a sequence of giving between the two *susu*. For example, this gift may reciprocate in kind a prior gift, and so end the sequence of giving between the two *susu*; or it may create a debt leaving the recipients beholden to the deceased's affinal kin. If this is the case, it is usually understood that the gift is intended to enable the children of the deceased to use some portion of their father's land in their lifetime. This arrangement can only last while their deceased father's kin remain beholden to them through unmatched or unreciprocated gifts.[16]

Negotiating Respect: Between Voyeurism and "I"-Witnessing

As I walked back to Gohiya my companions asked me why Roger had not stayed for the burial. I simply replied, "He was sick." Only three months into my fieldwork I did not have the words to explain that because he did not know Eric's father or his kin, and he was not an ethnographer, he felt like a voyeur. Although keen to participate in and observe Nuakatan people's knowledge and practices, his interest was motivated by a desire to forge friendships with people living on the island. Unlike my own, it was not motivated or bound by research imperatives. As a result, he felt morally compromised by observing others grieve merely to satisfy his sense of curiosity. He risked viewing this occasion as theater, thereby objectifying the bereaved as actors and their distress as mere performance. My walking companions seemed disappointed by my explanation. Their reaction was perversely reassuring to me, vindicating my own ambivalent decision to stay and witness the burial feast. Nevertheless, I remained uneasy.

Feeling compromised by my decision to attend the funeral I subsequently raised my ethical dilemmas with Wycliffe. My concerns were summarily dismissed. He claimed that people expected me to attend; it was important for me to see, for how else would I really know or understand their burial customs? Knowing Wycliffe for such a short time I could not discern whether these comments were politely deferential remarks designed to allay my guilt or his considered opinion about acceptable ethnographic practice on Nuakata.

Disturbed, and finding no convincing or acceptable consolation, I determined not to attend another death and burial, unless I knew the person or was obliged to attend because of my friendship and relationship with people. When another death occurred some three months later—an old woman to whom I had given medicine, but did not really know—I resisted my ethnographic impulses and reluctantly stuck to my earlier resolution. My resolve was tested, however, by a stream of people who, when passing by our house on the way to her funeral, stopped to ask when I was coming to the old woman's hamlet. To their questions I simply replied, "I am not going." They in turn asked, "Why?" "Because I don't know the old woman," was my reply. To this they added, *"nige teya hava, 'ulaoma* (No matter, you come!)." Three days later when these same people returned from the burial, they laughingly told how they had not slept for two nights. All through the nights they had been pelted with spiritual stones by the old woman's spirit. Explaining this as her act of retribution, they claimed she was unhappy with people's show of respect. She had not been buried properly. Again they asked, "Why didn't you come?"

On hearing this news I was filled with regret. Not only had I missed an opportunity to witness these events, but these people were clearly perplexed by my decision, if not my lack of respect. More questions presented themselves to me. For whom did my nonattendance at the burial feast demonstrate respect? In my desire to be ethical, had I denied people's capacity to accommodate me and my work? Whose "high moral ground" had I settled upon and to what end?

Several days after the death and burial of the old woman I passed through her hamlet while walking around the island. After inviting me to rest with them, her relatives—among them a woman I knew—asked me why I had not come to the hamlet when she died. Relieved by the opportunity to explain, I stated my reason. Dismissing my concerns, they stated that to understand their burial practices I must witness them. Then they could explain them to me. Not only would I honor them with my presence but I would honor the old woman. Once again I was reminded that—like it or not—because I was a white person in a region with a history of white colonization and Protestant mission involvement dating back over a century, my presence on these occasions conferred honor and respect on the deceased and her kin.

Chastened, I could not ignore this tide of opinion. Clearly, in both identifying myself and being identified as someone interested in local beliefs and practices, the people of Nuakata expected me to attend communal events, including burials. My presence was viewed as a measure of my genuine interest in understanding their customs (*kastom*).[17] Apparently many of the adults on Nuakata, both young and old, understood my ethnographic project as documenting practices they identified and privileged as customary/cultural. My presence, my time on Nuakata encouraged local people to understand and value their customary practices as unique.

Among the significant things I learned from my ethical equivocations at that time was that on Nuakata death was a tangible part of living, with direct personal, familial, and communal implications and effects. Many people directly participate in burial ceremonies: making wreaths, preparing food, singing, digging the grave, preparing the body. While familiarity and intimacy with the deceased and/or her *susu* compels some people to publicly mourn and respect the dead, many participate in burial ceremonies for a variety of other reasons. Some people attend mortuary ceremonies to express communal solidarity, others attend for fear that they may incite the wrath of the deceased and her *susu*. Some attend out of curiosity, while others wish to learn respectful practices. In reality, at Eric's father's burial, I was but one of many conspicuous learners, for many kin living on the mainland—people who had been away from their island villages for a long time—attended his burial and were also witnessing, even photographing, practices they had not seen for a long time, if ever. Perhaps like me their interest was ethnographic. By taking photographs they could describe and show what they had witnessed to friends and family "back home" in Port Moresby. Children's attendance at these events was unquestioned, if not encouraged. It was only by watching their elders, by listening to their explanations, by admonishment when they behaved disrespectfully, that children and young people learned expected customary ways.

Therefore, in deciding not to attend the funeral, I had reluctantly stood my (high moral) ground, but in so doing had lost shared ground. I had not only missed an opportunity to learn, but, more important, I had missed the opportunity to demonstrate respect by witnessing to others' witnessing of death and burial. I had failed to appreciate that as both a respected visitor and anthropologist on the island I had a responsibility to observe *and* witness such occasions.

Like an adolescent with an identity crisis I had come to grief somewhere between my childlike fascination and desire to see, learn, and participate and my adult impulse to know already, to be socially competent, to avoid mistakes. Scheper-Hughes speaks to my dilemmas when she writes:

> One hears of anthropological observation as a hostile act that reduces our "subjects" to mere "objects" of our discriminating, incriminating, scientific gaze.... [G]iven the perilous times in which we and our subjects live, I am inclined toward compromise, the practice of a "good enough" ethnography.... Not to look, not to touch, not to record can be the hostile act, an act of indifference and of turning away. (1995, 417)

I placed considerable emphasis on observation and participation in these mortuary sequences, and so did local people. Seeing was considered integral to knowing, participation to understanding, just as performing and witnessing mourning practices were crucial demonstrations of respect. "Seeing" on Nuakata, though, neither implied nor necessitated a form of dispassionate, scientific observation—observation that created (emotional, thoughtful, and spatial) distance between observer and observed. Nor did it necessarily lead to speculation. People often watched so that they could "do." In this sense, my seeing differed from theirs, motivated as it was by a wish to translate, interpret, and make meaningful what I saw. I wanted to see, therefore know and understand. I wanted to observe, in order to make the observed transparent, to conquer its mysteries. I wanted to see, so that I might render it faithfully in imagined texts, for example, field notes, articles, a book. In one sense, then, my observations were hostage to these imaginary, explanatory texts. Yet I had failed to anticipate the emotional effect and force of these events and therefore did not consider how my emotional responses to "seeing" and participating might influence my understanding of death and mourning. Perhaps most important in the context of this discussion, I had conveniently overlooked the ethical dilemmas and decisions that necessarily arise during, and ensue from, participant observation. To my genuine surprise I realized that I had thought of myself as an impassioned participant, but a dispassionate observer. I had inadvertently assumed and made a distinction—at once temporospatial, epistemological, and political—between doing, seeing, and knowing. It was a distinction that, in the interests of a dispassionate knowing, also enabled me to defer ethical decisions until after the "seeing" had occurred.

Understanding Respect and Respectful Understanding

My specific ethical dilemmas in the field can be dismissed as the trifling concerns of a fledgling ethnographer ensnared by her own well-meaning ambivalence or "a fact of research life" confronted by all ethnographers. However, I believe that they not only raise broad epistemological questions for ethnography, they also challenge us to consider how we represent these issues in our texts. Seemingly overlooked and/or displaced by research imperatives, ethical dilemmas in the field are often relegated to private texts—field notes, diaries, letters, and conversations. They surface in ethnographies as absences, elisions, or asides in introductions. Sometimes they emerge in articles as ethical practice issues in specific fieldwork contexts.[18] Occasionally they are detached and liberated from their uncomfortable living contexts, emerging in articles or books as theoretical questions about the merits of politically engaged ethnographic practice and writing (see Visweswaran 1988; Walter 1995; Wolf 1993), the possibilities of and for objective research (e.g., D'Andrade 1995; Denzin 1997; Scheper-Hughes 1995), and abstract reflections on ethical practice in anthropology (e.g., Adams 1981; Knauft 1994; Whittaker 1981). By compartmentalizing the ethical in this way, the impression is given, if not the assumption made, that dilemmas and questions of this kind have little direct bearing on what, how, and with whom we participate and observe in the field, how this influences our understanding, and how our experiences are subsequently represented and/or interpreted beyond it. When detached from their experiential context, ethical issues simply become "ends in themselves," independent objects of study, rather than "integral dimensions of" and "means to" understanding the context from which they emerged. Clearly, this was not consonant with my own ethnographic experience—my own interpretation, misinterpretation, and *negotiated* reinterpretation of what I could respectfully witness in the field and extrapolate beyond it (see Scheper-Hughes 1992, 14–23). For it was in a specific context (a burial ceremony) that I became preoccupied with my own respectful ethical practice on Nuakata. My response was both the effect of and affected by the context.[19] It was a context in which people's actions express, and are primarily intended to elicit, demonstrations of respect. Conversely, it could be claimed that my preoccupation with respectful/ethical practice led me to understand respect and respectful understanding as a central dimension or purpose of mourning practices on Nuakata. Of course neither proposition is mutually exclusive. Both offer a valuable perspective on the way practices associated with death or mourning are understood and represented in this text.

My practical ethical dilemmas were sparked by my failure to anticipate the emotional impact of seeing and participating in mortuary ceremonies. Perhaps this is not surprising given my prefield reading of the ethnographic accounts of death in Melanesia and Milne Bay in particular (Battaglia 1990; Damon and Wagner 1989; Munn 1986). These texts mostly offer nonspecific, dispassionate accounts of death, detailing the author's interpretation of the strategic purpose, meaning, and comparative significance of the ensuing mortuary sequence and associated prestations. In these texts the gravity of the loss is often buried in the page. So, too, is the multifaceted response of the witnessing ethnographer. The impression is given that the feelings evoked and expressed by participants and witnesses on these occasions, especially those of the ethnographer, contribute little to an understanding of the social effect and meaning of mortuary practices. Equally, the significance of emotional expressions as forms of social action that create social effects is underemphasized. As a result the view that expressions of feeling (and the possible ethical impulses that may flow from them) reflect the inner subjective states of individual selves is perpetuated by the form, if not the content, of such texts (Abu-Lughod and Lutz 1990; Lutz 1988, 1990). So, too, are the related assumptions that thinking is separable from feeling, and understanding detachable from experience (Jackson 1989; Rosaldo 1989; Wikan 1991). Widely acknowledged by both anthropologists and feminist philosophers as ethno- and phallocentric, these assumptions, grounded as they are in Western, Enlightenment philosophy, valorize knowing and understanding founded on dispassionate and disembodied Reason and the objectifying gaze of the implicitly male Subject. However, on Nuakata observing, doing, and experiencing the social effects of this seeing and doing are integral to understanding. Understanding is neither dispassionate nor value free (Mallett 1995, 1997).

Overt resistance to consideration of feelings/emotions in ethnographic texts, especially those of the ethnographer, remains well entrenched in anthropology.[20] Opponents argue that feelings contaminate the text, that they are inimical to reasoned analysis and preclude objective knowledge. As a consequence the status and strategic political import of ethnographic knowledge are undermined. In his article "Ethnography Without Tears" Roth (1989) seems to speak for those in the discipline who ignore feminist ethnographies and explicitly reject the (nonfeminist) reflexive and dialogical ethnographic genres that reveal the ethnographer's feelings and experiences. He argues that both the authors and proponents of dialogic, reflexive texts (e.g., Clifford, Fabian, Rosaldo, Asad) mistakenly attribute epistemological significance to their strategic political efforts to redress inequitable post-/colonial power relations by producing representative texts. They attempt to diffuse their authority, gain credibility, and establish authenticity by including multiple voices and confessing to feelings of uncertainty and vulnerability in their texts. Rejecting these efforts as "epistemologically innocuous" and politically misrepresentative, he claims they merely affirm the widely held belief that all truths are partial. This, though, accuses these ethnographers of seeking an authenticity they do not claim. More important, it mistakenly interprets their projects to acknowledge and explore the historical, political, and relational "contingency" of ethnographic knowledge with vain attempts to develop superior epistemologies and "guilt free" methodologies (Clifford 1989).

I do not wish to imply that all ethnographic responses to death and mortuary practices, including textual representations, should focus on the specific ethical/emotional expressions and responses of participants, including ethnographers; rather, following writers such as Clifford (1986, 1988, 1989), Rosaldo (1984), and Danforth (1982), I argue that there should be room in the discipline for methodologies/epistemologies and genres of ethnographic writing that can. When represented in abstract terms and forms, the experience and significance of death for the people studied risk becoming completely foreign, *other* to the reader's own. In telling the stories of particular deaths, ethnographers risk promoting the idea that the practices associated with these examples, and the significance and intent attributed to them, are representative of a given culture that, in terms of affection, coincides with the reader's and/or the ethnographer's own. By representing their own experience in the text, ethnographers risk becoming the focus of the account, thereby devaluing the experiences, the stories of those with whom they researched. Despite these and many other "risks" there is much to be gained by making reflexivity and the encounter between researcher and researched "ethnographic rather than contemplative projects" (Herzfeld 1989, 563). For such encounters invite us to reflect on the contemporary anthropological project, the multifaceted role and responsibilities of the ethnographer, ethical practice in the field, and what and how we can claim to understand and/or know in our ethnographic texts. Specifically, they expose the limitations of speculative ways of knowing that valorize dispassionate observation while inviting us to consider a way of understanding that values the ethical and emotional responses invoked by our participation and observation.

Tau'ala'alahi: One Who Burns

Following my discussion with the old woman's kin, I decided to attend the *tau'ala'alahi* feast held five or six days after her burial. At dawn on the day of the feast I set out alone for the old woman's hamlet. When I arrived at the entrance to her hamlet, a group of women who were preparing food together beckoned me to join them. Spirits were high. Wresting my camera from my backpack, I tried to capture this levity on film. Absent was the solemnity and mournful weeping that marked Eric's father's burial. Absent, too, were the ethical ruminations that marked my participation in, and observation of, that occasion. But unmistakably present throughout this day—as with all other "events" I attended, mournful or otherwise—was a sense of time, suspended.

Freed of time's demands, festive events on Nuakata seemed to claim their own unique space. It was a space/time in which the present was privileged, a space/time that did not clearly delineate between an event and the preparations necessary for that event to occur. On these occasions, in this "space," people did not "wait" for things to happen; rather, they seemed to accept that events simply unfolded.

Sitting there, talking, eating, I found myself waiting expectantly for something to happen. Eventually a senior woman belonging to the old woman's clan invited me to join her in the center of the hamlet, so that she and several other older people could explain the day's events. These same people, mainly older men, instructed the two women primarily responsible for the feast—members of the dead woman's *susu*—in the proper and respectful ways to proceed.

Noah and Yamesi variously described *tau'ala'alahi* as the "feast for those two *galiyauna*" and the "resurrection feast." They added that "after the feast the deceased's spirit departs for Bwebweso." Confused by their explanations I asked Wycliffe about the significance of the feast's name. *Tau'ala'alahi* literally translates as "one who burns." He replied:

> I don't know why they say *tau'ala'alahi*. But those two *galiyauna*, once . . . [the members of the deceased's *susu*] cook this feast, they'll make those two *galiyauna* maybe strong. I am not sure how *tau'ala'alahi* works.

Months later, when speaking with Wycliffe and, through him, Antiya and Noah about mortuary practices in the olden days, Wycliffe added:

> Before, the three burial feasts—*tau'ala'alahi, bwabwale,*[21] *guyau*—used to be all joined together, but now they have become separate. Before, [when] I heard my grandfather[22] talking he did not mention *tau'ala'alahi*. Once he said, if a person dies and they take [the] skull off, that is *guyau*. And when they are bringing pig and food to the grave [for the two *galiyauna* and their assistants], then that was *bwabwaleta*. *Bwabwaleta* was the feast that follows *tau'ala'alahi*. Now *tau'ala'alahi* and *bwabwaleta* are mixed together. This is a bit different from Duau.[23] We call it *tau'ala'alahi* here, but at Duau this feast is called *pwaipwai*. If a person dies [at Duau] he remains on his sleeping mat until they kill a pig. When a person dies, a pig must die for the *galiyauna* and his family. *Ai'ai bwabwale* is food that is eaten by those *galiyauna* and their family and relatives.

These comments only served to confuse me more, for how were they to be understood? Was *tau'ala'alahi* to be considered a relatively modern phenomenon, or did it exist in the precolonial and early colonial past? If so, what was the significance of its past to its present form? What, if any, remnants remained embedded in current practices? If, as Wycliffe suggested, it was then a combination of two feasts, how, when, and why did this transformation occur? Also, what was resurrection? Who or what was resurrected? Given the influence of Christianity, what was meant by "resurrection"?

Of course, simple and direct answers to these questions were not forthcoming, but Leenhardt's general observations about the meaning of death in Melanesia were suggestive. If in Melanesia death does not mean "annihilation" or consignment to "oblivion," then resurrection in this context cannot be considered a physical or spiritual reclamation or return from "the nothingness of death" (see Leenhardt 1979, 40–43). At no time does the spirit cease to exist, it merely stays for a time in its natal hamlet to ensure its work is complete before departing to dwell with its spiritual kin.

Before long, I caught sight of two *galiyauna* and their fellow grave diggers, entering the hamlet by the main path. Earlier in the day these grave workers had left the hamlet—where they had remained since the old woman's burial—to wash and prepare themselves for the feast. Until this time they had been fed and attended to by the old woman's granddaughter. They made their way past the people gathered on the edge of the hamlet, then sat down on several mats placed a short distance from the houses. Members of the *susu* and clan of the deceased assembled close by, yet—with the exception of several older men and the two women coordinating the feast—they remained distant from the grave workers. Like other members of their clan before them, the grave diggers and the two *galiyauna* were issued with red hibiscus or white frangipani flowers to place in their hair, thereby signaling the beginning of the end of their customary observances. The colors of the flowers were significant. Red flowers were given to members of the clan who had already lost one or both of their parents. White flowers were distributed to those whose parents were still living.

Soon after, the two *galiyauna* positioned themselves in front of the deceased woman's house. A small crowd gathered around them. In the doorway of the house stood the old woman's granddaughter, the principal mourner. Looking up to her, the *galiyauna* asked if she had *beda* [betel nut]. With this, she threw several handfuls of *beda* in their direction, scattering the crowd who clamored and clambered to get it. Everyone was joking and laughing. Next, the two *galiyauna* asked for mustard, lime, and, finally, tobacco. The woman flung her replies at them with theatrical flourish. And with each throw a new group formed around the *galiyauna* as everyone tried to snatch these offerings. Someone explained to me that the two *galiyauna* were now free to partake of these things.

Following these proceedings, the crowd dissipated, and with this the excitement and laughter faded away. One final sign remained to be enacted for the two *galiyauna*. A woman from the old woman's *susu* placed two pots containing fish, tapioca, yams, and sweet potato before them. The two *galiyauna* bent down to smell the food, which had been cooked in coconut juice, before it was whisked away.

Talking afterward with Wycliffe and Antiya, Wycliffe explained in English that

> in the olden days, when the *galiyauna* came back from the grave, they would have to stay and fast until the big feast called *guyau*. When the *guyau* was over, they were allowed to eat fish or pig or any type of protein, or work in the garden, or go and fish. Those people who helped them with digging the soil or working around the cemetery, they could do anything. But now some of the culture is already changed.... Usually we cook only the *tau'ala'alahi*, and that's it. We will be staying and the *galiyauna* will be fasting from protein for how many weeks, and then they are allowed to eat or do anything they want. Now ... between death and the *tau'ala'alahi* feast, [the *galiyauna*] will not eat fish and pig until the feast. Only [roasted] yams would be eaten. If [there aren't any] then we use sweet potato, good tapioca or bananas. The people cleaning around the cemetery after the funeral, they will wash in a strong current and drink a coconut shell of salt water each day to purify themselves. The people who are digging cannot eat protein. The *galiyauna* will not eat protein after the feast either. They believe they will get sick. Some [*galiyauna*] will take about one month before they eat fish; some don't eat pig at all.

By these men's account, in the "olden days" the two *galiyauna*, like the widow/widower, observed food taboos until the final feast in the mortuary sequence. For the two *galiyauna*, maintenance of these taboos was precautionary. Made vulnerable and susceptible to illness by their efforts with the dead body, *galiyauna* could only be restored to full strength by the reciprocal efforts of the deceased's *susu*. Although, in the past, taboos may have been customarily lifted following a feast (either *bwabwaleta* or *tau'ala'alahi*) held long prior to *guyau*, the two *galiyauna* (and by association their kin) lived with some threat to themselves while the spirit of the deceased remained at Nuakata. In the past, the spirit's rising—or resurrection—was possible only when its life had been duly honored and, if necessary, its death avenged. Living kin had to settle the cause of death, avenging their loved one when sorcery or witchcraft was believed to be involved. Now, however, when both the talk and practice of witchcraft and sorcery are actively discouraged by the church, and when the burden for the spirit's passage beyond death has increasingly fallen to God rather than living kin, people no longer speak openly about avenging the death of their kin through witchcraft. Despite the church's influence, though, many deaths are still surrounded by rumors of sorcery and witchcraft.

Just as the expression and period of mourning observed by the widow have evidently compacted over time, so too the fasting period for the two *galiyauna* has been reduced. As Wycliffe suggested, in its contemporary form the *tau'ala'alahi* feast aims to restore strength to the two *galiyauna* and—through them—members of their matrilineage. In this sense, perhaps the living were also thought to be resurrected; wounded by the loss of death, perhaps it was they who were restored to health. Although the visible work of the feast was important, the invisible or concealed work—namely, the spirit's departure—remained a necessary, if unexplained, consequence.

With these activities completed, the *galiyauna* retreated to their mats, where they played cards, chewed betel nut, smoked, and ate roasted food provided by the old woman's granddaughter. Attention was focused on the final preparations for the feast, overseen by the female members of the deceased's *susu*. Two lines of food were laid out on mats in the center of the hamlet. I was directed to sit at one with some members of the deceased's *susu*, and at the other were clan members, including members of the *susu* of the *galiyauna* together with their in-laws. Everyone else sat further away, gathering around several mats laden with food. Following the meal some older members of the deceased's clan complained that the food had been laid out incorrectly. They declared that a separate "table" should be laid for men and women of the clan and that members of different clans should not eat together as one. Resigned to yet saddened by these violations of customary practices, they assured all those people within earshot that they would continue to observe these customs.

With nightfall imminent, the feast completed, many people slipped away, back to their hamlets. I joined a small procession that stumbled its way back in the dark along the path that winds its way through Bolime and Yalasi. Coconut palm flares lit our way. Many, particularly the young people, remained in the old woman's hamlet for the night, singing and playing cards. Passing by our house the next day on his way back from the old woman's hamlet, Yamesi dropped in to see us. Obviously weary, he told us that he had not slept. All throughout the night the old woman had been throwing stones—spiritual stones—and crying. She was still angry that she had not been shown proper respect. His comment launched a discussion about Christianity, culminating with the question, "Where does the spirit go when your time is over?" Laughing, musing with us, issuing us a challenge, Yamesi replied, "Do you know where the spirit goes?" Pausing, he added:

> When we are living on the earth we are watching carefully to see where the spirit goes, but we don't know. Before, they thought that they go to Bwebweso. But this time, nobody knows where they go. They go to Bwebweso or they go to heaven. . . . [Nobody knows] where is their living place, where they are staying. The Bible teaches the spirit goes somewhere, but it does not explain how or why the spirit comes back and does these things.

That the spirit of the deceased endures beyond death was not questioned by the people I spoke to on Nuakata. Some, however, questioned where the spirit goes after death. Of these, some older people stridently believed that the spirit goes to Bwebweso. Others were troubled by their inability to decide. Many people told me that the spirit goes to Heaven, while others responded to my inquiries with indifference or amusement, declaring "ta'i'ita (Who knows!—and by implication, Why care!)—Bwebweso? Heaven? What's the difference?" The spirit continues wherever it stays.

Forgetting Guyau

Hoping that memories of past mortuary practices would reveal the significance of current ones, I turned my attention to the final, climactic feast in the mortuary sequence: *guyau*. According to Daphne Lithgow's unpublished dictionary of Auhelawa, the terms *guyau* and *soi* are interchangeable. Both mean "to distribute." No longer made or enacted, *guyau* was barely remembered on Nuakata. People prefaced their remarks about *guyau* with expressions of relief at its passing. *Guyau* belonged to the ancestors' time. Noah, a man in his early fifties, told us that it was discontinued in his generation when their marriages were young and the birth of a new generation had barely begun. By his account the last *guyau* held on Nuakata was in 1960, one year prior to Wycliffe's birth. Conducted or sponsored by Wycliffe's namesake, a senior member of the Bo'e clan, it was held at Gogobohewa—the Yalasi hamlet, where Wycliffe's maternal uncle Hosea, sister Geteli, brother-in-law Justin, and their children were living. This *guyau* was attended by relatives from Duau and Koyagaugau and people from Nuakata. Wycliffe's namesake died two or three months after the feast, and with his passing it was decided among his *susu,* clan, and affinal kin that, given the immense amount of work involved in hosting this feast, it would be the final *guyau* for the Bo'e clan. It seems that this decision was subsequently adopted by all the clans on Nuakata. Born of pragmatism and necessity, this decision was apparently not influenced by European or local missionaries or government personnel.

As a result of the decisions and actions of their parents, grandparents, and in some cases great-grandparents, the succeeding generations did not know about *guyau*. When asked about this feast, they merely repeated the refrain learned from their elders: "We no longer do this, it was too much work." Not only did these generations not perform or remember *guyau,* it seemed they did not want to know about it. Perhaps, more to the point, they wanted to forget this feast. When asked about it, younger (married and unmarried) people referred me to Antiya or Wycliffe, and when present while Wycliffe and Antiya attempted to describe some aspect of the feast, they invariably became bored and distracted. Unable or unprepared to contribute to the discussions, they gradually drifted off to do some other activity.

Both the language and practices of remembering and forgetting on Nuakata suggest that, like the people of Sabarl, the people of Nuakata have traditionally had no "concept of memory as a faculty" (see Battaglia 1990, 8; 1992, 5)—an internal, neural epicenter located in the mind. Remembering was understood as a particular expression of thinking-feeling—thinking-feeling directed toward the person, place, thing, or activity to be remembered. Spoken of as an alienable or semialienable possession, remembrance was an activity that could be spoken, performed, placed. Three words were used to describe remembering in Alina Nu'ata. The first, *nuwatawulobai,* means to think-feel (*nuwatawu*) and finally find it (*lobai*). Remembering in this sense was to search and locate something;

to direct thinking-feeling toward something and thereby find it. A second word, rarely used, *nuwamomohi*, means thinking-feeling pulled or squeezed together tightly. Described in this way, remembering was a bringing or gathering together of thinking-feeling—a re-collection of that which was to be remembered (cf. Battaglia 1990, 55). The third word, *nuwatawu'avivini*, more difficult to translate, means something like thinking-feeling (*nuwatawu*) that is cared for (*'avivini*)—thinking-feeling that is nurtured. These memories and rememberings were nurtured, supported, and maintained. People generally used *nuwatu'avivini* when their thinking-feeling (remembering) was directed to and placed with people, events, customary practices that they held dear. Remembering of this kind drew past, present, and future together. By directing thinking-feeling to that which went before, the present and future were also nurtured.

If remembering was to nurture thinking-feeling by bringing the past into the present, then forgetting (*nuwapwanopwanowei*—from *nuwa*, meaning heart, think-feel, and *pwanoli*, meaning adultery, mistake, to do or make something wrongly) was to think-feel something incorrectly. Implied was a sense of transgression, of acting improperly, disrespectfully. Forgetting was not so much an inability to bring something to mind, as it is often conceived in English, but more like its reverse—an inability, or even a reticence, to direct or take thinking-feeling to something, whether that something be a place, time, object, event, individual, or action. Inferred was a loss of empathy—an inability or reluctance to place one's thinking-feeling with someone, something, or activity to be remembered. By forgetting, the forgotten may be defiled, diminished, displaced, and dispossessed. Conversely, it may be finished or completed. When used in the latter sense, forgetting was a deliberate, intentional, indeed necessary act—an act that completed the past (actions and relations) to make way for the present and the future. This interpretation of forgetting does not suggest that all traces of the past were necessarily erased, but rather that the present and future were absolved of the past.

In day-to-day living, isolated acts of recollection, remembrance, or simple forgetfulness passed unnoticed. However, in "customary" matters, forgetfulness or the ability to remember assumed a broader significance and meaning. For example, when someone forgot the names of people and places in a story, they were reluctant to tell it, for they were unable to wholeheartedly place themselves in the story's time and space. The converse was also held to be true. Without entering the time and space of the story, the storyteller would forget pertinent names and details. If the story told of ancestral connections to the land, then a flawed retelling was considered improper. When details of a mortuary feast were forgotten or overlooked or incorrectly performed, as was the case in the *tau'ala'alahi* feast that occurred following the old woman's death, then older people in particular considered it highly disrespectful to the deceased and her kin. Forgetfulness of this kind was not only a failure to recall and/or reenact the customary ways of one's forebears but it also expressed, embodied (see Eves 1996b), and displayed a lack of empathy with the deceased and her living kin—an inability or reluctance to place oneself in her time and space.

As implied previously, though, forgetfulness, like recollections, may also be strategically or pragmatically motivated acts to complete the past, as was the case for the *guyau* feast. The community chose to discontinue this practice and thereby forget an aspect of their past. Rendered irrelevant, it was only worth remembering the reason for abandoning it. Arguably, this interpretation of the significance of forgetting *guyau* on Nuakata is an extension of the claim made by many Melanesian and, especially, Massim ethnographers, notably Battaglia (1990, 1992, 1993), Macintyre (1989b), Thune (1989), Munn (1986), Eves (1996b), and Lattas (1996), of the centrality of remembering and forgetting the social relations embodied by the deceased and his or her kin in (Massim) mortuary practices. Reflecting on the Sabarl mortuary sequence and the gift exchanges integral to these practices, Battaglia (1992) states that "forgetting is an accomplishment of remembering." She argues for a "consideration of *forgetting as a willed transformation of memory*" (1992, 14, emphasis in original). In so doing, she suggests the "possibility of a collectively performed forgetting that actually has constructive social effects . . . forgetting [that] is linked to social re-construction and cultural re-evaluation," forgetting understood as a "desirable social goal" (1992, 14). In relation to the gift exchanges that accompany the mortuary sequence she asserts that "gift exchange performances make such a process explicit in that they foreground objects which embody the relations to be forgotten and sequentially articulate the course of their transformation and substitution" (1992, 14).

Remembering Guyau

Still wanting to know more about *guyau*, I talked with Antiya. When I initially asked him to explain this feast, he commented that it was the "feast for those dead bodies, those dead ancestors within the clan."

Knowing from Wycliffe that he had lived experience of *guyau*, I appealed to his memory of the witnessed event. Reluctant to elaborate, he deferred further discussion of the feast until he had time to consider things in private. Several weeks later he returned, this time volunteering what seemed like his final and complete word on the feast—a written description of the *muli* prestation. "But what was *muli*?" I asked. "How was it relevant to the feast?" Arrived at with some considerable effort, he could not be persuaded to discuss or expand upon his written recollections. When he left, Wycliffe explained:

> *Guyau* was a big feast that is held within the clan for those dead ancestors who have passed away a long time ago or a person who has just recently died. They take the skull and put it in a sacred place where all those ancestors died a long time ago. They have to put them together with the new dead person's skull. . . . That's how the custom goes.

He added that *muli* is an offering or gift made and performed by a man or woman—supported by their respective *susu*—affinally related to the matrilineage hosting the feast. At my request Wycliffe and I turned our attention to Antiya's text. Loosely translated it stated:

> If a man or woman together with his or her respective matrilineal kin were giving *'ai'ai nabwanabwa* (*guyau* food offering) and five pigs, they would take them to the hamlet where the *guyau* occurs. *Muli* comprising five pigs are called *'waiwai* (mango) in the Duau language. Two celebratory performances (*'anayaliyaliyamane*) integral to the prestation of *muli* are possible: one is called *'asawe* (mango) and the other *'wawa*. *Asawe* does not possess a magic chant (*'ana'alavahivahili*), but it is accompanied by dancing and happiness. But *'wawa* comes with its chant and with its happiness. The bird/clan called *bo'e*, the black crane—people see and perform its games, its actions, its ways. The *'wawa* chant is said like this:

Bo'e bo'e 'iya'o Bo'e auseloi auseloiya'o Bo'e aubigai aubigaiya'o Bo'e pauli lagana tauneteneteinaya'o. . . Bo'e pauli luguna tau'ava'avalainya'o	Black crane . . . Black cranes dance Black cranes mangrove branch cross over it Black cranes branch carried . . .

Bo'e 'ai'aisemwasemwaya'o	Black crane food . . .
Bo'e 'aena itatausigesigegeya'o	
Eyaeyaui 'ovaovaui'idalasaui'idalasaeui	
Kagu pukeui Kuguwaliyamauikubibiyamaui	
Didiladaui Buwobuwau 'ui'eee'iu'iowa'ui	
ilaoma'ui 'E	it comes . . .

Neither Antiya nor Wycliffe could fully translate the chant, written in the Duau language. From the remnant translation it was clear that it described the performance of the ways of the black crane. Still, I felt none the wiser about the *guyau* feast. I had been expecting, hoping for, a linear narrative accompanied by a brief synopsis of the purpose of the feast, and Antiya's seemingly obtuse account confused and confounded as much as clarified. Why had he explained *guyau* by means of the *muli* prestation? I felt I was being presented with pieces of a jigsaw, each piece a mere fragment yet apparently whole in itself; each reflecting a larger picture, which remained ultimately elusive. Where I wished to define the borders of this puzzle, thereby framing the picture, containing its possibilities, Antiya seemingly felt no such need.

Once again Wycliffe bore the brunt of my confusion. Plying him with questions, I asked, "What does *guyau* mean? What happens to the skull? Who supplies the food for the feast? How long does it last?" Spoken in English and in a linear narrative style that I could readily understand, his answers assumed an authority and authenticity that, at the time, Antiya's lacked. By Wycliffe's account, told to him by his grandfather, mother, and maternal uncle,

> each *guyau* was hosted by either the uncle or relative of the dead body within the clan. Once this person had made the decision to host a *guyau*, other members of the *susu* and clan had to respect that decision and begin preparation for the feast. *Guyau* was held during harvest time, particularly July and August, when there were plenty of yams. Gardens may be planted by both *susu* and . . . [affinal kin], especially for the *guyau* feast. [In preparation for the *guyau*, the sponsoring] *susu* would build a traditional saddle-backed house, [known as] a *pahoma*, or *'abanuwatuwu'avivini*, a place of remembrance. [As a remembering place] it remembered and honored the dead bodies, the dead ancestors, within the *susu* and clan. No one would live in the house, but yams collected and offered as gifts may be stored there in preparation for the

feast. [Several days] before the feast [was due to] begin, *hinevelam* and *wohiwa*—women and men who had married into the village of the feast-givers—together with their *susu* would present their *mulina* (marriage payment) to the awaiting host of the *guyau*. When they brought their gifts of food, they placed them on the shelves made for the *guyau*. [Particular note was taken of] how much they brought and if their gift was not [considered adequate] then the in-law was [said to be] of little worth to the clan. The clan would gossip about him and he would have to [fulfill his obligations] properly on another [festive occasion]. The *guyau* lasted up to a week. If the *guyau* was held for someone recently dead, then during this time the big *galiyauna* within the clan would carry the skull on a mat and place it in the ancestral skull cave. . . . The *guyau* began when the host declared it had started. Then he would climb onto a big shelf and begin the distribution of the uncooked food. He would call out the name of each person in turn, and when they come up to the shelf he gave them a piece of pig and some yams. The food would be given like this until there was no longer any left on the shelf. Once this distribution was completed, cooked food would be served. The *guyau* was declared finished when the host declared the last dance. After this, people would disperse and return to their villages.

Wycliffe's assertion that *guyau* (*soi*) was held for *each* dead body of the clan was at variance with Macintyre's (1989b, 143–44, 147) account of the Tubetube practice of *soi*. On Tubetube, in the past, *soi* was not held for each dead body within the clan, but, rather, marked the passing of a *susu* generation. In other details, though (e.g., the building of the shelf and the distribution of uncooked food), the ceremony seemed very similar.

Thinking Antiya's description and discussion of *guyau* was completed, I was pleasantly surprised when, in conversation several months later, he voluntarily elaborated on the affinal prestations. He added that

> at the place where the *guyau* was held they built a *pahoma* and put all the food. And when they arrived at that place, they used this type of dance called '*asawe 'wawa*. Someone beat the drum and men danced, and one man—his body decorated with charcoal—would break the '*asawe* branch. This man would go first, and then the drummers, and then the in-laws carrying food. Then they would put food inside the *pahoma*, and then the dance would finish and the owners of the *guyau* would prepare some food and they would eat. There was also a '*wawa*

dance, but the in-laws would do one or the other. For the *'wawa* dance strong men would put a tree on their shoulder. As they made their way carrying the tree—if something was blocking their way, they would bump it down (like a coconut tree), because they put a spell on the tree so that it would become sort of active or powerful. They would not go around trees. *Mulina* is for big feasts, like *guyau*, or when they are putting cement on bodies. Now when they put cement on a body there is a party.

Preoccupied with the past, I failed to ask Antiya about the party for the concrete headstones. Cement graves were by no means a common or necessary feature of the cemeteries scattered around Nuakata—their cost alone prevented this. Where possible, however, the graves of senior members of given *susu* were cemented, as a sign of permanent respect, much like the depositing of the skull in the skull cave.

The day after my conversation with Antiya I talked with Yamesi about *guyau*. He, too, described the shelves for the in-laws' food (*'waiwai*) and elaborated further on the baskets of yams brought for the feast. He noted that, although the host of the feast would not be told how much the in-laws brought, he would know whether or not the gift was an exact or equivalent payment for a prior gift of his own. There were four different ways in which yams could be collected together and presented at the *guyau*. The first, *nabwanabwa*, comprised a hundred or so yams, depending on their size, collected together in a string bag. The second, *baditutula*, consisted of yams placed in a five- to six-foot-square stick pen. The third group was called *sabaliya*; these were placed in front of the *pahoma*. They comprised one type of yam called *pwane'ahu* placed on a stretcher made of sticks. The last type, *lomwau*, were a bit like *nabwanabwa*, but were simply heaped on a shelf.

The significance of Antiya's account of *guyau* eluded me until I returned to Australia and reread the ethnographic writings on mortuary sequences in Massim communities. Only in writing down his words and attempting to recall the circumstances of their delivery did I appreciate why he focused on the *muli* prestation, and, indeed, why Wycliffe did not. Wycliffe's knowledge of *guyau* was based on the recollected experience of his matrilineage—hosts of Nuakata's final *guyau*. In contrast, Antiya's account privileged his own experience of this *guyau*. As an affinal kinsman to the Bo'e or Black Crane clan he contributed *muli* to this final *guyau*. Understood in this way, his elucidation of the *bo'e* chant was not offered as an example of a prestation chant, as I had first imagined, but as a specific recollection from his personal past. As a senior representative of his generation he, like Yamesi, was instrumental in the decision to abandon this mortuary practice. Although a hard worker, no doubt his experience of preparing *muli* for the feast gave impetus to his pragmatic push for change! Of course, other reasons for change existed. Exhumation of the dead had long been forbidden by law and frowned upon by the United Church. Accordingly, a significant part of the purpose and practice of the feast—the placement of a skull in its skull cave—was necessarily precluded.

There is a second, more speculative yet seemingly consistent, explanation for Antiya and Yamesi's preoccupation with the *muli* prestations. Believing that the main purpose of the feast was to place the skull of the deceased in the skull cave, thereby celebrating and honoring matrilineal clan ancestors—and with it the matrilineage/clan—I had assumed that the primary work for the feast would be performed by the hosts. In my thinking and questions about the feast I had focused on the host's role and activities.[24] While clearly interested in the descriptions of the affinal prestations by Antiya and Yamesi, I was preoccupied with the unspoken accounts of the host's role. As a result I did not fully explore the possibility that the affinal prestations themselves were pivotal to the celebrations honoring the host clan. Affines, friends, or members of the paired matrilineage of the hosts dance, chant, and perform the actions of the host clan bird as they present their substantial gifts to the feast-givers. They detail, celebrate, and imitate its ways, thereby celebrating the clan identity of the hosts. As in marriage and birth, the integrity and identity of a given *susu* and clan are reinforced and replenished by affinal kin. It could be argued, though, that it was not only the host *susu* whose reputation was enhanced by these *muli* prestations. On Vanatinai, where the same term—*muli*—is also used to denote the affinal prestation of valuables at the start of the final feast (*zagaya*) in the mortuary sequence, these affinal prestations can enhance the giving reputation of the entire affinal lineage. Lepowsky notes that "the whole *muli* procession . . . is a public display of the affines' wealth and generosity" (1989, 221). For this reason, *muli* prestations were a source of concealed pride for those who made them.

At birth a child on Nuakata was considered a living embodiment of past, present, and future relationships within its matrilineage—a babe who would continue to grow into someone who was distinct within this matrilineage. A child is a unique confluence in time, space, and place of the conjugal relationship that led to its conception. In death and the unfolding mortuary sequence the deceased's individuality was recognized as it was also completed. So, too, the mutual support between the deceased and her affinal kin was publicly recognized and ended by members of the deceased's *susu*. The integrity of the matrilineage, the maternal inheritance that sustained the deceased in life, was reaffirmed as her place within the matrilineage was finally consolidated in the realm of the dead with those clan members that "go before" (*bodaowa himugaiwa*—those who died before, those that went first). In this sense the "before" that death referred to was not thought of as an empty space, but rather as a transhistorical, communal, and familial place, a place where spirits dwell unconstrained by time's embodiment.

The women of any given *susu* bear and nurture living seeds, babies, *susu* members, thereby facilitating the continuity of the *susu*/clan. The men of any given *susu* prepare the ground for women to plant seeds, nurture *susu* members, and receive deceased bodies, so that their spirit may continue on to the realm of the dead. Therefore, through their bearing, nurturing activities the women belonging to a given *susu* facilitate the continuity of the *susu*/clan. But these activities are only made possible by the supportive work of *susu* and/or clan men. Neither women nor men alone, or together, are considered the source of continuity for their *susu*. As such, their actions facilitate rather than ensure the continuity of the *susu*/clan.

Conclusion: Remembering Nuakata

Dear Shelley,

I shall try to write a small letter to you both so that you might know that you and us are one family. From God we are staying on this earth and from God our strength comes.

    Shelley when you both left, I and your mother at Gohiya felt very sad and we cried for you. After your Gohiya mother slept and when she got up the next morning she saw your house and she was crying and she said to me, "Shelley and Roger are like my children, I carried them." She said, "All the time they were thinking-caring for me." And she asked me, "Will they come back some time or not?" And I said, "I don't know. Only God knows." And I said, "If Roger gets well Shelley will be happy and she will say to Roger, 'let's come back to Nuakata Island,' "and their study . . . they will finish it."[1] (Excerpt from a letter from Noah Siyae, 30 November 1993)

We received this letter from Wycliffe's father just before Christmas 1993. Reading it we felt both sorrow and joy. We had reluctantly left Nuakata by mid-October and returned to Melbourne. Our time there was abruptly foreshortened when, in early September, following a particularly perilous boat journey, Roger developed his tenth bout of what we assumed to be malaria. Although the frequency of his attacks was high in terms of the local population, the occurrence of what Western medicine identifies as malaria was not. It was rife on Nuakata. After taking the requisite course of quinine, Roger had felt well for a day or so before the all too familiar fever and headache returned. Seasonal winds, rain, and heavy seas meant that no one on the island was able to return to the mainland by sailing canoe or boat. Effectively stranded without radio or boat, and unable to seek medical advice from Moses, who was away at the time, I sought assistance from Eric, the local healer. Eric treated Roger on two separate occasions, his efforts bringing relief for several days, before the acute spleen pain and fever reemerged. More than a little anxious and distressed by this turn of events, I sought advice from Noah and Eunice, who urged Roger and me to leave the island and seek medical attention back in Australia. Bad weather prevented us from effecting this plan until four weeks later when, quite fortuitously, a yacht sailed into Duwaduwali Bay and its owners, a retired couple from Australia, kindly offered to transport us back to Alotau.

Overwhelmed by sadness when we left the island, we were struggling with life back in Melbourne. When left to wander, our thoughts invariably returned to Nuakata. We longed to be back there with our friends. We imagined what they were doing. It was summer—the pineapples and mangoes would be ripening. Children would be playing together in the water—jumping, splashing, and laughing. Wycliffe's mother and sisters would be heading off to their gardens at sunrise. They would return by midmorning to escape the full heat of the day. Perhaps his brothers were out fishing and diving on the reefs. Or maybe they were playing cards in our house. We wondered, Who was winning? Which teams had won the soccer and netball competitions? Was everyone well? Did they miss us as we missed them?

It was difficult to reconcile these compelling memories and imaginings with my project to write an ethnography detailing notions of the gendered person and reproductive health on Nuakata. How could I write about people who had become like kin, friends, or acquaintances without objectifying them? How should I represent and honor people's ways of thinking and acting? How would I create a sensible narrative from my disparate memories, field notes, transcripts, and diary accounts? How could I do all this while critically reflecting on ethnographic method, knowledge production, and writing? Noah's letter arrived just as I was contemplating the writing task. His words and the relayed comments of his wife, Eunice, not only brought comfort but also inspired a way that I might remember the people and places of Nuakata. His letter inadvertently touched on themes about knowledge, gender, belonging, difference, and remembering that had emerged as central to my ethnographic project to understand the significance or relevance of notions of the gendered person on Nuakata.

Knowledge and Knowing

That Noah should write this first letter, rather than Wycliffe, Eunice, or even Geteli, was telling in many ways. On one level, it simply reflected his role in orchestrating our stay on Nuakata and his comparative facility with written English. While it was Eunice's customary right, as a senior woman in her *susu*, to determine whether or not we could live at Gohiya, in practice Noah and Eunice's sister's husband, Antiya, were instrumental in making that decision. These men were conferred with this authority because of their respected status within the Nuakatan community, especially within the United Church, and because of their long-standing work on behalf of Eunice's *susu*. On another level, the fact that the author of this letter was a respected senior man reiterated the central irony of my fieldwork, namely, that despite my prefield assumptions and intentions, men as much as, if not more than, women proved pivotal to my research. While senior men did not presume to speak with me about women's experience of pregnancy, birth, contraception, menstruation, and gardening—deeming it women's knowledge or knowing—they often claimed an authority to speak on behalf of women and younger kin about other, related customary matters. On these occasions women routinely, but not always, deferred to them.

It was tempting to conclude from this that knowledge was gendered on Nuakata and that my research inflected a masculine sensibility. While I would not wish to deny the validity of both assertions, for they are partially true, they are ultimately too simplistic. On Nuakata, as discussed in chapter 3, people could know something without directly experiencing it, however this form of knowledge was less potent than experienced knowledge and understanding. For this reason, in any context where two or more people are present, only those with significant experience could claim authority to speak or perform this knowledge. While possession of knowledge defines someone's individuality, it did not constitute him or her as a person or an autonomous individual as such.

Before speaking about what they know then, people living on Nuakata took account of their relationship with those present and observed the rules governing what could be said or done in the presence of senior or junior, and male or female affines, *susu* members and other people. In this way it is possible to claim, somewhat clumsily, that age, seniority, status, kinship relations, gender, ethnicity, and religious affiliation influenced both the experience and expression of knowledge on Nuakata. I am highly reluctant to specify how this occurs, for people living on Nuakata would neither think of nor explain the local rules governing the dissemination of knowledge in these terms.

It follows, then, that the understanding of particular aspects of Nuakatan sociality that I gained through conversations and interviews with people was necessarily influenced by my informants and the speaking contexts in which the knowledge was elicited. My understanding was also filtered through Wycliffe who, as a single man of my age and my fictive affine, brought his own long-standing and highly attuned ethnographic sensibility to our research relationship. In recording and reproducing knowledge gained in the field, I felt compelled to report the speaking context—to specify who spoke, to what audience, where, and, if possible, with what intent. Without such details readers cannot begin to understand the potency of the knowledge shared and something of the speaker's intent in disclosing such information or understanding. Nor can they form an opinion about the efficacy of both my informants' and my own claims to know. By providing these contextual details, I provide readers with the opportunity to assess how interrelated factors such as the gender, age, kinship affiliations, status, and ethnicity of my informants are inflected in my representations of various aspects of Nuakatan sociality. This is not to suggest, however, that it is possible to fully grasp a speaker's intent or that my representations of these fieldwork encounters are transparent. Rather this narrative strategy serves to remind and reinforce the idea that anthropological knowledge production in and beyond the field is contingent on the intersubjective process of participant observation. Speakers, listeners, ethnographers, and readers are always positioned in these encounters. This narrative strategy also potentially alerts the reader to the absences and elisions in fieldwork encounters—to all that is unasked, unknown, or misunderstood.

Bearing, Birthing, and Gender

As I contemplated the writing task, Eunice's claim that we were like her children—that it was as if she had carried and born us—refocused my attention on reproductive health matters, while also reminding me of the evident yet understated significance of women's bearing and carrying practices on Nuakata. Although my research on women's reproductive health was foreshortened by our hasty departure from Nuakata, it was clear to me that women were making very thoughtful, if not pragmatic, decisions about their own and their children's health (see chaps. 2, 3, and 5). Aware of the risks to themselves and their infants associated with village births—namely, postpartum hemorrhage, retained placenta, and infection—many, but by no means all, were electing to birth at the hospital on the mainland. In this setting they could birth with female midwives in attendance. Medication and surgery were also available to them if required. By birthing in the hospital, rather than their villages, women were spared the embarrassment of having a single, male community health worker in attendance if complications arose during or after labor. Some also wished to avoid the intervention of village midwives during labor and birthing. Many women, however, continued to birth in their matrilineal villages, even if they had previously birthed in the hospital. The reasons for this were many and varied. Some could not raise the necessary money for the trip to the mainland and a prolonged stay in hospital. Some husbands refused to allow their wives to go to the hospital. Some felt healthy during their pregnancies and preferred to birth on familiar, matrilineal land with their kin present.

Women living on Nuakata largely relied on the advice and support of their female kin for prenatal and postnatal care. Too embarrassed to seek assistance from the male community health worker during birth, they were similarly reluctant to seek his advice, support, or intervention around contraception, prenatal, and postnatal care. In theory, female midwives from the mainland were meant to conduct prenatal clinics once a month on the island. In practice, however, these rarely occurred. Bad weather and inadequate funding prevented the midwives from regularly attending these clinics. As a result some young women felt unsure and even fearful of birth. Caught between the advice and practices of their older female kin and a conflicting preventive community health agenda encouraged by the community health worker and reinforced during their primary school education, these young women were, at times, unsure about what they should do in relation to their reproductive health. Sometimes familial and economic pressures prevented them from effecting their reproductive health choices.

As discussed in chapter 3, by bearing children and garden produce, women sustained their living *susu*. They ensured the continuity of their *susu* and its individual members for past, present, and future generations. Women said that only they bear children, for they alone possess the bodily form and maturity that enables them to perform this activity. While the form of girls' bodies reveals the potential to bear children, their inability to produce menstrual blood means they lack the capacity to sustain pregnancies. It was this capacity, and the capacity to sustain one's *susu*, rather than childbearing itself, that was considered most relevant to the category "woman" on Nuakata. A woman's capacity to bear children, and hence her identification as a woman, was known to be contingent upon the activities of those *susu* members (male and female, past and present) who sustained and nurtured her to maturity. It was contingent on all those who could enable her to realize this potential—principally non-*susu* men with whom she could have vaginal sexual intercourse.

If it was primarily women (rather than girls, boys, or men) who carried and bore, then it was men who made this possible by clearing and preparing the space for children and/or garden produce to grow. In this way, men facilitated and supported women's bearing activities. While they could not give birth, men could and did carry children and garden produce, just as women often assisted with the clearing of gardens. Despite their different activities and responsibilities, men and women could and did perform and engage in the same practices. As discussed in chapter 5, both men and women were involved in nurturing and growing themselves, their children, and, through them, their *susu*. People claimed that it was only when semen and menstrual blood co-mingle that the unborn child's blood develops and the child can then grow within the womb. The child is therefore grown, if not substantively constituted, by the combined labors of its parents. This understanding of the emergence and constitution of the unborn baby and, by implication, the child, the young man or woman, and the adult resonates with M. Strathern's (1988) claims about the Melanesian understanding of the constitution of the person and the unitary individual. As noted in the introduction, Strathern claims that the Melanesian person is understood as a social microcosm—the product of cross-sex, consanguineal, and affinal parts/relations. The person has dual origins, and it is only in specific relational contexts and through specific material exchanges that a person's internal, dualistic differentiation is de-emphasized to produce the unitary individual. It is only on these occasions that being male or being female emerges as a "holistic unitary state" (M. Strathern 1988, 14).

Similarly, people assumed that one is not born a woman (or a man), on Nuakata. One becomes a woman because of and in relation to people (both male and female, *susu*, and non-*susu*) who are not women, that is, young girls, men, etc. The terms *man* and *woman* only became meaningful, or in any sense prescriptive, in relation to others. While the specter of (child) bearing and vaginal sex between a man and woman (rather than heterosexuality) pervaded this category, the performance of these activities confirmed rather than created someone as a woman. Women who did not bear children and/or garden produce were still considered women, for the form of their body and their capacity to menstruate was indicative of their potential to do so. People felt sorry for these women. By having no one to nurture, grow, or sustain and, in turn, no one to care for them when they are old, their living, and that of their *susu*, was necessarily diminished.

As this discussion implies, the categorical and ethnocentric distinctions between the terms *sex, gender,* and *sexuality* were of limited value for the analysis of the categories "man" and "woman" and the relations within and between these types of people on Nuakata. Where the context demanded, two genders were differentiated on the basis of bodily form and perceived potential to bear children and thereby sustain and continue a given *susu*. Only those with the potential to bear children could, in time, with age and maturity, become women. Therefore, the difference between sex and gender on Nuakata was subtle. It could be described as the difference between form and action, potential and capacity. In my experience, neither the terms nor the difference between the terms was invoked. In fact, such a difference is best understood as an ethnocentric analytical contrivance. Similarly, people did not speak of sexuality, although they did speak of their wants or desires. People's desires—for food, sex, or other goods and services—were spoken of as alienable possessions or performative longings. The cause or underlying basis of their desires was neither questioned nor invoked. Desire itself was not understood as a substantive essence. Accordingly, someone's sexual desires did not define him or her as homosexual, heterosexual, bisexual, and so forth. They merely characterized the way he or she preferred to act in sexual relationships.

These reflections beyond the field made me reconsider my original ethnographic project to reflect on the significance or relevance of ideas about the gendered person on Nuakata. During my time on Nuakata people rarely spoke of human beings in abstract terms. In fact there was no equivalent term for the category person in Alina Nuʻata! As discussed in chapters 2 and 6, particular human beings were always identified in terms of their particular activities, their identifying characteristics and relationships, or their relationship to the speaker. Particular human beings were also described as "the one who . . . ," where the ellipses stand for a particular activity or way of doing things. It could be said that doing rather than being, social relationships rather than essential personal characteristics were fundamental to Nuakatan ways of understanding human beings. It was people's belongings to other people, places, and things, rather than their identities or status as persons, that mattered on Nuakata.

In contemplating how to write the ethnography I was faced with several immediate theoretical and political issues. How could I write in a way that addressed my own and other ethnographers' questions about the gendered person while also conveying the ethnocentric nature, if not irrelevance, of those questions for people living on Nuakata? How could the text reflect and respect how these people understand one another rather than anthropological debates about the comparison between Melanesian and Western persons? I also sought to highlight and reflect on the epistemological and methodological significance of a process that occurred during my own fieldwork and commonly occurs during ethnographic research. Put simply, many researchers enter the field with research topics, a set of questions, even research hypotheses, only to find, once in the field, that they must shift their foci because their research agendas are founded on false or irrelevant assumptions. This process is routinely elided in the ethnographic texts that follow.

In confronting these issues I made strategic decisions about the structure and content of the text. First I decided to privilege local people's ways of talking, explaining, and enacting their understandings of one and other. In effect this meant that difficult decisions had to be made about what could be de-emphasized or sacrificed in the text for the book to be of a readable, publishable length. I therefore decided to limit my discussion of regional and cross-regional comparisons and theoretical debates on the gendered person in the main body of the text. In my reflections on Nuakatan ways of understanding people, sociality, sickness, and childbearing, I was determined to avoid using ethnocentric analytical terms such as person, self, subject, gender, sexuality, and "the body." For this reason I decided to largely consign my conventional theoretical discussion of these issues to the Introduction. The other chapters engage with these theoretical debates but they do so through the form and narrative strategies employed in the text.

These textual strategies proved more difficult to implement than it might appear. At a most basic level it is difficult to avoid terms, categories, and syntax that one takes for granted. It is even more difficult to do this while also engaging with works that employ the terms one is determined not to privilege. And always the question remains, Who is the audience for such writing, such anthropological projects?

Accommodating Difference

Eunice's relayed claim that we were like her children also pointed to her understanding of living with difference. In the context of mutual care and tangible support born of living together, similarities and differences between people were accommodated—a shared place made, a common humanity discovered. Only by accommodating the similarities and differences between people (men and women, *susu* and affine, Papuan and *dimdim*) was one's *susu* revitalized, and a shared humanity established and confirmed. As a member of a given *susu* and clan, people had a recognized place on Nuakata. These allegiances determined how people of different ages, sex, and clan affiliation related with one another. They defined one's belonging and structured the interdependent and complementary relationships considered vital for one's living and staying. For these reasons people who came to stay from other places were always integrated into an existing *susu* and clan, whether or not they had known ancestral links to these groups.

Yet, integrating Roger and me proved more problematic than for most, as unlike all others who had come to stay we were white people, *dimdim*. This defined our difference. In a region with a long history of colonialism, where the remaining white missionaries and other expatriates are materially advantaged and continue to occupy positions of power and authority over local people, white skin was a difference that continued to make a difference. As white people we were assumed to eschew reciprocal, mutually dependent relationships, to value the individual, and to practice selfishness and arrogance. Access to money and material possessions was believed to lessen white people's need for others, including Papuans. Accordingly, white people acted as though their living was not contingent upon the past, present, and future activities of both their *susu* and affines. Although known to lack knowledge and understanding of Papuan ways, white people were generally thought of as intelligent, their ways sophisticated (if not bemusing) and therefore worthy of respect.

Skin color, then, did not constitute or fundamentally determine the difference between white and Papuan peoples on Nuakata, but rather signified historically different ways of living, understanding, and relating. While not essentialist in nature, these differences were nonetheless embodied. They were evident and recognized in postures and gestures, in people's differing occupations and in the organization of spaces, in the distribution of things, and in the ways people worked, spoke, ate, and thought. It therefore follows that Papuans could act like white people and vice versa. Accordingly, Papuans can and do act, to varying degrees, as if they are autonomous individuals rather than relationally constituted, just as white people can act as if they are relationally constituted. Only by redressing the material inequalities and transforming these embodiments will the postures of difference separating Papuan and white people diminish. Perhaps, only then will Noah's claim that all people on earth come from God and share a common humanity be more than a platitude in this context.

Although Roger and I wished to belong, to have a tangible connection with particular *susu* and the broader community on Nuakata, we too sought relations that could strengthen the similarities and accommodate the differences (both material and performative) between ourselves and local people. There were many reasons for taking this stance, among them ethical and methodological considerations as well as self-interest. I believed it disingenuous to position myself as a participant observer, who was, in effect, a tabula rasa prior to arrival on the island. I neither hoped nor attempted to act as though my participant observation on Nuakata would lead me to an indigenous understanding of local knowledge and practices. Nor did I pretend to lack opinions or beliefs. Apart from anything else, Roger's presence made it impossible to act otherwise. There as my partner, to offer support, Roger did not seek a research relationship with local people. Rather, he sought friendship founded on mutual respect and interest in one another's past, present, and future ways of living. Unlike mine, his relationships with people were not constrained by a pressing research agenda. Having my partner present also meant that local people could observe me in a relationship that extended beyond the field, one embedded in my own social world. Apart from respectfully refraining from demonstrations of affection in public, Roger and I maintained a way of relating to one another, including the way we organized our domestic life, that testified not only to cultural difference but to a sense of personal continuity.

As suggested earlier, despite their quiet misgivings about white people and their relations with Papuans, our hosts had good reason to reinforce and accommodate the similarities and differences between us. By housing and supporting us, the Nuakatan community in general and several families in particular could, by association, claim something of the respect and status historically asserted and bestowed upon white people in the region. Our presence and fascination with Nuakatan people's ideas and practices, our desire to learn their language, gave people cause to reflect on their customary ways and provided an opportunity for them to conceive of themselves as distinctive and knowledgeable. Therefore, our stay, and more particularly my research, reinforced, perhaps even created, a collective Nuakatan cultural identity, both on the island and in the region. More practically, our presence brought limited material benefits for our friends, fictive kin, and, to a lesser degree, the wider community.

Belonging and Remembering

That our place, our belonging among the Siyae *susu*, affines, and broader Nuakatan community, should be confirmed after we had gone was no coincidence. As the practices associated with death and burial on Nuakata revealed, it was only by looking backward on what had gone before—on someone's individual ways and living relationships—that his or her staying could be understood and encapsulated. Someone's habits, relationships, and things constituted the territory of his or her individuality and belonging. Indeed, these belongings to people (particularly *susu*), places, and things constitute someone (or "sum-one," the sum of the relational parts that together make one); they constitute what may loosely yet misleadingly be glossed as the person.

After death, the deceased could only enter the realm of the dead when he or she no longer belonged with the living and, conversely, when the living no longer belonged with the deceased. For this to occur, the living must respectfully acknowledge and appropriately remember the nature of their embodied relationship with the deceased. In so doing, they completed or finished this living, embodied relationship.

As other Massim ethnographers attest, the practice of remembering in order to complete or finish someone's life is a pivotal aspect of mortuary feasts across the region (Battaglia 1992; Damon and Wagner 1989). On Nuakata, as elsewhere, people often referred to this form of remembering as forgetting the deceased. Forgetting, in this context, did not mean erasing memories of the deceased, or denying the personal impact of his or her loss. On the contrary, forgetting was a process of recalling the social relationships integral to the former life of the deceased, and therefore his or her *susu*. By exchanging valued food, such as pigs, yams, and rice, the *susu* and/or affines of the deceased specifically demonstrated the deceased's prior contribution to the life and growth of their kin. These social relations between the deceased's *susu* and affines, and the debts, obligations, and responsibilities associated with them, were completed and forgotten through the process of gift exchange integral to the mortuary feasts. During the period of mourning following a death, people remembered to forget the deceased in other ways, typically through acts of avoidance—avoiding use of his or her name and engaging in activities particularly associated with him or her. How one remembered the deceased depended on one's relation to him or her.

On Nuakata, then, remembering was enacted, embodied, placed. People directed or projected their thinking-feeling to the knowledge, practices, events, or people to be recalled, thereby creating the past in the present. Remembering could also be a kind of imagining. For example, in remembering a story, someone evoked the seen and unseen, known and unknown alike. Only those with the necessary authority and experience were entitled to recall customary matters, be it a story or practice or some other form of knowledge. Knowing, like remembering, was neither emotive nor distant from experience and relationships. Through participation and observation people learned how to perform and thereby remember given activities, things, and places. Knowledge, particularly performed customary knowledge, was possessed by given people. They alone chose whom, if anyone, they would pass it on to, in effect deciding who could remember it. More often than not knowledge of this kind was entrusted to select junior members within one's matrilineage—kin who by their thoughtfulness, diligence, or astuteness had demonstrated their worthiness. But in some instances this knowledge was given to nonkin with whom one had a special relationship, or to trusted and respected people who were prepared to pay for it. Relationships of mutual respect and trust, if not affection, were therefore pivotal to the exchange of customary knowledge. Where qualified trust and respect exist, the information and ideas exchanged were incomplete or misleading. Failure to remember the details of customary stories or practices was thought to cause disrespect to those implicated in the performance. It was also thought to diminish the potency of the story or practice. Forgetfulness in these contexts demonstrated an inability to place oneself in (an)other's space, an inability to empathize. It was quintessentially a form of carelessness and disrespect—a lack of care and respect for one's kin and for the entrusted knowledge and practices. As such, there was a moral quality to both remembering and forgetting. Committing improprieties of this kind could be dangerous for such acts were thought to incite the ire of both the living and the dead.

For the people living on Nuakata, remembering and forgetting were often linked or related social practices. One might remember as a means of completing and forgetting given relationships, knowledge, or practices, or remember in order to nurture and continue them. Conversely, one might forget as a means of remembering. What was and was not said or done was often equally important. In fact, concealed or elided thoughts, feelings, and acts were often considered more potent forms of knowledge. Different obligations and conditions applied according to the perceived value and purpose of that which was remembered. How people remembered depended on their relationship to the people present and the ones remembered. People always remained mindful of their relative authority to speak or act.

As I reflected on the implications of these issues for the written ethnography, I wondered how I could remember my fieldwork experiences in a way that respected the moral purposes and effects bestowed upon remembering and forgetting on Nuakata. It seemed that my capacity to empathize, to imagine, if you like, was crucial. Among other things, I needed to demonstrate respect for details, remain aware of the extent and limitations of my own and others' knowledge, and, where possible, maintain clarity about the purpose of my own and others' remembering. In detailing the context in which knowledge or understanding was elicited I must also, where possible, remain mindful of my relationship to the people whose knowledge and remembering I represent. Not only must I strategically avoid writing about some things, but I must also make these elisions and their purposes evident, if not explicit.

Remembering Nuakata, Remembering Us

As I read Noah's letter, I interpreted Eunice's question about our possible return to Nuakata as an attempt to discern the future nature of our relationship with herself, her *susu*, and, more broadly, the people of Nuakata. In effect, it seemed that she was asking Noah, asking us, how should she remember us? Did we feel as she did? How should she think-feel and speak of our stay on Nuakata? Was the relationship continuing or completed? While unsure, Noah thought our relationship would continue. Requests made later in the letter for a Methodist hymnbook and for news of our well-being suggested that he wished to foster indebtedness. Noah also recognized that my research was incomplete and that this would necessitate my return to Nuakata. By doing this he recognized what we shared during our stay and highlighted our continuing interdependence. In writing the letter he engaged in an act of remembering aimed at recognizing and continuing our relationship.

The sentiments expressed in Noah's letter transported my thinking back to Nuakata and, more specifically, Gohiya. Perhaps this was Noah's intent. Thinking and feeling were spoken of as inseparable on Nuakata. Thoughts were felt and feelings were conceived and expressed thoughtfully, if not purposefully. When enacted or expressed, felt-thoughts could effect concealed purposes, causing others to act. As I focused on Nuakata I remembered times spent with friends and adopted kin and imagined what they might be doing now, how they might have changed. The feelings of alienation and difference that I experienced during our first days there mingled without merging with the sense of grief and loss I felt during and after our departure. Among other things, these responses revealed and highlighted both the extent and the limitations of my prefield imaginings—imaginings fundamentally influenced by a sense of prefieldwork nerves and anxiety. Feeling desolate when I first arrived, I only decided to stay because I imagined and hoped for a time when we belonged on Nuakata. This hope was founded on an assumption of a shared humanity and the compelling testimony of many anthropologists to fictive kin relationships with their fieldwork hosts. In remembering these feelings I was reminded of and confronted by the ways my prefield imaginings had positively and negatively influenced my research and relationships on Nuakata. If my prefield imaginings were shaped by memories of Pacific anthropology classes and texts, feminist theory and my father's wartime experiences, then my postfield remembering was shaped by these conjoined with experiences shared on Nuakata. My memories of these experiences and of particular people and places enabled me to reimagine Nuakata. Not only was my experience there limited, my memory of this experience was necessarily selective. Noah underlines this point in his letter when he notes that my research is not finished. In fact my research was just beginning.

Foreshortened by Roger's illness, our stay on Nuakata had ended at a time when familiarity and trust between us and Eunice's family (both *susu* and affines) was beginning to emerge. The research and the relationships were inextricably bound. Only through experience, by repeatedly doing and/or witnessing given practices, would I come to know and understand their local significance. Only by proving myself trustworthy over time, by repeatedly demonstrating care and respect for people, by establishing mutually indebted relationships, would I be entrusted with knowledge of valued customary ideas and practices. For me to more fully understand Nuakatan sociality and notions of the "I" or "one who . . . ," I must enliven these relationships with people, both by returning to and remembering the field imagined and lived.

Notes

INTRODUCTION

1. See Bell (1993); Bell, Caplan, and Karim (1993); Caplan (1993); del Valle (1993).
2. See Bourdieu and Wacquant (1992, 104).
3. See Fabian (1983, 89); Crick (1976).
4. Cf. Dumont (1978).
5. See Ingold (1991); Morton (1995); Clifford (1986, 1988); Marcus and Cushman (1982); Marcus and Fischer (1986).
6. See also Haraway (1991, 185–201).
7. See Alcoff (1991).
8. Cf. Neumann (1992, 40–49).
9. In his reflection on the Western philosophical *Sources of the Self,* Charles Taylor writes, "In fact, our visions of the good are tied up with our understandings of the self. We have already seen one facet of this connection in the close link . . . between identity and moral orientation. We have a sense of who we are through our sense of where we stand to the good. But this will also mean . . . that radically different conceptions of what the good is go along with quite different conceptions of what a human agent is, different notions of the self. To trace the development of our modern visions of the good, which are in some respects unprecedented in human culture, is also to follow the evolution of unprecedented new understandings of agency and selfhood" (1989, 105).
10. See for example, Carrithers, Collins, and Lukes (1985).
11. See Kovel (1981, 1988); Benjamin (1988).
12. Mauss concludes, "Who knows even whether this 'category,' which all of us here believe to be well founded, will always be recognized as such? It is formulated only for us, among us. Even its oral strength—the sacred character of the human 'person' (*personne*)—is questioned, not only throughout the Orient, which has not yet attained the level of our sciences, but even in our countries where this principle was discovered" (1985, 22, emphasis in original).
13. See also Morton (1995).
14. See Bhabha (1993); M. Strathern (1988); Taylor (1989).
15. See Bordo (1990, 144–45); Benhabib (1990).
16. See, for example, Fox-Keller (1985); Flax (1990a, 1990b); Jaggar (1989); Lloyd (1984); Merchant (1980); Butler (1988); de Lauretis (1986a).
17. See Derrida (1978, 1982); Foucault (1978, 1980); Grosz (1989); Taylor (1986).
18. See Rorty (1979); Jay (1993).
19. See Bell and Nelson (1989); Ram (1993); Alcoff (1991).

20. When Descartes, "sitting by the fire, wearing a dressing gown," began his quest to "establish something firm and constant in the sciences"—some irrefutable "knowledge of truth"—it was from the deceptive realms of the senses and the illusory world of his dreams that he fled. Beset by doubt and fear, he sought to eliminate all beliefs that were "not entirely certain." Through "peaceful solitude" and rigorous self-examination and destruction of the "principles on which all [his] previous opinions were based," he believed he might discover and articulate certainty and knowledge of truth. Not only did these musings reveal his conflation of truth with certainty but they also reflected Hegel's (1974) observation that Descartes made an epistemological link between self-consciousness and the exposition of truth (Hodge 1988, 155). Although he claimed to suspend and examine his beliefs, he neither abandoned nor considered his most basic assumptions. Reason, certainty, knowledge of truth, and his rational, self-reflective methodology remained beyond question (Descartes 1968, 95–97).

21. With reason as its progenitor, it is a self that is potentially the same as other selves and for which the experiences of its embodiment (for example, its gender and its parentage, its historical, sociocultural context) are rendered prejudicial and therefore irrelevant to true and certain knowledge. It is a great irony that Descartes is credited with instigating Western philosophy's preoccupation with the individual subject, and yet he attempted to subordinate individuality and morality to a transcendent, transhistorical rationality (Pelz 1974).

22. See Moore (1988); Haraway (1991, 127–81); di Leonardo (1991).

23. Where, for the sake of brevity, I conflate egalitarian and social constructionist feminism, feminist theorists such as Grosz (1994, 15–17) differentiate between the two.

24. See Haraway (1991, 127–48); Grosz (1994); Gatens (1983, 1991); Moore (1988, 1994c).

25. See, for example, Butler (1993); Wittig (1981).

26. See Moore (1994c); Mohanty (1991a, 1991b). Cf. Spivak (1984, 1988).

27. See Butler (1988, 1990); Irigaray (1985a, 1985b); Cixous (1981a, 1981b); de Lauretis (1986a, 1986b); I. Young (1990); Braidotti (1989); Flax (1990b).

28. See Taylor (1989); Pile and Thrift (1995, 24–25).

29. See Moore (1988, 187–98; 1994c, 26–27); de Lauretis (1986a).

30. I use the word *privilege* here with some irony. For, clearly, it is only because of privilege that the ethnographer can conduct fieldwork. What is more, to some extent, fieldwork inevitably reinforces this privilege and the relationship between privileged and underprivileged. However, I also use *privilege* to suggest that, without past experience of fieldwork, the intending fieldworker can romanticize the field and fieldwork relations. Fieldwork possibilities are not sullied by experience of the field.

31. See Dwyer (1977, 1979, 1982); Tedlock (1983); Hymes (1972); Scholte (1974).

32. See Bourdieu (1977); Bourdieu and Wacquant (1992); James (1976); Turner (1986); Rosaldo (1989); Jackson (1989).

33. See Rorty (1979); Merleau-Ponty (1962); James (1976, 1978); Heidegger (1975, 1993); Dewey (1929).

34. See Fabian (1983); Jay (1993).
35. See Jackson (1989, 136–55).
36. See Bell (1993); Caplan (1988a, 1988b); M. Strathern (1987a); Behar (1995).
37. When my father named some local people with whom he had particular friendships, he used the term *fuzzy wuzzies* as an affectionate collective term. The term *fuzzy wuzzy angels* was coined by Australian military personnel to describe the native people who assisted them in their wartime efforts.
38. See Damon (1989); Fortune ([1932] 1989); Battaglia (1990); Leach (1967); Leach and Leach (1983); Macintyre (1983, 1987); Malinowski (1922); Munn (1986, 1990); A. Weiner (1976, 1988); Thune (1980, 1990); Young (1989a, 1989b); Bromilow (1929).
39. See Macintyre (1995); Jolly (1992b); Thomas (1991); Biersack (1991).
40. See Carrier (1992); Thomas (1991); Gewertz and Errington (1991b).
41. M. Strathern notes that she replaced the word *deconstruction* with the terms *deconstitution* and *decompostion* in *The Gender of the Gift* to prevent readers from conflating Melanesian deconstructive practices with those promoted by Western postmodernist literary and philosophical theory. She notes that Melanesians "are not doing deconstruction in the Western sense because they do not hold constructionist premises" (1989a, 55–56).
42. Singer states that identifiable shortcomings in "conventional" medical anthropology include "microlevel circumscription" and "neglect of social relations," medicalisation, and ecological reductionism (1989, 193). Singer suggests that "microlevel" analyses in small-scale communities have often emphasized the ritual and symbolic dimensions of health and sickness "as if rituals and symbols or perhaps values and beliefs constitute society independent of a political economic context" (1989; 1990, 179). "Meaning centered," ecological, and comparativist forms of medical anthropology are targeted for criticism by these researchers. Meaning-centered anthropologists contend that "human illness is fundamentally . . . meaningful and that all clinical practice is inherently interpretive or 'hermeneutic'" (Good and Good 1981, 175; see also Kleinman 1973, 1980). They stress that "multiple interpretative frames and discourses are brought to bear on any illness event." Accordingly, "interpretations of the nature of an illness always bear the history of the discourse that shapes its interpretation, and are always contested in settings of local power relations" (Good 1994, 53). Critics of this approach argue that, in focusing on particular social relations (between, for example, doctor and patient), these studies often ignore the macrolevel forces that influence these interactions (Singer 1990).

Ecological forms of medical anthropology analyze health and sickness in a given community in terms of the adaptive measures adopted by people to their physical environment. By taking the environment as given or natural, however, these studies overlook the human construction of it and the health and sickness of people living in it (Hahn 1995; Singer 1990). While both these forms of medical anthropology have been accused of medicalizing medical anthropology by employing the language, concepts, and values of Western biomedicine to frame their analyses, comparative cultural studies of health and illness, like those of Lewis (1975) and Frankel (1986) in Papua New Guinea, have been particularly criticized by critical (interpretive) medical anthropologists. These studies fail to analyze Western biomedical epistemologies in the cultural constructivist terms reserved for so-called traditional medicine (Good 1994; Keck 1993; Lock and Scheper-Hughes 1990; A. Young 1982).

43. See also Morsy (1990); Good (1994); Scarry (1985).

44. See Clifford (1988); Geertz (1988); Stocking (1983); Said (1995); Abu-Lughod (1990); Trinh (1989).

45. See Scheper-Hughes (1995, 419–20); Clifford (1989, 562); M. Strathern (1989a, 565–66); Herzfeld (1989, 563); Rabinow (1996, 28–58).

46. Her dare, What if I talked like a woman? evokes Ursula Le Guin's comments to a college class in 1983. Le Guin asked, "Instead of talking power, what if I talked like a woman right here in public?" (1989, 115).

47. See Behar (1995); Behar and Gordon (1995); Marcus (1993); Gacs et al. (1989); Bell (1993).

48. See Caplan (1988a, 1988b); Moore (1988, 1994c); M. Strathern (1987c).

49. See D. Gordon (1988) and especially Gordon (1995) for a discussion of the implications of reading the history of feminist anthropology and ethnography through the conventional/experimental distinction.

50. Stacey (1990).

51. See, for example, Okely (1992); Okely and Callaway (1992); Callaway (1992); Cotterill and Letherby (1993).

52. See, for example, D. Gordon (1995); Josephides (1997); Trinh (1989); Moore (1994a, 1994b).

53. See, for example, D. Gordon (1993).

54. A feminist and an anthropologist but not a self-identified feminist anthropologist/ethnographer, Marilyn Strathern's contribution to debates about knowledge are unsurpassed in the discipline. See, for example, M. Strathern (1987c, 1988, 1989a, 1991).

55. See, for example, di Leonardo (1991); Cole and Phillips (1995); Behar (1995); Kirby (1993).

56. This point is also highlighted by Mascia-Lees, Sharpe, and Cohen (1989); Scheper-Hughes (1992).

57. See, for example, Caplan (1988b); Abu-Lughod (1991); Jennaway (1990); and compare with Rabinow (1996, 51–56).

CHAPTER 1

1. See Barker (1990, 7–10) and Forman (1990).

2. For a discussion of the role and impact of foreign missionaries in Melanesia (past and present) see Jolly and Macintyre (1989); Young (1989b, 1996); Burridge (1978); Boutilier, Hughes, and Tiffany (1978); Eves (1996a); Reed (1998); White (1992).

3. In 1993 there were at least ten Christian denominations represented in Alotau that had a permanent population of approximately 5,000 people. These included the Anglican, Catholic, Christian Revivalist, CLC (Christian Living

Center), Jehovah's Witness, Mormon, Seventh-Day Adventist, Tewala Bible College, and United Churches. The Baha'i were also represented.

4. Excluding its long point, Gadahoa, which is located on its southern margins, Nuakata is roughly 4.5 kilometers wide and 2.5 kilometers long.

5. Pidgin, Motu, and English are the lingua francas for much of Papua New Guinea; however, in Milne Bay Province, English and especially Dobu are the common languages.

6. This figure included the four sides of the island, the inhabitants of Daiwali, and people staying temporarily (several weeks or months) in places beyond Nuakata.

7. English equivalent not known.

8. Regional Methodist missions amalgamated with the Papua New Guinea and Solomon Islands United Church in 1968 (M. Young 1996, 105).

9. The Reverend George Brown, general-secretary of the Australasian Methodist Missionary Society, briefly visited the island in 1890.

10. The Bromilows sought to overturn cultural practices that they considered incompatible with Christianity, including: cannibalism, witchcraft, sorcery, and the enforced lengthy seclusion of widows following their husbands' death. Affronted by the perceived neglect of children, instances of infanticide, and premarital sex, they also attempted to impose "the European-Wesleyan-Victorian family model" values and daily practices on the Dobuans (M. Young 1989b, 122). Young (1989b, 124) notes that they met with considerable resistance. Commenting on the impact of Polynesian evangelical missionaries on Tubetube and throughout the Louisiades, Macintyre states that because of their harsh methods they, rather than the Australian missionaries, are "remembered as the agents of change" (1989b, 162).

11. For a discussion of missionaries as "heroes responsible for instituting the moral order as it is known today" see White (1992, 136) and M. Young (1996) in particular.

12. As both White (1992, 159, 179) and M. Young (1977; 1996, 96–100) attest, commemorative enactments of missionary first encounters are widespread throughout the Pacific. In detailing the characteristic components of these reenactments they note that the missionary is depicted as the primary agent, while local people are portrayed as passive savages, awaiting pacification and conversion.

13. My observations and comments here coincide with Thune's (1990, 104) reflections on the role of village pastors in the Loboda village United Church on Normanby Island.

CHAPTER 2

1. While the average life expectancy in PNG has been extended to fifty-four years and the national infant mortality rate has dropped from an estimated 500 deaths per 1,000 in 1949 (Gunther 1949, in Biddulph 1991) to 59 per 1,000 in 1990 (Grant 1990), the maternal mortality rate remains alarmingly high—approxi-

mately 930 per 100,000 live births (Kuble 1998). Decreases in the infant and maternal mortality rate have been achieved in urban areas of PNG, however these achievements have not been matched in rural or marginal areas (Biddulph 1991; Douglas 1991; Everett 1987; Gillett 1990; Mola 1985; 1989; Mola and Aitken 1984; see Mallett 2002).

2. Nancy Munn's first two field periods on Gawa stretched "from June 1973 to mid July 1974 and from late May 1975 through July 1975. A third period . . . extended from mid-October 1979 to early January 1981" (Munn 1986, xv). Moses was an infant during Munn's initial time on Gawa and was about nine when she returned for her third field trip.

3. Of course, Western researchers are not the only ones who express nostalgia (see Battaglia 1995).

4. In the Western world, over the past two centuries all stages or phases of reproduction, from conception to childbirth and breast-feeding, have become increasingly medicalized (Hahn 1995; Lewis 1990; Pierson, Arnup, and Levesque 1990, xiii). Responsibility and control over childbirth has been displaced from childbearing women themselves and their female midwives to medical practitioners, gynecologists, and obstetricians. As expertise and authority over birth has been subsumed by medical practitioners, the site of childbirth has gradually moved from home into doctors' working domains, i.e., the hospital. Similar changes have been observed in relation to pregnancy. In her detailed history of maternity care in Britain, Oakley (1984) documents the shifts from the seventeenth- and eighteenth-century view of pregnancy as a natural, biological state to the nineteenth- and twentieth-century view of it as pathology—as a medical phenomenon akin to illness, an "at risk" condition.

5. The development and use of NRT has generated vigorous and critical analysis by feminists. As Ginsburg and Rapp (1991) observe, some writers welcome these changes, claiming that the provision of safe and reliable forms of contraception, abortion, and obstetric care provides women with autonomy, control, and choice in relation to reproduction (see Gordon 1976; Petchesky 1984). However, many contest these assertions, suggesting that NRTs represent and perpetuate the extension of the medicalization of conception, pregnancy, and birth—a process inviting and effecting radical social transformation in whatever social contexts they are appropriated (see Rowland 1992). The monitoring of women's health necessitated by the use of these technologies institutes a new level of "social surveillance of reproductive practices" (Corea et al. 1987; Ginsburg and Rapp 1991, 315; Rowland 1987; 1992), presenting medical science with an ever-expanding platform for defining and prescribing healthy reproductive, maternal, and paternal behavior (Beck-Gernsheim 1989; Rapp 1993). It also makes possible ever more intrusive forms of birth and population control, particularly in third world contexts. Accordingly, women's choices and decisions to use reproductive technologies are constrained by issues such as class, ethnicity, location, religion (see Lazarus 1994; Nsiah-Jefferson and Hall 1989), and the complex interplays between local and global economic concerns—the vested interest of Western medical science, multinational pharmaceutical companies, and, in the Third World in particular, prescriptive social policies generated and, to varying degrees,

enforced by the World Bank and major aid organizations (Ginsburg and Rapp 1991; Yanoshik and Norsigan 1989).

6. Around the turn of the twentieth century, in the rapidly industrializing societies of Britain and Canada, the need for a healthy work force was perceived as crucial (Arnup, Levesque, and Pierson 1990; Lewis 1990; Oakley 1984). Major epidemics and wars in the first half of the twentieth century also focused political attention on the health of these populations. As a direct result, not only did public health become the concern of centralized policymakers, a concern that continues today, but greater attention was directed to infant care and nutrition, partially reflected in the collection and collation of more specific statistics about infant mortality (Oakley 1984, 36–37). This in turn led to an increasing preoccupation with maternal care. Mothers were held responsible for the health of their infants, and their behavior was subject to increased scrutiny, surveillance, and "education" by policymakers and health service providers who deemed themselves the arbiters of good "scientific" care (Hahn 1995; Oakley 1984; Pierson, Arnup, and Levesque 1990, xx). While improvements in infant mortality followed—largely, it seems, due to improved levels of hygiene, sanitation, and nutrition—similar improvements in maternal mortality were much slower to materialize.

7. Where in Britain policies on maternal practice and care were premised on a "class-based hierarchy of mothering," in parts of the Pacific they were premised on race-based hierarchies (Jolly 1998a; 1998b). See Manderson (1992, 1998) for a discussion of colonial Malaya.

8. For example, Jolly contends that, unlike the condominium government in Vanuatu, the British colonial administrators of Fiji worked to preserve indigenous race and culture. Accordingly, "state-sponsored surveillance and education of indigenous mothers w[ere] thus attempted far more vigorously in Fiji than in Vanuatu where such concerns remained those of the missions until very late in the colonial period" (1998b).

9. For a discussion of the essentialist, ahistorical, ethnocentric, and elitist qualities of the French *l'écriture féminine* theorists, see Moi (1985) and Suleiman (1985). See also Simone de Beauvoir's response to this form of feminism in Simons and Benjamin (1979). While welcoming the celebration of women's bodily experiences, she dismisses the preoccupation with the body that these French feminists instituted. For a counterchallenge and discussion of these claims, see Dallery (1989); Jones (1981).

10. Following Jolly (1992a, 34), I use this term as a means to highlight and reflect on the colonizing discourses and practices arising from within Western feminism.

11. Used alone, or in a phrase incorporating the first person personal pronoun *ya*, the emphatic pronoun *yabom* means "I alone" or "myself." In contradistinction to *yau*, this pronoun is used to draw attention to the "I" who is distinguished by particular act(s) performed alone, or unique features. Wycliffe revealed that it is also used to denote loneliness, considered a rare, highly undesirable, and, therefore, diminishing feeling or activity on Nuakata.

12. *Omiu* (you [pl.], yours); *'ita* (we, us, ourselves [inclusive]); *'ai* (we, us, ourselves [exclusive]); *hibom* (they, them, themselves).

13. Butler writes that "where there is an 'I' who utters or speaks and thereby produces an effect in discourse, there is first a discourse which precedes and enables that 'I' and forms in language the constraining trajectory of its will. Thus there is no 'I' who stands *behind* discourse and executes its volition *through* discourse. On the contrary, the 'I' only comes into being through being called, named . . . [I]t is the transitive invocation of the 'I.' Indeed, I can only say 'I' to the extent that I have first been addressed. . . . [P]aradoxically the discursive condition of social recognition *precedes* and *conditions* the formation of the subject; recognition is not conferred on a subject, but forms that subject" (1993, 225, emphasis in original).

14. Later, when people knew Roger better, they referred to him affectionately as *gagasa* (show-off).

15. The stated aim of the two-year CHW training program is to train frontline primary health-care workers whose role it is to "provide MCH [maternal and child health] care at every contact with mothers and children, basic obstetric care, nutritional surveillance and assist with immunizations. . . . [It is the broader] role of the CHW to improve the health of the rural population, especially that of mothers and children, through the promotion of self-reliance and improved health services in the village" (Health 1991, 223, 342).

16. Later, in my role as proxy health worker when Moses was absent from Nuakata, several reasons became apparent for people's resistance to take or complete treatment/prophylactic doses of chloroquine. Quinine acts as the generic term for all tablets on Nuakata. Since quinine is known to relieve discomfort during sickness, people request and take it to relieve symptoms associated with sickness. As with their use of local "medicines," they take "quinine" until the symptoms or discomfort has passed. While people acknowledge the need at times to use local protective "medicines" to prevent sickness caused by witchcraft, spirits, or sorcery, most publicly state that with the rise of Christianity these threats are fast becoming a thing of the past. Local medicines are more routinely used to heal existing conditions rather than prevent possible ones. Malaria is the only condition for which pregnant women, children, and infants are encouraged by Moses to take prophylactic doses of chloroquine to prevent sickness. However, the term *malaria* is rarely used on Nuakata. People generally say they have fever, hot or cold body, and headache, and they show little or no interest in the cause of these all-too-familiar forms of sickness.

17. This phenomenon is widely recognized by researchers and health service providers (Gillett 1990; Kolehmainen-Aitken 1990; Welsch 1991). It is the Health Department's stated aim "to improve maternal and child health by increasing the number of women" available for frontline health work (1991, 340).

18. See Garner (1989) for a critique of such schemes.

19. Their interests and efforts were focused on a five-year UNICEF-funded village birth attendants project that was about to be implemented to the north of Nuakata in the Milne Bay provincial districts of Losuia, Esa'ala, and Bolubolu. In 1995 UNICEF, together with the Milne Bay provincial government, initiated and implemented a similar project in the Rabaraba district of Milne Bay

Province. The reported aim of the project is to provide village birth attendant training to select village women (Maolai 1995).

20. Attendance figures were not collected for the Nuakata MCH clinics, however Moses indicated that it is usual for between fifteen and twenty women to attend. High priority is given to the clinic by women with sick children or children requiring immunization.

21. Reid (1984) observed that of the MCH clinics she witnessed in PNG, 70 percent of the consultations between the nurses and mothers with children took less than two minutes. Hughes (1994, 231) stresses that MCH nurses often spend a considerable amount of their potential consultation time traveling to and from rural clinics.

22. In describing the ritualized nature of maternal and child health clinics Denoon (1989a), following Reid (1984) and Mola and Aitken (1984), concludes that the effect of this "ritualization of function" is to deny rural mothers in particular "their only prospect of maternity care" (1989a, 103–4).

23. See Jackson's (1989) essays "Thinking through the body" and "Knowledge of the body" in particular.

24. As both Hughes (1994, 222–28) and Mull (1990) note, the PHC policy of the World Health Organization has been affected by controversy, conflict, economic constraints, and political will.

CHAPTER 3

1. Sleeping in the *misinali* (pastor's) house, we spent our days under a day shelter in the church grounds, learning the language with Wycliffe and myriad bystanders. We often felt like a living spectacle, objects of fascination and mirth, and, for young children, terror.

2. Several weeks later Mona distanced herself from me, commenting at the time that she must not be seen to be seeking special favor with me, otherwise people will talk or gossip about her.

3. I later discovered that many young women spoke basic English, but were too embarrassed to speak it with me.

4. Fabian writes that "confrontation is an epistemological prerequisite for ethnography. . . . [U]nder the conditions of shared time (or coevalness) field research is fundamentally confrontational and only superficially observational. To acknowledge that Self and Other are inextricably involved in a dialectical process will make anthropology not less but more realistic" (1991, 208).

5. M. Strathern (1988) argues that the idea that women make babies derives from the commodity logic integral to Western capitalist production. She claims that Melanesian women do not think that "women make babies" (1988, 311–18).

6. A knowledgeable person is known as *tauhanapui* (the one who knows).

7. The *Oxford English Dictionary* (1989) states that the word *conception* is derived from the Latin *concipere* (to take) and implies "to take to oneself, take in and hold." *Conception* is defined as, among other things, "the action of conceiving or fact of being conceived in the womb"; that which is conceived (the fetus,

the offspring); the action or faculty of conceiving in the mind, or of forming an idea or notion of anything; apprehension, imagination; that which is conceived in the mind, an idea, notion." In contrast, *Webster's Third New International Dictionary* (1966) defines conception as the "act of becoming pregnant (formation of a viable zygote); state of being conceived; that which is conceived (embryo, fetus); the capacity, function or process of forming ideas or abstractions or of grasping the meaning of symbols representing such ideas or abstractions; an idea or general notion." Subtle, yet significant, differences in the meaning of conception are conveyed by the two dictionaries. The former nominates where conception occurs (womb or mind), and the latter incorporates a scientific understanding of conception—the formation of a viable zygote—with its definition.

8. Bourdieu notes that Elias, following Benjamin Lee Whorf, points out that "Western languages tend to foreground substantives and objects at the expense of relations and to reduce processes to static conditions" (Bourdieu and Wacquant 1992, 241 n. 36).

9. In discussing the significance of the dead body in Western biomedicine, Leder asserts that modern medicine is based "first and foremost, not upon the lived body, but upon the dead, inanimate body" (1992, 17). It is a point reinforced by Jordanova (1989), who explores the gender assumptions, sex roles, and body images conveyed by (especially) late-eighteenth-century wax anatomical models of female bodies.

10. See M. Strathern (1992) for a discussion of the biologization of natural kinship in twentieth-century Euro-American culture. Strathern notes that, as a result of new reproductive technologies, the distinction between "social" and "biological" parenthood has been "introduced into regular parlance" (1992, 18–19).

11. See Roth (1903), cited in Leach (1967, 39).

12. Malinowski (1948, 216–18) claimed that Trobriand islanders believe that impregnation occurs when a spirit of the dead (*baloma*) enters a woman's vagina. The spirit belongs to the same subclan as the woman. It is the father's role to open the woman's vagina for the *baloma* to enter. Only the woman and her matrilineal kin contribute to the substantive constitution of the child.

13. While Malinowski recanted his initial assertion (1948, 220–37) that Trobriand island people's ignorance of physiological paternity confirmed Frazer's evolutionist argument that it was indicative of primitivism, he vigorously rejected the claim of Losuia district officer Alex Rentoul (1931) that knowledge of physiological paternity and magicoreligious beliefs coexisted on the island. Angered by this challenge to his ethnographic authority, he engaged the help of his friend Raphael Brudo, a regional pearl trader, to testify to the veracity of his claim. For further discussion of this conflict see "Footnotes to the History of Anthropology: Raphael Brudo on Malinowski's fieldwork" (*History of Anthropology Newsletter* 1996).

14. Malinowski (1932) concludes that Trobriand conception beliefs reflect an ideology centered on bodily and spiritual identity.

15. Widely accused of ethnocentrism, Spiro later backed away from his initial argument.

16. See Clifford's (1986) article "Partial Truths" for a discussion of these issues.

17. Advice also given by Bourdieu (1977) and M. Strathern (1988).

18. In English the verb "to know" is derived from the Old English *gecnawan,* which is related to the Old Norse *kna* (I can) and the Latin *noscere* (to come to know). This etymology suggests an understanding of "knowing" as both potential and a process that is active and/or passive.

19. Of interest, too, is the grafting of God the Father onto a female cosmology.

20. For a discussion of the strategic responses of informants to the discussions and questions posed by the ethnographer, see Jackson (1989, 6) and J. Weiner (1998). Both authors insist that the (personal, social, political, and historical) context for ethnographic inquiry is crucial to understanding the responses given.

21. As Ram (1993) notes, postcolonial writers such as Spivak and Kirby deny that intersubjectivity between persons of different cultures can exist.

22. Because of this translation in the Dobuan Bible, the Auhelawa Bible translations and several local storybooks developed by the Summer Institute of Linguistics literacy program, the word *'ate* is now translated as "heart" by some local people.

23. Another word, *lautowoi,* derived from *lau* (to go) and *towoi* (to try), together with various adjectives, denotes embodied feeling(s). This noun/verb is generally used to describe embodied feelings arising from activity or sickness (e.g., weariness, vigor). A third word, *'amna* (sweet taste or feeling), is used to describe the embodied feeling when someone is tired.

24. For a discussion of syncretism and multiple cultural perspectives see Carrier (1992, 15) and Thomas (1992).

CHAPTER 4

1. Translation of the term *dalava* as hamlet is not without problems. Local people familiar with English translate this word as "village." I have chosen to translate it as "hamlet" in accordance with anthropological convention and the precedence already established by Massim ethnographers, such as Thune, Macintyre, and Battaglia. Unlike in the islands of the northern Massim, including the Trobriands, people in the southern Massim live in small family groups of no more than ten or fifteen people.

2. An unpublished dictionary of the Auhelawa language states that *natu mohimohilina* denotes those children to whom a woman has given birth. Although I did not hear this term used on Nuakata, I could not say with any certainty that it or an equivalent term is not used there.

3. By using the terms *belong* and *belonging* I am trying to subvert through avoidance the convolutions of identity politics. I am not here talking of a person's "sense of belonging," as this seems too abstract, too voluntary, but instead hope to capture the unquestionable foundational nature of a Nuakatan person's belonging to their *susu.*

4. The taboo on sexual intercourse while a woman is lactating is consistent

with this interpretation. It is feared that semen will contaminate the mother's breast-milk, causing the suckling infant to become sick or die (see also Macintyre 1988, 52).

5. For example, all those who descend from this common ancestress two or three generations back are obliged to contribute to all marriage and mortuary exchanges for any member of their group.

6. Macintyre (1983, 46) states in relation to Tubetube social organization that usufructuary rights may also be given to non-*susu* women in recognition of their labor on non-*susu* land.

7. I use the expression "ground of living/staying" here deliberately for, as mentioned earlier, there is no verb "to be" in Alina Nu'ata.

8. For a description of these roles on Tubetube see Macintyre (1983, 52).

9. The term *mulolo* means freely given gift of love. While it is used to denote the gifts given by children to a father's *susu* at the time of his death, it has more recently been used as the name of the annual gift-giving ceremony for the United Church. Occurring annually, this event sees each hamlet obligated to give money to support the work of the regional church. In the past the amount given was unspecified, but in 1993 the church insisted that each hamlet should contribute at least 20 kina. This term is also used to denote God's love for people. Macintyre (1983, 52) notes that this term is used similarly on Tubetube.

10. Commenting on the two names bestowed on the people of Duau on northeast Normanby Island, Thune notes of the *susu* name that it "should never be used and is rarely known by those beyond their *susu* for it contains within itself *susu* and hence individual identity and essentiality which should not pass beyond the boundaries of the bearer's *susu*" (1980, 95 n. 62).

11. Thune writes of Loboda village, Duau, that a second, unrestricted name is used by non-*susu* members, often to remember experiences or friendships.

12. Thune states that in "many respects there is a general identity uniting all bearers of the same name who may even structurally substitute for one another both within a *susu* and with respect to *susu* beyond itself" (1980, 95 n. 62).

13. Fortune writes that "certain rules and observances govern . . . [the] communication [between owners of a village and their in-laws]. The incomers are called Those-resulting-from-marriage, or strangers [by] . . . Owners of the Village . . . Those-resulting-from marriage cannot use the personal name of any one of the owners down to the smallest child, except in the case of a father to his own child. They must use a term of relationship" ([1932] 1989, 5).

14. A person addresses his/her birth father, father's brother, and mother's sister's husband as *tamagu* (my father). When, in conversation, it is necessary to distinguish between these fathers, a person can name his/her birth father *tamagu 'agu taulabalaba* and birth father's brothers and mother's sister's husband *madiyagu*. The term *madiyagu* is also used to address one's stepfather. In contrast, a person's mother's brother(s) is addressed as *yagubada*. A person's father's sister's husband and mother's brother's wife are named *yayagu*. On Tubetube, like Nuakata, "all men who are married to women ego class as *sina* [mother] are called *tama* [father]" (Macintyre 1983, 362). But, in contrast to Tubetube, where the term *madia-* is used to distinguish a mother's sister's husband from a man

who is a father's brother, on Nuakata the term *madiya-* is used interchangeably for both these men. It is also the term of address for a stepfather and a spouse's father. Macintyre notes that the exclusive use of the term *madia-* on Tubetube "for men of the ascendant generation who marry into ego's *susu*" is consistent with Lounsbury's assertion that the "spouses of consanguineals in the ascending generation are not affines, but a variety of step kin (and that they are never classed with affines in any kinship terminology except where affines are classed with consanguineals)" (1983, 362).

15. This brief description by no means exhausts the kinship terminology and its use on Nuakata. The kinship terminology on Nuakata is almost identical to those described by Macintyre (1983, 360–67) for Tubetube and Fortune ([1932] 1989, 37) for Dobu. It is consistent with an "Iroquois system in which cross and parallel kin in the middle three generations are distinguished according to the relative sex of the linking kin but in which only the last links in a chain of genealogical connection determine cross/parallel status" (see also Keesing 1975, 66–71; Macintyre 1983, 360). The same alterations to kinship status and terminology occur at death as they occur on Dobu and Tubetube. For example, Wycliffe revealed that when his mother's brother dies, he will assume the status and term of "father" to his mother's brother's children—people whom he addresses as "cousin" prior to his mother's brother's death.

16. As Battaglia has noted for Sabarl, where similar naming practices associated with marriage are observed, it seemed that "far from merely 'bridging' relations between groups (as they are often depicted in anthropological literature), marriages reinforce distinctions and may actually introduce conceptual space between persons" (1990, 113).

17. It became clear that this was the case when one fellow, widely regarded as the most greedy man on the island (*tauhamgogoi,* "the one who eats it all"), incensed the people working on the house by repeatedly asking us for tobacco without contributing to the building project. His nickname, which means "all the rice," was conferred upon him because "he will always eat a plate of rice, or the like, without considering others" (Wycliffe). We were strongly advised to refuse his requests out of respect for those working on the house.

18. Of Dobu, Fortune writes: "Normally the house interior is as rigidly restricted to man, wife, and their children, as the graveyard that the house fronts is rigidly restricted to the corpses of brothers, sisters, and sisters' children, it being understood that the house is restricted to the one unit, the biological family only, whereas the graveyard is common to all the *susu* of the village" ([1932] 1989, 4).

19. This was done more to protect them from the annoyance of biting than from any attempt to prevent malaria.

20. Many of Munn's (1986, 35–37) observations about the living places and habits of unmarried youths on Gawa (during the 1970s) seemed to hold true for young people on Nuakata during my time there. For example, she describes Gawan courting activities as transitional behaviors or rites de passage:

> Instead of hierarchizing processes explicitly shaped by the authority of adults who impose regulation from the outside through direct control over initiates'

bodies, Gawan transition emphasises the relative autonomy of the youths while adults watch from behind the scenes, exerting covert influence on their children, but interfering directly only in cases of radical misbehaviour. (1986, 36–37)

21. Cf. Fortune, who specifies: "Those-resulting-from-marriage, while they are yet newly married, must approach an owner's family sitting beneath the owner's house by a roundabout way, circling in unobtrusively and bending apologetically while they do so, their own spouse being the only owner excepted. By the time one or two children are born this behavior is usually discarded towards the own mother-in-law's *susu*" ([1932] 1989, 5–6).

22. Battaglia claims that on Sabarl, where residence is virilocal following marriage, "a new bride has a fragile claim to control of the husband's house" (1990, 31). It is only through her services to her husband's kin that she establishes power and influence in this realm.

23. Wycliffe's initial tentative declaration that *maybe* Susan and Nowel were married reflected more widespread uncertainty about when and by what means a couple are considered married. Some people with whom I spoke about marriage thought it occurred when the couple began living with one another. Others considered this living-together a form of betrothal that was finally realized as marriage when gifts had been exchanged between the couple's respective *susu*, and family parties arranged in the couple's natal hamlets. Perhaps these differing opinions expressed by people within and across different *susu* reflect a process of transformation and contraction of marriage practices more uniformly upheld in the past. For example, Fortune ([1932] 1989, 21–30) indicated that for the people of Dobu during the late 1920s a young couple were considered betrothed once they were discovered sleeping together in the girl's natal hamlet. From that point onward the young couple would "avoid the personal names" of their potential in-laws. The young man would immediately commence work in his in-laws' garden, working alongside them. While he would sleep with his potential spouse at night, he would not eat or associate with his in-laws in their hamlet. After a year or so, when he had accumulated the necessary gifts to exchange between the *susu*, the respective exchanges would occur (see Fortune [1932] 1989, 25–26) and the marriage would be pronounced. In describing and elaborating upon Dobuan social organization, Fortune (5–30) highlights the fundamental differences between *susu* and non-*susu* encapsulated and, indeed, consummated in the marriage relationship. He stresses the alienation, born of difference, experienced by either a man or woman when they are living in their spouse's hamlet/village.

24. As Munn (1986) notes for Gawa, this freedom to wander around alone or with groups of young men or women is a feature of young people's behavior that changes upon marriage.

25. In Alina Nu'ata the word 'amwaha (more broadly meaning "stairs or entrance to a dwelling") can be used both as a concrete noun, e.g., 'amwa'amwahane (place or path), and in a more abstract sense when referring to a person's actions, attitudes, and ways of doing things, e.g., 'amwa'amwaha (the moving along that path, or someone's ways and the actual expression of those ways).

This etymological link between personal actions and path provides a local metaphor that gives expression to Nuakatan sociality, a link that also exists in other languages of the Massim.

26. As with Thune's observations of Dobu, the people living in any given hamlet are usually "either members of the owning *susu* or their spouses, or children" (Thune 1980, 14). But this is not always the case. At times individuals and, indeed, whole family groups live on non-*susu*/nonclan land.

27. Divorce was common in this community, and it was usual for the couple, whatever their ages, to separate and return to their own *susu*, where they remained until remarrying. Children of divorced couples remained with their mothers, but some visited at their fathers' place.

CHAPTER 5

1. See M. Strathern (1988) and Wagner (1977, 1981) for a discussion of analogous ways of thinking and knowing in Papua New Guinea.

2. Also the word for twins, *patubwau*, in Alina Nu'ata means two seeds.

3. Syntocinon is given to expedite the birthing of the placenta and prevent hemorrhage associated with retained placenta. Ergometrine is given to prevent hemorrhaging following birth of the placenta.

4. Eunice claimed that "it is good for women to have four or five children. It makes them strong, their blood strong. Ten or eleven [children] is not good for the blood. It is too many to look after properly."

5. In her unpublished dictionary of Auhelawa, Daphne Lithgow suggests that the stem word *laba* means line. Martha Macintyre indicated that in the Tubetube language *laba* refers to the sight line or watermark on a boat. It also means edge or boundary (personal communication). This accords with Thune's (1980, 89 n. 57) claim that on northeast Normanby *laba* means boundary, border, edge, limit, finish. Thune states, however, that *labalaba* does not carry these meanings. It refers to the individual referred to by Fortune ([1932] 1989, 14–15) as "boundary man" (see also Chowning 1989). Whereas on Dobu the son of a deceased man is addressed by members of the man's *susu* as "boundary man" (*labalaba*), on northeast Normanby a man's sons and daughters are addressed as *labalaba* by members of his *susu*, whether he is dead or alive. Although *laba* and *labalaba* in Alina Nu'ata are clearly cognates with the Dobuan terms, I did not hear them used in this way. Used as a verb, *labalaba* referred to process and time of birth. Used as a noun, this term denotes one who directly effects or makes birth possible. The fact that this term is used to describe birth mothers as well as birth fathers suggests local recognition of paternity in pregnancy and birth.

CHAPTER 6

1. In this text I trace my experiential account of a burial ceremony that I attended early in my fieldwork on Nuakata. I juxtapose this with a more abstracted reflection on the contemporary practices, social implications, and meaning of death, and part of the ensuing mortuary sequence on Nuakata. I do

not posit either of these forms of textual representation of death as more authentic, more factual, more or less interpretative or subjective than the other. Rather, these accounts are intended to resonate with one another at points, to sound discordant notes at others. I do this to strategically point to some of the epistemological and political consequences of the way death is represented in anthropological texts (see Mallett 1998).

2. Macintyre (1989b, 139) describes the same practices on Tubetube.

3. As on Nuakata, singing (*'wali*) is the first stage of the Tubetube mortuary sequence (Macintyre 1989b, 135–37).

4. Dewey writes: "Through habits formed in intercourse with the world, we inhabit the world. It becomes a home and the home is part of our every experience" (1958, 104). See Scarry (1985, 27–180) for an inspired discussion of the spatial and material territories of people's lives.

5. Although theoretically contentious, the term *personality* has been popularly and pragmatically appropriated by many people, even those who are opposed to this concept. It often seems to imply a fixed internal state or localized epicenter within the brain, which in concert with social forces and/or biological drives and imperatives directs a person's behavior. Accordingly, thinking and behavior are considered an expression of personality rather than personality itself. These expressions are subservient to hidden internal forces of (self-)consciousness or will, which are integral to the personality.

6. This understanding was inflected in the command *tau tau tau*, which means "go, go, go." In this context *tau* acts as a homonym of *lau* (to go).

7. In some ways this is similar to English expressions like "a body of people," or "the body corporate."

8. I use the term *selfish* cautiously here, as the term used to describe such people on Nuakata is *tau'aiduma*, which may be roughly translated as "the one who eats or claims all the food for him/herself."

9. On Tubetube the term *galiauna* or *yanasa* is used to denote both male and female members of the paired matrilineage who orchestrate the activities associated with burial (Macintyre 1989b, 139–40; also see Seligman [1910] 1976, 609–10). According to Chowning (1989, 100) the term *geyawuna* (the workers and eaters) is used in Molima, Fergusson Island, to denote those responsible for burial and handling the dead body. Usually this task falls to the deceased's sister's children or mother's brother. On northeast Normanby Island, as on Nuakata, the principal grave digger is usually a "favoured, more distant matrilineal mate or member of an associated matrilineage" (Thune 1989, 159–60).

10. The practice of referring to the deceased as ill has been noted by Leenhardt (1979), who asserts that for Melanesians in general and Canaques in particular the "nothingness" of death does not exist. "Death appears to him as a negative state of life and a different form of existence" (Leenhardt 1979, 35).

11. As previously discussed, embodiment on Nuakata is considered contingent upon the combined labors of matrilineal and affinal kin. Embodiment constitutes a confluence of mutually dependent relationships. See Munn (1986, 164).

12. In discussing Fortune's ([1932] 1989) descriptions of the significance of seed yams on Dobu, Bloch and Parry state: "[Yams] are *tomota*—'human beings.'

... But further than this, they are the lineage kin descended from the founding ancestress of the *susu*. Their flesh ... is planted in the garden as the corpses of the ancestors are planted in the village mound. ... What reproduces the lineage in a material sense, then is ... the flesh of its own kind. The consumption of yams ... grown from one's own lineage's seed strain, thus amounts to an act of symbolic endo-cannibalism" (1982, 28).

13. The term for widow, *hiwape*, is derived from *hiwa* (to pour out) and *'wapelu* (to wither). As on Tubetube and Duau, the widow/widower on Nuakata are considered the alienable possession of the grieving *susu*. By employing the alienable possessive pronoun *yama* (our), the *susu* of the deceased indicate the widow/widower's loss of status and integral connection with their matrilineage (see Macintyre 1989b, 135).

14. While an emotionally charged moment, I remained aware that I might be projecting emotions onto Waligeha.

15. Macintyre (1989b, 136) notes that on Tubetube it was colonial government officers, rather than missionaries, who forced people to abandon their practice of burying corpses in shallow graves and disinterring skeletons. Missionaries focused their efforts on transforming the treatment of the widow by her affines.

16. See Macintyre (1989b, 145–49) for a discussion of the gifts exchanged between *susu* and affines of the deceased following death on Tubetube.

17. See Foster (1995) for an analysis of the social processes that have led to local understanding of mortuary rites as *kastom* on Tanga Island, New Ireland.

18. A review of ethnographic articles dealing with notions of ethical practice reveals that while such issues have been addressed in specific contexts, they have yet to be considered in all (disciplinary and geographical) fields of anthropological inquiry. The specific contexts where these issues have been considered include medical settings/research (e.g., Schoepf 1991; Schuster 1996); applied anthropological research (e.g., Barrett 1997; Dominy 1990; Everhart 1984; Williams 1995); and ethnic conflict (Khazanov 1996).

19. For example, affected by the mortuary ceremony and people's visible demonstrations of distress, I risked misinterpreting their emotions. My impulse to project emotions onto people is evident in my discussion of Waligeha's grief associated with the loss of his daughter. While aware at the time that this was highly problematic, I nevertheless entertained these ideas and assumptions about the nature of his grief.

20. As Abu-Lughod and Lutz (1990) attest, it has only been in the past decade that the anthropology of emotion has emerged as a legitimate field of study in the discipline.

21. M. Young (1989a, 193–94) states that in Bwaidoka on southeast Goodenough Island *bwabwale* was a feast conducted by the owners of the deceased for the buriers. It was formerly held a year after the initial feast to remove food taboos from the principal mourners. This contrasts with the *bwabwali* sequence of feasts described by Thune (1989, 163–67), which were held in Loboda village on northeast Normanby Island. These feasts were variously conducted by the deceased's matrilineal mates and his/her affines, in order to sever the ties and erase the debts between the respective *susu*. Chowning (1989, 101) notes that for

the people of Molima, Fergusson Island, *bwabwale* is the feast that frees the bereaved spouse from mourning.

22. Originally from the Sigasiga region of Duau on Normanby Island, the grandfather mentioned in this account was considered a custodian of customary knowledge within Wycliffe's clan. With his passing in 1989 detailed knowledge and understanding of past ways practiced on Nuakata were all but lost, save for the fragments remembered by his living kin. Wycliffe had spent many hours with his grandfather learning about customary matters.

23. Many people living on Nuakata are descendants of people from Duau. On Nuakata many people consider Duau the place from which custom originates.

24. Daphne Lithgow defines *muli* in Auhelawa as a marriage payment (cf. Fortune [1932] 1989, 197–200; Lepowsky 1989, 228 n. 8).

CONCLUSION

1. I quote this letter while knowing that some may interpret it as an attempt to authenticate my research experience. In one sense, of course, it does perform this function (or one like it), but, more important, it demonstrates the centrality of the relationships between ethnographers and their subjects that underpin the participant observation method. I am also aware that some will see the content of this letter as romantic, but even if this is so (and I am not sure it is), given that my research and research relationships are only newly founded, is it unreasonable that romance should be a part of them? Is it not at least possible to have thinking romanticism? Could it also be true that romanticism is a significant aspect or phase of our thinking, feeling, relating—one that brings with it a unique and important form of knowing and understanding? (see de Zengotita 1989, 692; Hastrup 1995, 690).

Glossary of Nuakatan Terms

Glottal stops are common in Alina Nu'ata. Vowel pronunciation is as follows: *a*—as in car, *e*—as in met, *i*—as in machine, *o*—as in ought, *ai*—as in aisle *ei*—as in vein, *au*—as in loud, *ou*—as in loud, *oa*—sound the *o* and *a* but almost together.

There are eighteen letters in the Alina Nu'ata alphabet. English letters not found are *c, f, j, k, q, r, x,* and *z.* Regarding the accent, each syllable receives equal stress. Unlike other Milne Bay languages, the *k* phoneme does not exist in Alina Nu'ata. Glottal *a* ('*a*) is used instead.

aba'eno	Sleeping place
abanatu	Child's place, womb
abanuwatuwu'avivin	Place of remembrance
abi	Build
abilau	Start, begin to make
abimamole	Create
abita'alawahi	Joke
abiyemasele	Make clear, make visible
abiyemodi'ini	Make angry, become angry
abiyenamwanamwa	Make good, right, proper
abiyetowolo	Make stand up
abiye'wahiuyo	Make strong
adi	Their (semialienable possessive pronoun)
agu	My (semialienable possessive pronoun)
agu yaiyewa	Spouse's cross-sex sibling
ahoni	Gossip, to talk about someone and make them ill
ai'abi	Cat's cradle, (lit.) building, making in process
aiai	Food
ai'auhi	Contraception
aibika	Seed yams
aihale	Old woman/female
ainai	In or on
aiwa	Wood, tree, fire
aiwa tanitaniwagani	Tree fairies
ala	To open

ala'ala'wowowoli	Hot, heat
alamiya bwadana	Fish sickness
alawai	Witch
Alina Nu'ata	Language of Nua'ata, dialect of Auhelawa
alo	Bay
Alogau	(1) Hamlet on the north-northwest side of Nua'ata
	(2) United Church on the north-northwest side of Nua'ata
alu'aluwa	Spirit
am'oleya	Spiritual appearance
amwaha	(1) Path, stairs, and entrance to dwelling
	(2) Person's unique ways
anayaliyaliyamane	Celebratory performance at mortuary feast
ao'ao	Crow
apali	Sexual intercourse
Asailo	(1) Hamlet on the southwest side of Nua'ata
	(2) United Church on the southwest side of Nua'ata
asawe	Mango
asiyebwa	(1) Sickness
	(2) Respectful term for someone recently deceased
ate	(1) Heart
	(2) Liver
	(3) Center of emotions and feelings
atemuyamuya	Liver/feeling paining, embodied feelings
atehawawali	(1) Reddish liver, rash, or skin disease that occurs when someone is fearful
	(2) Embodied feeling of fear and/or anxiety
atovi	Palm leaves
au'aubabada	Story
auhelawa	Language of Kurada (South Normanby Island) and Nua'ata
avala	Carry or bear children or things
avalai	Give birth
bada	Already
baditutula	Type of presentation of yams
bailowolowo	Flying witches
bilai	Mortuary feast
balau	Sorcerers
bilibili	External walls of house
boda	People or ancestors from same clan
bo'e	Black crane, black crane clan
boha	Bags for carrying garden produce
Boirama	Uninhabited island belonging to Nua'ata on the southeast side of Nua'ata
Bolime	(1) Southeast side of Nua'ata
	(2) Southeast wind

Glossary 295

Bomatu	(1) North side of Nua'ata
	(2) North wind
bubuli	Mortuary taboos
Bulelala	Legendary spirit woman who carries the spirits of the yams
bwabwale	Mortuary feast
bwasiyagu	Father-in-law
bwasumo	Bird(s)
bwau	Two
Bwauli	(1) Northwest side of Nua'ata
	(2) Northwest wind
Daiwali	Inhabited island belonging to Nua'ata, located southwest of Nua'ata Nua'ata
dalava	Hamlet/village
dalavai	Hamlet, to it
dimdim	White person
dobi	To go down, toward the sea
dova dimdim	Like a white person
edewa	Dog
ehebo	One
ekelisiya	Church members
elepa	Bush knife
elolo	Bird clan, type of bird unknown
Gaimanugini	Hamlet on northwest side of Nua'ata
galiyauna	Men responsible for burial of the dead
gama	Child
gamahine	Young girl
gigini	Handle
ginaginauli	Wood already used as timber
ginauli	(1) Things
	(2) Plants used to heal
godu	Break or snap
godugodu	(1) Large clamshell
	(2) Womb
goduyoi	(1) Abortion
	(2) Miscarriage
goha	To cut when felling a tree
Gohiya	Hamlet on the southwest side of Nua'ata
guyau	Final feast of the mortuary sequence
Hana Kuba Kuba	Uninhabited island belonging to Nua'ata
hanapui	Know; knowledge that is certain; knowing/knowledge that is inherited or offered as a gift
Halewa'una	Name of a bay on the north-northwest side of Nua'ata
Hapela'awa'awa	Hamlet on the north-northwest side of Nua'ata

hae	To go up a mountain (used only when sun is rising or risen)
hauga	Time, weather, lifetime
hauga 'i'ovi	Time is over (used when someone has died)
heda	Child (male or female)
hedaheda	Children
heda yana'aba'eno	Womb
hesi	But
heva	Floorboards
hevali	Young man, youth
hina	Mother
hinagu	My mother
hinagu habaluna	My small mother
hinagu mwala'ina	My big mother
hinevela	Women who marry into a *susu*
hiuma	Pregnant, pregnancy
huhu	Another word for *susu*, maternal family group
Iabama	Small uninhabited island belonging to East Cape
ilalauputeiwa	Unsuitable, incompatible
ita	To see
ita'avivini	To care for
iamoihanane	True, correct, real
kakaleku	The call of a chicken
kastams	Customs
kundu	Wooden drum
labahi	To birth
labalaba	Transformative time of birth
labavai	The taking of a child's spirit by an ancestor
laga	To go up inland, away from the sea
lagahi	Conception
lau	To go, to move
laugagaiyo	Rule, law
lili'o	Parrot, parrot clan
logidi	House stumps
loheya	Man, men
loheyana	Its manliness, male
lomwau	Type of presentation of yams
lougu	Sibling of different sex
lougu tahigu	Younger sibling of different sex
lougu tuwagu	Older sibling of different sex
-ma	Verb suffix that signals that the action of the verb is in the direction of the speaker
mahalava	Arrive, happen, occur, become present, materialize in a place
maheya	Pig
mahul	Sign

Glossary 297

manibubu	Eagle, eagle clan
Maramatana	Local council to which Nua'ata belongs
masele	Bring into the open, become visible
mata	Today; will (intent to act)
mehe	Eyes
mehena	His/hers/its eyes
meimeituwu	Eternal spiritual beings
misinali	Junior pastor, missionary
miya	To sit, stay, remain, dwell
modi'ini	Angry
mugai	Go before, go in front
mulamula	Medicine, magic
molo	Semen
mulolo	Love, gift, good will
muli	Offering or gift made in mortuary feast
mulina	Marriage payment
mwala'ina	Big, large
mwalowoi	Death, dead
mwanegu	Spouse
na	And
nabwanabwau	Type of presentation of yams
namwanamwana	Good
natugu	My child
nibai	Brother/sister (cousin), e.g., mother's brother's child
niu	Coconut
nuwa	(1) The place where thinking-feeling arises
	(2) Inside the body
	(3) Want, wish, desire
nuwamasele	Understand, attitude, opinion, meaning
nuwapwanopwanowei	To forget
nuwanuwa	Gable roof
nuwatuwu	Thinking-feeling
nuwatuwuine	Thinking-feeling it, the thinking-feeling
nuwatuwudawani	Thinking-feeling hidden from elders
nuwa'epo	Chest
nuwamagi	Kidney
nuwavitai	Heavyhearted, depressed
nuwadaumwali	Calm heart, peaceful
nuwamomohi	Squeeze thinking-feeling, remember, memory
nuwanuwpuyo	Virginity, chastity
nuwadobi	Humble
nuwapotapota	Stubborn
oba	Magic words, spells
omiu	You (pl.)
owa	You (sing.)
oya	Garden

Pahilele	Inhabited island belonging to East Cape
paihowa	Work, do, enact, make
paihowai	Work it, make it, use it, do it
patubwau	Twins, two seeds
pehipehi	Umbilical cord, navel
pilopilo	Frangipani
poi	Pluck, or rip off flowers, to tear open
politiki	Politicking
puhoma	Traditional saddle-back house
pulipuli	Floor joists
pwane'ahu	Type of yam
pwanoli	(1) Mistake
	(2) Adultery
sabaliya	Type of presentation of yams
sagesagena	Bleeding
sailau	Sailing canoe
salana	Teeth
Silopan	Custodial spirit of Nua'ata's central mountain, Mount Tanalabwa
sinebada	Respectful term for white woman
sinelautegege	Good spiritual woman
sinemuyamuyalele	Bad spiritual woman
subu	Double-hulled canoe
susu	Family, particularly maternal
tahigu	*Susu* brother/sister (cousin), i.e., mother's sister's child
ta'i'ita	Who knows
tama	Father
tamagu	My father
tamagu 'agutaulabalaba	My birth father
tamagu habaluna	My small father
tamagu mwala'ina	My big father
tamahina	(1) (lit.) father, mother
	(2) food for a journey
tamumu	Placenta
Tanalabwa	Central mountain on Nua'ata
tau	(1) Body
	(2) The one who
tau'ala'alahi	Resurrection or transformation feast
taubada	Older, respected man
taudiwo	Their bodies
taugu	My body
tauhanpui	Knowledgeable person
taumudulele	Spirit-man
taumwalowoi	Dead body
tau'oba'oba	Sorcerers

tautaubada	Very old and respected man
tauve'ita	Teacher
tenem	That
tewala	Language of East Cape, Papua New Guinea
tom	To cut with axe or bush knife
tomowa	Group of people, humankind
tonitonibwa'wa	Spirit people who live on the ground or under rocks
to'wato'wai	Dwarfs
tubu	Grandparent, grandchild
tubui	Restored to health
umulitaedi	Ways or customs to be followed
usilahe	Accident, injury
uto	Brain
uve'ahihiyedi	You respect them
uwe	Vines used for building houses
vada	House
vahala	Young woman/female
vai	To get
-wa	Verb suffix signaling that the action of the verb is directed away from the speaker
wahiala	Strength, energy, vitality
waiena bwadana	Menstrual blood
waihiu	Girl, woman
waihiuna	Female
waiwaihiu	Girls, women
walata	Pot
waligeha	Namesake
waliwali	Singing
wapina	Blood
walonane	Words
wawa	Dance traditionally performed at mortuary feasts
wetuhu	Vines used in building houses
wo'e	Cry out, grieve for, deceased loved one
wohiwa	Man who marries into a *susu*
woiyawanane	Poison
wonu bwadana	Turtle sickness
wuwuna	Because
ya	I
yababana	Bad
yabom	I alone
yagu	My (alienable possessive pronoun)
yagulauwa	Mother-in-law
yagu'iva	Spouse's same-sex sibling
yaipoine	Sterility
Yalasi	(1) Southwest side of Nua'ata (2) Southwest wind

Yana	Its, hers, his (alienable possessive pronoun)
yawahi	Breath, life force
Yaubada	God
yauwedo	(1) Greeting
	(2) Thank you
yemedi	Believe, to rely upon
zagaya	Final feast in the traditional mortuary sequence

References

Abrahams, Roger. 1985. Ordinary and extraordinary experience. In *The anthropology of experience*, edited by V. Turner and E. Bruner. Chicago: University of Illinois Press.

Abu-Lughod, Lila. 1990. Can there be a feminist ethnography? *Women and Performance: A Journal of Feminist Theory* 5 (1): 7–27.

———. 1991. Writing against culture. In *Recapturing anthropology: Working in the present*, edited by R. Fox. Santa Fe, N.Mex.: School of American Research.

Abu-Lughod, Lila, and Catherine Lutz. 1990. Introduction: Emotion, discourse, and the politics of everyday life. In *Language and the politics of emotion*, edited by C. Lutz and L. Abu-Lughod. Cambridge: Cambridge University Press.

Adams, Richard. 1981. Ethical principles in anthropological research: One or many? *Human Organization* 40 (2): 155–60.

Alcoff, Linda. 1991. The problem of speaking for others. *Cultural Critique* (winter): 5–32.

Appadurai, Arjun. 1990. Topographies of the self: Praise and emotion in Hindu India. In *Language and the politics of emotion*, edited by C. Lutz and L. Abu-Lughod. Cambridge: Cambridge University Press.

Arens, W. 1979. *The man-eating myth: Anthropology and anthropophagy*. New York: Oxford University Press.

Arnup, Katherine, Andree Levesque, and Ruth Roach Pierson, eds. 1990. *Delivering motherhood: Maternal ideologies and practices in the nineteenth and twentieth centuries*. London: Routledge.

Barker, John, ed. 1990. *Christianity in Oceania: Ethnographic perspectives*. ASAO Monograph no. 12. Latham: University Press of America.

Barrett, Bruce. 1997. Identity, ideology and inequalities: Methodologies in medical anthropology, Guatemala 1950–1995. *Social Science and Medicine* 44 (5): 579–87.

Battaglia, Debbora. 1985. "We feed our father": Paternal nurture among the Sabarl of Papua New Guinea. *American Ethnologist* 12 (3): 427–41.

———. 1990. On the bones of the serpent: Person, memory and mortality in Sabarl Island Society. Chicago: University of Chicago Press.

———. 1992. The body in the gift: Memory and forgetting in Sabarl mortuary exchange. *American Ethnologist* 19 (1): 3–18.

———. 1993. At play in the fields (and borders) of the imaginary: Melanesian transformation of forgetting. *Cultural Anthropology* 8 (4): 430–42.

———. 1995. On practical nostalgia: Self-prospecting among urban Trobrianders. In *Rhetorics of self-making,* edited by D. Battaglia. Berkeley: University of California Press.

Beck-Gernsheim, Elizabeth. 1989. From the pill to test-tube babies: New options, new pressures in reproductive behaviour. In *Healing technology: Feminist perspectives,* edited by K. Ratcliff. Ann Arbor: University of Michigan Press.

Behar, Ruth. 1995. Introduction: Out of exile. In *Women writing culture,* edited by R. Behar and D. Gordon. Berkeley: University of California Press.

Behar, Ruth, and Deborah Gordon, eds. 1995. *Women writing culture.* Berkeley: University of California Press.

Bell, Diane. 1993. Introduction 1: The context. In *Gendered fields: Women, men and ethnography,* edited by D. Bell, P. Caplan, and W. J. Karim. London: Routledge.

Bell, Diane, Pat Caplan, and Wazir Jahan Karim, eds. 1993. *Gendered fields: Women, men, and ethnography.* London: Routledge.

Bell, Diane, and Topsy Narappula Nelson. 1989. Speaking about rape is everyone's business. *Women's Studies International Forum* 12 (4): 403–16.

Benhabib, Seyla. 1990. Epistemologies of postmodernism: A rejoinder to Jean-François Lyotard. In *Feminism/postmodernism,* edited by L. Nicholson. New York: Routledge.

———. 1992. *Situating the self: Gender, community and postmodernism in contemporary ethics.* Oxford: Polity Press.

Benjamin, Jessica. 1988. *The bonds of love.* New York: Pantheon Books.

Benveniste, Emile. 1966 [1956]. La nature des pronoms. In his *Problèmes de linguistique générale.* Paris: Gallimard.

———. 1971. *Problems in general linguistics.* Translated by Mary Elizabeth Meek. Miami Linguistics Series, no. 8. Coral Gables, Fla.: University of Miami Press.

Bhabha, Homi. 1993. *The location of culture.* London: Routledge.

Biddulph, John. 1991. Child health in Papua New Guinea: A 30 year perspective. *Medical Journal of Australia* 154:439–40.

Biersack, Alietta. 1991. Thinking difference: A review of Marilyn Strathern's *The gender of the gift. Oceania* 62:147–54.

Bloch, Maurice, and Jonathan Parry, eds. 1982. *Death and the regeneration of life.* Cambridge, Mass: Cambridge University Press.

Bordo, Susan. 1986. The Cartesian masculinization of thought. *Signs: Journal of Culture and Women in Society* 11 (31): 439–56.

———. 1990. Feminism, postmodernism, and gender-scepticism. In *Feminism/postmodernism,* edited by L. Nicholson. New York: Routledge.

Bourdieu, Pierre. 1977. *Outline of a theory of practice.* Translated by Richard Nice. Cambridge: Cambridge University Press.

———. 1990a. *In other words: Essays towards a reflexive sociology.* Translated by Matthew Adamson. Cambridge: Polity Press.

———. 1990b. *The logic of practice.* Cambridge: Polity Press.

Bourdieu, Pierre, and Loïc Wacquant. 1992. *An invitation to reflexive sociology.* Cambridge: Polity Press.

Boutilier, James, Daniel Hughes, and Sharon Tiffany, eds. 1978. *Mission, church*

and sect in Oceania. ASAO Monograph no. 6. Ann Arbor: University of Michigan Press.
Braidotti, Rosi. 1989. The politics of ontological difference. In *Between feminism and psychoanalysis,* edited by T. Brennan. London: Routledge.
———. 1991. *Patterns of dissonance: A study of women in contemporary philosophy.* Translated by Elizabeth Guild. Oxford: Polity.
Bromilow, William. 1929. *Twenty years among primitive Papuans.* London: Epworth Press.
Burridge, Kenneth. 1978. Introduction: Missionary occasions. In *Mission, church and sect in Oceania,* edited by J. Boutilier, D. Hughes, and S. Tiffany. Lanham, Md.: University Press of America.
Butler, Judith. 1988. Performative acts and gender constitution: An essay in phenomenology and feminist theory. *Theatre Journal* 40 (4): 519–31.
———. 1990. Gender trouble, feminist theory, and psychoanalytic discourse. In *Feminism/postmodernism,* edited by L. Nicholson. New York: Routledge.
———. 1993. Bodies that matter: On the discursive limits of "sex." New York: Routledge.
Callaway, Helen. 1992. Ethnography and experience: Gender implications in fieldwork and texts. In *Anthropology and autobiography,* edited by J. Okely and H. Callaway. London: Routledge.
Caplan, Pat. 1988a. Engendering knowledge: The politics of ethnography (part 1). *Anthropology Today* 4 (5): 8–12.
———. 1988b. Engendering knowledge: The politics of ethnography (part 2). *Anthropology Today* 4 (6): 14–17.
———. 1993. Introduction 2: The volume. In *Gendered fields: Women, men and ethnography,* edited by D. Bell, P. Caplan, and W. J. Karim. London: Routledge.
Carrier, James. 1992. Introduction. In *History and tradition in Melanesian anthropology,* edited by J. Carrier. Berkeley: University of California Press.
Carrithers, Michael, Steven Collins, and Steven Lukes, eds. 1985. The category of the person: Anthropology, philosophy, history. Cambridge: Cambridge University Press.
Chodorow, Nancy. 1978. The reproduction of mothering: Psychoanalysis and the sociology of gender. Berkeley: University of California Press.
Chowning, Anne. 1989. Death and kinship in Molima. In *Death rituals and life in the societies of the Kula ring,* edited by F. Damon and R. Wagner. De Kalb: Northern Illinois University Press.
Cixous, Hélène. 1981a. The laugh of the Medusa. In *New French feminisms,* edited by E. Marks and I. D. Courtivan. New York: Harvester Press.
———. 1981b. Sorties. In *New French feminisms,* edited by E. Marks and I. D. Courtivan. New York: Harvester Press.
Clifford, James. 1986. Introduction: Partial truths. In *Writing culture: The poetics and politics of ethnography,* edited by J. Clifford and G. Marcus. Berkeley: University of California Press.
———. 1988. The predicament of culture: Twentieth-century ethnography, literature and art. Cambridge: Harvard University Press.

———. 1989. Comment. *Current Anthropology* 30 (5): 561–62.
Clifford, James, and George Marcus, eds. 1986. *Writing culture: The poetics and politics of ethnography.* Berkeley: University of California Press.
Cole, Sally, and Lynne Phillips, eds. 1995. *Ethnographic feminisms.* Ottawa, Ontario: Carleton University Press.
Corea, Gena, et al., eds. 1985. Man-made women: How new reproductive technologies affect women. 1st Midland Book ed., International Interdisciplinary Congress on Women (2d ed., Groningen, Netherlands, 1984). London: Hutchison.
Cotterill, Pamela, and Gayle Letherby. 1993. Weaving stories: Personal auto/biographies in feminist research. *Sociology* 27 (1): 67–79.
Crapanzano, Vincent. 1992. Hermes' dilemma and Hamlet's desire: On the epistemology of interpretation. Cambridge: Harvard University Press.
Crick, Malcolm. 1976. Explorations in language and meaning: Towards a semantic anthropology. London: Malaby Press.
Dallery, Arleen. 1989. The politics of writing (the) body: Ecriture feminine. In *Gender/body/knowledge: Feminist reconstructions of being and knowing,* edited by A. Jaggar and S. Bordo. New Brunswick: Rutgers University Press.
Damon, Frederick, and Roy Wagner, eds. 1989. *Death rituals and life in the societies of the Kula ring.* De Kalb: Northern Illinois University Press.
Dandrade, Roy. 1995. Moral models in anthropology. *Current Anthropology* 16 (3): 399–408.
Danforth, Loring. 1982. *The death rituals of rural Greece.* Princeton: Princeton University Press.
de Certeau, Michel. 1988. *The practice of everyday life.* Translated by Stephen Rendell. Berkeley: University of California Press.
de Lauretis, Teresa, ed. 1986a. *Feminist studies/cultural studies,* edited by T. de Lauretis. Bloomington: Indiana University Press.
———. 1986b. Introduction: Feminist studies/critical studies. In *Feminist studies/cultural studies,* edited by T. de Lauretis. Bloomington: Indiana University Press.
del Valle, Teresa. 1993. *Gendered anthropology.* London: Routledge.
Dening, Greg. 1980. Islands and beaches: Discourse on a silent land, Marquesas, 1774–1880. Carlton, Vic.: Melbourne University Press.
———. 1996. *Performances.* Chicago: University of Chicago Press.
Denoon, Donald. 1989a. Medical care and gender in the Pacific: Domestic contradictions and the colonial impact. In *Family and gender in the Pacific: Domestic contradictions and the colonial impact,* edited by M. Jolly and M. Macintyre. Cambridge: Cambridge University Press.
———. 1989b. Public health in Papua New Guinea: Medical possibility and social constraint, 1884–1984. Cambridge: Cambridge University Press.
Denzin, Norma. 1997. *Interpretive ethnography: Ethnographic practices for the twenty-first century.* Thousand Oaks, Calif.: Sage.
Derrida, Jacques. 1978. *Writing and difference.* Translated by Alan Bass. London: Routledge and Kegan Paul.

———. 1982. Differance. In *Margins of philosophy,* edited by J. Derrida. Chicago: University of Chicago Press.
Descartes, René. 1968. *Discourse on method and the meditations.* Translated by F. E. Sutcliffe. London: Penguin.
Devereaux, Lesley. 1986. Gender relations: A note on universals. *Canberra Anthropology* 9 (1): 68–77.
Dewey, John. 1929. *Experience and nature.* London: Allen and Unwin.
———. 1958. *Art as experience.* New York: Capricorn Books.
De Zengotita, Thomas. 1989. Romantic perfusion and cultural anthropology. In *Romantic motives: Essays on anthropological sensibility,* edited by G. W. Stocking Jr. Madison: University of Wisconsin Press.
di Leonardo, Micaela. 1991. Introduction: Gender, culture, and political economy: Feminist anthropology in historical perspective. In *Gender at the crossroads of knowledge: Feminist anthropology in the postmodern era,* edited by M. di Leonardo. Berkeley: University of California Press.
Dinnerstein, Dorothy. 1977. *The mermaid and the minotaur.* New York: Harper and Row.
Dominy, Michele. 1990. New Zealand's Waitangi Tribunal: Cultural politics of an anthropology of the high country. *Anthropology Today* 6 (2): 11–15.
Douglas, Michael. 1991. Supervision of rural health centres in Papua New Guinea: Consolidation of the delivery of health services. *Papua New Guinea Medical Journal* 34:144–48.
Dreyfus, Hubert, and Paul Rabinow. 1993. Can there be a science of existential structure and social meaning? In *Bourdieu: Critical perspectives,* edited by C. Calhoun, E. LiPuma, and M. Postone. Oxford: Blackwell.
Dumont, Jean-Paul. 1978. The headman and I: Ambiguity and ambivalence in the fieldworking experience. Austin: University of Texas Press.
Dureau, Christine. 1993. Nobody asked the mother: Women and maternity on Simbo, Western Solomon Islands. *Oceania* 64:18–34.
———. 1994. Mixed blessings: Christianity and history in women's lives on Simbo, Western Solomon Islands. Ph.D., Department of Anthropology, Macquarie University, North Ryde.
———. 1998. From sisters to wives: Changing contexts of maternity on Simbo, Western Solomon Islands. In *Maternity and modernities: Colonial and postcolonial experiences in Asia and the Pacific,* edited by K. Ram and M. Jolly. Cambridge: Cambridge University Press.
Dwyer, Kenneth. 1977. On the dialogic of fieldwork. *Dialectical Anthropology* 2:143–51.
———. 1979. On the dialogic of ethnology. *Dialectical Anthropology* 4:205–24.
———. 1982. *Moroccan dialogues: Anthropology in question.* Baltimore: Johns Hopkins University Press.
Edwards, Keith. 1987. Childhood malaria: Aspects of immunity affecting morbidity and mortality. *Papua New Guinea Medical Journal* 30:135–41.
———. 1992. Editorial: Maternal survival and village delivery. *Papua New Guinea Medical Journal* 35:79–83.
———. 1994. Editorial: Rural health service crisis in Papua New Guinea: Causes,

implications and possible solutions. *Papua New Guinea Medical Journal* 37:145–51.

Eipper, Chris. 1990. Imagining anthropology: Wherein the author journeyed to exotic Ireland, was initiated as an ethnographer, but questioned the discipline's image of itself. *Canberra Anthropology* 13 (1): 48–77.

———. 1996. Ethnographic testimony, trust and authority. *Canberra Anthropology* 19 (1): 15–30.

Eisenstein, Hester. 1984. *Contemporary feminist thought*. London: Allen and Unwin.

Enslin, Elizabeth. 1994. Beyond writing: Feminist practice and the limitations of ethnography. *Cultural Anthropology* 9 (4): 537–68.

Everett, Valerie. 1987. The M of MCH. *Papua New Guinea Medical Journal* 30:121–25.

Everhart, Robert B. 1984. Dilemmas of fieldwork in policy research. *Anthropology and Education Quarterly* 15 (3): 252–58.

Eves, Richard. 1996a. Colonialism, corporeality and character: Methodist missions and refashioning of bodies in the Pacific. *History and Anthropology* 10 (1): 85–138.

———. 1996b. Remembrance of things passed: Memory, body and the politics of feasting in New Ireland, Papua New Guinea. *Oceania* 66:266–77.

Fabian, Johannes. 1983. *Time and the other: How anthropology makes its object*. New York: Columbia University Press.

———. 1991. *Time and the work of anthropology: Critical essays, 1971–1991*. Chur, Switzerland: Harwood Academic Publishers.

Fernandez, J. 1989. Response to Roger Keesing's "Exotic readings of cultural texts." *Current Anthropology* 30 (4): 470–71.

Fine, Michelle. 1994. Working the hyphens: Reinventing self and other in qualitative research. In *Handbook of qualitative research*, edited by N. K. Denzin and Y. S. Lincoln. Thousand Oaks: Sage.

Flax, Jane. 1990a. Postmodernism and gender relations in feminist theory. In *Feminism/postmodernism*, edited by L. Nicholson. New York: Routledge.

———. 1990b. Thinking fragments: Psychoanalysis, feminism, postmodernism in the contemporary West. Berkeley: University of California Press.

Forman, C. 1990. Some next steps in the study of Pacific Island Christianity. In *History and tradition in Melanesian anthropology*, edited by J. Carrier. Berkeley: University of California Press.

Fortune, Reo. [1932] 1989. *Sorcerers of Dobu: The social anthropology of the Dobu islanders of the western Pacific*. Illinois: Waveland Press.

Foster, Robert. 1995. *Social reproduction and history in Melanesia*. Cambridge: Cambridge University Press.

Foucault, Michel. 1978. *History of sexuality*. Vol. 1, *An introduction*. Translated by Robert Hurley. Middlesex: Penguin Books.

———. 1980. *Power/knowledge: Selected interviews and other writings, 1972–1977*. Translated by Colin Gordon, Leo Marshall, John Mepham, and Kate Soper; edited by C. Gordon. New York: Pantheon.

Fox-Keller, Evelyn. 1985. *Reflections on gender and science.* New Haven: Yale University Press.
Frankel, Stephen. 1986. *The Huli response to illness.* Cambridge: Cambridge University Press.
Frankenberg, Ruth. 1993. *White women, race matters: The social construction of whiteness.* Minnesota: University of Minnesota Press.
Fuss, Diana. 1989. *Essentially speaking: Feminism, nature and difference.* New York: Routledge.
Gacs, Ute, Aisha Khan, Jerrie McIntyre, and Ruth Weinberg, eds. 1989. *Women anthropologists: Selected biographies.* Urbana: University of Illinois Press.
Gadamer, Hans-Georg. 1975. *Truth and method.* New York: Seabury Press.
Garner, Paul. 1989. Voluntary village health workers in Papua New Guinea. *Papua New Guinea Medical Journal* 32:55–60.
Gatens, Moira. 1983. A critique of the sex/gender distinction. In *A reader in feminist knowledge,* edited by S. Gunew. London: Routledge.
———. 1991. Feminism, philosophy, and riddles without answers. In *A reader in feminist knowledge,* edited by S. Gunew. London: Routledge.
Geertz, Clifford. 1988. *Works and lives: The anthropologist as author.* Stanford: Stanford University Press.
Gewertz, Deborah, and Frederick Errington. 1991a. *Twisted histories, altered contexts: Representing the Chambri in a world system.* Cambridge: Cambridge University Press.
———. 1991b. We think, therefore they are?—On occidentalizing the world. *Anthropological Quarterly* 64:80–91.
Gillett, Jillian. 1990. *The health of women in Papua New Guinea.* Madang, Papua New Guinea: Kristen Press.
Gilligan, Carol. 1982. *In a different voice.* Harvard: Harvard University Press.
Ginsburg, Faye, and Rayna Rapp. 1991. The politics of reproduction. *Annual Review of Anthropology* 20:311–43.
Good, Byron. 1994. *Medicine, rationality, and experience: An anthropological perspective.* Cambridge, Mass: Cambridge University Press.
Good, Byron, and Mary-Jo DelVecchio Good. 1981. *The semantics of medical discourse,* edited by E. Mendelsohn and Y. Elkana. Dordrecht: D. Reidel.
Gordon, Deborah. 1988. Writing culture, writing feminism. *Inscriptions* 3 (4): 7–26.
———. 1993. Worlds of consequences: Feminist ethnography as social action. *Critique of Anthropology* 13 (4): 429–43.
———. 1995. Conclusion: Culture writing women: Inscribing feminist anthropology. In *Women writing culture,* edited by R. Behar and D. Gordon. Berkeley: University of California Press.
Gordon, Linda. 1976. *Woman's body, woman's right.* New York: Penguin.
———. 1990. *Woman's body, woman's right: Birth control in America.* Rev. and updated ed. New York: Penguin.
Grant, J. 1990. *The state of the world's children: UNICEF.* Oxford: Oxford University Press.
Gregory, Chris. 1982. *Gift and commodities.* London: Academic Press.

Grosz, Elizabeth. 1989. *Sexual subversions: Three French feminists.* Sydney: Allen and Unwin.
———. 1994. *Volatile bodies: Toward a corporeal feminism.* St. Leonards, NSW: Allen and Unwin.
Hahn, Robert. 1995. *Sickness and healing: An anthropological perspective.* New Haven: Yale University Press.
Haraway, Donna. 1990. A manifesto for cyborgs: Science, technology, and socialist feminism in the 1980's. In *Feminism/postmodernism,* edited by L. Nicholson. New York: Routledge.
———. 1991. Simians, cyborgs, and women: The reinvention of nature. New York: Routledge.
Harding, Sandra. 1987a. Conclusion: Epistemological questions. In *Feminism and methodology: Social science issues,* edited by S. Harding. Bloomington: Indiana University Press.
———. 1987b. Introduction: Is there a feminist method? In *Feminism and methodology: Social science issues.* Bloomington: Indiana University Press.
Harstock, Nancy. 1987. The feminist standpoint: Developing the ground for a specifically feminist historical materialism. In *Feminism and methodology: Social science issues,* edited by S. Harding. Bloomington: Indiana University Press.
Hastrup, Kirsten. 1995. *A passage to anthropology: Between experience and theory.* New York: Routledge.
Health, PNG Department of. 1991. *Papua New Guinea National Health Plan: 1991–1995.* Port Moresby, Papua New Guinea: Department of Health.
Hegel, Georg. 1974. *Hegel's lectures on the history of philosophy.* Trans. E. S. Haldane and F. H. Simon. London: Routledge and Kegal Paul.
Heidegger, Martin. 1975. Building dwelling thinking. In *Poetry, language, thought.* New York: Harper and Row.
———. 1977. *The question concerning technology and other essays.* Translated by William Lovitt. New York: Harper and Row.
———, ed. 1993. *Basic Writings,* edited by D. F. Krell. London: Routledge and Kegan Paul.
Heller, Agnes. 1990. Death of the subject. *Thesis Eleven* 25:22–38.
Herdt, Gilbert. 1994. Mistaken sex: Culture, biology and the third sex in New Guinea. In *Third sex, third gender: Beyond sexual dimorphism in culture and history,* edited by G. Herdt. New York: Zone Books.
Herzfeld, Michael. 1989. Comment. *Current Anthropology* 30 (5): 563.
Hodge, Joanna. 1988. Subject, body and the exclusion of women from philosophy. In *Feminist perspectives in philosophy,* edited by M. Griffiths and M. Whitford. Bloomington: Indiana University Press.
hooks, bell. 1982. *Ain't I a woman: Black women and feminism.* London: Pluto Press.
———. 1984. *Feminist theory: From margin to center.* Boston: South End Press.
———. 1991. Sisterhood: Political solidarity between women. In *A reader in feminist knowledge,* edited by S. Gunew. London: Routledge.
Hughes, Jenny. 1994. WHO is working for international health. In *Anthropology*

and third world development, edited by B. Geddes, J. Hughes, and J. Remenyi. Geelong, Australia: Deakin University Press.
Hymes, Dell, ed. 1972. *Reinventing anthropology.* New York: Pantheon Books.
Ingold, Timothy. 1991. Becoming persons: Consciousness and sociality in human evolution. *Cultural Dynamics* 4:355–78.
Irigaray, Luce. 1985a. *Speculum of the other woman.* Translated by Gillian C. Gill. Ithaca: Cornell University Press.
———. 1985b. *This sex which is not one.* Translated by Catherine Porter and Carolyn Burke. Ithaca: Cornell University Press.
Jackson, Michael, ed. 1989. *Paths toward a clearing: Radical empiricism and ethnographical inquiry.* Bloomington: Indiana University Press.
Jackson, Peter. 1997. Kathoey <> Gay <> Man: The historical emergence of gay male identity in Thailand. In *Sites of desire, economies of pleasure,* edited by L. Manderson and M. Jolly. Chicago: University of Chicago Press.
Jaggar, Alison. 1983. *Feminist politics and human nature.* New Jersey: Rowman and Allanheld.
Jaggar, Alison, and Susan Bordo, eds. 1989. *Gender/body/knowledge: Feminist reconstructions of being and knowing.* New Brunswick: Rutgers University Press.
James, William. 1976. *Essay in radical empiricism.* Cambridge: Harvard University Press.
———. 1978. *Pragmatism.* Cambridge: Harvard University Press.
Jay, Martin. 1993. Downcast eyes: The denigration of vision in twentieth century French thought. Berkeley: University of California Press.
Jennaway, Megan. 1990. Paradigms, postmodern epistemologies and paradoxes: The place of feminism in anthropology. *Anthropological Forum* 6 (2): 167–90.
Jolly, Margaret. 1991. "To save the girls for brighter and better lives": Presbyterian missions and women in southern Vanuatu, 1848–1870. *Journal of Pacific History* 26 (1): 27–48.
———. 1992a. Colonizing women: The maternal body and empire. In *Feminism and the politics of difference,* edited by S. Gunew and A. Yeatman. Sydney: Allen and Unwin.
———. 1992b. Partible persons and multiple authors: Book review forum on Marilyn Strathern (1988) "The Gender of the Gift": Problems with women and problems with society in Melanesi. *Pacific Studies* 15:137–49.
———. 1998a. Introduction: Colonial and postcolonial plots in histories of maternities and modernities. In *Maternities and modernities: Colonial and postcolonial experiences in Asia and the Pacific,* edited by K. Ram and M. Jolly. Cambridge: Cambridge University Press.
———. 1998b. Other mothers: Maternal "insouciance" and the depopulation debate in Fiji and Vanuatu, 1890–1930. In *Maternities and modernities: Colonial and postcolonial experiences in Asia and the Pacific,* edited by M. Jolly and K. Ram. Cambridge: Cambridge University Press.
Jolly, Margaret, and Martha Macintyre. 1989. Introduction. In *Family and gender in the Pacific: Domestic contradictions and the colonial impact,* edited by M. Jolly and M. Macintyre. Cambridge: Cambridge University Press.

Jones, Ann. 1981. Writing the body: Toward an understanding of l'Ecriture feminine. *Feminist Studies* 7 (2): 247–63.
Jordanova, Ludmilla. 1989. Sexual visions: Images of gender in science and medicine between the eighteenth and twentieth centuries. New York: Harvester Wheatsheaf.
Jorgenson, Daniel. 1983a. The facts of life, Papua New Guinea style. *Mankind* 14 (1): 1–12.
———. 1983b. Mirroring nature? Men's and women's models of conception in Telefolmin. *Mankind* 14 (1): 57–65.
Josephides, Lisette. 1991. Metaphors, metathemes, and the construction of sociality: A critique of the New Melanesian ethnography. *Man*, n.s., 26:145–61.
———. 1997. Representing the anthropologist's predicament. In *After writing culture*, edited by A. James, J. Hockey, and A. Dawson. London: Routledge.
Kanfert, Patricia, and John O'Neil. 1993. Analysis of a dialogue on risks in childbirth: clinicians, epidemiologists, and Inuit women. In *Knowledge, power, and practice: The anthropology of medicine and everyday life*, edited by S. Lindenbaum and M. Lock, 32–54. Berkeley: University of California Press.
Keck, Verena. 1993. Two ways of explaining reality: The sickness of a small boy of Papua New Guinea from anthropological and biomedical perspectives. *Oceania* 63:294–313.
Keesing, Roger. 1974. Theories of culture. *Annual Review of Anthropology* 3:73–97.
———. 1975. *Kin groups and social structure*. Fort Worth: Holt, Rinehart and Winston.
———. 1985. Conventional metaphors and anthropological metaphysics: The problematic of cultural translation. *Journal of Anthropological Research* 41:201–18.
———. 1987. Anthropology as interpretive quest. *Current Anthropology* 28 (2): 161–69.
———. 1989a. Creating the past: Custom and identity in the contemporary Pacific. *Contemporary Pacific* 1:16–35.
———. 1989b. Exotic readings of cultural texts. *Current Anthropology* 30 (4): 459–79.
———. 1989c. Sins of a mission: Christian life as Kwaio traditionalist ideology. In *Family and gender in the Pacific: Domestic contradictions and the colonial impact*, edited by M. Jolly and M. Macintyre. Cambridge: Cambridge University Press.
———. 1990. Theories of culture revisited. *Canberra Anthropology* 13 (2): 56–69.
Keesing, Roger, and Margaret Jolly. 1992. Epilogue. In *History and tradition in Melanesian anthropology*, edited by J. Carrier. Berkeley: University of California Press.
Keesing, Roger, and Robert Tonkinson. 1982. Reinventing traditional culture: The politics of kastom in Island Melanesia. *Mankind* (special issue) 13 (4): 297–399.
Khazanov, Anatoly M. 1996. Anthropologists in the midst of ethnic conflicts. *Anthropology Today* 12 (2): 5–8.

Kirby, Vicki. 1989. Capitalising difference: Feminism and anthropology. *Australian Feminist Studies* 9:1–24.
———. 1993. Feminisms and postmodernisms: Anthropology and the management of difference. *Anthropological Quarterly* 66 (3): 127–33.
Kleinman, Arthur. 1973. Medicine's symbolic reality: On the central problem in the philosophy of medicine. *Inquiry* 16:206–13.
———. 1980. *Patients and healers in the context of culture: An exploration of the borderland between anthropology, medicine, and psychiatry.* Berkeley: University of California Press.
Knauft, Bruce. 1989. Bodily images in Melanesia: Cultural substances and natural metaphors. In *Fragments for a history of the human body,* Part 3, edited by M. Feher. New York: ZONE Books.
———. 1994. Pushing anthropology past the posts: Critical notes on cultural anthropology and cultural studies by postmodernism and existentialism. *Critique of Anthropology* 14 (2): 117–52.
Kolehmainen-Aitken, Riitta-Liisa. 1990. *Aid post and hospital orderlies: A vanishing breed?* Alotau, Papua New Guinea: Milne Bay Provincial Health Office.
Kovel, Joel. 1981. *The age of desire.* New York: Pantheon.
———. 1988. *The radical spirit: Essays on psychoanalysis and society.* London: Free Association Press.
Kristeva, Julia. 1980. *Desire in language: A semiotic approach to literature and art.* New York: Columbia University Press.
———. 1986. Women's time. In *The Kristeva reader,* edited by T. Moi. Oxford: Blackwell.
Kuble, Ennio. 1998. Spotlight on high maternal mortality rate. *National,* 19 February 1998.
Kuehling, Susanne. 1998. The name of the gift: Ethics of exchange on Dobu Island. Ph.D., Department of Anthropology, RSPAS, Australian National University, Canberra.
Lakoff, George. 1989. Response to Roger Keesing's exotic readings of cultural texts. *Current Anthropology* 30 (4): 472–73.
Lakoff, George, and Mark Johnson. 1980. *Metaphors we live by.* Chicago: University of Chicago Press.
Lattas, Andrew. 1996. Memory, forgetting and the New Tribes Mission in West New Britain. *Oceania* 66:286–304.
Lazarus, Elizabeth. 1994. What do women want? Issues of choice, control, and class in pregnancy and childbirth. *Medical Anthropology Quarterly* 8 (1): 25–46.
Le Guin, Ursula. 1989. *Dancing at the edge of the world: Thoughts on words, women, places.* London: Victor Gollancz.
Leach, E. 1967. Virgin Birth. Proceedings of the Royal Anthropological Institute, 1966.
Leach, Jerry, and Edmund Leach. 1983. *The Kula.* Cambridge: Cambridge University Press.
Leder, Drew, ed. 1992. *The body in medical thought and practice.* Dordrecht and Boston: Kluwer Academic Publishers.

Leenhardt, Maurice. 1979. *Do Kamo: Person and myth in the Melanesian world.* Translated by Basia Miller Gulati. Chicago: University of Chicago Press.

Lepowsky, Maria. 1989. Death and exchange: Mortuary ritual on Vanatinai (Sudest Island). In *Death rituals and life in the societies of the Kula ring,* edited by F. Damon and R. Wagner. De Kalb: Northern Illinois University Press.

———. 1993. *Fruit of the motherland: Gender in an egalitarian society.* New York: Columbia University Press.

Lewis, Gilbert Aguilar. 1975. *Knowledge of illness in a Sepik society: A study of the Gnau, New Guinea.* Monographs on Social Anthropology, no. 52. London: Athlone Press.

Lewis, J. 1990. "Motherhood issues" in the late nineteenth and twentieth centuries. In *Delivering motherhood: Maternal ideologies and practices in the nineteenth and twentieth centuries,* edited by K. Arnup, A. Levesque, and R. R. Pierson. London: Routledge.

Lindstrom, Lamont. 1994. Traditional cultural policy in Melanesia (kastom, policy, long kastom). In *Culture, kastom, tradition: Developing cultural policy in Melanesia,* edited by L. Lamont and G. White, 1–20. Suva, Fiji: Institute of Pacific Studies, University of the South Pacific.

Lindstrom, Lamont, and Geoffrey M. White, eds. 1994. *Culture, kastom, tradition: Developing cultural policy in Melanesia.* Suva, Fiji: Institute of Pacific Studies, University of the South Pacific.

Lithgow, David. 1976. Austronesian languages: Milne Bay and adjacent islands (Milne Bay Province). In *New Guinea area languages and language study,* edited by S. Wurm. Canberra: Research School of Pacific Studies, Australian National University.

Lloyd, Genevieve. 1984. *The man of reason: "Male" and "female" in Western philosophy.* London: Methuen.

———. 1991. Reason as attainment. In *A reader in feminist knowledge,* edited by S. Gunew. London: Routledge.

Lock, Margaret, and Nancy Scheper-Hughes. 1990. A critical-interpretative approach in medical anthropology: Rituals and routines of discipline and dissent. In *Medical anthropology: A handbook of theory and method,* edited by T. Johnson and C. Sargent. New York: Greenwood Press.

Lukes, Steven. 1985. Conclusion. In *The category of the person: Anthropology, philosophy, history,* edited by M. Carrithers, S. Collins, and S. Lukes. Cambridge: Cambridge University Press.

Lutz, Catherine. 1982. The domain of emotion words on Ifaluk. *American Ethnologist* 9:113–28.

———. 1988. *Unnatural emotions: Everyday sentiments on a Micronesian atoll and their challenge to Western theory.* Chicago: University of Chicago Press.

———. 1990. The erasure of women's writing in sociocultural anthropology. *American Ethnologist* 17 (4): 611–27.

Lutz, Catherine, and Geoffrey White. 1986. The anthropology of the emotions. *Annual Review of Anthropology* 15:405–36.

Lutz, Catherine A., and Lila Abu-Lughod, eds. 1990. *Language and the politics of emotion.* Cambridge: Cambridge University Press.

Macintyre, Martha. 1983. Changing paths: An historical ethnography of the traders of Tubetube. Ph.D., Australian National University, Canberra.

———. 1987. Flying witches and leaping warriors: Supernatural origins of power and matrilineal authority in Tubetube society. In *Dealing with inequality: Analysing gender relations in Melanesia and beyond*, edited by M. Strathern. Cambridge: Cambridge University Press.

———. 1988. Nurturance and nutrition: Change and continuity in concepts of food and feasting in a southern Massim community. *Journal de la Société Océanique* 85 (3): 51–59.

———. 1989a. Better homes and gardens. In *Family and gender in the Pacific: Domestic contradictions and the colonial impact*, edited by M. Jolly and M. Macintyre. Cambridge: Cambridge University Press.

———. 1989b. The triumph of the Susu: Mortuary exchanges on Tubetube. In *Death rituals and life in the societies of the Kula ring*, edited by F. Damon and R. Wagner. De Kalb: Northern Illinois University Press.

———. 1990. Christianity, cargo cultism and the concept of the spirit in Misiman cosmology. In *Christianity in Oceania: Ethnographic perspectives*, edited by J. Barker. Lanham, Md.: University Press of America.

———. 1993. Fictive kinship or mistaken identity? Fieldwork on Tubetube Island, Papua New Guinea. In *Gendered fields: Women, men and ethnography*, edited by D. Bell, P. Caplan, and W. J. Karim. London: Routledge.

———. 1995. Violent bodies and vicious exchanges: Personification and objectification in the Massim. In *Persons, bodies, selves, emotions*. In *Social Analysis* 37 (Apr.): 29–43.

Malinowski, Bronislaw. 1922. *Argonauts of the western Pacific: An account of native enterprise and adventure in the archipelagoes of Melanesian New Guinea*. London: Routledge and Kegan Paul.

———. 1932. *The sexual life of savages in North-Western Melanesia: An ethnographic account of courtship, marriage, and family life among the natives of the Trobriand Islands, British New Guinea*. 3d ed. London: Routledge.

———. 1948. *Magic, science and religion and other essays*. London: Souvenir Press.

———. 1962. *Sex, culture, and myth*. New York: Harcourt Brace and World.

Mallett, Shelley. 1995. Burying Lazarus: A feminist psychoanalytic critique of the death of the Subject. *Social Analysis* 37 (Apr.): 82–100.

———. 1997. Conceiving cultures: Person, health and place on Nua'ata, Papua New Guinea. Ph.D., Sociology, politics and anthropology, La Trobe University, Bundoora.

———. 1998. Living Death: Understanding respect and respectful understanding on Nua'ata. Papua New Guinea, *Canberra Anthropology* 21 (1): 1–25.

———. 2002. Colonial Impregnations: Reconceptions of Maternal Health Practice on Nua'ata. Papua New Guinea. In *Birthing in the Pacific: Beyond Tradition and Modernity*, edited by V. Lukere and M. Jolly. 125–47. Honolulu: University of Hawai'i Press.

Manderson, Lenore. 1992. Women and the state: Maternal and child welfare in colonial Malaya, 1900–1940. In *Women and children first: International maternal and infant welfare, 1870–1945,* edited by V. Fildes, L. Marks, and H. Marland. London: Routledge.

———. 1998. Shaping reproduction: Maternity in early twentieth century Malaya. In *Maternities and modernities,* edited by K. Ram and M. Jolly. Cambridge: Cambridge University Press.

Maolai, Paul. 1995. Village birth attendant's programme for Rabaraba. *Eastern Star,* 29 May, 9.

Marcus, George, and Dick Cushman. 1982. Ethnographies as texts. *Annual Review of Anthropology* 11:25–69.

Marcus, George, and Michael Fischer, eds. 1986. *Anthropology as cultural critique: An experimental moment in the human sciences.* Chicago: University of Chicago Press.

Marcus, Julie, ed. 1993. *First in their field: Women and Australian anthropology.* Melbourne: Melbourne University Press.

Martin, Emily. 1987. The woman in the body: A cultural analysis of reproduction. Boston: Beacon Press.

———. 1991. The egg and the sperm: How science has constructed a romance based on stereotypical male-female roles. *Signs* 16 (3): 485–501.

Mascia-Lees, Frances, Patricia Sharpe, and Colleen Ballerino Cohen. 1989. The post-modernist turn in anthropology: Cautions from a feminist perspective. *Signs* 15:7–33.

Mauss, Marcel. 1973. Techniques of the body. *Economy and Society* 2:70–78.

———. 1985. A category of the human mind: The notion of person, the notion of self. In *The category of the person: Anthropology, philosophy, history,* edited by M. Carrithers, S. Collins, and S. Lukes. Cambridge: Cambridge University Press.

Mead, Margaret. 1949. Coming of age in Samoa: A psychological study of primitive youth for Western civilization. New York: New American Library.

Merchant, Carolyn. 1980. *The death of nature.* San Francisco: Harper and Row.

Merlan, Francesca, and Alan Rumsey. 1991. Ku Waru: Language and segmentary politics in the western Nebilyer Valley, Papua New Guinea. Cambridge: Cambridge University Press.

Merleau-Ponty, Maurice. 1962. *The phenomenology of perception.* Translated by Colin Smith. London: Routledge.

Merrett-Balkos, Leanne. 1998. Just add water: Remaking women through childbirth, Anganen, Southern Highlands, Papua New Guinea. In *Maternities and modernities,* edited by K. Ram and M. Jolly. Cambridge: Cambridge University Press.

Mohanty, Chandra. 1991a. Cartographies of struggle: Third world women and the politics of feminism. In *Third world women and the politics of feminism,* edited by C. Mohanty, A. Russo, and L. Torres. Bloomington: Indiana University Press.

———. 1991b. Under Western eyes: Feminist scholarship and colonial discourses. In *Third world women and the politics of feminism,* edited by C. Mohanty, A. Russo, and L. Torres. Bloomington: Indiana University Press.

Moi, Toril. 1985. *Sexual/textual politics: Feminist literary theory*. London: Methuen.
Mola, Glen. 1985. Maternal health services and maternal mortality in Papua New Guinea. *Papua New Guinea Medical Journal* 28:241–45.
———. 1989. Maternal death in Papua New Guinea, 1984–1986. *Papua New Guinea Medical Journal* 32 (1): 27–31.
———. 1991. Making family planning more effective—Papua New Guinea Style. *Papua New Guinea Medical Journal* 34:85–86.
Mola, Glen, and Iain Aitken. 1984. Maternal mortality in Papua New Guinea. *Papua New Guinea Medical Journal* 27 (2): 65–71.
Moore, Henrietta. 1988. *Feminism and anthropology*. Cambridge: Polity Press.
———. 1994a. The feminist anthropologist and the passion(s) of new Eve. In *A passion for difference*, edited by H. Moore. Cambridge: Polity Press.
———. 1994b. Master narratives. In *A passion for difference*, edited by H. Moore. Cambridge: Polity Press.
———. 1994c. *A passion for difference*. Cambridge: Polity Press.
Moraga, Cherrie, and Gloria Anzaldua. 1983. *This bridge called my back: Writings by radical women of color*. New York: Kitchen Table, Women of Color Press.
Morris, Rosalind. 1994. Three sexes and four sexualities: Redressing the discourses on gender and sexuality in contemporary Thailand. *Positions* 2 (1): 15–43.
Morsy, S. 1990. Political economy in medical anthropology. In *Medical anthropology: A handbook of theory and method*, edited by T. Johnson and C. Sargent. New York: Greenwood Press.
Mortimer, Lorraine. 1990. What if I talked like a woman right here in public? *Arena* 92:43–65.
Morton, John. 1995. The organic remains: Remarks on the constitution and development of people. In *Persons, bodies, selves, emotions*. In *Social analysis: Journal of cultural and social practice* (special issue), edited by J. Morton and M. Macintyre. Adelaide: University of Adelaide.
Mosko, Mark. 1992. Motherless sons: "Divine kings" and "partible persons" in Melanesia and Polynesia. *Man*, n.s., 27:697–717.
Mull, J. D. 1990. The primary health care dialectic: History, rhetoric and reality. In *Anthropology and primary health care*, edited by J. Coreil and D. Mull. Boulder: Westview.
Munn, Nancy. 1986. *The fame of Gawa: A symbolic study of value transformation in a Massim (Papua New Guinea) society*. Durham: Duke University Press.
———. 1990. Constructing regional worlds in experience: Kula exchange, witchcraft and Gawan local events. *Royal Anthropological Institute Journal* 25 (1): 1–17.
Neumann, Klaus. 1992. *Not the way it really was: Constructing the Tolai past*. Pacific Islands Monographs, no. 10. Honolulu: University of Hawaii Press.
Nsiah-Jefferson, Laurie, and Elaine Hall. 1989. Reproductive technology: Perspective and implications for low-income women and women of colour. In

Healing technology: Feminist perspectives, edited by K. Ratcliff. Michigan: University of Michigan Press.

Oakley, Ann. 1980. *Women confined: Towards a sociology of childbirth*. Oxford: Martin Robertson.

———. 1984. *The captured womb: A history of the medical care of pregnant women*. New York: Basil Blackwell.

Okely, Judith. 1992. Anthropology and autobiography: Participatory experience and embodied knowledge. In *Anthropology and autobiography*, edited by J. Okely and H. Callaway. London: Routledge.

Okely, Judith, and Helen Callaway, eds. 1992. *Anthropology and autobiography*. London: Routledge.

Oxford English Dictionary. 1989. 2d ed. Oxford: Clarendon Press.

Pelz, Werner. 1974. The scope of understanding in sociology: Towards a more radical reorientation in the social and humanistic sciences. London: Routledge and Kegan Paul.

———. 1992. The dream of reason produces monsters. Manuscript.

Petaliyaki, Bartholomew, and Daphne Lithgow. n.d. The use of the suffixes -wa and -ne in Auhelawa. Unpublished ms.

Petchesky, Rosalind. 1984. *Abortion and woman's choice: The state, sexuality, and reproductive freedom*. New York: Longman.

Pierson, Ruth Roach, Katherine Arnup, and Andree Levesque. 1990. Introduction. In *Delivering motherhood: Maternal ideologies and practices in the nineteenth and twentieth centuries*, edited by K. Arnup, A. Levesque, and R. R. Pierson. London: Routledge.

Pile, Steve, and Nigel Thrift. 1995. Mapping the subject. In *Mapping the subject: Geographies of cultural transformation*, edited by S. Pile and N. Thrift. London: Routledge.

Pratt, M. 1986. Fieldwork in common places. In *Writing culture: The poetics and politics of ethnography*, edited by J. Clifford and G. Marcus. Berkeley: University of California Press.

Probyn, Elspeth. 1993. *Sexing the self: Gendered positions in cultural studies*. London: Routledge.

Rabinow, Paul. 1996. *Essays on the anthropology of reason*. Princeton: Princeton University Press.

Ram, Kalpana. 1993. Too "traditional" once again: Some post-structuralists on the aspirations of the immigrant/Third World female subject. *Australian Feminist Studies* 17:5–28.

———. 1998. Maternity and the story of enlightenment in the colonies: Tamil coastal women, South India. In *Maternities and modernities*, edited by K. Ram and M. Jolly. Cambridge: Cambridge University Press.

Ram, Kalpana, and Margaret Jolly, eds. 1998. *Maternities and modernities: Colonial and postcolonial experiences in Asia and the Pacific*. Cambridge: Cambridge University Press.

Rapp, Rayna. 1991. Moral pioneers: Men, and fetuses on a frontier of reproductive technology. In *Gender at the crossroads of knowledge: Feminist anthropology in the postmodern era*, edited by M. di Leonardo. Berkeley: University of California Press.

———. 1993. Accounting for amniocentesis. In *Knowledge, power and practice: The anthropology of medicine and everyday life,* edited by S. Lindenbaum and M. Lock. Berkeley: University of California Press.

———. 1995. Heredity, or: revising the facts of life. In *Naturalising power: Essays in feminist cultural analysis,* edited by R. Rapp. New York: Routledge.

Reed, Adam. 1998. Contested images and common strategies: Early colonial sexual politics in the Massim. In *Sites of desire, economies of pleasure: Sexualities in Asian and the Pacific,* edited by L. Manderson and M. Jolly. Chicago: University of Chicago Press.

Reid, Janice. 1984. The role of maternal and child health clinics in education and prevention: A case study from Papua New Guinea. *Social Science and Medicine* 19:291–303.

Rich, Adrienne. 1976. *Of woman born: Motherhood as experience and institution.* London: Virago.

Rorty, Richard. 1979. *Philosophy and the mirror of nature.* Princeton: Princeton University Press.

Rosaldo, Michelle. 1980. *Knowledge and passion: Ilongot notions of self and social life.* Cambridge: Cambridge University Press.

Rosaldo, Renato. 1984. Grief and a headhunter's rage: On the cultural force of emotions. In *Text, play, and story: The construction and reconstruction of self and society,* edited by E. Bruner. Washington, D.C.: Americal Ethnological Society.

———. 1989. *Culture and truth: The remaking of social analysis.* Boston: Beacon Press.

Ross, Malcolm. 1988. *Proto Oceanic and the Austronesian Languages of Western Melanesia.* Pacific Linguistics Series C, no. 98. Canberra: Research School of Pacific Studies, Australian National University.

Roth, Paul. 1989. Ethnography without tears. *Current Anthropology* 30 (5): 555–61.

Rowland, Robyn. 1987. Technology and motherhood: Reproductive choice reconsidered. *Signs* 12 (3): 512–28.

———. 1992. *Living laboratories: Women and reproductive technologies.* Bloomington: Indiana University Press.

Rozario, Santi. 1998. The dai and the doctor: Discourses on women's reproductive health in rural Bangladesh. In *Maternities and modernities,* edited by K. Ram and M. Jolly. Cambridge: Cambridge University Press.

Ruddick, Sara. 1980. Maternal thinking. *Feminist Studies* 6:342–64.

———. 1989. *Maternal thinking: Toward a politics of peace.* Boston: Beacon Press.

Rumsey, Alan. 1989. Grammatical person and social agency in the New Guinea Highlands. Paper read at 25th Annual Regional Meeting of the Chicago Linguistic Society; Part Two: Parasession on Language in Context, at Chicago.

———. 2000. Agency, personhood and the "I" of discourse in the Pacific and beyond. *Journal of the Royal Anthropological Institute* 2000 (6): 101–15.

Sahlins, Marshall D. 1981. *Historical metaphors and mythical realities.* Ann Arbor: University of Michigan Press.

———. 1985. *Islands of history.* Chicago: University of Chicago Press.

Said, Edward. 1995. Secular interpretation, the geographical element, and the methodology of imperialism. In *After colonialism: Imperial histories and postcolonial displacements,* edited by G. Prakash. Princeton: Princeton University Press.

Scarry, Elizabeth. 1985. *The body in pain: The making and unmaking of the world.* New York: Oxford University Press.

Scheper-Hughes, Nancy. 1985. Culture, scarcity and maternal thinking: Maternal detachment and infant survival in a Brazilian shantytown. *Ethos* 13 (4): 291–317.

———. 1992. *Death without weeping: The violence of everyday life in Brazil.* Berkeley: University of California Press.

———. 1995. The primacy of the ethical: Propositions for a militant anthropology. *Current Anthropology* 36 (3): 409–20.

Schoepf, Brooke Grundfest. 1991. Ethical, methodological and political issues of AIDS research in Central Africa. *Social Science and Medicine* 33 (7): 749–63.

Scholte, Bob. 1974. Towards a reflective and critical anthropology. In *Reinventing anthropology,* edited by D. Hymes. New York: Vintage Books.

Schuster, Elizabeth. 1996. Ethical considerations when conducting ethnographic research in a nursing home setting. *Journal of Aging Studies* 10 (1): 57–67.

Seligman, Charles Gabriel. 1976 (1910). *The Melanesians of British New Guinea.* New York: A.M.S. Press.

Simons, Margaret, and Jessica Benjamin. 1979. Simone de Beauvoir: An interview. *Feminist Studies* 5 (2): 330–45.

Singer, Merrill. 1989. The coming of age of critical medical anthropology. *Social Science and Medicine* 28:1193–1203.

———. 1990. Reinventing medical anthropology: Toward a critical realignment. *Social Science and Medicine* 30:179–87.

Spiro, Melford. 1968. Virgin birth: Parthenogenesis and physiological paternity: An essay in cultural interpretation. *Man* 3:242–61.

Spivak, Gayatri Chakravorty. 1984. *In other worlds.* New York: Routledge.

Stacey, Judith. 1988. Can there be a feminist ethnography? *Women's Studies International Forum* 11 (1): 21–27.

———. 1990. *Brave new families.* New York: Basic Books.

Stack, Carol. 1974. *All our kin: Strategies for survival in an urban black community.* New York: Harper and Row.

Stocking, George. 1983. *Observers observed: Essays on ethnographic fieldwork.* Madison: University of Wisconsin Press.

Stoler, Ann. 1991. Carnal knowledge and imperial power: gender, race, and morality in colonial Asia. In *Gender at the crossroads of knowledge,* edited by M. di Leonardo. Berkeley: University of California Press.

Strathern, Andrew. 1972. *One father, one blood.* Canberra: Australian National University Press.

Strathern, Marilyn. 1968. Popokl: The question of morality. *Mankind* 6:553–61.

———. 1987a. An awkward relationship: The case of feminism and anthropology. *Signs* 12:276–92.

———. 1987b. Introduction. In *Dealing with inequality: Analysing gender rela-*

tions in Melanesia and beyond, edited by M. Strathern. Cambridge: Cambridge University Press.

———. 1987c. Out of context: The persuasive fictions of anthropology. *Current Anthropology* 28 (3): 251–81.

———. 1988. *The gender of the gift.* Berkeley: University of California Press.

———. 1989a. Between a Melanesianist and a deconstructive feminist. *Australian Feminist Studies* 10:49–69.

———. 1989b. Comment on "Capitalising Difference." *Australian Feminist Studies* (autumn): 25–29.

———. 1991. *Partial connections.* Savage, Md.: Rowman and Littlefield.

———. 1992. Reproducing the future: Anthropology, kinship and the new reproductive technologies. New York: Routledge.

———. 1993. Entangled objects: Detached metaphors. *Social Analysis* 34:88–101.

———. 1995. Nostalgia and the new genetics. In *Rhetorics of self-making,* edited by D. Battaglia. Berkeley: University of California Press.

Suleiman, Susan. 1985. Writing and motherhood. In *The m(other) tongue: Essays in feminist psychoanalytic interpretation,* edited by S. Garner, C. Kahane, and M. Sprengnether. Ithaca: Cornell University Press.

Taufa, Tukutau. 1978. Malaria and pregnancy. *Papua New Guinea Medical Journal* 21:197–206.

Taussig, Michael T. 1993. *Mimesis and alterity: A particular history of the senses.* New York: Routledge.

Taylor, Charles. 1989. *Sources of the self: The making of the modern identity.* Cambridge: Cambridge University Press.

———. 1993. To follow a rule. In *Bourdieu: Critical perspectives,* edited by C. Calhoun, E. LiPuma, and M. Postone. Cambridge: Polity Press.

Taylor, Mark, ed. 1986. *Deconstruction in context: Literature and philosophy.* Chicago: University of Chicago Press.

Tedlock, Dennis. 1983. *The spoken word and the work of interpretation.* Philadelphia: University of Pennsylvania Press.

Thomas, Nicholas. 1991. Entangled objects: Exchange, material culture and colonialism in the Pacific. Cambridge: Harvard University Press.

———. 1992. Substantivization and anthropological discourse: The transformation of practices into institutions in neo-traditional Pacific societies. In *History and tradition in Melanesian anthropology,* edited by J. Carrier. Berkeley: University of California Press.

———. 1994. *Colonialism's culture: Anthropology, travel and government.* Melbourne: Melbourne University Press.

Thomason, Jane, and William Newbrander. 1991. A survey of Papua New Guinea's health sector financing and expenditure. *Papua New Guinea Medical Journal* 34:129–43.

Thune, Carl. 1980. The rhetoric of remembrance: Collective life and personal tragedy in Loboda village. Ph.D., Department of Anthropology, Princeton University.

———. 1989. Death and matrilineal reincorporation on Normanby Island. In

Death rituals and life in the societies of the Kula ring, edited by F. Damon and R. Wagner. De Kalb: Northern Illinois University Press.

———. 1990. Fathers, aliens, and brothers: Building a social world in Loboda Village church services. In *Christianity in Oceania: Ethnographic perspectives*, edited by J. Barker. Lantham: University Press of America.

Trinh, T. Minh-Ha. 1989. *Woman, native, other: Writing postcoloniality and feminism*. Bloomington: Indiana University Press.

Turner, Victor. 1986. Dewey, Dilthey, and drama: An essay in the anthropology of experience. In *The anthropology of experience*, edited by V. Turner and E. Bruner. Chicago: University of Illinois Press.

Turner, Victor, and Edward Bruner. 1986. *The anthropology of experience*. Chicago: University of Illinois press.

Urban, Greg. 1989. The "I" of discourse. In *Semiotics, self and society*, edited by B. Lee and G. Urban. Berlin: Mouton de Gruyter.

Visweswaran, Kamala. 1988. Defining feminist ethnography. *Inscriptions* 3 (4): 27–57.

———. 1994. The betrayal: An analysis in three acts. In *Fictions of feminist ethnography*, edited by K. Visweswaran. Minneapolis: University of Minnesota Press.

Wagner, Roy. 1972. *Habu: The innovation of meaning in Daribi clan definition and alliance in New Guinea*. Chicago: University of Chicago Press.

———. 1977. Analogic kinship: A Daribi example. *American Ethnologist* 4:623–42.

———. 1981. *The invention of culture*. 2d ed. Chicago: University of Chicago Press.

———. 1983. The ends of innocence: Conception and seduction among the Daribi of Karimai and the Barok of New Ireland. *Mankind* 14 (1): 75–83.

———. 1989. *Death rituals and life in the societies of the Kula ring*, edited by F. Damon and R. Wagner. De Kalb: Northern Illinois University Press.

Walter, Lynn. 1995. Feminist anthropology? *Gender and Society* 9 (3): 272–88.

Weiner, Annette. 1976. *Women of value, men of renown: New perspectives on Trobriand exchange*. Austin: University of Texas Press.

———. 1988. *The Trobrianders of Papua New Guinea*. New York: Holt, Rinehart and Winston.

Weiner, James. 1998. Must our informants mean what they say? *Canberra Anthropology* 20 (1–2): 84–97.

Welsch, Robert. 1991. Traditional medicine and Western medical options among the Ningerum of Papua New Guinea. In *The anthropology of medicine: From culture to method*, edited by L. Romanucci-Ross, D. Moerman, and Laurence Tancredi. New York: Bergin and Garvey.

Wheatley, Elizabeth. 1994. How can we engender ethnography with a feminist imagination? A rejoinder to Judith Stacey. *Women's Studies International Forum* 17 (4): 403–16.

White, Geoffrey. 1992. *Identity through history: Living stories in a Solomon Island society*. Cambridge: Cambridge University Press.

Whittaker, Elvi. 1981. Anthropological ethics, fieldwork and epistemological disjunctures. *Philosophy of the Social Sciences* 11 (4): 437–51.

Wikan, Unni. 1991. Toward an experience-near anthropology. *Cultural Anthropology* 6 (3): 285–305.
Williams, Brackette F. 1995. The public I/eye: Conducting fieldwork to do homework on homelessness and begging in two U.S. cities. *Current Anthropology* 36 (1): 25–39.
Wilshire, Donna. 1989. The uses of myth, image and female body in re-visioning knowledge. In *Gender/body/knowledge: Feminist reconstructions of being and knowing,* edited by A. Jaggar and S. Bordo. New Brunswick: Rutgers University Press.
Wittgenstein, Ludwig. 1953. *Philosophical investigations.* Translated by G. E. M. Anscombe. Oxford: Blackwell.
Wittig, Monique. 1981. One is not born a woman. *Feminist Issues* 2:47–54.
Wolf, Diane, ed. 1993. Feminist dilemmas in fieldwork. *Frontiers* 13 (3): 1–103.
Yanagisako, Sylvia, and Jane Collier. 1987. Toward a unified analysis of gender and kinship. In *Gender and kinship: Essays toward a unified analysis,* edited by J. Collier and S. Yanagisako. Stanford: Stanford University Press.
Yanoshik, Kim, and Judy Norsigan. 1989. Contraception, control and choice: International perspectives. In *Healing technology: Feminist perspectives,* edited by K. S. Ratcliff, M. M. Ratcliff, G. Mellow, B. D. Wright, G. Price, K. Yanoshik, and M. Freston. Ann Arbor: University of Michigan Press.
Young, Allan. 1982. The anthropologies of illness and sickness. *Annual Review of Anthropology* 11:257–85.
Young, Iris Marion. 1986. The ideal of community and the politics of difference. *Social Theory and Practice* 12 (1): 1–26.
———. 1990. *Throwing like a girl and other essays in feminist philosophy and social theory.* Bloomington: Indiana University Press.
Young, Michael. 1977. Dr Bromilow and the Bwaidoka wars. *Journal of Pacific History* 12:30–153.
———. 1980. A tropology of the Dobu mission. *Canberra Anthropology* (1): 86–104.
———. 1983. *Magicians of Manumanua: Living myth in Kalauna.* Berkeley: University of California Press.
———. 1989a. "Eating the dead": Mortuary transactions in Bwaidoka, Goodenough Island. In *Death rituals and life in the societies of the Kula ring,* edited by F. Damon and R. Wagner. De Kalb: Northern Illinois University Press.
———. 1989b. Suffer the children: Wesleyans in the D'Entrecasteaux. In *Family and gender in the Pacific: Domestic contradictions and the colonial impact,* edited by M. Jolly and M. Macintyre. Cambridge: Cambridge University Press.
———. 1992. Gone native in isles of illusion: In search of Asterisk in Epi. In *History and tradition in Melanesian anthropology,* edited by J. Carrier. Berkeley: University of California Press.
———. 1996. Commemorating missionary heroes: Local Christianity and narratives of nationalism. In *Narratives of nation in the South Pacific,* edited by T. Otto and N. Thomas. Amsterdam: Harwood Academic Publishers.

Index

abortion, 128
Abu-Lughod, Lila, 34–35
adoption, 142, 144
aesthetics, 165–66
agency, 75, 77–78, 215
    and habitus, 94–95
    Melanesian, 18, 21, 116
    and the person, 20
    and sex and gender, 73
    in Western-style medicine, 93
'ai'abi, 196–203
aid post, 46, 49, 88, 91
    childbirth at, 86–87
    clinics at, 83–85, 96
    medical supplies and equipment, 88–90
allegory, 17
Alina Nu'ata. *See* languages
Alotau, 2, 44, 56, 62, 260
    hospital, 83
        as birthing site, 190–92, 198, 263
        prenatal clinic at, 92–93
    proximity to Nuakata, 41
alterity, 120–21
ancestors, 214, 220
    embodiment of, 234
    and *guyau*, 254
    and land, 251
    spirits of, 230–31
    time of, 250
anthropological imagination, 5
anthropological knowledge creation, 3–4, 31
    contingency and, 9
anthropological method. *See* method; participant observation

anthropology. *See also* feminist anthropology
    ethics of, 3, 42, 222, 237–41, 244, 268
    and ethnocentrism, 13, 265–66
    and exoticism, 18, 23–24, 120–21, 131–32
    and the feminist imaginary, 36
    Melanesian, 18–19, 25, 111
    nostalgia in, 68
    and (post)colonialism, 40–43, 65–66, 113, 243
    and postmodernism, 113, 121
    and romanticism, 40, 66–71
    scope of, 29
    and social inequality, 35
anthropology of experience, the, 15–19. *See also* lived experience
    and the search for meaning, 32
Ao'ao. *See* clans
arrival story, 44
    as trope, 49–50
Auhelawa. *See* languages
Averill, Roger, 1–2, 71, 163, 197
    and fictive kinship, 142, 150–51, 174
    and first trip to Nuakata, 44–45
    and malaria, 224, 259–60, 273
    photograph of, 64
    and relationships, 268–69
    and voyeurism, 224–25, 237

Bataille, Georges, 6
Battaglia, Debbora, 188, 214
    and conception beliefs, 114–15
    and definition of *nuwa*, 125
    and gardening/pregnancy metaphor, 177
    and gendered spaces, 168

Battaglia, Debbora (*continued*)
  and kinship, 146, 148
  and memory, 250–52
  and the relational person, 216
bearing, as gendered, 136
belief, 138
  and 'ai'abi, 197
belonging, 141, 152, 266, 269
  and *kastom*, 181
Benhabib, Seyla, 12
Benjamin, Jessica, 5
Benveniste, Emile, 77–78
betel nut, 161, 181, 208
Biersack, Alietta, 18–19
binary pairs, 19
birth. See childbirth
birthdays, 204–5
blood
  and growing babies, 117
  menstrual, 105–6, 116
  in pregnancy and birth, 192–94, 264
body, the, 6–10, 81, 108, 121, 217
  in Alina Nua'ata, 215
  and Cartesian epistemology, 9
  in critical interpretative anthropology, 27
  cultural construction of, 26
  female, 12, 69, 79
  and habitus, 128
  maternal, 69, 96–97
  and Melanesian personhood, 23, 264
  /mind distinction, 10
  as partible, 21, 96
  parts, names for, 122–25
  as separated from spirit, 231
  as sexed, 11, 72–73, 100
  and social theory, 31–33
  as text, 13
Bo'e. See clans
Bordo, Susan, 9
Bourdieu, Pierre, 4, 15, 166
  and language, 108
  and methodological pluralism, 30
  and notion of field, 98–99

  and notion of habitus, 94–95, 98–99, 128
  and praxis, 95, 99–100
  and reflexivity, 28
  and subjectivity, 94–95
Braidotti, Rosi, 11, 73–74
breast-feeding, 26, 84–85, 99
breast-milk, significance of, 142–43
Bromilow, William, 59–60
burial feasts. See mortuary practices
Butler, Judith, 81
Bwebweso, Mt., as realm of the dead, 218, 224, 228, 232–33, 245, 249

cannibalism, 18, 59, 60, 229
Caplan, Patricia, 36
Carpenter, 156, 161–62, 164, 170
Carrier, James, 120–21
Cartesian epistemology, 6–10, 24
cat's cradle. See 'ai'abi
census, 55–56
childbirth, 26, 66–67, 189–98, 231, 264
  attendants, 87–88
  and blood, 192–94
  and customary practices, 84–88, 178
  and gender relations, 82
  and health, 83, 88
  mortality during, 86, 88, 93
  phenomenological renderings of, 68
  place of, 87, 92, 99, 263
  as represented in 'ai'abi, 197–203
  and *susu* continuance, 204
  Western medicine's prescriptions for, 99
  women's understanding of, 54
children, 80
  and gender, 79–80
  and spirits, 138, 230–31
  and yams, 137
Chodorow, Nancy, 70
Christianity, 205–6, 246, 249. See also missionaries; United Church
  and conception beliefs, 103, 105, 107, 117–18, 139
  and the creation story, 118

and dualisms, 138–39
  increased influence of, 180–82
  Melanesian, 121
Cixous, Hélène, 12
clans, 56–57, 142, 148, 171, 258
  Ao'ao, 229–30
  Bo'e, last *guyau*, 250, 253–57
  spirits of, 212
Clifford, James, 15
  and anthropology, 40–43, 65–66
  and cultures as dynamic, 23
  and ethnographic writing, 27–31, 243
  and feminist ethnographies, 34
  in Melanesia, 23, 25
  and missionizing, 40–41, 60
  and Western appropriation of space/time, 31
colonial relations, 53, 82, 100–101, 225–26, 228, 239, 267
  and fertility control, 186
  in fieldwork, 66
  and health provision, 89
community health worker. *See also* Diawasi, Moses
  authority of, 91
  and gender and service provision, 85, 93, 263
  and Primary Health Care policies, 98
  role of, 83
conception, 105–7, 127–28
  and bearing, 135–36
  and gardening metaphor, 209
  and identity, 114
  and Massim anthropology, 108–16
  Nuakatan beliefs about, 103–8, 116–23, 126, 130, 135, 137–39
  and Virgin Birth, 111–13
  Western beliefs about, 108–10, 114, 135
contraception, 54, 185–88
  Western, 189
Crapanzano, Vincent, 15

Critical Interpretative Anthropology, 27
Critical Medical Anthropology, 26–27
cultural evolutionists, 111
cultural studies, 4
culture(s)
  as distinct from nature, 19
  as dynamic, 23
  notion of, 66, 120
  Western definitions of, 183
custom, 16, 126. *See also kastom*
  regarding marriage, 158–61
  regarding pregnancy and childbirth, 84–85, 90, 97, 178

Danforth, Loring, 243
death, 206–7. *See also* mortuary practices
  and afterlife, 218, 224, 228, 232–33, 245, 249
  customs relating to, 211–58
  as embodiment of illness, 220
  of Eric's father, 211
  as imminent, 196
deconstruction, 24, 28. *See also* postmodernism
de Lauretis, Teresa, 13
Dening, Greg, 120–21
Derrida, Jacques, 6
Descartes, René, 8, 13, 110–11
desire, 124
Dewey, John, 15, 94–95, 128, 166
dialectical anthropology, 14–15
dialogue
  critique of, 15
  and ethnography, 14
  in fieldwork, 15
  in texts, 15
diarrheal diseases, 66, 83, 89
Diawasi, Moses, 65–66, 69, 189, 260. *See also* community health worker
  attitude to
    kastom, 181
    traditional contraception, 186

Diawasi, Moses (*continued*)
  author's relationship to, 45–49, 71
  clinical practices of, 82–100
  photograph of, 102
diet, 55, 170
  and breast-feeding, 90
  and contraception, 188–89
  and health, 84
  and postpartum food taboos, 85
  in pregnancy, 90, 92, 178
difference, 82
  accommodation of, 5–6, 14, 49–50, 163
  author's desire for, 131
  and belonging, 141
  cultural, 25, 45, 48, 119–21, 134, 165, 233
    and possessions, 170–71
  ethnic, 2
  and ethnography, 223
  female, 10
  gender, 22, 107
  and lived experience, 14
  production of, 33
  sexual, 10–11, 14, 17, 72–74
  and similarities, 13, 18, 259, 267
  skin color and, 100–101
Dilthey, Wilhelm, 15
dimdims, 37
disease, 26. *See also* diarrheal diseases; malaria
disenchantment, and social theory, 31–32
District Health Department, 63
Dobu
  Island, 59
  and kinship, 143–44, 146
  and totems, 57
  language, 51, 229
Dreyfus, Hubert, 95
dualisms, 73
  Christian, 138–39
  as troubled by maternal thinking, 68
Dureau, Christine, 67, 69, 184
  and colonial fertility control, 186
dwelling, 75

East Cape, 41, 47, 51
  language, Tewala, 45, 104
  and local council, 63
  maternal and child health nurses from, 89, 97
economy, 55
education, 51
  and Bible colleges, 62
  and culture, 181–82
  and gender, 80, 84
Eipper, Chris
  and ethnographic testimony, 28–29
  and ethnographic trust, 29–31, 223
  and idea of humankind, 5
Eisenstein, Hester, 26
embodiment, 12, 22, 37, 73–74, 81, 100, 167, 252. *See also* body, the
  of customs, 183
  and death, 227–28
  and epistemology, 32, 116
  and habitus, 94
  of illness, 220
  and maternity, 12, 36
  of matrilineal relations, 257–58
  Melanesian notions of, 23
  of relationships, 234, 269
  and social theory, 31–33
  and subjectivity, 11, 14, 76–78
  and temporality, 196, 220
Emma, 84–85, 188, 194
  and baby Reni, 133–34, 204
  and conception beliefs, 132
empathy
  in ethnography, 223, 271
  and memory, 251
  and motherhood, 70
  as way of knowing, 14
enchantment, 44, 49
encompassment, 77–78
Enlightenment, the, 6–10, 244
  epistemology, 20
Enslin, Elizabeth, 35
epistemology, 3–4
  Cartesian, 6–11, 24

and embodiment, 16, 32
and empathy, 14, 223, 271
Enlightenment, 9, 20
feminist, 7
Melanesian, 18–25
relational, 32
and temporality, 16
Eric, 164, 211, 225, 235
as traditional healer, 260
Errington, Frederick, 42–43
essentialism, 69, 73
and ethnography, 42
in feminist theory, 10, 14
ethics, 5, 70
and anthropology, 3, 42, 222, 237–41, 244
and Western-style medical practices, 96
ethnocentricism, 13
in ethnographic writing, 28
ethnographer, 3–4, 53
as author, 27–31, 33
and colonialism, 14, 65–66, 120
as health worker, 100
as witness, 29, 37
ethnographic authority, 4, 6, 15, 27–28, 30, 53
ethnography, 18, 23–25, 239, 241. *See also* feminist ethnography
and authority, 27–28, 30
authorship of, 28, 53
characteristics of, 3–4, 14, 28, 30, 35
dialogue in, 27
and emotion, 240, 242–44, 260
and empathy, 223
experimental, 16, 19, 34
as gendered, 71, 91
and imagination, 3
with a partner, 268–69
politics of, 4, 35
reflexivity in, 28, 35
and relational knowing, 54
and subjectivity, 3, 28
as testimony, 29–31, 37
and trust, 29–31, 223
and uncertainty, 31

Eves, Richard, 68, 86, 186, 252
existentialism, 16, 23
exoticism, 18, 23

Fabian, Johannes, 31, 65, 119–20
fathering, 146–47
feeling/emotion, 124–26
and ethnography, 240, 242–44, 260
/thinking and memory, 250–51
feminist anthropology, 17, 35, 67
history of, 26, 33–36
feminist critiques of Western biomedical discourse, 109
feminist ethnography, 33–36, 243
collaboration in, 34
parameters of, 34
politics of, 34
reflexivity in, 28, 35, 243
feminist philosophy, 4–7, 10, 215, 242
Fernandez, James, 132
fictive kinship, 174, 259–60, 262, 272. *See also* kinship
and authenticity, 142
field, the
Bourdieu's concept of, 98–99
conduct in, 30
dialogue in, 15
and feminist ethnography, 35
as imagined, 1–4, 18, 50, 142, 222, 272
as lived experience, 133, 207
parameters of, 25–26
preparation for, 1
as remembered, 2
as text, 27–31
fieldnotes, 2
fieldwork, 1–4, 18, 27–28
assumptions, 2, 5, 37, 72–74, 82, 119, 261, 266
decision to do, 5, 14, 17
and enchantment, 44
equipment, 2, 36–37, 132
methods, 2, 49, 53, 84, 106, 141–42, 219
relationships, 35, 65–66
gendered, 91

fieldwork (*continued*)
  remembered, 271
  as rite of passage, 45, 133
  and romanticism, 15, 66–67
  and temporality, 3
Fine, Michelle, 15
fishing, 55
Flax, Jane, 6
food, 204, 208–9, 232. *See also* mortuary practices
  in pregnancy, 178, 180
  and sociality, 90
  taboos
    for *galiyauna*, 218, 246–47
    mourning, 213, 227, 235
    postpartum, 85
Fortune, Reo, 57, 115, 157
  and kinship, 143–44, 146
  and yams as humans, 177
Foster, Robert, 23–25
Foucault, Michel, 73–74, 166
  and subjectivity, 6–7
Frankenberg, Ruth, 100
Frazer, James, 111

Gadamer, Hans-Georg, 15
galiyauna, 217, 221, 225
  current duties of, 218, 230
  past practices of, 226–29, 234
    and *guyau*, 255
    and *tauʻalaʻalahi* (resurrection feast), 245–48
gardens, 55, 72, 85, 174, 207–10
  design, 208
  harvesting, 178
  and marriage, 160
  plants in, 208–10
  and pregnancy and birth, 177–78, 185, 209–10
  and *susu*, 144
Gatens, Moira, 10
Geertz, Clifford, 4
  and ethnographic writing, 27–31
gender
  in Alina Nuʻata, 78
  assumptions about, 26, 71–76, 82

and bearing, 136
and category of woman, 17, 264–65
and children, 79–80
and diet, 84
difference, 22, 107–8
and division of labor, 76, 80–81, 84, 145, 153, 163, 233
and education, 80, 84
and ethnocentrism, 12
and female sustenance of *susu*, 258, 263
and knowledge, 261
Melanesian epistemology of, 18
Melanesian personhood, 22
and personhood, 261
relations and childbirth, 84–86
and sex, 72, 81–82
/sex distinction, the, 10–11
and subjectivity, 4–7, 94–97, 178
Gewertz, Deborah, 42–43
gift exchange, 138, 154–55, 171, 204. *See also* Kula; *mulolo*
  anthropological, 1
  and connectedness, 270
  and gift/commodity distinction, 19, 21
  in marriage, 161
  and Melanesian personhood, 24
  and mortuary practices, 236–37
Gilligan, Carol, 70
Gohiya, 151, 154, 158–61, 167, 178
  as location for author's house, 48, 170
  as Siyae hamlet, 48, 54
Goodenough Island, 49
Gregory, Christopher, 21
Grosz, Elizabeth, 11

habitus, 94–95, 98–99
  and the body, 128
hamlets, 56, 212. *See also* Gohiya
  as birthing sites, 190–92, 196
  characteristics of, 46
  living arrangements in, 158–61
  pathways connecting, 167–68
Haraway, Donna, 10, 109

health. *See also* health clinics; maternal and child mortality
  cultural constitution of, 26
  and gender, 84
  preventative strategies for, 88, 97
  reproductive, 263
  research on, 26, 41
health clinics
  family planning, 189
  maternal and child, 66, 82–85, 88–91
    attendance patterns, 91
    reflections on, 91–92
  reflections on, 96
  and temporality, 206
health patrol, 82–85, 91, 100
Heidegger, Martin, 15, 17, 95
  and dwelling, 75
  and the scientific method, 8
Heller, Agnes, 7
Henry, Jennifer, 43–45, 49
house(s)
  abandoned on owner's death, 213
  author's, as communal, 161–62
  bachelor, 157
  building, 152–54
  design, 155
humanism, 5–6
humankind, concept of, 5
humility, 49

identity, 16, 120, 141
  and biology, 108–10
  clan, 257
  and conception, 114
  and gender, 107–8, 265
  Nuakatan cultural, 269
  relational, 145–47
  susu, 115, 150, 224, 257
imaginary
  anthropological, 5, 18
  Cartesian, 8
immunization, 83–85, 89
individualism, 20, 24, 205, 261
  lack of concept, on Nuakata, 216
  Western concept of, 107–8, 267
intersubjectivity, 14, 16, 65
and temporality, 31
Irigaray, Luce, 11–12
  and difference, 12
I'unia, 137–39

Jackson, Michael
  and aesthetics, 165–66
  and *'ai'abi*, 198
  and the anthropology of experience, 15–17
  and metaphor, 128–29, 132
  and subjectivity, 94–95
  and symbols, 163–64
Johnson, Mark, 130
Jolly, Margaret
  and anthropological exoticism, 23–24
  and colonial fertility control, 186
  and postcolonialism, 121
Jorgenson, Dan, 111–13
Josephides, Lisette, 24

kastom, 180–83. *See also* custom
Keesing, Roger
  and anthropological exoticism, 23–24, 120–21, 131–32
  and critical interpretative anthropology, 27
  and postcolonialism, 121
kinship, 141–48, 267. *See also* fictive kinship; matrilineage/*susu*
  affinal relationships, 145, 217, 221–22, 236–37
  and identity, 224, 257
  Euro-American, 110
  matrilineal, 18
  and pathways, 169
  ties, 77
Kirby, Vicki, 36
Knauft, Bruce, 107, 113
knowing
  as concept in Alina Nua'ata, 106, 126
  vs. doing, 117, 126
  and embodiment, 116
  experiential, 53, 55

knowing (*continued*)
  and identity, 110
  intersubjective, 17, 119
  materialist theory of, 95
  and Melanesian epistemology, 18, 184
  performative nature of, 270
  relational, 32, 53–54, 65
  seeing as mode of, 240–41
  Western, 19, 184
knowledge
  of bush, 153
  customary, 53, 106, 136
    entrusted, 270
  ethnographic, 243–44
  of gardening/birthing practices, 210
  as gendered, 261
  spectator view of, 166
Kovel, Joel, 5
Kuehling, Susanne, 214
Kula, 18, 51, 171. *See also* trade, history of

Lakoff, George, 130–31
land
  ancestral connections to, 251–52
  clearing, 207–8
  division of, 46, 58
  lived knowledge of, 55
  matrilineal ownership of, 144, 150, 208, 210, 237
languages
  Alina Nu'ata
    definition of "understanding," 123–26
    gender in, 78
    learning, 129–30
    linguistic features of, 75–78, 104–6
    and memory, 250–51
    and pregnancy, 178
    as taught in schools, 182
    translation of, 121–23, 126
    word for "bearing," 136
    word for "blood," 193
    word for "contraception," 187
    words relating to the body, 122–26, 215
    words relating to the person, 214–15, 266
  Auhelawa, 50–52
    characteristics of, 51–52
  Dobu, as church language, 229
  English, 100
    definition of "conception," 109–10, 114
    definition of "understanding," 123
    spoken locally, 51, 89, 92, 103
  Tewala, 45, 104
Leach, Edmund, 111–13
Leenhardt, Maurice, 246
Lepowsky, Maria, 115, 127, 257
life cycle, 207, 209
Lithgow, Daphne, 50, 249
Lithgow, David, 50–52, 123
lived experience, 14–17, 28. *See also* anthropology of experience, the
  the author's, 2, 133
  and Cartesian epistemology, 9
  and difference, 14, 113
  and embodiment, 12
  as gendered, 72
  of Nuakata, 50
  phenomenological theory of, 11, 16
  and place and space, 55
  and relational knowing, 54
  and research, 14
  and the sexed body, 73
  and social theory, 32
  as way of understanding, 15, 104, 127
living/staying, 205–7
Lloyd, Genevieve, 8–9
local council, 63
London Missionary Society, 59. *See also* missionaries
Lutz, Catherine, 54, 130

Macintyre, Martha
  and author, 17–18, 132
  and blood metaphor, 194
  and colonial administrators, 59

and conception, 115
and emotion, 124
and garden design, 208
and *guyau* (*soi*), 255
and kinship, 143–44, 147, 150
and Kula, 51, 171
and marriage customs, 161
and Melanesian personhood, 22–24, 138–39
and memory, 252
and totems, 57
and Tubetube, 124–26
magic, 182
  and journey to Bwebweso, 233
  words (*'oba*), 218
malaria, 82–84
  as health issue on Nuakata, 66
  prevention of, 90, 157
  prophylaxis for, 82–84
  treatment of, 89, 100
Malinowski, Bronislaw, 42, 130, 133
  and Trobriand conception beliefs, 111–13
Mallett, Frank
  experiences of World War II, 39
  memories of Milne Bay, 17–18
Mari, 179–80, 183
  and baby, 198, 204
  and childbirth, 190–91
  photograph of, 102
marriage, 134, 158–61
Marriot, McKim, 20
Martin, Emily, 109
Marx, Karl, 95
Massim
  definition of, 44
  depopulation in, 67
  ethnographies, 17, 120, 124–26, 143, 158, 177, 252, 269–70
  importance of death in, 206–7
  languages, 124
  missionaries in, 59, 86, 148
  and *susu*, 143
maternal and child health clinics. *See* health clinics
maternal and child mortality, 67, 70–71, 83, 99
  in childbirth, 86, 88, 93
maternalism, as expression of neo-colonialism, 69
maternity, 146
  and birth mothers, 195
  and embodiment, 36
  Melanesian, 67
  pragmatics of, 69–70
  and ways of thinking, 68
  Western, 67
matrilineage/*susu*, 56–57, 167–68
  and belonging, 142–48, 152
  and blood, 194
  female sustenance of, 258, 263
  hamlet spaces, 168
  and identity, 115, 144, 150, 224, 257
  and maternal and child health care, 97, 179
  and mortuary practices, 211–12, 236
  naming and, 148, 151
  relations, 257–58
  and seed yams, 177
Mauss, Marcel, 128
  and the person, 5–6, 94–95
Mead, Margaret, 67
medicine
  preventative, 88, 90, 97
  traditional, 41, 67, 82–88
    and contraception, 185–88
    and pregnancy, 97
  Western-style, 26, 41, 67, 70, 82–88, 186, 259
    availability of, 189, 191
    knowledge, 93, 96–99, 139
    Moses Diawasi as embodiment of, 92–94
    and pregnancy, 97
    and space, 88, 91–99
    spatial and power relations in, 91–92
    and temporality, 93
Melanesia, 17
  anthropological writing on, 18–19, 25, 111
  identity, 113–16

Melanesia (*continued*)
  colonialism in, 23, 25
  status of women in, 18
Melanesian personhood. *See also* person, the
  and agent/person distinction, 21–22
  and the body, 23
  and gender difference, 22
  notions of, 18–25
  and reproduction, 22, 264
  as social microcosm, 21
memory, 250–51
menstruation, 105–7, 116, 128, 194–95, 264
  and female identity, 265
Merleau-Ponty, Maurice, 17, 164
  and subjectivity, 94–95
  and theory of sexuality, 11–12
Merrett-Balkos, Leanne, 69
metaphor(s), 16–17
  discussion of, 128–32, 213–14
  postmodern, for self, 24
method. *See also* participant observation
  and difference, 223
  ethnographic, 2, 28–29, 49, 53, 84, 106, 141–42, 219, 222–23, 260, 266
    traditional model of, 55
  intersubjective, 14–15
  and lived experience, 16–17
  and pluralism, 30
  relation of the subject to, 9
  and scientific empiricism, 8, 15
Meyau, Antiya, 54, 56, 59, 63
  and knowledge of body parts, 123–25
  and mortuary practices, 212–13, 217, 221, 226–34, 236
    last *guyau*, 250, 252–57
    tauʻalaʻalahi (resurrection feast), 245–48
Meyau, Malida, 54, 146, 149, 171
  and childbirth, 192
  and contraception, 185–88
  and gardens, 207

Meyau, Roger, 142, 149, 150, 217, 223–24
Meyau, Sinetana, 191, 217
Milne Bay, 39
  fieldwork in, 18, 132–33
  Giligili airbase, 17
  Health Department, 83, 88
  Province, first Methodist mission in, 47
miscarriage, 128
missionaries. *See also* Christianity; London Missionary Society
  and Bible translation, 50–51, 123, 148
  and colonialism, 40–41, 120–21, 267
  and fertility control, 186
  and local pastors, 61, 62
  and maternal practices, changes to, 67–68
  and mortuary practices, changes to, 225–26, 228
  Polynesian, 59
  relationships with anthropologists, 39–41
  and sexual propriety, 86
Mona, 128, 130, 133
  and beliefs about conception, 103–8, 114, 116–22, 137–39
  and birth, 194, 196
Moore, Henrietta, 26, 69, 73–74
  and belonging, 141
  and cultural meanings and values, 94
  and the cultural relativism of humanism, 6
  and difference, 13
  and reflexivity in ethnography, 28
Mortimer, Lorraine, and embodied social theory, 31–33
mortuary practices, 18, 211–58. *See also* death
  burial feasts, 225–37
  guyau, 249–58
  tauʻalaʻalahi (resurrection feast), 244–49
Mosko, Mark, 21, 77

mourning, 211–13, 219–22, 225
  as performance, 236
mulolo, 146–47
  and mortuary practices, 237
  and yams, 138
Munn, Nancy, 127, 154, 157, 252
  and matriclans, 57
  as remembered by Moses Diawasi, 66
  and *susu* belonging, 144

names
  nick-, 51
  as relational, 148, 151
  and *waligeha*, 142, 148
National Health Plans, 97–98
Neumann, Klaus, 31, 121
New Melanesian Anthropology, 23–25
New Melanesian History, 23–25
Normanby Island, 41, 49–50, 214
  Bunama region of, 58, 159
  Bwasiyayai region of, 58
  distance from Nuakata, 46
  Duau region of, 58
    burial feasts in, 245
    conception beliefs in, 136–38
    and kinship, 147
  links with Nuakata, 63
Nuakata
  arrival at, 43–44
  climate of, 173
  daily rhythms on, 53
  early weeks there, 99
  economy of, 55
  geographical division of, 46, 169
  health risks on, 70
  intended research of, 41–42
  isolation of, 48, 70, 89
  landscape of, 46, 55
  lived experience of, 50
  location of, 41, 55
  population of, 56
  regional status of, 63
  seascape of, 46, 55
  seasons on, 206
  settlement of, 58–59
  trip around, 45–49
nuwa-, 123–26

occidentalism, 23
other, the, 101, 120–21
  and cannibalism, 229
  and subjectivity, 16

Papua New Guinea, 41–43, 55
  anthropologists in, 87
  colonial medical administrators in, 68
  education in, 51 (*see also* education)
  infant deaths in, 71
  languages of, 125
  rural places in, 87
  Southern Highlands, birth in, 69
participant observation, 3, 14–15, 54, 142, 222–23, 262
  ethics of, 237–41, 268
  and ethnographic writing, 28
pathways, 236
  connecting hamlets, 167–68
  and kinship, 169
  as personal inscriptions, 213, 216–17
Pelz, Werner, 8, 123
person, the. *See also* Melanesian personhood
  and agency, 116
  anthropological quest for, 131
  and gender, 178, 261
    and primary health care, 26
  inalienable aspects of, 52
  notions of, 5–6
    Nuakatan, 69
  as partible, 18–25
  and pathways, 213–14
  and postmodernism, 7
  as relational, 5, 7–8, 10, 75–78, 210, 216
  in relation to self, 5
  semi-alienable aspects of, 52, 106
  and the sex/gender distinction, 10
  and Western individual, 20, 24, 107–8
  word for, in Alina Nu'ata, 75

personality, 213–14
phallogocentrism, 13
phenomenology, 11, 14–15
philosophy
   existentialism, 16
   feminist, 4–7
   phenomenology, 11, 14–16
   Western, 15, 17
Pile, Steve, 4
place(s), 62–63
   and anthropology, 46
   of birthing, 87, 92, 99, 190–92
   cooking, 162–63
   dwelling, 75
   embodiment of, 167
   and housing, 46, 152–69
   and pathways, 169
   and *susu*, 144
   and temporality, 206
population of Nuakata, 56
postcolonialism, 113, 120–21
postmodernism, 4. *See also* deconstruction
   and anthropology, 113, 121
   and multiplicity, 24
   and partibility, 24
   and person, 7
   and representation, 7
pragmatism, 69–70
   Melanesian, 135
Pratt, Mary Louise, 49
praxis
   Bourdieu's theory of, 95
   regarding pregnancy, 99
pregnancy, 26, 41, 66, 184–85
   and *'ai'abi*, 197–203
   as analogue for gardening, 177–78, 185
   and blood, 192–94
   customary practices regarding, 97, 178
   experiences of, 189–91
   and health, 84
      risks, 97
   and hospitalization, 83
   husbands' role in, 97
   phenomenological renderings of, 68
   treated as health issue, 83
   women's understanding of, 54
Primary Health Care policy, 26, 98
Probyn, Elspeth, 4
pronouns, possessive, 51

Rabinow, Paul, 95
reason
   and Cartesian epistemology, 9
   as Enlightenment metanarrative, 6–10
reflexivity
   in ethnographic writing, 28, 243
      feminist, 35
   in modernism, 29
   in romanticism, 29
relativism, 6–10
   cultural, and critical interpretative anthropology, 27
remembering, 269–71
representation, crisis of, 4
research
   approval for, 41, 45, 49
   assistant, role of, 48, 53 (*see also* Siyae, Wycliffe)
   intentions, 41, 65
   plan, 2
respect, 79, 91, 142, 145
Rich, Adrienne, 73
Roda, 85
romanticism
   and anthropology, 40, 66–71
   of fieldwork, 15
   and reflexivity, 29
Rorty, Richard, 15–16, 130
Rosaldo, Michelle, 3–4, 130, 243
Rosaldo, Renato, 66–67
Rosemary, 185–88
Ross, Malcolm, 51
Roth, Paul, 111
Rozario, Santi, 70
Ruddick, Sara, 70
Rumsey, Alan, 77–78

Sabarl
  conception beliefs on, 114–15
  and definition of *nuwa*, 125
  and memory, 250–51
Sahlins, Marshall, and encompassment, 77
sailing canoes, 47, 147
salvage ethnography, 66–68
Scheper-Hughes, Nancy
  and the ethics of ethnography, 240–42
  and the ethnographic field, 3
  and the pragmatics of motherhood, 69–70
school, Community Primary, 47
self/I, the
  and Cartesian epistemology, 9
  and commodity logic, 184
  as contingent, 72–73
  and ethnocentrism, 13
  embodiment of, 6–10
  Melanesian epistemology of, 18
  and the Melanesian person, 21
  Nuakatan notions of, 69, 106
  as processual, 72–74
  and reason, 8
  as relational, 5, 7–8, 10, 75–78, 210, 265, 269
  as substantive, 72–73
sex
  assumptions about, 82
  as discursive phenomenon, 74
  and ethnocentrism, 13
  and gender, 72, 81–82
  /gender distinction, the, 10–11, 265
  and subjectivity, 95–97
sexual intercourse
  and blood, 193
  and growing babies, 115–17, 127
sexuality, Merleau-Ponty's theory of, 11–12
sexual liaisons, 157
sickness
  cultural constitution of, 26
  research on, 26
Sideia Island, 47

Sineliko, 178, 210
Singer, Merrill, 26
Siyae, Douglas, 149, 173
Siyae, Eba, at high school in Alotau, 54, 172
Siyae, Eunice, 54, 141–42, 149, 171, 174–75, 204, 259–60, 262, 267, 271–73
  and childbirth, 192
  and *ʻaiʻabi*, 197–98
  photographs, 199–203
  and contraception, 188
  and marriage customs, 158–61
  and parenting, 146
  and pregnancy, 178
Siyae, Geteli, 54, 150, 160, 204–5, 250
  and gardens, 175, 178, 207–10
  and pregnancy, 184
Siyae, Jane, 54, 149, 207–8
Siyae, Misako, 2, 172
Siyae, Noah, 54, 56, 123–24, 145, 151, 172, 174–75
  as Bible translator, 50, 156
  letter from, 259–60, 271–73
  and marriage customs, 159–61
  and mortuary practices, 212–13, 226, 230–31, 236, 250
  tauʻalaʻalahi (resurrection feast), 245–48
Siyae, Nowel, 142, 144, 159–61, 172
Siyae, Roger, 2, 150, 172
Siyae, Washington, 2, 37, 172
Siyae, Wycliffe, 2, 37, 56, 147–48, 151, 164, 170–74, 177, 209
  and *ʻaiʻabi*, 197
  and belief, 138
  as Bible translator, 50, 156
  and birthdays, 204–5
  and ethics of fieldwork, 238
  ethnographic sensibility of, 262
  and conception beliefs, 121–23, 136
  and knowledge of customary practices, 53, 183
  and marriage customs, 159–61
  and mortuary practices, 211–13, 217, 221, 225–37, 250

Siyae, Wycliffe (*continued*)
   guyau, 253–57
   tau'ala'alahi (resurrection feast), 245–48
   photograph of, 64
   as research assistant, 48, 53–54, 129–30, 186, 262
   and *susu*, 141–48
Siyae *susu*, 54, 149–50, 171–75
soccer, 46–47
social construction metaphor, 10
sociality
   Melanesian, 19–24
   Nuakatan, 118
social theory
   and disenchantment, 31–32
   and embodiment, 31–33
society
   Melanesian, 19
   in relation to the individual, 10, 19
solipsism, 4
sorcery, 18, 226–27, 248
space
   and colonialism, 31
   communal, 60, 161–62, 167, 244
   and health clinics, 96
   lived, 46, 166
   sleeping, 157
   as socially structured, 94, 99
   and temporality, 206
   and Western-style medicine, 88, 91–99
spirit(s)
   ancestral, 127, 230–31, 236
   Bulelala, story of, 137–39, 177
   and children, 138, 230–31
   of clans, 212
   of Mt. Tanalabwa (Silopan), 127
   of yams, 137–38
Spiro, Melford, 112
sport, 260
   social and organizational role of, 46–47, 63, 81
Stacey, Judith, and feminist ethnography, 34–36
Strathern, Marilyn
   and blood metaphor, 194
   and commodity logic, 183–84
   and conception, 113
   and Euro-American kinship, 110
   and feminist anthropology, 35–36
   and gender, 74
   and Melanesian agency, 116
   and Melanesian epistemology, 18–26
   and Melanesian personhood, 264
   and partibility, 24, 26, 77
   and the relational person, 216
subject, the
   and agency, 5, 10, 116
   and being, 75
   Bourdieu's philosophy of, 94
   Cartesian, 7
   and commodity logic, 184
   as contingent, 72–73
   definitions of, 7
   discursive positions and, 78
   as distinct from object, 19
   as female, 12
   feminist critiques of, 11
   as gendered, 4–7, 13
   and partibility, 77–78
   as processual, 72–73
   relatedness of, in Auhelawa, 51–52
   relation of knowing and method to, 9
   in relation to the other, 16
   as substantive, 72–73
   as text, 12
   as unitary, 194
subjectivity
   and the body, 215
   as discursive, 94–95
   embodied, 11, 14, 73–74
   as gendered, 95
   and the other, 16
subu
   description of, 43
   trip in, 43–45
Summer Institute of Linguistics
   and Bible translation, 50
   Diwala Center, 39

Susan, 178, 180, 183, 188, 191
susu. *See* matrilineage/*susu*

Tanalabwa, Mt., 44, 47
    Silopan as spirit of, 127–28
Taylor, Charles, 9, 95
temporality, 3, 60, 119, 206, 210, 244, 251
    and embodiment, 220, 258
    of human action, 94
    and intersubjectivity, 31
    Nuakatan notions of, 52
    and phenomenology, 16
    and the sexed body, 74
    and Western-style medical practice, 91, 93
testimony, ethnography as, 29–31, 133
Tewala. *See* languages
Thomas, Nicholas, 121
Thrift, Nigel, 4
Thune, Carl, 41, 115, 214, 252
    and gardening/pregnancy metaphor, 177
    and kinship, 143–44, 147
tithing. *See mulolo*
totems, 57–58
trade, history of, 57. *See also* Kula
tradition, 16
transport, lack of, 63
trunk, as metaphor, 1–2, 36–37
trust
    and the ethnographer, 29–30
    and witnessing, 29
truth
    as absolute, 7
    Cartesian pursuit of, 8
    ethnographic, 34
    in Western philosophy, 15
Tubetube
    and conception beliefs, 115
    and garden design, 208
    and *guyau* (*soi*), 255
    and kinship, 143–44, 147
    language of, 124–26
    marriage customs, 161
    notions of personhood, 138–39
    as site of Macintyre's fieldwork, 24, 132
    and totems, 57

understanding
    allegory, role in, 17
    definitions of, 123, 127
    experience as a means to, 15, 104
    metaphor, role in, 17
    narrative, role in, 17
    as processual, 25
    as relational, 25, 53–54
    as revelation, 126
UNICEF, 98
United Church, 77, 180, 257. *See also* Wesleyan Methodist Christian Mission
    Bunama circuit, 62
    and *kwato*, 62
    on Nuakata, 60, 257
        gender roles within, 61–62
        hierarchical relationships within, 60–62
        influence on communal life, 60
    location of, 46–47
    pastors of, 229
Urban, Greg, 78

visualization, 15
Visweswaran, Kamala, 34–36
voice, 120
    politics of, 4, 7

Wacquant, Loïc, 4
    and reflexivity, 28
    and subjectivity, 94–95
Wagner, Roy, 113, 121
warfare, 18, 57, 127
Weiner, Annette, 67, 137
Wesleyan Methodist Christian Mission, 18
    centenary celebration of, 59
West, the, 13
    as problematic construct, 42
Wheatley, Elizabeth, 36

whiteness, as marker of difference, 100–101
witchcraft, 18, 79, 127, 137, 164, 231, 248
witnessing
  and ethnography, 37, 55
  and the "I-witness," 28
Wittengenstein, Ludwig, 95, 129
woman/women
  assumptions about, 71–76
  because I am a, 75–76
  category of, 264–65
  concept of, 78–79
  and contraception, 185–89
  in feminist theory, 10
  as mother, 12
  shyness of, 91, 100, 104
  and social theory, 31–33
  talking as, 31–33
  as universal, 11, 33
Women's Fellowship, 60, 72, 103, 133, 180, 204, 229

workboats, 44, 48, 49
World Health Organization (WHO), 98
World War II, 17–18, 39, 47

yam(s), 136–38, 156–57, 207, 209–10, 220
  and *'ai'abi,* 197–98
  in burial, 231–32
  as child metaphor, 137, 177
  as gifts, 161, 207
  and *guyau,* 254, 256
  harvest, 172, 210
Yamesi, 217, 221, 226–34, 245–48
  discussing Christianity, 249
  and *guyau,* 256
Young, Iris, 11–12
Young, Michael
  and the history of Milne Bay missions, 59
  and inalienable aspects of the person, 52